The European Constitution

The European Constitution

Cases and Materials in EU and Member States' Law

Giuliano Amato

Vice-President of the European Convention 2002–2003, Professor, European University Institute, former Prime Minister of Italy

Jacques Ziller

Professor at the European University Institute, Italy, formerly at Université de Paris I – Panthéon-Sorbonne, France

With the collaboration of Rebeca Lizasoain Brandys, Research Assistant, European University Institute

Edward Elgar

Cheltenham, UK • Northampton, MA, USA

Published by
Edward Elgar Publishing Limited
Glensanda House
Montpellier Parade
Cheltenham
Glos GL50 1UA
UK

Edward Elgar Publishing, Inc.
William Pratt House
9 Dewey Court
Northampton
Massachusetts 01060
USA

A catalogue record for this book
is available from the British Library

Library of Congress Cataloguing in Publication Data

Amato, Giuliano.
The European Constitution : cases and materials in EU & member states' law / Giuliano Amato, Jacques Ziller.
p. cm.
Includes bibliographical references and index.
1. Constitutional law—European Union countries. 2. European Union countries—Politics and government. I. Ziller, Jacques. II. Title.
KJE4445.A45 2007
342.24—dc22 2007000156

ISBN 978 1 84720 129 4 (cased)

Typeset by Cambrian Typesetters, Camberley, Surrey
Printed and bound in Great Britain by MPG Books Ltd, Bodmin, Cornwall

Contents

Abbreviations

CFSP	Common Foreign and Security Policy
CoR	Committee of the Regions
COSAC	Conference of the Community and European Affairs Committees of EU Member States
CT	Constitutional Treaty, that is, treaty establishing a constitution for Europe
EC	European Community
ECB	European Central Bank
ECHR	European Convention of Human Rights
ECJ	European Court of Justice
EU	European Union
EUI	European University Institute
IGC	Intergovernmental Conference
SEA	Single European Act
TEC	Treaty establishing the European Community
TEU	Treaty on the European Union
UK	United Kingdom
UN	United Nations

Foreword

At the meeting of the European Council on 16–17 June 2005, two weeks after the negative referendums on the Treaty establishing a Constitution for Europe, the Heads of State and Government agreed upon a period of reflection 'to enable a broad debate to take place in each of our countries, involving citizens, civil society, social partners, national parliaments and political parties'. While some declared the Constitutional Treaty dead and others carried on with the processes leading to its ratification, the academic debate continued. As a modest contribution to this academic debate, we held a seminar on 'the ratification of the Constitution for Europe' at the European University Institute in Florence from January to March 2005. Edward Elgar Publishing showed interest in publishing the materials we used in the framework of this seminar to prompt discussion with post-graduate students and post-doctoral fellows in law and political science.

The present book offers a selection of these materials, including excerpts of the European Convention's work; selected statutory and constitutional provisions of the Member States; related passages from pertinent court decisions – from both European courts as well as Member States' constitutional courts; institutional and doctrinal analyses; and relevant excerpts from the Constitutional Treaty itself. Many of these documents directly relate to the provisions of the Constitutional Treaty, while the others, although not directly related, are nevertheless relevant to the debate surrounding it. These documents should help the reader to better understand some of the most important changes that would be introduced by the Constitutional Treaty in the EU legal and political system. They might also help to assess the need for the reforms embedded in the Constitutional Treaty as well as the quality of the formulations agreed upon at the European Council of 18 June 2004, which resulted in the Treaty signed in Rome on 29 October of the same year.

The book is divided into nine chapters. Chapters 1 and 2 are designed to have a broad overview of the ratification process as a whole and especially of the referendums which took place in four Member States in 2005. They are not meant only as documents on contemporary history but as a contribution to the reflections of lawyers, political scientists, politicians and practitioners on the procedures to be adopted for future amendment of EU treaties. Chapter 3 presents a general but not exhaustive overview of the numerous innovations introduced by the Constitutional Treaty, from mere codification to institutional reforms. This should also be useful for the reflection on the future of the European Union, both from the perspective of the possible entry into force of the Constitutional Treaty (either in its form as of 2004 or in an amended version) and from the perspective of a prolonged pause in constitutional reform at EU level. Chapters 4 to 9 explore in more depth several dimensions of these innovations: the wording of essential EU law principles such as the principle of primacy (Chapter 4), the transformation into a legally binding instrument of the Nice Charter of Fundamental Rights (Chapter 5), the streamlining of EU competences, instruments and legal bases (Chapter 6) and a specific aspect of the institutional changes which have an impact at both EU and Member State level, namely, the role of national parliaments. The two final chapters are devoted to the two policy areas where the constitution for Europe would introduce the biggest changes as compared to the present situation, that is, in the area of freedom, security and justice (the so-called 'third pillar' of the EU – see Chapter 8) and, last but not least, in the field of the common foreign, security and defence policies (Chapter 9).

We have tried to present a wide variety of documents, including translations of documents which do not exist in the English language, so as to give the readers as much information as possible in order for them to make up their minds in an independent way. We also avoided cutting the documents down too much, and we have kept our introductory comments to a very short introduction, in order to allow for discussion by those who will use this book as a teaching instrument to each chapter. We hope and expect that the discussions generated by these documents will be intense and fruitful.

Giuliano Amato and Jacques Ziller
July 2006

Acknowledgements

We would like to thank Rebeca Lizasoain Brandys, who helped us to collect and present the materials for our seminar and who assisted us in the preparation of this book, and Mel Marquis, who handled the English language revisions of our introductions to each chapter and of the Foreword. We would also like to thank the EUI researchers who translated those documents which were not available in the English language:[1] Luke Mason,[2] Tobias McKenney[3] and Thomas Roberts.[4]

Notes

1. Translations made under our responsibility are signalled by the indication '[translation]' in the title of the Document.
2. Documents 2.2, 2.14 and 8.11.
3. Documents 2.9, 2.10, 3.3 and 4.4.
4. Documents 1.10, 1.11, 2.5, 2.12, 4.6, 4.9, 7.9, 8.8, 8.9, 8.10 and 9.2.

1. The ratification of the Treaty of Rome of 29 October 2004 establishing a constitution for Europe

Document summary

Doubts about a smooth referendum process, parliamentary votes and possibly judicial review thus explain the wording of Article IV-447 CT [Document 1.2] and the corresponding Declaration (or 'rendez-vous clause') of the IGC [Document 1.3]. Unlike the corresponding provisions of the SEA and the Treaty of Maastricht, the setting of a deadline corresponded not to naïve optimism but, on the contrary, to a cautious diffidence.

By the time the Heads of States and Governments agreed upon the Constitutional Treaty during the European Council of 18 June 2004, British Prime Minister Tony Blair had already announced that a referendum would be held in the United Kingdom. Opinion polls, however, indicated strong support for the Treaty in all the other 'old' Member States, starting with France and The Netherlands. The ratification process was launched in the new Member States in the autumn of 2004, at a time when doubts were surfacing with respect to the outcome of the French referendum. The forebodings of some proved to be prophetic when, on 29 May 2005, a majority of French voters rejected ratification of the Constitutional Treaty, followed on 1 June by a majority of Dutch voters [Document 1.4].[4] Six days later, the British government decided to postpone the referendum it had started preparing.[5] At its meeting in Brussels on 16 and 17 June 2005, the European Council agreed that a period of reflection was necessary [Document 1.5]. This has often been referred to as a 'pause for reflection', as the European Council agreed that those governments electing to change their ratification calendar in light of the French and Dutch votes could do so.

Yet there was no pause in the ratification process. At the time of the June 2005 European Council, ten Member States had completed the process allowing for ratification – either by a vote of parliament only or by both a referendum and a parliamentary vote. A year later, five other Member States had done so [Document 1.4]. However, in a strict legal sense, it is wrong to say that 15 Member States had ratified the text by June 2006, as was stated in the Conclusions of the Austrian Presidency [Document 1.13]. In fact, by that time only 12 Member States had deposited their instruments of ratification of the Constitutional Treaty. Romania and Bulgaria could be added to these 12, as they formally signed on 25 April 2005 a Treaty of Accession to the Constitutional Treaty – which however contained a clause providing that these countries would accede instead to the TEC and the TEU if the CT had not entered into force at the moment of their accession. Meanwhile, three of the 15 Member States which were purported to have ratified the Constitutional Treaty [Document 1.4] had not done so: the Heads of State of Belgium, Germany and Slovakia each had to wait for a decision of their respective Constitutional Courts or, in the case of Belgium, for the lapse of the deadline for a possible application for judicial review. In Finland, the ratification process was under way, and the competent standing committee of the

Parliament had already endorsed the Treaty. In the remaining nine countries, the procedure had been slowed down or even halted.

From a legal point of view, the attitudes of these nine Member States, as well as those of France and The Netherlands, must be seen in light of their obligations under Article 18 of the Vienna Convention on the Law of Treaties [Document 1.6]: the Declaration of the European Council of June 2005 [Document 1.5] is a recognition of the validity of a pause in the ratification process for those Member States which were so inclined. The Conclusions of the Presidency of the European Council of June 2006 [Document 1.13] extend this permission until June 2008 at the latest. Both documents demonstrate that the Constitutional Treaty, far from being 'dead', has the validity of a multilateral treaty which has been signed but has not yet entered into force. It may thus be used as an instrument of interpretation, and indeed it may be regarded as the formulation of an agreement on the wording of those clauses which are to be considered as a codification of existing law.[6]

As pointed out above, therefore, the 'pause for reflection' is not a pause in the ratification process. But in this regard another question arises. Is there any 'reflection' in the Member States and EU institutions, as called for in both documents of the European Council?

There has indeed been reflection in those Member States which had not yet completed their process of authorisation for ratification in June 2005 but have done so since then. This is demonstrated by the referendum in Luxembourg and by the number of parliamentary debates, with a record of seven parliamentary debates in Belgium, thanks to the federal structure of the kingdom and to the significant competences assigned to the regions and to the (language-based) communities in external relations [Document 1.4]. Some reflection has also taken place in the EU institutions and organs: the European Parliament [Document 1.7] has been the place where debate never ceased, while the Committee of the Regions [Document 1.8] also had its share in the reflection, as compared to the quite limited amount of debate in a number of Member States, especially in France and The Netherlands, where silence has been the clearest answer to the referendums. From November 2005 onwards, the German government [Document 1.9] has been the flagship of those in favour of trying to ratify the Constitutional Treaty, while the French Socialist Party clearly preferred a new, renegotiated treaty – without saying to what extent such a new text should differ from the existing one [Document 1.10].

The scholarly literature envisages several different scenarios at EU and at national level [Documents 1.11 and 1.12], which are all compatible with the positions expressed at the European Council of June 2006 [Document 1.13]: the 'pause of reflection' could continue as a 'wait and see' period, as happened from June 2005 to June 2006. Alternatively it could also develop into a genuine period of discussion, in academia as well as in the political arena, which could lead to a resolute conclusion about the future of the CT.[7]

Document 1.1: Treaty on European Union, Article 48 (ex Article N)

The government of any Member State or the Commission may submit to the Council proposals for the amendment of the Treaties on which the Union is founded.

If the Council, after consulting the European Parliament and, where appropriate, the Commission, delivers an opinion in favour of calling a conference of representatives of the governments of the Member States, the conference shall be convened by the President of the Council for the purpose of determining by common accord the amendments to be made to those Treaties. The European Central Bank shall also be consulted in the case of institutional changes in the monetary area.

The amendments shall enter into force after being ratified by all the Member States in accordance with their respective constitutional requirements.

Document 1.2: Treaty Establishing a Constitution for Europe, Article IV-447 'Ratification and entry into force'

1. This Treaty shall be ratified by the High Contracting Parties in accordance with their respective constitutional requirements. The instruments of ratification shall be deposited with the Government of the Italian Republic.

2. This Treaty shall enter into force on 1 November 2006, provided that all the instruments of ratification have been deposited, or, failing that, on the first day of the second month following the deposit of the instrument of ratification by the last signatory State to take this step.

Document 1.3: Declaration no. 30 on the ratification of the Treaty establishing a Constitution for Europe, Treaty Establishing a Constitution for Europe, annexed to the Treaty Establishing a Constitution for Europe

The Conference notes that if, two years after the signature of the Treaty establishing a Constitution for Europe, four fifths of the Member States have ratified it and one or more Member States have encountered difficulties in proceeding with ratification, the matter will be referred to the European Council.

Document 1.4: European Commission, Summary Table – Procedures planned for the Ratification of the European Constitution, Updated: 10 May 2006 available at www.europa.eu/constitution/ratification_en.htm

Summary table – Procedures planned for the ratification of the European Constitution. Some of the information in this table is subject to change. In particular, certain Member States might decide to hold a referendum.

Table 1.1 Procedures planned for the ratification of the EC

Member state	Procedure	Date scheduled	Previous European referendums
Austria	Parliamentary (*Nationalrat* and *Bundesrat*)	Approval by the *Nationalrat* 11 May 2005 Approval by *Bundesrat* 25 May 2005	1994: accession
Belgium	Parliamentary (Chamber and Senate and Assemblies of Communities and Regions) Indicative referendum ruled out	Approval by the Senate: 28 April 2005 Approval by the Chamber: 19 May 2005 Approval by the Brussels regional parliament: 17 June 2005 Approval by the German Community Parliament of Belgium: 20 June 2005 Approval by the Walloon regional Parliament: 29 June 2005 Approval by the French Community Parliament: 19 July 2005 Approval by the Flemish regional Parliament: 8 February 2006.	No
Cyprus	Parliamentary	Approval by the House: 30 June 2005	No
Czech Republic	Referendum. But no final decision so far	Referendum postponed to end of 2006–beginning of 2007	2003: accession
Denmark	Referendum	Referendum postponed (no new date has been set)	1972: accession 1986: Single European Act 1992: Maastricht Treaty (twice)

Table 1.1 continued

Member state	Procedure	Date scheduled	Previous European referendums
			1998: Amsterdam Treaty 2000: euro
Estonia	Parliamentary	Approval by Parliament: 9 May 2006	2003: accession
Finland	Parliamentary	Presentation by the Government of a report to the parliament: 25 November 2005 Ratification expected during the presidency of the Council in the second half of 2006	Consultative referendum: 1994: accession
France	Referendum	Referendum 29 May 2005 negative (No: 54.68%; turnout: 69.34%)	1972: enlargement EEC 1992: Maastricht Treaty
Germany	Parliamentary (*Bundestag* and *Bundesrat*)	Approval by *Bundestag*: 12 May 2005 Adoption by *Bundesrat*: 27 May 2005	No
Greece	Parliamentary but the Left parties submitted a joint proposal for a referendum	Approval by Parliament: 19 April 2005	No
Hungary	Parliamentary	Approval by Parliament: 20 December 2004	2003: accession
Ireland	Parliamentary and Referendum	Referendum postponed (no date has been set) A White paper was presented to the Parliament on 13 October 2005	1972: accession 1987: Single European Act 1992: Maastricht Treaty 1998: Amsterdam Treaty 2001 and 2002: Nice Treaty

Member state	Procedure	Date scheduled	Previous European referendums
Italy	Parliamentary (Chamber and Senate)	Approval by the Chamber on 25 January 2005 and by the Senate on 6 April	Consultative referendum 1989: possible draft Constitution
Latvia	Parliamentary	Approval by the chamber on 2 June 2005	2003: accession
Lithuania	Parliamentary	Approval by Parliament: 11 November 2004	2003: accession
Luxembourg	Parliamentary (two votes) and consultative referendum	Approval by the Chamber (first reading) 28 June 2005 Positive Referendum 10 July 2005: 56.52% in favour, 43.48% against Final approval by the Chamber 25 October 2005 (57 votes in favour, 1 against)	No
Malta	Parliamentary	Approval by Parliament: 6 July 2005	2003: accession
Netherlands	Parliamentary (First and second Chambers) and consultative referendum	Referendum 1 June 2005 negative (No: 61.6%, turnout: 62.8%)	No
Poland	No decision so far	The Parliament failed on 5 July 2005 to vote on the ratification procedure Ratification postponed (no date has been set)	2003: accession
Portugal	Referendum	Referendum postponed (no date has been set)	No
Slovakia	Parliamentary	Approval by Parliament: 11 May 2005	2003: accession

Table 1.1 continued

Member state	Procedure	Date scheduled	Previous European referendums
Slovenia	Parliamentary	Approval by Parliament: 1 February 2005	2003: accession
Spain	Parliamentary (Congress and Senate) and consultative referendum	Referendum 20 February 2005: 76.7% in favour. Turnout: 42.3% Approval of the Congress on 28 April Approval of the Senate on 18 May 2005	No
Sweden	Parliamentary No referendum envisaged at this stage	Ratification postponed (no date has been set)	Consultative referendums: 1994: accession 2003: euro
United Kingdom	Parliamentary (House of Commons and House of Lords) and referendum	Parliamentary ratification process suspended (suspension announced by UK government, 6 June 2005)	1975: Continued membership of the EC

Document 1.5: Declaration by the Heads of State or Government of the Member States of The European Union on The Ratification of the Treaty Establishing a Constitution For Europe (European Council, 16 and 17 June 2005), Brussels, 18 June 2005 SN 117/05, available on the website of the Council of the European Union at www.consilium.europa.eu

We have held a wide-ranging review of the process of ratification of the Treaty establishing a Constitution for Europe. This Treaty is the fruit of a collective process, designed to provide the appropriate response to ensure that an enlarged European Union functions more democratically, more transparently and more effectively.

Our European ambition, which has served us so well for over 50 years and which has allowed Europe to unite around the same vision, remains more relevant than ever. It has enabled us to ensure the well-being of citizens, the defence of our values and our interests, and to assume our responsibilities as a leading international player. In order to fight unemployment and social exclusion more effectively, to promote sustainable economic growth, to respond to the challenges of globalisation, to safeguard internal and external security, and to protect the environment, we need Europe, a more united Europe presenting greater solidarity.

To date, 10 Member States have successfully concluded ratification procedures, thereby expressing their commitment to the Constitutional Treaty. We have noted the outcome of the referendums in France and the Netherlands. We consider that these results do not call into question citizens' attachment to the construction of Europe. Citizens have nevertheless expressed concerns and worries which need to be taken into account. Hence the need for us to reflect together on this situation.

This period of reflection will be used to enable a broad debate to take place in each of our countries, involving citizens, civil society, social partners, national parliaments and political parties. This debate, designed to generate interest, which is already under way in many Member States, must be intensified and broadened. The European institutions will also have to make their contribution, with the Commission playing a special role in this regard.

The recent developments do not call into question the validity of continuing with the ratification processes. We are agreed that the timetable for the ratification in different Member States will be altered if necessary in response to these developments and according to the circumstances in these Member States.

We have agreed to come back to this matter in the first half of 2006 to make an overall assessment of the national debates and agree on how to proceed.

Document 1.6: Vienna Convention on the Law of the Treaties of 22 May 1969, Article 18

Article 18 'Obligation not to defeat the object and purpose of a treaty prior to its entry into force'

A State is obliged to refrain from acts which would defeat the object and purpose of a treaty when:

(a) it has signed the treaty or has exchanged instruments constituting the treaty subject to ratification, acceptance or approval, until it shall have made its intention clear not to become a party to the treaty; or

(b) it has expressed its consent to be bound by the treaty, pending the entry into force of the treaty and provided that such entry into force is not unduly delayed.

Document 1.7: European Parliament, Resolution on the period of reflection: the structure, subjects and context for an assessment of the debate on the European Union (selected extracts), Session document A6-0414/2005, 16.12.2005, available on the website of the European Parliament at www.europarl.europa.eu/eu

European Parliament – 2004–2009, Report on the period of reflection: the structure, subjects and context for an assessment of the debate on the European Union (2005/2146(INI)), Committee on Constitutional Affairs, Co-rapporteurs: Andrew Duff and Johannes Voggenhuber

[. . .]

The European Parliament,

- having regard to the Treaty of Nice,
- having regard to the Treaty establishing a Constitution for Europe,
- having regard to its resolution of 12 January 2005 on the Treaty establishing a Constitution for Europe,
- having regard to the Declaration of 18 June 2005 by the Heads of State or Government on the ratification of the Treaty establishing a Constitution for Europe, at the conclusion of the European Council of 16 and 17 June 2005,
- having regard to the Treaty concerning the Accession of the Republic of Bulgaria and Romania to the European Union,
- having regard to the opinions on the period of reflection delivered by the Committee of the Regions on 13 October 2005 and the European Economic and Social Committee on 26 October 2005 at the request of the European Parliament,
- having regard to Rule 45 of its Rules of Procedure,
- having regard to the report of the Committee on Constitutional Affairs and the opinions of the Committee on Foreign Affairs, the Committee on Industry, Research and Energy, the Committee on Regional Development, the Committee on Agriculture and Rural Development, the Committee on Culture and Education, the Committee on Legal Affairs, the Committee on Civil Liberties, Justice and Home Affairs and the Committee on Women's Rights and Gender Equality (A60414/2005),

Whereas

A. The Treaty establishing a Constitution for Europe was signed by the Heads of State and Government of the twenty-five Member States of the European Union on 29 October 2004, and confirmed again by the European Council in its Declaration of 18 June 2005,

B. The Constitution was drafted by the European Convention which, compared to previous procedures to prepare new treaties, achieved new levels of openness, pluralism and democratic legitimacy,

C. The European Parliament endorsed the Constitution by a majority of over two-thirds as 'a good compromise and a vast improvement on the existing treaties . . . [which] will provide a stable and lasting framework for the future development of the European Union that will allow for further enlargement while providing mechanisms for its revision when needed' in its Resolution of 12 January 2005,

D. The reforms for which the Treaty establishing a Constitution for Europe provides are intended, inter alia, to cope with the consequences of the enlargement of the Union on 1 May 2004, and the success of this and future enlargements will be in jeopardy unless a constitutional package is ratified,

E. Thirteen Member States, representing a majority of the Member States of the Union, have since ratified the Constitution in accordance with their own constitutional requirements, including by means of a referendum in both Spain and Luxembourg,

F. France and the Netherlands, following referendums held on 29 May and 1 June 2005 respectively, have failed to ratify the Constitution – with the result that the ratification process has subsequently stalled in most of the remaining ten Member States,

G. Under Article 48 of the Treaty on European Union, the Constitution will not enter into force unless and until it is ratified by all Member States,

H. Declaration 30 annexed to the Treaty Establishing a Constitution for Europe, states that 'if 2 years after the signature of the Treaty Establishing a Constitution for Europe, four fifth of the Member States have ratified and one or more Member States have encountered difficulties with proceeding with ratification, the matter will be referred to the European Council',

I. It is necessary to respect those Member States and their peoples which have ratified the Constitution as well as those which have not, and to analyse carefully the reasons for the negative results in France and the Netherlands,

J. The No votes appear to have been rather more an expression of dissent at the present state of the Union than a specific objection to the constitutional reforms, but, paradoxically, the result of the Noes is to maintain the status quo and block reform,

K. The European Council confirmed this analysis by taking the view, in its Declaration of 18 June 2005, that 'these results do not call into question citizens' attachment to the construction of Europe' but that 'citizens have nevertheless expressed concerns and worries which need to be taken into account'; the European Council therefore decided on a 'period of reflection . . . to enable a broad debate to take place in each of our countries, involving citizens, civil society, social partners, national parliaments and political parties'; the heads of government agreed that in the first half of 2006 they would 'make an overall assessment of the national debates and agree on how to proceed',

L. In that Declaration, the heads of government declared that the ratification process could continue, and also agreed that the original timetable for the entry into force of the Constitution (1 November 2006) would be extended,

M. The European Council, however, failed to give a clear focus to the period of reflection or to define the methods and the framework for drawing conclusions from this debate, and has since been seen to lack both the political will and the capacity to stimulate and manage the European dialogue,

N. The absence of an agreement on the policy challenges and budgetary means of the enlarged Union for the period 2007–2013 further undermines the present and future Union,

O. The period of reflection has started with debates on the context rather than the text, with issues such as the future of the European social model, European economic prospects, the speed of enlargement, the medium term budget and the single market in services, all featuring prominently,

P. The Commission has published its contribution on the period of reflection with the aim of restoring public confidence in the European Union by supporting national debates and promoting initiatives at community level, but this should not prevent all of Europe's political institutions from making a combined effort or from exercising leadership which takes seriously the strategic importance of the Constitution and the political reality of the preconditions upon which its success depends,

Q. The national parliaments have declared their support for a series of joint parliamentary meetings that will 'stimulate, steer and synthesize' the European dialogue,

1. Reaffirms its conviction that the Treaty of Nice is not a viable basis for the continuation of the European integration process;

2. Confirms its commitment to achieving without undue delay a constitutional settlement which strengthens parliamentary democracy, transparency and the rule of law, anchors fundamental rights, develops citizenship, and enhances the capacity of the enlarged Union to act effectively at home and abroad; fears that without such a constitutional settlement it will not be possible for the Union to expect the support of its citizens, to maintain the momentum of integration and to become a credible partner in world affairs; recalls its endorsement of the Treaty establishing a Constitution for Europe as achieving these objectives; calls also on the European Council of June 2006 solemnly to declare the same commitment to a constitutional settlement on the future of Europe;

3. Stresses that it is not possible to further enlarge the Union after the accession of Bulgaria and Romania on the basis of the Treaty of Nice;

4. Recalls that the political problems and institutional weakness that the Convention was set up to address will persist – and, indeed, grow unless and until the reforms enshrined in the Treaty establishing a Constitution for Europe are brought into force;

5. Notes that many of the concerns expressed relate more to general and specific problems of context than to the text itself; considers that if progress can be made in such issues, it will be easier to find a solution regarding the text;

6. Resists proposals to establish core groups of certain Member States while the constitutional process is still in train; deplores any suggestion that coalitions of certain Member States could be formed outside the EU system; points out that forms of enhanced cooperation should promote the achievement of the Union's aims, preserve its interests and reinforce the process of integration, and be open to all the Member States at any time; also stresses that these possible forms of cooperation should not be implemented to the detriment of the efforts being made to arrive at a Constitution for Europe without undue delay;

7. Warns that a strategy based on the selective implementation of the Constitution risks destroying the consensus that achieved a balance between the institutions and among Member States, thereby aggravating the crisis of confidence;

8. Notes that there are only a limited number of democratic reforms that can be introduced at this stage without treaty change but by revision of rules of procedure or interinstitutional agreement – such as transparency of law-making in the Council, introduction of a form of citizens' initiative, improvements to the comitology procedure, full use of the 'passerelle' clauses in the field of justice and home affairs, and the more rigorous scrutiny by each national parliament of its government's conduct of EU affairs;

9. Proposes to use the current period of reflection to re-launch the constitutional project on the basis of a broad public debate about the future of European integration; resolves that this European dialogue – whose results should not be prejudged – should aim to clarify, deepen and democratise the consensus around the Constitution and address criticisms and find solutions where expectations have not been met;

10. Welcomes the beginnings of a broad debate about the Union's policy direction but stresses that this must take place within the context of overcoming the constitutional crisis, and that policy prescriptions at EU level must relate directly to the rules, powers and procedures of the EU institutions as well as to the competences conferred on the EU by the Member States and should identify the issues that are common throughout Europe;

11. Suggests that this new dialogue, which should be seen as a chance to promote European democracy, should be conducted and coordinated across the Union, structured by common themes and in realistic stages according to an agreed framework for evaluation, and designed to lead to decisive political choices;

12. Insists that the public debate be engaged within both the European and the national framework; warns that narrowly focussed national debates will do

little to change national stereotypes, and also that an imposed dialogue without political goals would become nebulous, even vacuous, thereby giving rise to increased disaffection on the part of European citizens;

13. Proposes that the European Parliament invite national parliaments to a series of conferences ('Parliamentary Forums') in order to stimulate the debate and to shape, step by step, the necessary political conclusions; will invite the other EU institutions to contribute to the Forums;

14. Recognises the critical importance for the European Union and in particular for Parliament of avoiding another setback in the constitutional process; commits itself therefore to playing a leading role in the European dialogue, in particular by publishing 'European Papers' on each of the big issues facing the Union, which may be used as a common European template for the national debates and which, together with contributions from national parliaments, should be used as the basis for the deliberations of the Parliamentary Forums;

15. Recognises that it is strategically important for political institutions to encourage a pro-active attitude on the part of the media (in particular television, the press and local radio) and to enlist them for the purpose of publicising and intensifying the debate;

16. Proposes that the first Parliamentary Forum be convened in the spring of 2006, in advance of the June meeting of the European Council, in order to hear reports from the French and Dutch Parliaments about their suggestions for a way forward and to discuss, on the basis of this Resolution, the structure of the European dialogue, the aim of this Forum being to make comprehensive recommendations to the European Council about how the Union should proceed to find the way out of the crisis;

17. Proposes that the first Parliamentary Forum should identify a limited number of priority questions about the future of Europe and the governance of the Union which should be addressed in subsequent Forums and in the broader public debate, such as:

(i) what is the goal of European integration?

(ii) what role should Europe have in the world?

(iii) in the light of globalisation, what is the future of the European social and economic model?

(iv) how do we define the boundaries of the European Union?

(v) how do we enhance freedom, security and justice?

18. Believes that a rich debate on these fundamental issues will open up new perspectives for European integration and prepare the ground for reform of the common policies in those areas where dissension exists;

19. Believes, moreover, that the European dialogue will only overcome the constitutional crisis if it engages not only each EU institution but also national and regional parliaments, local government, political parties, social partners,

civil society, the academic community and the media; puts particular value in this regard upon practical contributions from the European Economic and Social Committee and the Committee of the Regions;

20. Requests Member States to organise a large number of public meetings and media debates on the future of Europe ('Citizens' Forums') at national, regional and local level, structured along the commonly agreed themes, with the assistance of the Commission; urges the social partners and civil society organisations to get engaged in these debates;

21. Expects political parties to give much more prominence to the European dimension in both their internal debates and electoral campaigning;

22. Would welcome citizens' petitions that contribute to shaping the debate;

23. Urges the Union to give much greater priority to cultural and educational policy in order to give life to the Constitution's formula of 'unity in diversity';

24. Points out that a European dialogue will be impossible without adequate funding, and reiterates its budgetary proposal for increased funding of the PRINCE programme; in this regard, urges a rapid settlement of the Financial Perspective of the Union for the period 2007–2013;

25. Suggests that the conclusions of the period of reflection should be drawn at the latest in the second half of 2007, and that a clear decision be reached at that stage about how to proceed with the Constitution;

26. Notes that there is in theory a number of options available to the Union ranging from abandoning the constitutional project altogether, continuing to try to ratify the present text unamended, seeking to clarify or add to the present text, restructuring and/or modifying the present text with the aim of improving it, or embarking upon a complete re-write;

27. Considers that a positive outcome of the period of reflection would be that the current text can be maintained, although this would only be possible if accompanied by significant measures to reassure and convince public opinion;

28. Calls on the members of the European Council to accept both individual and collective responsibility for bringing into force a Constitution for Europe; and insists that they coordinate more closely both the content and timing of the national campaigns and give evidence to the citizen of their political will and mutual solidarity;

29. Takes note of Commission's 'Plan D for Democracy, Dialogue and Debate'(COM(2005)0494), but calls on the Commission not only to deliver its communications strategy but also to show decisive political commitment to help the Union emerge from its current constitutional difficulties;

30. Underlines that Romania and Bulgaria must be involved in all the actions referred to above;

31. Calls upon all civil-society associations and organisations to include the

entry into force of the Constitution as one of their priorities for discussion and debate;

32. Demands in any case that every effort be made to ensure that the Constitution enters into force during 2009;

33. Instructs its Committee on Constitutional Affairs to monitor the period of reflection, especially as regards the preparation of the Parliamentary Forums, the elaboration of the working documents ('European Papers') the summarising of the institutional and citizens' debates, conclusions and the proposals for action that may emerge from them;

34. In this spirit, asks the Constitutional Affairs Committee to work closely with all other committees directly interested in the preparation of the Parliamentary Forums and the drafting of the working documents for them;

35. Instructs its President to forward this Resolution to the members of the European Council, the Council, the Commission, the national and regional parliaments of the Member States, the Committee of the Regions, the European Economic and Social Committee, the former Members of the European Convention, and the parliaments and governments of the accession and candidate countries.

Document 1.8: Committee of the Regions, Opinion on the Period of Reflection: the Structure, Subjects and Context for an Assessment of the Debate of the European Union, Const-032, 21 October 2005 (selected extracts), available on the website of the Committee of the Regions at www.cor.europa.eu

The Committee of the Regions

(A) CONTEXT

1. believes that, in order to safeguard peace, freedom and prosperity, a politically strong and democratic European Union, strong European leadership and strong interinstitutional cooperation to relaunch the European project are needed;

2. expresses concern that too long a period of reflection would damage the EU's public image, and urges all institutions to work to reclaim and relaunch the core European ideal and project;

3. considers it advisable to use this period for reflection to examine what the public in the Member States thinks about the European Union and to consolidate the fundamental aims, values and principles of the EU, such as solidarity, effectiveness, transparency and cooperation, based on the support of its citizens;

4. reiterates the importance of the fundamental rights of the Union as enshrined in the charter included in the Constitutional Treaty;

5. believes that the European Union must take the results of the French and Dutch referenda seriously and must be seen to do so; considers that to proceed with the ratification process of the Constitutional Treaty without altering the original schedule and without serious reflection at European level would send a negative message to Europe's citizens and might engender further rejections in Member States;

6. recognises however that the reasons for those rejections are many and varied and in some cases may not be in response to the Treaty itself; thus considers it fundamental to concentrate efforts above all on the context of the debate, focusing it on a successful agreement of the financial perspectives; reiterates however that more than a half of all Member States have already ratified the Treaty by their chosen method and the decisions of these Member States must count as much as those who voted against;

7. reaffirms its commitment to the Constitutional Treaty and its advances which guarantee better European governance through its considerable improvement in the functioning, simplicity and transparency of the EU compared to the existing treaties;

8. considers that in broadening out the debate on the future of the European Union its institutions should focus on the actual and potential practical benefits that membership and citizenship bring to its citizens;

9. in order to rebuild the trust of European citizens in the European project, calls on the EU institutions to:

- take decisions which are pending in those areas where the Union brings real added value to Europe's citizens;
- begin functioning in a much more decentralised manner, respecting and promoting the subsidiarity principle, which should be applied also on subnational levels;
- pro-actively demonstrate that a political union will not undermine Europe's cultural and linguistic diversity;
- show that Europe will provide its citizens with opportunities to develop their personal and professional experience at a European level;
- establish a permanent two-way dialogue with Europe's citizens;
- develop a culture of enhanced transparency, especially by making the workings of the Council more accessible, to enable citizens to better understand the EU decision-making process;

10. calls for the continuation of activities promoting the principle of subsidiarity in all areas and drawing on the advantages that the greater proximity of regional and local institutions can offer to citizens;

11. calls upon the Member States to deepen political integration of the EU, which constitutes a fundamental basis to develop an enlarged Union, defining

the aims, potential geographical limits and long term objectives of the integration process within the European Union; whereas EU membership shall entail respect for local and regional democratic self-government within the established constitutional framework of each country;

12. calls on politicians at Member State, regional and local levels to take the responsibility for their own actions in the areas falling in their responsibility and to refrain from the common habit of using 'Brussels' as scapegoat; underlines that the European Union can only succeed if politicians at European, national, regional and local level divide duties responsibly and acknowledge that institutional respect is essential for success, as a prerequisite for good governance;

[. . .]

(C) SUBJECTS FOR REFLECTION

GENERAL SCOPE

20. considers that the provisions of the Constitutional Treaty relating to the Union's territorial dimension and the involvement of local and regional authorities, both institutionally through the CoR and more generally, constitute an important and positive development;

21. calls upon the EU institutions to help to develop a real 'subsidiarity culture' within the Union, its Member States, and its regional and local authorities, and to apply without delay the principles of subsidiarity and proportionality provided for in the Constitutional Treaty as a simple and effective way to demonstrate to citizens that the Union will act only where the added value is clear and in respect for its principle of better lawmaking;

22. calls for application of the concept of 'proximity' in the application of EU policies and law, as this would be a visible sign of the will to implement procedures for more transparency as an immediate reaction to citizens' concerns; in this context the introduction of a new legal instrument facilitating interregional and cross-border cooperation, including economic and social cooperation, could be seen, for instance, as a clear sign towards a closer Europe of the citizens;

23. underlines that whereas it would be desirable for these elements to have a place in the Treaty, many of the actions and obligations arising from these provisions can be integrated immediately into the Community's activities, such as extending impact assessments to include the financial and administrative impact of new EU law on local and regional authorities;

- has in particular welcomed the following points in the Treaty as articles of good governance and wishes to ensure that their safeguard and implementation are fully considered during the period of reflection:

- recognition of the role of local and regional authorities in EU governance;
- better consultation prior to publication of legislative proposals;
- account to be taken of the financial and administrative burden falling on local or regional authorities;
- a broader definition of subsidiarity to incorporate local and regional government; recognition of the cultural and linguistic diversity as a source of wealth to be preserved, alongside the fundamental principle of cooperation and integration;
- enhancement of the role of the Committee of the Regions, in particular introduction of the right of recourse to the European Court of Justice in respect of its own prerogatives or breaches of subsidiarity;
- reference to representative associations (for example of local or regional government);

(D) ASSESSMENT

35. invites the EU institutions and the Member States to listen to the citizens in order to evaluate the results of the debate during the period of reflection;

36. is conscious that during the period of reflection various different scenarios are likely to be discussed, but is against abandoning this Constitutional Treaty in favour of the Nice Treaty, and calls for a consensual approach towards ratification by 2009;

37. wishes to actively participate in the relaunching of the constitutional process and offers to the European Parliament support for its efforts to secure a successful outcome.

Document 1.9: German Federal Government, Angela Merkel's Government Policy Statement, 30 November 2005, English translation by the German Government's services (selected extracts), available at http://www.bundesregierung.de/en/-,10001.929347/regierungserklaerung/Policy-Statement-by-Federal-Ch.htm

Policy Statement by Federal Chancellor Dr Angela Merkel in the German Bundestag 30 November 2005

[. . .] Ladies and gentlemen, as you can see we have an ambitious agenda because we are sure that a great deal can be achieved. We have done so because we know that economic strength is once again possible. Then we can experience once again what made Germany's social market such a success. Then we will be able to overcome the contradiction between labour and capital and help those for whom life is tough going. If we can accomplish that we can also be a strong partner in Europe and in the world at large. German foreign and European policy is based on values and informed by interests. A policy serving German interests needs, as we know, alliances and cooperation with our partners.

I am aware that they have great expectations of us as I found again during my recent visits to Paris, Brussels and London. The reason they are so high is that Europe is now in a deep crisis. The fundamental cause of this crisis is a lack of trust:

- The Constitutional Treaty has suffered major setbacks.
- On EU finances there are serious conflicts of interest between the Member States.
- Progress on the Lisbon Process is well behind target.
- The future of European enlargement increasingly calls for answers to a number of fundamental issues: Where does Europe end? What is the purpose of European unification?

Moreover, those who are serious about strengthening the EU's and its institutions' ability to act must continue to support the European Constitution project.

Let me state clearly: we want to make the Constitution Treaty a success.

Document 1.10: French Socialist Party, Le Mans Conference 18 to 20 November 2005 – Final Motion 'Winning From the Left With the Socialists: Consensus–Truth–Unity', available at http://www.parti-socialiste.fr (selected extracts) [translation]

The European Left holds the key to the future of Europe. Within this context, we have a particular responsibility in resolving the crisis and meeting the expectations, requirements and dissatisfactions of our fellow citizens which were expressed on 29 May. In order to overcome this crisis, we must move beyond differences between yes and no, have a clear vision of our project for Europe, and agree amongst ourselves over the methods for its implementation.

During the debate on the European Constitution, we differed over the best response to bring in order to build up a strong Europe marked by its solidarity. But this goal was and remains shared by all socialists: as militants in favour of the European Union, and as its true architects, we want to refocus it around a political consensus that is more in tune with social issues. We socialists reaffirm our commitment to the federal perspective.

Having remained on the sidelines in 2002, the debate over the future of Europe shall be one of the key issues in the presidential election of 2007. The heads of state and government have already planned to examine the issue of the institutional future of the Union and the Constitutional Treaty in mid-2007. On 29 May, the Constitutional Treaty was rejected by a majority of our citizens. We socialists take note of this rejection and shall respect this popular consensus. We propose to redefine the basis for the revival of the European project.

We propose a recovery plan for Europe based on the following elements:

- repeal of anti-social directives (services directive, working time directive, and so on) and development of a framework directive on public services;
- bolstering of the Euro zone with the goals of employment, growth and innovation clearly affirmed in the economic policy of the zone;
- reform of the stability pact, establishment of an economic government, democratic control of the ECB by the European Parliament. The objectives of the Central Bank must include growth and full employment;
- development of a Social Treaty, outlawing fiscal and social dumping in an enlarged Europe and curbing unchecked relocations within this space. The appearance of a minimum European wage would be a symbolic step;.
- drafting of a constitutional text that is legible and democratic, centred around the institutions and values of the Union; such a text could be drafted in a constituent process;
- doubling of the European budget to 2 per cent of GDP. The Union must in future be able not only to borrow but also to levy a European tax which could be a surcharge on the wealth tax [Impôt de Solidarité sur la Fortune];
- more stringent action on the common external tariff: the existing instruments are not satisfactory, in particular because they are not sufficiently used. We socialists undertake to assess the implementation of measures that are better able to protect European industry and its future, in particular against relocations outside Europe. The establishment of minimum standards in social and environmental matters applying to suppliers of the Union, along the lines of those concerning technical standards which already apply to imported products, could be the conditio sine qua non for free importation into the EU. This will therefore constitute a powerful lever for bringing about levelled up convergence of social models;
- it is necessary to move towards budgetary federalism and to permit the Union to levy taxes and to issue loans to finance a plan for European integration, following the pattern of the programme that was necessary to finance the first wave of adherence to the Euro.

Document 1.11: Translated with the permission of *La Revue du Marché Commun et de l'Union européenne*, Jacques Ziller, 'The Constitution for Europe, let's talk about it!' [La Constitution pour L'Europe, Parlons en!], in *Revue du Marché Commun et de l'Union européenne*, no. 426, March 2006, pp. 1–6 (selected extracts) [translation]

[. . .]

II Putting the Constitutional Treaty back on the agenda while respecting the will of the electorate of all countries of the Union

It is more than legitimate to put the Constitutional Treaty back on the European agenda, and above all to seek out the means for implementing the solutions which Europe needs, at the same time respecting the will of the electorate – of all voters, including those who voted against ratification just as those who voted in favour in referenda, as well as those who have elected parliamentary majorities which have spoken out in favour of the Treaty. No solution can be found which focuses on the concerns of an individual country in isolation. It is necessary both to understand what the Union needs and what is feasible in the light of the legitimate differences in interests between the Member States and the extent of that which citizens are prepared to accept.

The European Convention worked for eighteen months to hammer out a draft which satisfied the Union's apparent needs. It is all too easy for all and sundry to criticize the gaps or to propose alternative versions for a text which Valéry Giscard d'Estaing branded in June 2003 as 'imperfect but beyond what could be hoped for'. The unfolding of events during the intergovernmental conference from October 2003 to June 2004 threw into relief the restrictions inherent in any attempt to reach agreement between the governments of the 25 countries, in the face of all the differences in their respective political orientations, their views on the future of Europe, and above all their perceptions of the interests of their respective countries and of the expectations of their voters. The context has not fundamentally changed since then, beyond the change in status of ten of the 13 countries whose delegates participated in the European Convention from that of candidates to full blown members, which can only fuel their desire to achieve recognition for their own special circumstances. This is one of the main reasons which make it so difficult to set aside the contents of the Treaty of 29 October 2005, the other being that the 14 countries whose parliaments or electorates have already expressed their agreement might well have more difficulties in accepting a text which differed from the present one than those which have not yet ratified this text. This situation creates various constraints which significantly circumscribe the room for manoeuvre of those who genuinely look for a solution to the vote of 29 May in France and that of 1 June in the Netherlands.

Respecting the electoral results means trying to understand the arguments made during the campaign, in order then to offer an alternative solution, both to those who voted 'no' as well as to those who voted 'yes' or who abstained. The available means for understanding these arguments are limited in number and rudimentary: on the one hand there are a couple of opinion polls from the day of the referendum or from its immediate aftermath, whilst on the other hand there are the campaign arguments. Two strands of criticism were levelled against the European Constitution during the referendum campaign, in responses to opinion pollsters as well as, as the case may be, during the debates which followed it. In the first place there were substantive critiques, which can be summed up in the fear that the European Convention could be the direct or indirect cause of job losses or of a weakening of social protection, or of a loss of sovereignty or autonomy of governments and national parliaments. Procedural critiques on the other hand pointed to the length and complexity of a text which the French electorate analysed in detail during the weeks leading up to the referendum, whilst Dutch voters basically complained of a lack of information.

The Response to Substantive Criticisms of the Constitutional Treaty: a Declaration of the European Council

The response to substantive criticisms cannot consist in the opening of negotiations for a new constitutional treaty, since practically all of the provisions of the Constitution which have been criticized during these debates are included in the texts of the treaties currently in force and which have been accepted by the 25 Member States, mostly since the Treaty of Rome, which came into force on 1 January 1958, or alternatively – in relation to provisions pertaining to economic and monetary union – following the Maastricht Treaty, which came into force on 1 November 1993. The response to these critiques can in fact be found in the provisions of the Constitutional Treaty which constitute a step forward from the existing treaties: the fundamental social rights of the second part, the crosscutting social clause of article III-117, the rebalancing of powers between the European Parliament and the Council, the affirmation of the respect by the Union for the diversity of its Member States and the new organization of relations between its institutions and the national parliaments as well as regional and local authorities.

There is a need in this area for a declaration of the European Council or some other formal act establishing the importance of an interpretation of the Constitution which promotes the development of employment and social protection. Although it is possible to find a formulation for a formal declaration that is acceptable to all governments which would not be wholly devoid of effects in that it would inform future interpretations of the Constitutional Treaty by the institutions of the Union, it is unrealistic to hope that new chapters on social policy could be added to the Constitution, and still less that the core of the internal market (formerly the common market), in existence since the end of the transition period provided for under the Treaty of Rome (1 January 1970), could be thrown into question.

A solution of this type was used to address the fears of the Danish electorate in 1992: rather than granting new derogations to Denmark, as is often claimed, the European Council of Edinburgh simply repeated formally by means of a ‘Decision’ of heads of state and government that which had already been granted to Denmark in the Maastricht Treaty, while at the same time clarifying the provisions inserted into the EC Treaty in 1986 by the Single European Act with article 100A(3) and (4), according to which the Treaty 'does not prevent any Member State from maintaining or introducing more stringent protection measures compatible with the EC Treaty, . . . in the field of working conditions and in social policy, . . . in order to attain a high level of consumer protection, . . . in order to pursue the objectives of protection of the environment' and which 'permit each Member State to pursue its own policy with regard to distribution of income and maintain or improve social welfare benefits'.[8]

The Response to Procedural Criticisms of the Constitutional Treaty: the Division of the Treaty into Two Parts

The response to procedural criticism must bear one limitation in particular in mind: the Constitutional Treaty was drafted in 21 official languages, without counting the Bulgarian and Romanian versions which will be necessary after the next enlargement, or the translations into Basque, Catalan, Galician and Valencian deposited by the Spanish government. This accordingly reduces both the interest in and possibility of trying to formulate particular provisions differently, not to speak once again of the fact that the essence of the text contained in the third part of the Constitution is taken word for word from the treaties already in force. For this reason they cannot be subject to discussion which would risk spinning out negotiations indefinitely.

The solution of separating the third part of the Constitution from the other provisions seems to be more straightforward. It had been proposed in particular by vice-president Amato during the working sessions of the European Convention. The contents of the third part of the Constitution are indispensable for the proper functioning of the Union, because it is this part that delineates the Union's competences in relation to those of the Member States, and which specifies relevant decision-making procedures: ordinary legislative procedure, special legislative procedures, or implementing acts. But it is not absolutely necessary that this content be included in the same text as the constitutional provisions of part one, the Charter of Fundamental Rights of part two, or the final provisions of part four. This would therefore leave us with a treaty establishing a Constitution for Europe, containing parts I, II and IV of the current text, alongside a treaty which contained the text of part three. This could for example be called the Basic Treaty of the European Union; this title could easily be translated into the other languages and be distinguished from that of the Constitution, in spite of their similarities. The only amendments to the texts would consist in a replacement of the references in particular articles of parts one and four of the Constitution to articles in part three with references to the articles of the Fundamental Treaty. Such an amendment could be made in an extremely short protocol: one article dividing the parts into two different treaties, and a second article setting out relevant numbering changes, to which a modified version of part IV could be attached as an appendix.

For all countries in which ratification procedures have already been concluded, it would be easy within a very short time frame to organize new procedures authorizing the ratification of this protocol, which would not require any substantive debate. An identical procedure was used to take note of the refusal of the Norwegian electorate to join the European Community and European Union in 1972 and 1994, respectively. For countries which have not yet finished their ratification procedures, things would be even simpler, and there would be no need to take the debate back to its initial stages.

This leaves France and the Netherlands. The precedents of Denmark in 1992–3 or Ireland in 2001–02 show that it is possible to reopen discussions on a 'no' vote without modifying the Treaty originally offered for referendum. This, however, must occur within a new context, which might include declarations or 'decisions' of the European Council as were made for those two countries; declarations of the respective governments of the countries concerned, as the Danish and Irish governments did in 1992 and 2002, respectively, before putting the matter in the hands of their electorates a second time; even a constitutional amendment, as in Ireland where the second referendum in 2002 related not only to the Treaty of Nice which had been put before the electorate the year before, but also to a constitutional reform which made any future participation of Ireland in the common defence policy subject to approval by the two houses of the Irish *Oireachtas*. Similarly, it is necessary to put the present matter before the electorate, not so much on legal grounds – the Dutch referendum was consultative, and the French Constitution did not expressly prevent the legislature from ignoring the popular vote in the referendum – but more simply out of respect for democracy.

There are various ways of putting this issue before the electorate again: in addition to a specific referendum, it may also occur through parliamentary or presidential elections, provided that the commitments made by those elected are clear. As is known, by Spring 2007 at the latest there will have been parliamentary elections both in the Netherlands and in France, as well as presidential elections in France. Parliamentary and presidential candidates will certainly need some political courage to take up an unambiguous position in favour of the ratification of the European Constitution, but this is not beyond the realms of the possible. And anyway has not one of the potential candidates for the presidential election in 2007 already stated that a referendum in his opinion would not be absolutely necessary? One particular constraint stems from commitments that the socialist party in France has already made, calling for a shorter constitutional text, although the party still supports the principle of a European Constitution, as has the majority of people questioned in opinion polls on this issue in France. If the European debate during 2006 can show that the only alternative to the Treaty of 29 October 2005 is its division into a Constitution for Europe and a Fundamental Treaty of the European Union, accompanied by a declaration on Social Europe, it will be difficult for it to argue against this alternative project.

Referendum or Constitutional Amendments in the Member States: Different Ways of Resolving the Crisis

Is a referendum really necessary? The problem of referenda on European treaties lies in the fact that they leave the fate of the peoples of all European countries in the hands of the electorate of one single country. Still, one cannot really ask the French or Dutch electorates to take not only their own aspirations into account, but also those of their neighbours who have no vote – which is by contrast foreseeable in the context of a parliamentary debate. As far as France in particular is concerned, where both presidential and parliamentary elections will be held in quick succession, it would make little sense to call for a referendum after these elections if both the new President of the Republic and the majority in the National Assembly had, prior to the vote, clearly spoken out in favour of ratification. After all, nobody would dream of asking a newly elected President of the Republic to invite voters to decide in separate referenda over each of the points in his or her programme.

A constitutional reform, which could be linked to an authorization to ratify, is possible and undoubtedly attractive as an argument against those who accuse politicians of wanting to manipulate public opinion. This was the solution chosen by the Irish government when putting the matter before the electorate after receiving a new mandate in the parliamentary elections of 7 May 2002: the new referendum not only concerned the ratification of the Nice Treaty, as in 2001, but also a constitutional reform crystallising the commitments undertaken by the Irish government before the European Council.

In the Netherlands, the constitutional amendment procedure requires the dissolution of the Chamber of Deputies, in order to ensure that the election campaign focuses on the proposed amendment. Rather than awaiting the end of the legislature in 2007, the Dutch parliament could set such a constitutional amendment in motion, by incorporating the authorization to ratify the constitutional treaty and the fundamental treaty into provisions of internal law which it deems necessary to ensure a better participation of the Dutch electorate in the future of the Union.

In France, constitutional amendments are also possible, and even if this is by no means necessary, it is nonetheless desirable. During the amendment of 28 February 2004, the drafters in fact neglected to take two important innovations in the Constitution for Europe into consideration. In the first place, the prospective article 88-6 of the French Constitution provides that 'Parliament may, after a motion is passed in identical terms by the National Assembly and the Senate, oppose any modification of the rules governing the passing of Acts of the European Union under the simplified revision procedure as set forth in the Treaty establishing a Constitution for Europe' as currently provided for under article IV-444 of the Constitutional Treaty. But no provision is made for the implementation of article IV-445 governing the simplified revision procedure concerning internal Union policies and action. It would therefore be logical, according to a specific procedure, to involve the French Parliament more closely in the amendment of articles concerning internal Union policies and action, especially if those articles currently included in part three became the text of a Fundamental Treaty distinct from the Constitution proper. Although of course the national parliaments must in any case give an opinion on any decision of the European Council taken on the basis of article IV-445, this would occur too late in the day to have any chance of affecting its enacted form. It would therefore be useful to enact a specific procedure.

Secondly, article IV-440(7) of the Constitutional Treaty provides for the possibility, on the initiative of the Member State concerned, to change the status of Danish, French or Dutch (overseas) countries or territories from that of outermost region integrated in the Union to that of associated overseas country or territory, and vice versa. In February 2004 the constitutional draftsmen failed to establish the internal aspects within the French Constitution of this procedure. This is all the more surprising in view of the fact that, since the amendment in 2003 concerning territorial units, the consent of the electorate is required in order to modify the status of departments, regions and overseas territorial units by transferring them from the article 73 regime to that of article 74 of the Constitution. These provisions are not technically applicable to a change in their European status, and it would therefore be useful to make further specific provision here.

Were a decision to be made in the European Council of June or December 2006 in favour of the division of the Treaty of 29 October 2004 into a constitutional treaty proper and a fundamental treaty, associated with a declaration on the social future of the European Union, then, as far as the French were concerned, the current crisis could be resolved by the acquisition of commitments from candidates in the presidential and parliamentary elections in favour of the ratification of these two treaties by way of an amendment, consisting of the two additions proposed here, of the text of the Constitution of the Fifth Republic. This would ensure that the authorization to ratify would be subject to the conditions for amendment of the 1958 Constitution, namely an identical vote of the two chambers of Parliament, followed either by a referendum or by a three-fifths majority vote of Parliament convened in Congress.

Surely that which is sufficiently democratic to modify the French Constitution is also appropriate to authorize the ratification by France of the Constitution for Europe?

In order for such a solution to be feasible it is imperative not to wait any longer: voters must know what is at stake before the 2007 elections in France and the Netherlands, as well as voters in other Member States, especially if ratification has not yet been authorized in their own country.

1 February 2006

Document 1.12: Reprinted with the permission of the author: Bruno De Witte, 'How Might the EU's Constitutional Arrangements be Settled? Escape Routes from the Constitution Trap and their Legal Feasibility', 1 February 2006

After the initial shock following the French and Dutch referenda, a number of political actors have started delineating scenarios for organizing the European Union's escape from the dead end in which the Constitutional Treaty process seemed to have ended. In this contribution, I do not intend to comment on the political feasibility of these various scenarios but on their legal feasibility, assuming that they get sufficient political support. Law is treated here as a semi-independent variable in the constitutional reform debate. Law serves as an instrument, providing means by which political ideas can be translated into written arrangements that bind participants of the system and have practical consequences; but law is also a value, in the sense that the European integration project has traditionally (compared to other regimes of international cooperation) given central importance to compliance with legal rules, and this respect for the rule of law is considered to be one of the ingredients of the overall success of the European integration project. In view of this, 'escape routes' from the constitutional dead end should be based on respect for the rule of law. This is not an evident assumption. In fact, at earlier, more confident, stages of the constitutional reform process, respect for the law was considered to be of secondary importance by some leading actors. For example, Giscard d'Estaing stated in the summer of 2004 that, if a large majority of the citizens of Europe and of the member states approved the Constitution, problems would arise for the states that refused to ratify it, and not for the Constitution itself.[9] He thus flatly ignored the 'rule of the game' (repeated in the Constitutional Treaty itself) that the Constitution cannot enter into force unless all Member States agree and ratify. Indeed, many of the statements calling for the Constitutional Treaty to go ahead in case of a ratification crisis indicated that such an initiative should not be stopped by 'legal technicalities'. In other words, the 'vanguard states' could also choose to 'ignore the law' and sweep away the current EU and international law rules if this were needed to extricate themselves from a ratification crisis. The countries willing to forge ahead would be prepared to break the law and explode the long-established institutional arrangements on the ground that the unreformed European Union no longer allows them to pursue their most cherished political goals and interests. Such a revolutionary move requires strong political resolve and close cohesion among the members of the breakaway group. At the present time, neither the resolve nor the cohesion seem to be there. It might therefore be better to keep an eye on the 'legal technicalities' and to evaluate the feasibility of the political scenarios also on the basis of their legal implications.

One scenario that I do not consider in the following pages is the broad public debate (including 'Parliamentary Forums') called for by the European Parliament in its recent resolution of 19 January 2006. This does not, as such, produce any legal consequences, but is merely the prelude to the possible adoption of legal 'rearrangements'.

1. Constitutional Treaty 'Plus'

The first political scenario consists in trying to accommodate positively the dissenting states (or their dissenting electorate) within the bounds of the Constitutional Treaty as it was agreed by all governments at the IGC. This is, in fact, what happened earlier on after the unsuccessful Danish referendum on the Maastricht Treaty, and again after the unsuccessful Irish referendum on the Nice Treaty. The diplomatic 'dialogue', in those two cases, did not aim at a modification of the treaty as signed, but at a separate legal or political agreement that could pave the way for a second referendum on that same treaty. In the case of Denmark, this separate agreement was the Decision on Denmark approved during the European Council meeting in Edinburgh (December 1992), which was presented as a binding legal document, and therefore can legally be qualified as an international agreement in simplified form. It did not purport to modify the Treaty of Maastricht, but only to offer a particular interpretation of it. However, it is undeniable that the Decision on Denmark has cast its shadow on the European Union: it is directly responsible for the complicated and almost unworkable Protocol on Denmark agreed in connection with the Treaty of Amsterdam, and the Constitutional Treaty, again, contains a special protocol on Denmark as well as a Declaration on that protocol. In the case of Ireland, the effects of its first negative referendum on the Nice Treaty became less visible at the EU level. Common action at the European level took the form of two Declarations made at the European Council meeting of Seville (the 'Seville Declarations'),[10] one by the Irish government and one by the European Council as a body. Both stated that the Treaty of Nice would not prevent Ireland from preserving the essence of its neutrality despite the development of a common security and defence policy.

However, the neutrality question was arguably not the central concern for most no-voters, and the main measures to convince the electorate to approve the Nice Treaty in a second referendum were taken at the domestic level, namely the creation of a National Forum on Europe, and the strengthening of national parliamentary control mechanisms on Irish EU policy making.[11]

Whether this 'vote-again' scenario could be repeated this time is politically very doubtful. However, it has been suggested, for example by the German government, that the addition to the Treaty of a non-binding declaration on the 'social dimension of Europe' (without changing the text of the Treaty itself) might do the trick.[12] It is possible to call this added text a Decision of the Heads of State and Government (as with the Edinburgh Decision on Denmark in December 1992), rather than a Declaration, emphasizing that the governments consider the added text to be a binding international agreement. Still, it would have to be compatible in every respect with the Constitutional Treaty: this is the condition on which the European Council could validly adopt such a decision without the need for parliamentary ratification. Otherwise, if there were an attempt at modifying even one single provision of the Constitutional Treaty, there would be a legally more complex situation, which I describe below.

2. Constitutional Treaty 'Minus'

It seems that one of the causes of hostility to the Constitutional Treaty among French and Dutch voters was its length and complexity as well as (in the French case particularly) the uninspiring content of Part III, the part on the policies of the European Union. In order to address these misgivings, one could 'hive off' Part III from the rest and make it into a separate treaty that could be called the 'Basic Treaty on the European Union', but without changing any of its content.[13] This could rather easily be done through a mini-treaty, and would presumably not require a new ratification round in those countries that have already ratified the 'complete' Constitutional Treaty. Whether it would be sufficient to convince a sufficient number of opponents in France, the Netherlands, the UK and elsewhere is quite another matter.

The French minister of the Interior Sarkozy proposed more radically that only the first part (or perhaps parts I, II and IV) of the Constitutional Treaty be retained, and the rest be quietly dropped.[14] Part III would therefore not need to be ratified by those countries that have not already done so, and, in his view, France could even ratify the slim version of the Constitutional Treaty without another referendum. Annoyingly, however, Parts I, II and IV cannot operate on their own without a complementary Part III. Many provisions of Part I expressly refer to Part III. This is very clearly the case with the Article on EU competences which specifies that the detailed and legally relevant division of competences between the EU and its Member States is made in Part III.

Similarly, the agreement to make the co-decision procedure into the 'ordinary legislative procedure' could be obtained only on condition that numerous exceptions to that principle were made in Part III. There are numerous other examples of the inextricable links between the various parts of the Constitutional Treaty.

It would not help at all to consider instead that the 'rump Constitution' (without its Part IV) would be complemented by the current rules of the EC and EU Treaty. On numerous points, Part I of the Constitution and the current Treaties would clearly be contradictory and incompatible. Simply dropping Part III is therefore just not possible. Misgivings about its content can only be addressed through its renegotiation, leading to a modification of the Constitutional Treaty as signed in October 2004. This amounts therefore to a 'revision of the revision', the hypothesis I consider immediately below.

3. Revising the Revision

Since the Constitutional Treaty came into legal existence upon its signature in October 2004, renegotiation of its terms would involve the drawing up of another Treaty that would aim both at replacing the Constitutional Treaty and revising the current EC and EU Treaties. All the states that have already ratified would then have to lodge a new act of ratification, which would require a new approval by their national parliaments but probably not a new referendum in countries where a referendum on the (original) Constitution had already been successful. Much would depend on the nature of the changes made to the original text (whether a mere opt-out for the dissenters or more), in the light of national constitutional requirements and national political dynamics.

In the political debate, a distinction is often made between two starting points: taking the Constitutional Treaty as a starting point (and to make only those changes that are necessary and sufficient to enable it to be accepted in every Member State), or taking the current Treaties as the starting point (and to make only those changes that are indispensable and are acceptable also for countries that reject the idea of a Constitution). From an EU law perspective, the two options are rather similar, because in both cases there is a need to abide by the rules set out in Article 48 EU Treaty that apply to the revision of the current Treaties, namely (essentially) a general consensus by all governments followed by individual ratifications in each country. In terms of national constitutional law there may be more of a difference between the two approaches, since minimal changes based on the current texts could more easily be approved by an ordinary vote in the national parliament, without the need for national constitutional revisions or referenda. Another advantage of a 'minimal' revision based on the current Treaties would be that it could be formally agreed on the occasion of the accession of the next new Member States, rather than at a separate IGC. Since Accession Treaties must anyway be ratified by all the Member States (cf. Article 49 EU Treaty), accession-cum-revision in one text is legally admissible (and in fact, Accession Treaties invariably do involve some slight changes to the Treaties, if only to accommodate the changes in composition of the EU institutions).

4. Piecemeal Reform under the Current Treaties ('Nice Plus')

The most orthodox scenario in the case of a clear failure by one or more Member States to ratify the Constitutional Treaty is for the European Council to acknowledge that the Constitutional Treaty will not enter into force and that the relations between the Member States (and the legal position of the EU institutions and the citizens) will continue to be governed by the EC and EU Treaty as last amended by the Treaty of Nice and the Accession Treaties. In fact, doing nothing at all, that is, forgetting about the Constitutional Treaty altogether, is a quite plausible 'non-scenario'. However, the European Council could also agree that efforts will be made to realize some constitutional reforms on the basis of the current Treaties. There would be ample scope for tinkering with the current post-Nice Treaty regime, so that some of the contents of the Constitutional Treaty can be taken on board without actually changing the present Treaties. This could be done in, essentially, two different ways: (a) through application of parts of the Treaty by means of secondary law or mere institutional practice, and (b) through the use of forms of closer cooperation.

(A) INFORMAL APPLICATION

With 'informal application', I mean the application of some of the institutional or substantive rules contained in the Constitutional Treaty without basing it on the formal authority that would have resulted from the entry into force of that Treaty. Today, we are already familiar with this phenomenon with regard to one important part of the Constitutional Treaty, namely the second part containing the text (with minor modifications) of the Charter of Fundamental Rights. This part of the Constitutional Treaty is already being applied by the political institutions of the Union (who committed themselves to do so when solemnly proclaiming the Charter in December 2000) and its content is effectively being used by the European Courts, although formally they continue to apply those rights as 'general principles of Community law'. A recent example of the enactment of a Constitutional Treaty innovation under current law is the establishment of the European Defence Agency.[15] More generally, a number of innovations contained in the Constitutional Treaty that are not incompatible with the present Treaties could be implemented in this way. For example, the role of national parliaments could be enhanced by a combination of reforms in national laws and interinstitutional agreements between the EU institutions. The interinstitutional agreement is a legal instrument that has been used repeatedly in the past to anticipate later Treaty reforms, and could be used again to achieve a variety of reforms proposed in the Constitutional Treaty. The Council can make its meetings more open to public observation by a change of its rules of procedure, or even through simple informal conclusions (as it started doing on 20/22 December 2005).[16] Some of the new policy advances of the Constitutional Treaty could be enacted by using the residual powers clause of Article 308 EC Treaty which has historically allowed the EU to enter into new policy fields without a specific competence basis elsewhere in the Treaties. An extreme (and unlikely) example of the 'Nice Plus' approach would be for the Member State governments to agree among themselves to forgo the use of their veto power in areas in which the Constitutional Treaty replaces unanimity by qualified majority voting. The Ioannina Agreement of 1994 could be invoked as a precedent for this: this was an informal agreement between governments dealing with the exercise of their voting rights in Council.[17]

When agreeing to such informal applications of the Constitutional Treaty, the government of the countries that have thus far failed to ratify the Constitutional Treaty would have to tread with particular care for domestic constitutional and political reasons. Also a price to be paid for the informal application of an unratified Constitutional Treaty would be an even greater lack of 'legibility' of the EU system whereas one of the main aims of the Constitutional Treaty was precisely to ensure greater simplicity and transparency.

(B) CLOSER COOPERATION

A second, complementary, way in which a Nice Plus scenario could be set in place is through increased recourse to forms of closer cooperation inside the European Union system. The enhanced cooperation mechanism, which was created by the Treaty of Amsterdam but has remained unused since 1999, could operate in order to perform one of its original aims, namely to allow 'willing and able' Member States to pursue deeper integration without passing through an intergovernmental conference.[18] In using the enhanced cooperation mechanism in order to achieve 'among themselves' some of the reforms contained in the Constitutional Treaty, the pro-Constitution states would be constrained by the numerous rules and conditions set by the Nice Treaty (even though that Treaty relaxed the even more stringent rules set by the Amsterdam Treaty). First, the Nice Treaty would not allow the 'pioneers' to select the members of the club, since enhanced cooperation regimes must be open to all states who wish to participate. Secondly, the Nice rules require enhanced cooperation initiatives to be taken by at least eight countries, so that for instance an initiative of the six original Member States of the EC would not qualify. Thirdly, the Nice rules do not allow for enhanced cooperation in areas that are outside EU competences as defined by the Treaties as they stand, and also expressly prohibit enhanced cooperation with military or defence implications. This means, for instance, that the Nice mechanism could not be used for the ambitious new defence policy delineated in the draft Constitution.

5. Reform under a Separate International Treaty

In view of the restrictions imposed by the Nice regime for enhanced cooperation, the states wishing to move ahead in accordance with the content of the Constitutional Treaty could also launch forms of cooperation between themselves outside the EU institutional framework. In its resolution of 19 January 2006, the European Parliament 'deplores any suggestion that coalitions of certain Member States could be formed outside the EU system', and this deploring is quite understandable from the EP's standpoint, since the major characteristic of acting 'outside' is that the institutional balance that exists 'inside' (with its complex and careful design of the respective roles of Commission, Council, Parliament and Court of Justice) ceases to apply. It is possible, of course, to 'recreate' the same institutional balance with a new set of institutions, but such a cumbersome scheme would only be justified if the new framework would be very broad in its scope and constitute a genuine 'Core Europe'. Verhofstadt's scheme for a 'United States of Europe'[19] is conceived like this, it seems. His plan would therefore, presumably require that little 'clones' of the existing institutions, with similar powers, would be set up to serve the members of this USE group. Any direct 'borrowing' of the existing institutions by the core group would require a revision of the existing Treaties, and therefore the agreement of those remaining outside the core.

More generally, partial agreements between only some of the Member States are clearly allowed in principle, and there are numerous examples of them. The most famous ones were probably the Schengen Agreement of 1985 and Schengen Convention of 1990. A more recent example, inspired by Schengen, is the Prüm Convention, concluded on 27 May 2005 between Belgium, Germany, Spain, France, Luxembourg, the Netherlands and Austria, in order to develop their cross-border cooperation in combating terrorism, cross-border crime and illegal migration.[20] However, when concluding partial agreements, the Member States must remain within the limits set by their EU law obligations. Briefly said, this means that such agreements may not be concluded in areas of exclusive EU competence (for example, in the field of trade or monetary policy), that they may not affect the normal operation of the EU institutional mechanisms (in view of the duty of sincere cooperation) and that they may not include any provisions that conflict with EU law or undermine existing EU policies, for example by discriminating on grounds of nationality in favour of citizens of some Member States only. Intergovernmental cooperation between a limited number of Member States of the EU is thus perfectly possible, but membership of the EU imposes major legal constraints on the scope and content of such cooperation. The formation of a true core group, adopting binding laws in a large range of crucial policy areas, is scarcely imaginable because it would unavoidably affect the rights which the other Member States and their citizens have under current EU law. A more limited regime of extra-EU closer cooperation, restricted for example to one policy area (such as defence) would be legally feasible, but it would have the negative side-effect of creating political fragmentation between Member States, and of undermining the institutional balance. It would also add to the complexity and opaqueness of the EU system and reduce the scope for democratic control of the decision-making process.

6. Rewriting the Rules of the Game

The final scenario that I would like to consider is currently not discussed at all in 'political Europe', but is one that I add myself, because it is a scenario that may have to be considered if and when the previous options prove to be politically or legally unfeasible. It consists in leaving the content of the Constitutional Treaty on one side, for the time being, and first launching a process for the revision of one single article of the current EU Treaty, namely Article 48 which defines the procedure for revision of both the EC and the EU Treaty – the procedure which has been followed for the adoption of the Constitutional Treaty so far. Article 48 contains the 'double veto' (general consensus on the content of revisions by all governments at an IGC, followed by separate ratification of the text in all 25 Member States) which contributes to causing the present impasse. It could be argued that, before continuing their substantive argument about the content of future reforms, the Member State governments and EU institutions should first reflect on how to amend the rules of the game, so as to avoid any future agreement again becoming liable to be 'shot down' by a veto expressed by a single government, a single national parliament or a single national electorate acting through a yes/no referendum. In the margins of the Convention, the European Commission had proposed something of this kind in its Penelope study: to have first a mini-agreement modifying the conditions for the enactment of the Constitutional Treaty (by modifying the conditions for revision of the EC and EU Treaty), followed later by the 'real' Constitutional Treaty. This idea came too late since the substantive discussion on the Constitutional Treaty was already in full swing, and it was therefore discarded without serious discussion. It may be worth reconsidering it as a way out of the constitutional cul-de-sac.

The practice of multilateral international organizations shows that their founding charter is usually subject to an amendment procedure that does away with the unanimity rule. For instance, the Treaties establishing the United Nations Organization,[21] the International Labour Organization (ILO)[22] and the

World Health Organization (WHO)[23] in principle require a two-thirds majority of the Member States for their amendment, which must include the five permanent Security Council Members as regards the UN Charter, and five of the ten members of 'chief industrial importance' for the ILO Constitution. A two-thirds majority is also required for amending the Statute of the Council of Europe.[24] The founding instrument of the International Monetary Fund (IMF) can be amended with the agreement of three fifths of the Member States having 85 per cent of the weighted votes (the votes being weighted according to the financial contribution of each member).[25]

The European Union is exceptional among international organizations with a large membership in requiring the unanimous consent of all the Member States for changes in the constitutional instrument. The unanimity rule for revision of the European Treaties can be explained by the fact that, originally, there were only six members. In a Union with 25 member states (for now), the unanimity rule for Treaty amendment becomes a major obstacle to change. It involves the risk that the dynamics of integration be halted, or made subject to blackmail, by a single Member State. The states favouring the status quo are, in fact, put in a structurally favourable position compared to those favouring changes in the European Union's constitutional framework. This is, in a way, turning the consent rule on its head, since the outcome favoured by a large majority of the states can be blocked by one state.[26]

In a report on possible reforms of the revision procedure, submitted by the European University Institute to the European Commission in 2000, it was suggested to replace the consensus rule by some kind of super-qualified majority decision rule for amending the Treaties, combined with the possibility for reluctant Member States to opt out of the non-institutional amendments.[27] This idea did not fly in the context of the Convention. Since the Convention was unable to reach a consensus on replacing the unanimity rule by qualified majority voting for the adoption of European Union legislation, it logically could not agree either on a shift to a (super-)qualified majority decision for Treaty amendment. Article 443 of the Constitutional Treaty maintains for the future the two basic elements of rigidity in Treaty revisions: the common accord to be reached in an intergovernmental conference (preceded normally by a Convention), and the separate ratifications to be delivered by each country. If the Constitutional Treaty were to enter into force, the EU's rules of change would therefore continue to be much more rigid than those applying to any national constitution, but also more rigid than those applying to the founding instruments of other, less integrated, international organizations. It is true that the Constitutional Treaty also provides for two 'simplified revision procedures', described in Articles 444 and 445, which are applicable for the amendment of specific parts of the Constitution. However, these two simplified procedures still retain the unanimity rule. The (real or symbolic) simplification is sought elsewhere, namely in the replacement of an intergovernmental conference by a decision of the European Council, and by the lack of a formal ratification requirement.

The drafters of the Constitution assumed optimistically that the rigid revision formula would not stop the Constitution from evolving in the future. That optimism seems misplaced in view of the difficulties faced by the Constitutional Treaty itself. It might be better, therefore, to continue to live under the current Treaties (the 'Nice Plus' option) while waiting for the moment when all states agree to introduce a more realistic and manageable revision formula, adapted to an organization of 25 or more Member States.

Document 1.13: Brussels European Council, 15 and 16 June 2006, Presidency Conclusions (selected extracts), available on the website of the Council of the European Union at www.consilium.europa.eu

Council of the European Union – Brussels, 16 June 2006 – 10633/06

1. The meeting was preceded by an exposé by Mr Josep Borrell, President of the European Parliament, followed by an exchange of views.

I. Europe Listens

2. In June 2005 the Heads of State or Government called for a period of reflection during which a broad debate should take place in all Member States, involving citizens, civil society, social partners, national parliaments and political parties, with the contribution of European institutions. The European Council welcomes the various initiatives taken in the Member States in the framework of national debates, as well as a series of events organized by the Austrian Presidency, in particular the conference 'The Sound of Europe' in Salzburg on 27/28 January 2006. The European Council expresses its gratitude to the Commission for having contributed to the reflection period in the context of its Plan D and to the European Parliament for having organized together with the Austrian Parliament the joint parliamentary meeting on the 'Future of Europe' on 8/9 May 2006. The European Council welcomes the intention of institutions and Member States to carry on their activities aimed at involving citizens in the debate about what Europe should stand for in the 21st century. It also welcomed the Commission's contribution, 'A Citizens' Agenda for Europe'.

3. The European Council carried out a first assessment of the reflection period. This took place on the basis of the written report prepared by the Presidency and Council Secretariat drawing on information provided by Member States on their national debates (doc. 9701/1/06 REV 1), the 'Plan D' initiative and the White Paper on a European Communication Policy. While worries and concerns have been voiced during all public debates, citizens

remain committed to the European project. Reinforced dialogue with the citizens requires adequate means and commitment. Citizens expect the Union to prove its added value by taking action in response to the challenges and opportunities facing it: ensuring peace, prosperity and solidarity, enhancing security, furthering sustainable development and promoting European values in a rapidly globalising world.

4. The Union's commitment to becoming more democratic, transparent and effective goes beyond the reflection period. The European Council reaffirms its commitment to a Union that delivers the concrete results citizens expect, in order to strengthen confidence and trust, as set out in Part II.

II. Europe at Work

[. . .]

III. Looking to the Future

(A) PURSUING REFORM: THE CONSTITUTIONAL TREATY

[. . .]

42. At the meeting of the European Council on 16/17 June 2005, Heads of State and Government agreed to come back to the issue of the ratification of the Constitutional Treaty in the first half of 2006 in order to make an overall assessment of the national debates launched as part of the period of reflection and to agree on how to proceed.

43. Since last June a further five Member States have ratified the Constitutional Treaty, bringing the total number of ratifications to 15. Two Member States have been unable to ratify, and eight have still to complete the ratification process, one of which has recently launched the procedure to that effect. It is hoped that this process will be completed in line with the conclusions of June 2005.

44. Recalling its conclusions of June 2005, the European Council welcomes the various initiatives taken within the framework of the national debates as well as the contributions of the Commission and Parliament to the reflection period. The significant efforts made to increase and expand the dialogue with Europe's citizens, including the Commission's plan D initiative, should be continued.

45. The reflection period has overall been useful in enabling the Union to assess the concerns and worries expressed in the course of the ratification process. It considers that, in parallel with the ongoing ratification process, further work, building on what has been achieved since last June, is needed before decisions on the future of the Constitutional Treaty can be taken.

46. After last year's period of reflection work should now focus on delivery of concrete results and implementation of projects. The European Council

agrees on a two-track approach. On the one hand, best use should be made of the possibilities offered by the existing treaties in order to deliver the concrete results that citizens expect.

47. On the other hand, the Presidency will present a report to the European Council during the first semester of 2007, based on extensive consultations with the Member States. This report should contain an assessment of the state of discussion with regard to the Constitutional Treaty and explore possible future developments.

48. The report will subsequently be examined by the European Council. The outcome of this examination will serve as the basis for further decisions on how to continue the reform process, it being understood that the necessary steps to that effect will have been taken during the second semester of 2008 at the latest. Each Presidency in office since the start of the reflection period has a particular responsibility to ensure the continuity of this process.

49. The European Council calls for the adoption, on 25 March 2007 in Berlin, of a political declaration by EU leaders, setting out Europe's values and ambitions and confirming their shared commitment to deliver them, commemorating 50 years of the Treaties of Rome.

(B) ENLARGEMENT

[. . .]

Notes

1. *Crotty* v. *An Taoiseach* [1987] IR 713.
2. On referendums, see Chapter 2 of this book.
3. Judgment of 12 October 1993, 2 BvR L 134/92.
4. See also Chapter 2.
5. See Chapter 2.
6. See Chapters 3, 4 and 5.
7. See the Introduction to this book.
8. For a detailed analysis of the provisions adopted for Denmark in 1992 and Ireland 2002, see J. Ziller, 'La ratification des traités européens après des référendums négatifs: que nous disent les précédents danois et irlandais?', in *Rivista Italiana di Diritto Pubblico Communitario*, no. 2–2005, pp. 365–76.
9. V. Giscard d'Estaing, 'Vite, la Constitution de l'Europe!', *Le Monde,* 10 July 2004.
10. Annexes III and IV to the Presidency Conclusions of the Seville European Council, 21 and 22 June 2002.
11. See B. Laffan, 'Ireland and Europe: Continuity and Change', *Notre Europe, Research and European Issues* 30, December 2003, at pp. 22–6 (www.notre-europe.asso.fr).
12. 'Merkel to present plan to save EU constitution', Euobserver.com, 19 December 2005.
13. Proposal developed by Jacques Ziller, professor of law at the EUI.
14. 'Sarkozy wants freeze on enlargement and slimmer EU charter', *euobserver.com* of 13 January 2006.
15. Council Joint Action 2004/551/CFSP of 12 July 2004 on the establishment of the European Defence Agency, OJ 2004, L 245/17. Recital 6 of the Joint Action mentions that the Agency 'is also envisaged in the draft Treaty establishing a Constitution for Europe'.

16. Conclusions of the Council (Agriculture and Fisheries) meeting of that day, pp. 53–4. See Jo Shaw, 'Transparency in the Council of Ministers', *The Federal Trust European Newsletter*, January 2006, p. 3.
17. See Editorial Comments, 'The Ioannina Compromise – Towards a wider and a weaker European Union?', *Common Market Law Review* (1994), p. 453.
18. A. Stubb, *Negotiating Flexibility in the European Union. Amsterdam, Nice and Beyond* (2002), at p. 165.
19. Speech at the CSIS in Washington, 17 January 2006.
20. The text of this Convention can be found in Council document 10900/05 of 7 July 2005.
21. Articles 108 and 109 of the United Nations Charter.
22. Article 36 of the Constitution of the ILO.
23. Article 73 of the Constitution of the WHO.
24. Article 41 of the Statute of the Council of Europe.
25. Article XXVIII of the Articles of Agreement of the IMF.
26. The argument is developed, for example, by C. Lord, *A Democratic Audit of the European Union* (2004), at pp. 79–80.
27. EUI, Robert Schuman Centre, *Reforming the Treaties' Amendment Procedures. Second Report on Reorganization of the European Union Treaties*, July 2000 (available on europa.eu.int/comm/archives/igc2000/offdoc/discussiondocs).

2. Referendums in the ratification process: constitutional bases, results, consequences

Document summary

2.1 Article 93, Spanish Constitution of 27 December 1978
2.2 Summary of Referendum results in Spain, 20 February 2005, Europarlamento
2.3 Article 11, French Constitution of 4 October 1958
2.4 Decision n° 2004–505 DC of 19 November 2004 of the French Constitutional Council (selected extracts)
2.5 CSA Institute opinion poll: The Vote on the Referendum on the European Constitutional Treaty: Explanations to the Vote and Political Perspectives, May 2005, (selected extracts)
2.6 European Commission – Eurobarometer on the European Constitution: post-referendum survey in France (selected extracts), June 2005
2.7 European Commission – Eurobarometer on the European Constitution: post-referendum survey in The Netherlands (selected extracts), June 2005
2.8 Document 2.8: 'French and Dutch should vote again on EU Treaty, says Belgian Foreign Minister', *EU Business*, 6 July 2005
2.9 Luxembourg: the referendum of 10th July 2005
2.10 'Le Luxembourg dit "oui" a la Constitution Européenne', Fondation Robert Schuman (selected extracts)
2.11 EU Constitutional Treaty: Statement of British Foreign Secretary Straw to the House of Commons, 6 June 2005
2.12 CSA Institute opinion poll: Should the Process of the Ratification of the European Constitutional Treaty be Pursued? June 2005 (selected extracts)
2.13 Patricia Jerónimo, 'Adoption and Entry into Force of the Constitution of Europe' (extract)
2.14 Judgment n° 704/2004 of the Portuguese Constitutional Tribunal (selected extracts)

Introduction

Referendums are not an unusual means in the process of ratification of EU treaties.[1] Frequently, referendums have been used in candidate countries aspiring to accede to the European Communities or to the EU, either to allow for the ratification of the relevant treaty of accession or as a way of confirming membership, as was the case in the United Kingdom in 1975. In Norway, referendums twice precluded the country from joining the Communities and the Union, and a referendum may even present an occasion for a Member State's population to decide upon the accession of a new Member State, as in the case of France in 1972 regarding the envisaged accession of Denmark, Ireland, Norway and the United Kingdom. However, such referendums only affect the relevant candidate countries; they do not have an impact on the future evolution of the basic Treaties on which the EC and EU are founded.

By contrast, referendums on amending treaties are a key to the entry into force of those amendments[2] and may thus be seen overall as having a more fundamental impact than referendums on accession treaties. Such referendums are nevertheless only governed by Member States' constitutional rules. Only in the case of Ireland can it be said that a referendum is a formal legal condition of ratification of an EU treaty, and this with two caveats: first, this condition is not rooted in the text of the Irish Constitution but derives from the Irish Supreme Court's jurisprudence in the *Crotty* case;[3] and second, it only applies if the relevant treaty contains clauses amounting to a transfer of sovereignty.

Although the question remains in discussion for some new Member States, especially in Slovakia, where it is the main question to be resolved in the pending case on the Constitutional Treaty before the Slovak Constitutional Court,[4] it may be said that, in other EU Member States, the decision to opt for a referendum is never obligatory for the government.

In some countries, such as France (Document 2.3) and Spain (Document 2.1), the national constitution either formally allows for such a referendum, without making it an obligation, or makes it a requirement for ratification in the absence of a sufficiently strong majority in parliament, as in the case of Denmark.[5] No constitutional provision in these countries sets specific conditions regarding the validity of the vote, for example, with respect to a required quorum of voters, and there is no prohibition on a second referendum on the same question and no minimum time limit within which such a new referendum must be held.

In a number of countries, such as Italy, Luxembourg, The Netherlands and the United Kingdom, there is no formal constitutional provision concerning such a referendum, and it is therefore up to the government and parliament to decide whether to organize one and whether they will be bound by the results. In Germany, a referendum on a nationwide basis is regarded as being implicitly prohibited by the Basic Law. This led some German politicians to consider amending the Basic Law in order to allow for a referendum on the Constitutional Treaty, but in the end this idea was not taken up, and ratification by Germany was subject to the traditional approval of the German Parliament (Bundestag) and Federal Council (Bundesrat).[6]

Only Portuguese constitutional law has established conditions for a referendum leading to the approval of a treaty. In particular, the question put to voters must be sufficiently legible and clear, as regards both its contents and its outcome, and the Constitutional Court must verify that those conditions are satisfied before allowing such a referendum to take place. Thus, for example, in 1998, the Portuguese Constitutional Court rejected the proposed text of the referendum on the ratification of the Treaty of Amsterdam (Document 2.13). This happened again in 2004 in connection with the Constitutional Treaty (Document 2.14), which prevented a referendum from taking place in Portugal in early 2005. In both cases, parliamentary approval was sufficient for ratification, but, whereas in 1998 the government eventually opted for parliamentary ratification only, in the case of the Constitutional Treaty the government indicated that it wanted to organise a new referendum once the text of the relevant question to submit to the electorate was finalised. Even after the French and Dutch negative referendums, and after a change of government due to the opposition winning the elections, the position of the government has remained the same, as stated unofficially in the context of the European Council of June 2006.

The diversity of constitutional provisions – or in some cases the absence of such provisions – relevant to referendums on EU treaties could be an interesting subject matter for an essay in comparative constitutional law. Among other implications, it has specific consequences at EU level, as it creates obstacles for the organisation of a possible EU-wide referendum. Although these difficulties are not impossible to overcome, they provide good reasons – or good pretexts – for those governments which are hostile to such a procedure. Even if the governments unanimously agreed upon a change in that direction, quite some time would still be needed in order for the Member States to adopt the legal provisions necessary for the organisation of a European referendum, as in the case of Germany, where a constitutional amendment would be required.

Beyond the specific case of Portugal (Documents 2.13 and 2.14), there seems to be little room for legal analysis going beyond the procedural aspects of referendums. However, the four votes organised in 2005 provide ample food for thought regarding the political and sociological dimensions of referendums on EU treaties. In order to draw conclusions from the relevant documentation (Documents 2.1 to 2.12), it should be taken into consideration that none of the four countries' governments was obliged to organise a referendum, although the announcement of a referendum in the UK by Prime Minister

Tony Blair in May 2004 set a 'moral precedent' that was probably one of the reasons behind the decisions of certain governments to hold them.

Furthermore, in order duly to appreciate the results of the four referendums held in 2005, it might be useful to recall the figures for the most relevant precedents, that is, the Treaties of Maastricht and Nice. In the case of Maastricht, turnout in Denmark was 82 per cent in 1992 (with 50.07 per cent No votes) and 85 per cent in 1993 (56.8 per cent Yes votes), and 69.69 per cent in France (51.01 per cent Yes votes). As for Nice, turnout in Ireland was 34.8 per cent in 2001 (53.9 per cent No votes) and 49.5 per cent in 2002 (62.9 per cent Yes votes). The main difference between the negative referendums of 1992 and 2001, on the one hand, and the 2005 votes on the other, is that in the first two cases the governments of the countries where referendums were held immediately decided that the ratification process should continue and that a closer look at the reasons for the 'no' vote should be undertaken by the relevant countries. This paved the way for efforts to reach a solution in agreement with the President of the European Commission and the incoming President of the European Council (Luxembourg and UK, both in 1992 and 2005). In 2005, neither the French nor the Dutch governments made serious efforts to understand the reasons for the negative votes. They only stated that the people had rejected the proposed ratification, without however indicating that their country would refuse ratification in the future.[7]

Document 2.1: Spanish Constitution of 29 December 1978, Article 93, English translation by the Congress of Deputies, available at http://www.congreso.es/ingles/funciones/constitucion/const_espa_texto.pdf

Title III – Chapter 3 – International Treaties

ARTICLE 93

Authorization may be granted by an organic act for concluding treaties by which powers derived from the Constitution shall be transferred to an international organization or institution. It is incumbent on the Cortes Generales or the Government, as the case may be, to ensure compliance with these treaties and with resolutions originating in the international and supranational organizations to which such powers have been so transferred.

Document 2.2: Summary of Referendum results in Spain, 20 February 2005, Source:www.europarl.es [translation]

The European Constitution was put to a referendum on Sunday 20 February 2005. Although Spanish ratification could have taken place through the passing of an ordinary Organic Law (Ley Organica) in the Cortes Generales, the

Spanish Parliament (in accordance with Article 93 of the Spanish Constitution) the Government, with the intention of encouraging debate and the participation of society and citizens, called a referendum. The question put to citizens was: 'Do you approve the Treaty establishing a Constitution for Europe?' In the Autonomous Regions with joint official languages, it was asked in both languages.

The Spanish Referendum in Figures
Data and results
Registered electorate
Eligible voters resident in Spain 33 562 119
Eligible voters resident abroad 1 130 159
Total 34 692 278
Total number of votes cast 14 204 663
Valid votes cast 14 081 966
Invalid votes 122 697
Abstention (eligible voters who did not vote) 19 359 017
% votes counted 100.00
% total voters 42.32
% valid votes 99.14
% abstention 57.68
% invalid votes 0.86
Options Spain
No. of votes (percentage)
Yes 10 804 464 (76.73)
No 2 428 409 (17.24)
Ballot paper left blank 849 093 (6.03)

Document 2.3: French Constitution of 4 October 1958, Article 11, translation by the French National Assembly, available at http://www.assemblee-nationale.fr/english/8ab.asp

Article 11

The President of the Republic may, on a proposal from the Government when Parliament is in session or on a joint motion of the two assemblies, published in either case in the *Journal officiel*, submit to a referendum any government bill which deals with the organization of the public authorities, or with reforms relating to the economic or social policy of the Nation and to the public services contributing thereto, or which provides for authorization to ratify a treaty that, although not contrary to the Constitution, would affect the functioning of the institutions.

Where the referendum is held in response to a proposal by the Government, the latter shall make a statement before each assembly which shall be followed by a debate.

Where the referendum decides in favour of the government bill, the President of the Republic shall promulgate it within 15 days following the proclamation of the results of the vote.

Document 2.4: Decision no. 2004-505 DC of 19 November 2004 of the French Constitutional Council (selected extracts), translation by the Constitutional Council, available at http://www.conseil-constitutionnel.fr/decision/2004/2004505/eng.htm

[. . .]

On October 29 2004 the Constitutional Council received a referral from the President of the Republic pursuant to Article 54 of the Constitution with regard to the question of whether authorisation to ratify the Treaty establishing a Constitution for Europe signed in Rome on the same date requires a prior revision of the Constitution;

[. . .]

With Respect to Applicable Norms of Reference:

5. The French Republic belongs to the European Communities and the European Union in the conditions provided for by Title XV of the Constitution; in particular, pursuant to article 88-1 thereof, 'The Republic shall participate in the European Communities and in the European Union constituted by States that have freely chosen, by virtue of the Treaties that established them, to exercise some of their powers in common';

6. These texts having constitutional value enable France to participate in the creation and development of a permanent European organization, vested with separate legal personality and powers of decision making by reason of the transfer of powers agreed to by the Member States;

7. When however commitments entered into for such purposes contain a clause running counter to the Constitution, call into question constitutionally guaranteed rights and freedoms or adversely affect the fundamental conditions of the exercising of national sovereignty, authorisation to ratify such measures shall require a prior revision of the Constitution;

8. It is on the basis of such principles that it is incumbent upon the Constitutional Council to examine the Treaty 'establishing a Constitution for Europe', together with the protocols and annexes thereof; those provisions of the said Treaty which merely reiterate commitments already entered into by France are however excluded from any such examination as to their conformity with the Constitution;

With Respect to the Primacy of the Law of the European Union:

9. Firstly, the provisions of the 'Treaty establishing a Constitution for Europe', and in particular those pertaining to the entry into force and revision thereof and the possibility for signatories to withdraw therefrom, show that said instrument retains the nature of an international treaty entered into by the

States signatory to the Treaty establishing the European Communities and the treaty on European Union;

10. The name given to this new Treaty does not require as such any ruling as to its constitutionality; Article I-5 thereof, pertaining to the relations between the European Union and the Member States thereof, shows that the title of said treaty has no effect upon the existence of the French Constitution and the place of the latter at the summit of the domestic legal order;

11. Secondly, pursuant to Article 88-1 of the Constitution: 'The Republic shall participate in the European Communities and in the European Union constituted by States that have freely chosen, by virtue of the Treaties that established them, to exercise some of their powers in common'; that the drafters of this provision thus formally acknowledged the existence of a Community legal order integrated into the domestic legal order and distinct from the international legal order;

12. Article 1-1 of the Treaty states that 'Reflecting the will of the citizens and States of Europe to build a common future, this Constitution establishes the European union, on which the Member States confer competences to attain objectives they have in common. The Union shall coordinate the policies by which the Member States aim to achieve these objectives, and shall exercise on a Community basis the competences they confer on it'; pursuant to article 1-5, the Union shall respect the national identities of Member States 'inherent in their fundamental structures, political and constitutional'; pursuant to Article 1-6, 'The Constitution and law adopted by the institutions of the Union in exercising competences conferred on it shall have primacy over the law of the Member States'; a declaration annexed to the Treaty shows that this Article does not confer on the principle of primacy any greater scope than that which it previously had;

13. If Article 1-1 of the Treaty replaces the bodies established by previous treaties by a single institution, the European Union, upon which Article 1-7 confers legal personality, the provisions of this Treaty, particularly the close proximity of Articles 1-5 and 1-6 thereof, show that it in no way modifies the nature of the European Union, or the scope of the principle of the primacy of Union law as duly acknowledged by Article 88-1 of the Constitution, and confirmed by the Constitutional Council in its decisions referred to herein-above; that hence Article 1-6 submitted for review by the Constitutional Council does not entail any revision of the Constitution;

With Respect to The Charter of Fundamental Rights of The European Union:

14. It is therefore necessary to rule on the conformity with the Constitution of the 'Charter of Fundamental Rights of the European Union' which constitutes the second part of the Treaty submitted for review by the Constitutional Council;

15. Firstly, pursuant to Article II-111 of the Treaty and excluding Articles II-101 to II-104, which only concern the 'institutions, bodies, offices and agencies of the Union', the provisions of the Charter are addressed to the Member States 'when they are implementing Union law', and 'only' in this case; pursuant to paragraph 5 of Article II-112, the Charter contains, in addition to 'rights' directly enforceable before national courts, 'principles' which constitute aims which may only be invoked in relation to acts of a general scope pertaining to their implementation; that among such 'principles' are found 'the entitlement to social security benefits and social services'; the 'right to work', the 'right of the elderly to lead a life of dignity and independence and to participate in social and cultural life', the 'principle of sustainable development' and 'a high level of consumer protection';

16. Secondly, paragraph 4 of Article II-112 of the Treaty provides that, insofar as the Charter recognizes fundamental rights as they result from the constitutional traditions common to the Member States, 'these rights shall be interpreted in harmony with those traditions'; the rights defined in Articles 1 to 3 of the Constitution, which proscribe any recognition of collective rights of any group defined by origin, culture, language or beliefs are thus respected;

17. Thirdly, the Preamble of the Charter states, 'The Charter will be interpreted by the courts of the Union and the Member States with due regard to the explanations prepared under the authority of the Praesidium of the Convention which drafted the Charter'; paragraph 7 of Article II-112 of the Treaty also provides that 'The explanations drawn up as a way of providing guidance in the interpretation of the Charter of Fundamental Rights shall be given due regard by the courts of the Union and of the Member States';

18. In particular, if the first paragraph of Article II-70 recognises the right of everyone, whether individually or in community with others, to manifest religion or belief in public, the explanations of the Praesidium specify that the right guaranteed by this article has the same meaning and same scope as the right guaranteed by Article 9 of the European Convention for the protection of Human Rights and Fundamental Freedoms; this right is subject to the same limitations, in particular those involving public safety, the protection of public order, health or morals and the protection of the rights and freedoms of others; Article 9 of the Convention has been constantly applied by the European Court of Human Rights, on the latest occasion in the decision referred to hereinabove, in harmony with the constitutional traditions of each Member State; the Court has thus given official recognition to the principle of secularism recognized by various national constitutional traditions and leaves States considerable leeway to define the most appropriate measures, taking into account their national traditions, to reconcile the principle of freedom of religion and that of secularism; the provisions of Article 1 of the Constitution whereby 'France is a secular republic' which forbid persons to

profess religious beliefs for the purpose of non compliance with the common rules governing the relations between public communities and private individuals are thus respected;

19. Moreover the scope of Article II-107 of the Treaty, pertaining to the right to an effective remedy and a fair trial, is wider than that of Article 6 of the European Convention, since it concerns not only disputes involving civil rights and obligations or the grounds for a criminal prosecution; it nevertheless emerges from the explanations given by the Praesidium that public access to court hearings may be subject to the limitations provided for in this article of the Convention; thus 'the press and public may be excluded from all or part of a trial in the interests of morals, public order or national security in a democratic society, where the interests of juveniles or the protection of the private life of the parties so require, or to the extent strictly necessary in the opinion of the court in special circumstances where publicity would prejudice the interests of justice';

20. Furthermore, if, pursuant to Article II-110, 'No one shall be liable to be tried or punished again in criminal proceedings for an offence for which he or she has been finally acquitted or convicted within the Union', the very wording of this Article, as is confirmed by the explanations of the Praesidium, means that these provisions apply solely to criminal law and not to administrative or disciplinary proceedings; that, furthermore, the reference to offences, and not to the acts involved, leaves French courts of law free, subject to due respect for the principle of proportionality of sentences, to punish those crimes and offences which prejudice the fundamental interests of the nation as provided for by Title I of Book IV of the French Criminal Code, taking into account the ingredients of such crimes and offences and the specific interests involved;

21. Fourthly, the general limitation clause contained in paragraph 1 of Article II-112 provides: 'Subject to the principle of proportionality, limitations may be made only if they are necessary and genuinely meet objectives of general interest recognised by the Union or the need to protect the rights and freedoms of others', that the explanations of the Praesidium specify that the 'general interests recognised by the Union' include in particular interests protected by the first paragraph of Article I-5, whereby the Union shall 'respect their essential State functions, including ensuring the territorial integrity of the State, maintaining law and order and safeguarding national security';

22. As is shown by the foregoing, the Charter, as regards either the contents of the articles thereof or the essential conditions pertaining to the exercise of national sovereignty, does not require any revision of the Constitution;

With Respect to The Provisions of the Treaty Pertaining to The Policies and The Functioning of the Union:

23. Pursuant to Article 88-2 of the Constitution, as amended subsequent to the revisions of the Constitution dated June 25 1992, January 25 1999 and March 23 2003: 'Subject to reciprocity and in accordance with the terms of the Treaty on European Union signed on February 7 1992, France agrees to the transfer of powers necessary for the establishment of the European Economic and Monetary Union – subject to the same reservations and in accordance with the terms of the Treaty establishing the European Community, as amended by the Treaty signed on October 2 1997, transfers of powers necessary for the determination of rules concerning freedom of movement for persons and related areas may be agreed upon. A statute shall determine the rules governing the European arrest warrant pursuant to instruments adopted under the Treaty on European Union';

24. The clauses of the Treaty which transfer to the European Union powers affecting the essential conditions of the exercise of national sovereignty in areas or on terms other than those provided for in the Treaties referred to in article 88-2 require a revision of the Constitution;

25. The 'principle of subsidiarity' as set forth in Article I-11 of the Treaty implies that, in areas which do not fall within its exclusive competence, the Union shall act 'only if and insofar as the objectives of the proposed actions cannot be sufficiently achieved by the Member States, either at central level or at regional and local level, but can rather, by reason of the scale or effects of the proposed action, be better achieved at Union level'; however the implementation of this principle may not suffice to prevent transfers of competence authorised by the Treaty from taking on a dimension or being carried out in such a way as to affect the essential conditions of the exercise of national sovereignty;

26. Pursuant to Article I-34 of the Treaty, unless otherwise provided for, the 'European law' and the 'European framework law' due to replace the 'Community regulation' and 'Community directive' shall be adopted, on the basis of proposals put forward solely by the Commission, jointly by the Council of Ministers, with the qualified majority provided for in Article I-25, and the European Parliament under the ordinary legislative procedure provided for in Article III-396; all matters coming under the competence of the Union, in particular those involving the 'area of freedom, security and justice' referred to in Chapter IV of Title III of the third part of the Treaty will therefore, unless excluded, be subjected to this ordinary legislative procedure;

[. . .]

With Respect to the New Manners of Exercising Powers Already Transferred Applicable Upon the Entry Into Force of the Treaty:

29. Any provisions of the Treaty which, in a matter inherent to the exercise of national sovereignty and already coming under the competences of the

Union or the Community, modify the applicable rules of decision making, either by replacing the qualified majority vote by a unanimous vote in the Council, thus depriving France of any power to oppose such a decision, or by conferring decision-making powers on the European Parliament, which is not an emanation of national sovereignty, or by depriving France of any power of acting on its own initiative, require a revision of the Constitution;

30. Consequently, once the measures involved are dependent upon a decision of the Council acting by a qualified majority, in particular under the provisions of Articles III-270 and III-271, when relating to powers already transferred in the field of judicial cooperation in criminal matters, of articles III-273 and III-276, which concern the structure, functioning, mission and tasks of Eurojust and Europol, and those of b) of paragraph 2 of Article III-300 relating to actions or positions of the Union decided on the proposal of the Minister of Foreign Affairs of the Union, they require a revision of the Constitution;

31. The same applies to provisions conferring decision-making powers on the European Parliament, in particular those of Article III-191, which provide that a European law or framework law shall determine the measures necessary for the use of the Euro, and those of the first paragraph of article III-419, which in matters concerning the area of security, freedom and justice, makes the establishing of any 'enhanced cooperation' within the Union dependent upon the approval of the European Parliament;

32. The same applies to the provisions of Article III-265 insofar as they replace the individual power of initiative vested in each Member State under previous Treaties by a joint right of initiative of a quarter of Member States, allowing the latter to put forward a draft European Act in matters concerning the area of freedom, security and justice, such as those mentioned in Article III-273 concerning Eurojust, and in Articles IIII-275 to III-277 relating to police cooperation;

With Respect to The Adoption of Qualified Majority Voting Under a Subsequent European Decision:

33. Any provision of the Treaty called a 'bridge provision' by those negotiating the same, and which, in a matter inherent to the exercise of national sovereignty makes it possible, even though making such a change dependent upon a unanimous decision of the European Council or the Council of Ministers, to replace a system of unanimity voting with one of a qualified majority, requires a revision of the Constitution; such modifications will not require any ratification or approval at national level likely to entail a review of the constitutionality of the same on the basis of Article 54 or 61, paragraph 2, of the Constitution;

34. Such is the case in particular as regards the measures pertaining to family law with cross-border implications provided for by paragraph 3 of

Article III-269, the minimum rules of criminal procedure provided for by d) of paragraph 2 of Article III-270 and the minimum rules pertaining to the definition and punishment of particularly serious crimes with cross-border dimensions provided for by the third indent of paragraph one of Article III-271; the same applies to paragraph 7 of Article 1-40 and paragraph 3 of Article III-300, which make it possible for decisions relating to foreign policy and common security and defence policy, the scope of which is not limited by the Treaty, to be henceforth taken by the Council acting by a qualified majority, upon a unanimous decision to said effect taken by the European Council, but without any ratification at national levels;

With Respect to the Simplified Revision Procedures Provided for by Articles IV-444 And IV-445 of the Treaty.

35. Firstly, for the reasons set forth hereinabove, the general 'bridge clause' found in Article IV-444 instituting a simplified revision process for the Treaty also requires review by the Constitutional Council; the first paragraph of this Article allows the European Council to authorise the Council, except in defence matters, to act by a qualified majority in an area or case where the Treaty requires unanimity, while the second paragraph authorises the adoption of laws in accordance with ordinary legislative procedure whenever Part III provides for a special legislative procedure; in the absence of any national ratification procedure making it possible to review the constitutionality of said laws, these provisions require a revision of the Constitution, notwithstanding the faculty given to each national Parliament to oppose the implementation thereof;

36. Furthermore, Article IV-445 institutes a simplified revision procedure concerning internal policies and action of the Union; it provides that, on the proposal of a Member State, the European Parliament or the Commission, the European Council, acting unanimously, 'may adopt a European decision amending all or part of the provisions of Title III of Part III' relating to the internal policies and action of the Union; that pursuant to the second indent of paragraph two, this European decision shall only come into force once it has been approved by the Member States 'in accordance with their respective constitutional requirements'; this reference to the constitutional rules of the Member States refers, where France is concerned, to the Parliamentary authorisation provided for by Article 53 of the Constitution.

With Respect to the New Powers Vested in National Parliaments in the Framework of the Union:

37. The Treaty submitted to the Constitutional Council increases the participation of national Parliaments in the activities of the European Union; it grants them new prerogatives and as such it is necessary to decide whether these prerogatives can be exercised within the framework of the current provisions of the Constitution;

38. Firstly, Article IV-444 introduces, as mentioned above, a simplified revision procedure of the Treaty; it provides for the notification of national Parliaments of any initiative taken in this respect and adds: 'If a national Parliament makes known its opposition within six months of such notification, the European decision . . . shall not be adopted'.

39. Secondly, the second indent of paragraph 3 of Article I-11 provides that national Parliaments shall ensure compliance with the principle of subsidiarity by the institutions of the Union in accordance with Protocol 2; that under articles 6 and 7 of the latter taken together with article 3 of Protocol 1, a national Parliament or, as may be, one of the Chambers thereof, may henceforth, within six weeks of the transmission to it of a draft European legislative act, send the Presidents of the European Parliament, Council and Commission a reasoned opinion on why it feels that the draft legislative act does not comply with the principle of subsidiarity; the draft act must be reviewed when these reasoned opinions represent one third of the votes allocated to the national Parliaments, or one quarter of the votes in areas of judicial cooperation in criminal matters or police cooperation; to this effect, each national Parliament has two votes, with each Chamber in a bicameral Parliament having one vote; after such review, the body from which the draft originates may decide to maintain, amend or withdraw the draft.

40. Thirdly, article 8 of Protocol 2 provides that the Court of Justice, which has jurisdiction in actions on the grounds of infringement of the principle of subsidiarity, may also examine actions brought by a Member State 'in accordance with its legal order on behalf of its national Parliament or a Chamber of it';

41. The recognized right of the French Parliament to oppose a modification of the Treaty under the simplified revision procedure provided for by Article IV-444 requires a revision of the Constitution in order to allow it to exercise this prerogative; the same applies to the faculty given to it, if need be according to the specific procedures of each of its two Chambers, to send a reasoned opinion or to bring an action before the Court of Justice in the framework of the monitoring of the respect for the principle of subsidiarity;

With Respect to the Other Provisions of the Treaty:

42. None of the other provisions of the treaty submitted to the Constitutional Council pursuant to Article 54 of the Constitution requires any revision of the latter;

With Respect to the Whole of The Treaty:

43. Authorisation to ratify the Treaty establishing a Constitution for Europe requires a revision of the Constitution on the grounds set forth hereinabove, [. . .]

Table 2.1 CSA opinion poll

Question – When voting today, did you think more about . . .?

	Percentage of voters	Based on vote	
		Percentage of Yes voters	Percentage of No voters
. . . the construction of Europe	60	82	42
. . . national problems	35	15	52
No answer	5	3	6
Total	100	100	100

Question – When voting, which issues were most important for you?

(Answers given with the help of a list)	%	Based on vote	
		Percentage of Yes voters	Percentage of No voters
The social situation in France	41	23	55
France's role in Europe	26	38	17
Europe's place in the world	24	50	4
The contents of the text of the European Constitution	21	19	24
The possible entry of Turkey into the European Union	14	6	20
The orientations, whether liberal or social, or European policy	14	10	17
Globalization	11	10	12
Your opinion of the government of Jacques Chirac	8	6	9
The enlargement of the Union to 25 countries	8	6	8
The positions taken by political personalities in favour of a Yes or No vote	5	4	6
No answer	4	3	5
Total	(1)	(1)	(1)

[1] Total greater than 100%; those questioned were able to choose more than one issue.

Document 2.5: CSA opinion poll: The Vote in the Referendum on the European Constitutional Treaty: Explanation of the Vote and Political Perspectives. May 2005, available at http://www.csa-fr.com (selected extracts) [translation]

CSA – Radio France – Le Parisien – Aujourd'hui en France
Referendum Vote on the European Constitutional Treaty: Explanation of the Vote and Political Perspectives
Institut CSA Opinion Poll
May 2005

Document 2.6: European Commission – Eurobarometer on the European Constitution: post-referendum survey in France (selected extracts), June 2005, available at http://ec.europa.eu/public_opinion/index_en.htm

[. . .]

Presentation

France chose to organise a referendum on the treaty establishing a Constitution for Europe. The referendum was held on Sunday, 29 May 2005. The very high turnout rate of 69.3 per cent is proof of the interest aroused by the campaign. The 'no' obtained 54.70 per cent of votes cast, thereby breaking the trend of previous referenda on European construction.[8]

The aim of this post-referendum survey, commissioned by Directorate-General Press and Communication of the European Commission, is to gain a better understanding of the reasons why people abstained, what motivated how they voted, the perceived effects of the Constitution and the possible scenarios following what some people have called a 'political earthquake'.

To that end, EOS Gallup Europe, through its partner institute in France, TNS-Sofres, carried out 2015 interviews over the two days following the vote, that is, on 30 and 31 May, with registered French voters, using the methodology adopted for the Flash Eurobarometer (telephone) surveys.

[. . .]

Conclusion

The issues at stake in this referendum on the ratification of the European Constitution in France clearly motivated the French and explain the turnout rate of 70 per cent. Two thirds of the people interviewed in this post-referendum survey declared that they had sufficient information to make a decision at the time of the referendum. Moreover, almost four out of ten citizens consider that the debates in the European Constitution started at the right time (39 per cent) but for others they started too late (37 per cent).

Although the high turnout rate is comparable to that recorded for the referendum on the Maastricht Treaty in 1992, 30 per cent of registered voters abstained on 29 May 2005. The abstention level in this referendum was highest among citizens aged under 40. The main reasons given by respondents for abstaining were, over and above being prevented from voting by material reasons (66 per cent), the complexity of the text (60 per cent) and the lack of information (49 per cent). Only 14 per cent of those who abstained explained their decision on the basis of their opposition to the European Union or European construction.

Support for the 'no' vote, which carried the referendum with almost 55 per cent of the votes cast, was most marked among French citizens aged between 40 and 54 (63 per cent) or in the 18 to 24 age group (59 per cent), people living outside the large urban centres (61 per cent in rural areas and 59 per cent in other towns) but above all among manual workers (76 per cent) and even more strikingly among those close to the FN/MNR (95 per cent) and the CP (94 per cent).

The main motivation of the 'yes' lies in the perception of the pursuit of European construction being indispensable (39 per cent) and in long-standing support for European construction (16 per cent). The reasons given for voting 'no' are far more diversified and are related to social concerns. Thus 'no' voters mentioned mainly the potentially negative effects of the Constitution on employment (31 per cent), France's poor economic situation (26 per cent), the perception of the Constitution as being too liberal from an economic point of view (19 per cent), but also their opposition to the President of the Republic or the government (18 per cent). More generally, the key element which motivated the majority of the 'yes' supporters is their general view of the European Union, while a majority of these who voted 'no' were guided by their view of France's economic and social situation.

Despite the 'no' victory, French citizens are still in favour of the European Union and 88 per cent of respondents consider that France's membership of the European Union is a good thing. That positive view is shared by not only all the 'yes' supporters (99 per cent) but also by a very large majority of the 'no' voters (83 per cent). In addition, three quarters of respondents declared that the European Constitution is indispensable in order to pursue European construction (75 per cent). That proposal is supported by 90 per cent of 'yes' voters and 66 per cent of 'no' voters. Finally, the European institutions conjure up a good image for the majority of the persons interviewed (53 per cent), but especially among those aged between 18 and 24 (62 per cent), despite the fact that the majority of that age group rejected the Constitution.

The majority of French citizens believe that the 'no' victory will allow a renegotiation of the Constitution in order, on the one hand, to come to a more social text (62 per cent) and, on the other hand, to defend better the interests of France (59 per cent).

French opinion seems to be divided on the question of the reduction of

France's influence within the European Union: 48 per cent of respondents seem certain that will be the case, while 47 per cent do not think so. Finally, 52 per cent of the people interviewed believe that the 'no' victory will make it more difficult for new countries to join the European Union.

Document 2.7: European Commission – Eurobarometer on the European Constitution: post-referendum survey in The Netherlands (selected extracts), June 2005 Document, available at http://ec.europa.eu/public_opinion/index_en.htm

[. . .]

Presentation

The Dutch referendum was held on 1 June 2005. A high turnout rate of 62.8 per cent was observed for this vote. A large majority of voters rejected the Constitution: the 'No' obtained 61.6 per cent of votes against only 38.4 per cent for the 'Yes'.

Directorate-General Press and Communication of the European Commission conducted a post-electoral survey in order to better understand the factors which determined the result of the referendum, but also the reasons for abstention, the motivations of voters and the possible scenarios following the 1 June vote.

EOS Gallup Europe, through its partner institute in the Netherlands, TNS NIPO, carried out 2000 interviews from 2 to 4 June. The methodology used is that of the Flash Eurobarometer (telephone) surveys.

In the following pages the report analyses the following themes:

- Turnout in the referendum: the profile of abstainers, the reasons for abstention, the role of information and the debates;
- Analysis of the results: the motivations leading to the choice of vote;
- The consequences of the 'No'.

[. . .]

Conclusion

The turnout of 62.8 per cent was indicative of the relevance of the European Constitution for the Dutch population, surpassing the turnout rate recorded in the last European elections (39.3 per cent).

Although citizens complain about the lack of information on the Constitution and the fact that debates started too late, the reasons for the overwhelming rejection of the Constitution (at 61.6 per cent) are more complicated than a simple lack of information. Indeed, in the Netherlands, the referendum has not only been used as a channel for criticising the Government (14 per cent) but it has also shown that 'no' voters are worried about a loss of sovereignty within a political union (19 per cent) and also complain about the cost of Europe for taxpayers (13 per cent).

On the other hand, the main motivation of the 'Yes' vote was to further the process of European construction, as was the case for Spain and France. Indeed, 24 per cent of all respondents who voted 'Yes' in the referendum cite this reason. The fact that 'it strengthens the feeling of a European identity' and that 'it strengthens the role of the Netherlands within the Union and in the World' are motivations which come in second place with an equal result of 13 per cent of respondents mentioning these.

One out of four of those who were in favour of the Constitution indicate that they are satisfied with the outcome of the referendum; that is, the 'No' victory. Furthermore, more than two thirds of those who abstained are satisfied with this result.

Regardless of whether or not citizens voted and whether or not they expressed their support or rejection of the Constitution, their country's membership of the European Union is far from being questioned: 82 per cent consider EU membership as being a good thing.

However, while the Spanish and French widely support the notion of a Constitution for Europe being essential for European construction, the Dutch are far less convinced and most of them disagree.

For a majority of respondents, EU institutions do not conjure up a good image. EU institutions have an image problem even among groups which have historically supported European construction, that is to say, the Government coalition (CDA, VVD and D66) and the Social-Democrats (PvdA).

As far as the consequences of the 'No' victory are concerned, a clear majority of Dutch respondents (65 per cent) agree that the rejection of the Constitution will allow for its renegotiation in order to place greater emphasis on the social aspects. Moreover, two in three (66 per cent) also believe that the 'No' victory will allow for the renegotiation of the Constitution in order to better defend Dutch interests. A majority of those who supported the Constitution at the polling stations share this opinion and believe in a renegotiation in both directions.

Document 2.8: 'French and Dutch should vote again on EU Treaty', says Belgian Foreign Minister', ***EU Business*****, 6 July 2005, at http://www.eubusiness.com/Institutions/050706142153.rqqsivk1**

France and the Netherlands should vote again on the European Union's constitution despite rejecting the treaty in referendums, Belgian Foreign Minister Karel De Gucht said on Wednesday.

He said both countries, founder members of the bloc, were due for elections early in 2007, which might provide an opportunity for the treaty to be put to the people a second time.

'We can create a climate in which the treaty could finally be adopted in France and the Netherlands,' he told reporters in Brussels.

'We must not rule out a second round, which could not take place before 2007. This second round could take several forms, but we have to proceed with a second vote,' he said.

'I could not foresee that the procedure be changed and that a parliamentary ratification take place instead,' he added.

By rejecting the treaty, French and Dutch voters helped throw the bloc into its biggest crisis in five decades. EU leaders announced last month a 'period of reflection' in which to reconsider the union's future direction.

Eleven countries have already adopted the treaty, only one by plebiscite, but several other members have since put their ratification plans on hold.

Luxembourg will hold a referendum on it on Sunday.

All 25 members must ratify the treaty, aimed in part at improving decision making in the expanding bloc, if it is to legally take force.

Document 2.9: Luxembourg – The referendum of 10 July 2005, Luxembourg Government, available at http://www.verfassung-fir-europa.lu/fr/referendum/index.html [translation]

The referendum on the Treaty establishing a Constitution for Europe takes place in the Grand-Duchy of Luxembourg on Sunday 10 July 2005.

That day, all the Luxembourgers registered on the electoral rolls are asked to express an opinion on the Constitution for Europe, by answering either 'oui', 'jo', 'ja' (yes) or 'non', 'nee', 'nein' (no) to the question, 'Are you in favour of the Treaty establishing a Constitution for Europe, signed in Rome on 29 October 2004?', formulated in three languages:

'Êtes-vous en faveur du Traité établissant une Constitution pour l'Europe, signé à Rome, le 29 octobre 2004?'

'Sidd Dir fir den Traité iwwert eng Konstitutioun fir Europa, ënnerschriwwen zu Roum, den 29. Oktober 2004?'

'Sind Sie für den Vertrag über eine Verfassung für Europa, unterzeichnet in Rom, am 29. Oktober 2004?'

Polling offices will be open from 8.00am to 2.00pm. It is a consultative referendum and voting is mandatory for all those registered on electoral roles for the purpose of voting in the legislative elections.

In June, the Chambre des Députés (the sole chamber of the Luxembourg parliament), proceeded with a first vote on the Constitution for Europe. In accordance with the constitution of Luxembourg, the second vote of the bill must take place at least three months after the first vote. The Chamber undertook to respect the vote of voters as expressed in the referendum of 10 July.

Document 2.10: 'Luxembourg says "yes" to the European Constitution, Fondation Robert Schuman (selected extracts) available at http://www.robert-schuman.org/ [translation]

On Sunday 10 July Luxembourg became the thirteenth member state (and third founding member state) to ratify the Treaty establishing a Constitution for Europe, with a 56.52 per cent share of the vote in favour of the text. 43.48 per cent of voters chose to vote against ratification of the Treaty. Luxembourg is thus the second country to ratify the European Constitution by referendum, following Spain, which had largely approved the text on 20 February (76.73 per cent of 'yes' votes). On 29 May, the French had rejected the treaty (54.67 per cent of 'no' votes), followed by the Dutch on 1 June (61.6 per cent of 'no' votes).

Nine out of 118 communes voted. Nine such communes rejected the Constitution. These include seven communes from the old industrial and mining area, located alongside the French border – Differlange (40.83 per cent of 'yes' votes), Rumelange, the second largest town of the country and stronghold of the left-wing opposition (43.52 per cent), Esch-sur-Alzette (46.76 per cent), Kayl (47.23 per cent), Sanem (47.33 per cent), Pétange (47.11 per cent) and Schifflange (47.41 per cent) – and two communes from the centre of the country which host refugee centres: Esch-sur-Sûre (41.84 per cent) and Beaufort (49.35 per cent).

Voting is compulsory in Luxembourg, and 98.18 per cent of the 220 717 registered voters went to the voting booths; 11 201 had chosen to cast postal votes and 5 894 voters dropped a blank or void ballot paper in the ballot box.

On 28 June, the Chambre des Députés (the single chamber of parliament) had unanimously approved the Treaty establishing Constitution for Europe. The 55 members of parliament present had voted in favour of the text while the five members of Action for democracy and justice in matters relating to pensions (the ADR party), opposed to the Treaty, had not taken part in the vote. Following the 'yes' vote of the Luxembourgers (the members of parliament had decided to respect the people's decision), the members of parliament must vote for a second time for the ratification of the European Constitution to take effect. However, the vote will not take place before 28 September, as article 59 of the Constitution of the Grand Duchy provides for a mandatory three-month interval between the two votes of the Chamber.

Document 2.11 EU Constitutional Treaty: Statement of British Foreign Secretary Straw to the House of Commons, 6 June 2005, Foreign and Commonwealth Office News available at http://www.fco.gov.uk/servlet/Front/TextOnly?pagename=OpenMarket/Xcelerate/ShowPage&c=Page&cid=1007029392547&to=true&a=KArticle&aid=1115144244649

Mr Speaker,

To give effect to the UK's commitment to ratify the Treaty by referendum, we introduced the European Union Bill in the last Parliament, and it was given a second reading by this House by a majority of 215 on 9 February. The Bill fell on the calling of the General Election. It was reintroduced in this new Parliament on 24 May – before either the French or Dutch referenda – and it would in normal circumstances have been scheduled for its Second Reading very shortly.

However, until the consequences of France and the Netherlands being unable to ratify the Treaty are clarified, it would not in our judgement now be sensible to set a date for Second Reading. There is also the need for further discussions with EU partners and further decisions from EU governments. The first opportunity for collective discussion within the EU will take place at the end of next week when Heads of State and Government meet in the European Council.

We shall of course keep the situation under review, and ensure that the House is kept fully informed.

I should emphasise that it is not for the UK alone to decide the future of the Treaty; and it remains our view that it represents a sensible new set of rules for the enlarged European Union. We reserve completely the right to bring back for consideration the Bill providing for a UK referendum should circumstances change. But we see no point in doing so at this moment.

[. . .]

Document 2.12 CSA opinion poll No. 0500744C June 2005: Should the Process of the Ratification of the European Constitutional Treaty be Pursued? June 2005 (selected extracts), available at http://www.csa-fr.com [translation]

Question – Do you think that the process of ratification of the Constitutional Treaty in the other European countries should continue or should be halted?

- Should be continued 63
- Should be halted 26
- No answer 11

Total 100

Document 2.13: Reprinted with the permission of L'Harmattan: Patricia Jerónimo, 'Adoption and Entry into Force of the Constitution of Europe' in J. Ziller (ed.) L'Européanisation des droits constitutionnels à la lumière de la Constitution pour l'Europe (The Europeanisation of Constitutional Law in the Light of the Constitution for Europe), Paris, L'Harmattan, 2003, p. 186. (extract)

It is worth mentioning that the Portuguese Constitutional Court, in its decision 531/98, dismissed the first (and to date the only) referendum with a European content held in Portugal precisely on the grounds outlined above. The question proposed by the Parliament – 'Do you agree with the continuance of the Portuguese participation in the construction of the European Union, within the framework provided by the Amsterdam Treaty'[9] – was deemed to be neither sufficiently clear nor precise, and therefore violating Art. 115/6 of the Portuguese Constitution. Taking as reference the private law concept of the 'teoria da impressão do destinatário' (theory of impression of the recipient), the Court pointed to the need to take into consideration the perception that a normal voter would have of a question stated in such ambiguous terms. Not only would a normal voter fear that his 'no' would force Portugal out of the EU, but what would have been the consequence of a no vote? He would hardly understand what it means to approve the Amsterdam Treaty. To fully understand the question, the Court argued, a good knowledge of what is the present state of the EU integration process is required, as well as of the content of the Amsterdam Treaty and of what it takes for Portugal to approve and ratify that same Treaty. These circumstance interfere with the intelligibility and clarity that must characterise any referendum question, and which guarantee that the referendum is genuinely democratic.

Document 2.14: Judgment no. 704/2004 of the Portuguese Tribunal Constitucional, available at http://www.tribunalconstitucional.pt/tc (selected extracts) [translation]

Judgment No. 704/2004 – Case no. 1025/04 – Full Session – Reporter: Conselheira Maria João Antunes

[. . .]

2. The resolution in question is of the following wording:

'Resolution of the Assembly of the Republic no. 74-A/2004 Proposal to hold referendum on the Constitution for Europe.

'The Assembly of the Republic resolves, in accordance with the effects of art. 115 and paragraph j) of art 161 of the [Portuguese] Constitution, to present to the President of the Republic the proposal to hold a referendum in which Portuguese citizens eligible to vote in Portugal and Portuguese citizens eligible to vote in Member States of the European Union will be called to answer the following question:

"Do you agree with the Charter of Fundamental Rights, the rule of voting by qualified majority and the new institutional framework of the European Union, in the terms included in the Constitution for Europe?" '

7.1. From the way in which the question is formulated (Do you agree with the Charter of Fundamental Rights, the rule of voting by qualified majority and the new institutional framework of the European Union, in the terms included in the Constitution for Europe?) one can see that it in fact contains a combination of three questions in a single formulation to which one replies with a single answer. From a syntactical point of view, it is possible to separate out three parts which correspond to three different direct objects, while both the verb ('Do you agree') and the preposition ('with') are missing before the last two objects. An equivalent sentence could have been constructed with the following formulation: 'Do you agree with the Charter of Fundamental Rights, do you agree with the rule of voting by qualified majority and do you agree with the new institutional framework of the European Union, in the terms included in the Constitution for Europe?'

We are dealing with a formulation of the referendum question which is not clear, taking into consideration the constitutional and legal requirement that this must be formulated in an unequivocal, explicit manner, without ambiguities (cf. Luís Barbosa Rodrigues, 'O referendo português a nível nacional', Coimbra Editora, 1994, p. 208). Lack of clarity occurs as an automatic consequence of the fact that a single question contains three issues. Following the Tribunal Constitucional's judgment no. 398/99 (Diário da República, II Série, 11 October 1999), one should hold that 'the formulation of the question to be put to the electorate (. . .) cannot help but give rise to some perplexity. At hand, we are dealing with a question in which are contained three issues, which, obviously, renders the question complicated'. In effect, it begins by asking about the Charter of Fundamental Rights, and then goes on to refer to qualified majority voting, finally alluding to the new institutional framework.

Bearing in mind the final part of the question put to referendum – the formulation of which results from the Constitution for Europe – the title of the Resolution of the Assembly of the Republic (Proposal to hold a referendum on the Constitution for Europe), and the travaux préparatoires of the Resolution, we are however confronted with the possibility that the Assembly of the Republic intended to pick out three aspects of the Treaty in order to give some content to the referendum proposal, to illustrate and clarify, in order for judgment stemming from a global reflection. However, if this is the case, we can draw attention to the similarities to the Tribunal Constitucional's judgment no. 93/2000 (Diário da República, II Série, 30 March 2000), 'that, in the way in which it is formulated, the question in hand conceals or renders nebulous the point which is contained therein, namely to ask only whether one agrees' with the Constitution for Europe. In the way in which it is formulated, the question is not clear, in the sense that its purpose is to ask the voter whether he or she agrees with the Constitution for Europe.

The formulation of the question also allows one, as we saw above, to conclude that its purpose is to ask whether the voter agrees with the Charter of Fundamental Rights, whether he or she agrees with the rule of qualified majority voting and whether he or she agrees with the new institutional framework of the European Union, all three of these aspects in the terms of the Constitution for Europe. Now, as has been repeated by this Tribunal, 'the mere possibility that one can attribute more than one meaning to the question denotes its equivocal nature and the consequent lack of clarity' (cf. Judgment of the Tribunal Constitucional no. 531/98 and, among those which follow, judgments no. 93/2000 and no. 94/2000, the latter published in Diário da República, II Série, 29 March 2000). The mere possibility that one can attribute more than one meaning to the question raises doubts regarding the requirement of intelligibility and comprehensibility and clarity of referendum questions, the raison d'être of which is to 'ensure that the will expressed by the voters is not falsified due to misleading presented questions' [. . .]

III

10. On this basis, the Tribunal Constitucional decides:

a) It considers that the proposal to hold a referendum on the Constitution for Europe, approved by the Resolution of the Assembly of the Republic no. 74-A/2004, of 19 November, does not respect the requirements of clarity and of formulation of questions for yes/no answers mandated by article 115, point 6, of the Constitution of the Portuguese Republic and article 7, point 2, of the Portuguese Law on Referenda (Lei Orgânica do Regime do Referendo);

b) Consequently, it regards as unproven the constitutionality and the legality of the referendum proposed by Resolution of the Assembly of the Republic no. 74-A/2004, of 19 November.

Notes

1. For a full list of those referendums, see Chapter 1, Document 1.4, p. 00.
2. See Chapter 1, introduction.
3. Ibid.
4. Ibid.
5. Ibid.
6. See Chapter 1, Document 1.4, p. 00.
7. See Chapter 1, introduction.
8. The referendum of 23 April 1972 on the enlargement of the European Communities to include the United Kingdom, Ireland, Denmark and Norway (which in the end did not ratify

its accession) had a turnout rate of 60.2 per cent and produced a 'yes' victory, with 68.3 per cent of the votes cast. For the referendum of 20 September 1992 on the ratification of the Maastricht Treaty, 69.7 per cent of registered voters turned out to vote; the result was a 'yes' victory, with 51.05 per cent of the votes cast.

9. 'Concorda com a continuação da participação de Portugal na construção da União Europeia no quadro do Tratado de Amsterdão?' Resolução da Assembleia da República no. 36-A/98.

3. Innovations in the constitution for Europe

Document summary

3.1 Jacques Ziller, 'The possibility of incorporating the relevant provisions on the monitoring of subsidiarity and proportionality in a different form', in Jacques Ziller and Charlie Jeffery, The Committee of the Regions and the implementation and monitoring of the principles of subsidiarity and proportionality in the light of the Constitution for Europe, Study by the European University Institute for the Committee of the Regions, Brussels, Committee of the Regions, 2006 (selected extracts)

3.2 Giuliano Amato, 'Will it be a new Europe after the Constitution?', in Christine Kaddous and Andreas Auer (eds), *Les Principes Fondamentaux de la Constitution Européene*, Collection des Dossiers de droit Européen, No 15, Helbing & Lichtenhahn, Geneva/Bâle/Munich, 2006

3.3 Jacques Ziller, 'Social Europe in the Constitution for Europe', *Droit Social*, no. 2, février 2005, pp. 188–99 (selected extracts)

Introduction

In this chapter, the innovations contained in the Constitutional Treaty are examined from two different but connected angles. Firstly, they are assessed in relation to the legal acts formally needed to adopt them, which allows us to understand where and when ratifying the Constitution is indispensable to availing ourselves of the reforms embedded in its clauses. Secondly, these innovations are considered in relation to their substantive nature, as measured against the path of the incremental changes that had been going on since the birth of the European Community. One might expect a Constitution to be a break more than a continuation of an incremental process, but this is not necessarily so.

Why are these two angles connected to each other? Because we discover that some of the innovations that may enter into force only by amending the Treaty are not at all breaks, but are instead further steps in current developments. And we also discover that some of the boldest innovations are not at all among the reasons for the rejection of the Constitution by the French and

Dutch voters. The consequent lesson is that the approach to the debate on the future of the constitutional text should be much more pragmatic than it currently is. First of all, opposing ratification out of hostility towards the break that a Constitution as such represents is much more ideological than realistic. Secondly, opposing the boldest innovations of the new text out of respect for the 'Nos' of the voters would similarly be based on false assumptions inconsistent with the facts. And finally, picking only those pieces that do not need Treaty amendments is an operation to be judged on the merits of such pieces, for in several cases it is just a formal choice, completely disconnected from the substance.

Notable examples are offered by the articles reproduced in the following pages. We read that Treaty amendments are needed both to allow the Committee of the Region to bring actions before the ECJ for violations of the subsidiarity principle (Document 3.1) and to abolish the so-called 'pillars' by merging the Union and the Community into one single entity with legal personality (Document 3.2). The former is a minor and sound improvement, not attainable otherwise, and its approval by Treaty amendment certainly would not lead to any breaking of the existing European architecture. The latter is a much more significant innovation, and yet, even as regards this reform, speaking of a 'break' would not be appropriate. To the contrary – as is argued in the second article of this chapter (Document 3.2) – since the three pillars were invented in Maastricht, their abolition and the legal personality of the Union itself were anticipated by the facts.

The fact of the matter is that not even the Constitution, despite its promising (or threatening) name, is free of the path dependence typical of the developments that have occurred in our common architecture throughout the years. To the contrary, whatever we read in it has precedents in which its innovations were partially contained (Document 3.3). Moreover, the legal force formally given to the Charter of Fundamental Rights is not entirely new. The Charter was originally conceived as a restatement of a longstanding European case law by which individual rights had been found in the general principles of Community law and in the constitutional traditions common to our Member States. Furthermore the Treaty on European Union had already referred to such rights (precisely in these terms) in Article 6.[1] Therefore, discussing the boldness of the Constitution in giving legal force to the Charter is a practical nonsense.

Actually, there are constitutional innovations that must be considered potential turning points, despite being based on precedents. But their potentialities have nothing to do with their being inserted in an article of the Constitution or in a protocol annexed to it, nor with the form legally necessary for their approval. In the following pages, we read that such is the case for the new Protocol on Subsidiarity, for the Area of Freedom, Security and Justice as amended in Part III of the Constitution, and for the expanded right to be informed (and no more than informed) of the European Parliament vis-à-vis the Council and its activities, according to articles from both Part I and Part III.

Hopefully, this articulated context will be subject to the attention of those who will decide on the future of the Constitution and who quite likely will be inclined eventually to approve only selected parts of it, namely, those parts that might spare the fatigue of the amendment procedure. Much has to be learnt before adopting such assumptions.

Document 3.1: Reprinted with the permission of the Committee of the Regions, from Jacques Ziller, 'The possibility of incorporating the relevant provisions on the monitoring of subsidiarity and proportionality in a different form', in Jacques Ziller and Charlie Jeffery, The Committee of the Regions and the implementation and monitoring of the principles of subsidiarity and proportionality in the light of the Constitution for Europe, Study by the European University Institute for the Committee of the Regions, 7 November 2005, Brussels, Committee of the Regions, 2006 (selected extracts)

In the absence of ratification of the Treaty of 29 October 2004, the possibility of incorporating some of the innovations of the Constitutional Treaty in different forms (whether they are referred to as a new treaty or new protocols is of little importance) has also been raised and is quite conceivable both legally and politically.

Legally, a distinction must be drawn between three types of provisions based on their binding force and their novelty. Politically, the distinction is different. Beyond the issue of how to maintain the momentum which the adoption of the draft Treaty establishing a Constitution for Europe had created, the development of new practices based on the ideas expressed in it requires that a distinction be drawn between two types of provisions of the Constitution depending on whether or not they appear to have been rejected by the votes on 29 May and 2 June and depending on whether they constitute concessions granted by certain Member States in return for other concessions in the 'package deal' resulting from an intergovernmental conference.

(a) The Provisions Requiring a New Treaty

The Constitution contains provisions which are not compatible with the present wording of the founding treaties and the protocols annexed to them. That is the case, for example, with the binding nature of the Charter of Fundamental Rights and a number of consequences of abolishing the pillar structure of the Union and more generally all the provisions which change the procedure for adopting Community acts, in particular those which replace unanimity in the Council by qualified majority voting or those which grant a co-decision power to the Parliament where it currently only has the right to be consulted. It is also the case as regards the creation of an EU Minister for Foreign Affairs,[2] but not necessarily as regards a President of the European Council.[3]

A new treaty amending the present Treaty would be necessary in order to implement these innovations. The name given to such a treaty (constitution, protocol, decision and so on) is unimportant. What is important is that such amendment would be subject to the present procedure for amending Community Treaties laid down in Article 48 TEU which requires an initiative on the part of a Member State or the Commission, a conference of representatives of the governments of the Member States (IGC), the unanimous adoption of the provision by those governments, and its ratification by all the Member States in accordance with their constitutional requirements.

Only two innovations concerning monitoring of the principles of subsidiarity and proportionality would appear to fall within this category of provision.

i. On the one hand, the possibility of the Committee of the Regions bringing an action for annulment to review the principle of subsidiarity – as provided by Article 8 of the Subsidiarity Protocol – certainly requires amendment of the Treaties. As regards the right of the Committee of the Regions to bring an action to protect its prerogatives (Article III-365(3)), the matter is more debatable. The Court granted Parliament such a right to bring an action, without it being laid down in the Treaties, in 1990.[4] On the other hand, since this right has been laid down in the EC Treaty, by an amendment to the Treaty of Maastricht which entered into force on 1 November 1993, there could be an attempt conversely to use this legislation to contend that at present an express provision of the Treaties is necessary for an institution or body of the Union to have a right to bring an action for annulment to protect its prerogatives.[5] Nonetheless, it should be noted that Article 245 EC permits amendment of the Statute of the Court of Justice by a unanimous decision of the Council at the request of the Court and after consulting the Commission, with the exception of the provisions on the status of the members of the Court. It is certainly unlikely, but not entirely impossible, that the Council will agree to granting the CoR access to the Court. It is easier to anticipate the Constitutional Treaty by amending Article 37 of the Statute to open up to the CoR the possibility of intervening, which will be examined in Chapter 9.

ii. On the other, the requirement on an institution or a State to re-examine its proposed legislation (laid down in Article 7 of the Subsidiarity Protocol) can follow only from an amendment to the Treaty insofar as the possible decision to maintain the proposal, for which reasons must be stated, could be the subject of an action for annulment before the Court.[6] However, no legislative basis is required for the institutions to enter into a moral commitment to re-examine their proposals.

(b) Provisions which can be Implemented on the Basis of Legislation Adopted by the Institutions of the Union or by Member States without the Need for Ratification

A significant number of provisions need to be laid down in legislation in order to be mandatory, even though they are not incompatible with the present wording of the Treaties. This is the case in particular as regards the non-procedural aspects of the new nomenclature of acts[7] and certain minor institutional provisions.

With regard to the innovations concerning the monitoring of the principles of subsidiarity and proportionality, the early warning mechanism could be established on the basis of two types of legislation which do not need to be in the form of a treaty.

i. As Community law now stands, there is nothing to prevent a national parliament from adopting a resolution on a draft Community act. The question arises only in the law of the Member States.[8] The question whether or not the country's permanent representation to the Communities and the Union is required officially to communicate such a resolution is also a matter of national law and is secondary once a parliament is resolved to make its position public. The Member States could undertake, where necessary by means of a declaration in the European Council, to lay down rules authorizing such resolutions and to have them notified to the Community institutions.

ii. As regards the notification of draft Community or Union acts to the national parliaments, it would likewise be sufficient for the Member States to enter into voluntary commitments under which their permanent representation would send such documents directly to the parliaments without delay. These commitments could be expressed during a meeting of the European Council, for example.

iii. As regards consideration of possible opinions issued by national parliaments, an interinstitutional agreement could be sufficient – subject, once again, to any disputed aspect.

iv. As for the possibilities of bringing an action to protect subsidiarity on behalf of national and regional parliaments, since the Protocol can only be regarded as an invitation to the Member States – and not an obligation or even less an authorization, which is not necessary – there is nothing to prevent them from introducing such measures without any basis in European legislation.

Some Member States have already adopted the national measures to implement the early warning mechanism and the mechanism for notifying actions, while at the same time making the applicability of the new legislation subject to the entry into force of the Constitutional Treaty, as France did by the constitutional amendment of February 2005 and Germany did by the law of May 2005 (see Chapter 8). If this entry into force is delayed significantly, there is nothing to prevent national legislation from being amended to make it immediately applicable and there is in any event nothing to prevent the government from undertaking to bring an action at the request of its parliament pending completion of the procedure for amending national law.

This may appear extremely complicated because the various factors to be taken into account have been broken down in the reasoning set out. In practice, two acts are sufficient:

- the adoption by the Member States, during a meeting of the European Council, of a commitment to put in place the procedures needed to allow their parliaments to play the role provided for in the Protocol, in the form of conclusions of the presidency or declarations, and
- the adoption, on the same occasion, by the Commission, the Parliament and the Council, of a commitment to adopt an interinstitutional agreement on the procedure for considering the opinions issued by national parliaments. Both these types of instruments could simply reproduce the early warning system provided for in the Protocol.

(c) Provisions which do not Need a New Legislative Basis

Apart from the fact that it proclaims important principles in terms of values, the Constitution for Europe is largely a work of codification and reorganization of present Treaties. This codification and reorganization could change the interpretation which the Court places on a number of provisions, in particular following the abolition of the pillars and because the Constitution places greater importance on the individual than on the economy.

One of the most significant consequences of this work from a legal point of view is the abolition of the pillars, which results in all the acts adopted in the field of freedom, security and justice being subject to review by the Court of Justice. However, many provisions of the Constitution already appear as such in the Treaties, apart from the designation of the acts. It should be noted that in substantive terms the difference between legislative and non-legislative acts has appeared in the Treaties since the Treaty of Maastricht which established the notion of the Council acting in its capacity as legislator, by the amendment of Article 207(3) (formerly Article 151) EC. This notion is reinforced by the Treaty of Amsterdam though the extension of the scope of co-decision and the simplification of the co-decision procedure and, with the adoption of the Subsidiarity Protocol annexed to the Treaty of Amsterdam, the term 'legislative act' actually appears in the Treaties.

1. It is clearly not necessary to make a detailed comparison of the Treaties in their present form and of the wording of the Constitution[9] and of the

Subsidiarity Protocol before adopting a definitive position, but it should already be noted that the principles of subsidiarity and proportionality appear in the EC Treaty and the TEU and have already been relied upon before the Court of Justice, and that the Protocol annexed to the Treaty of Amsterdam imposes a number of duties on the institutions – and in particular the Commission – as regards drafting and stating of reasons for its legislative proposals.

(d) Provisions that can be Regarded as a Reason for the Voters' Rejection of the Constitution in Countries where the Referendum Produced a 'No' Vote

Until proper and detailed studies of the reasons for the rejection of the Constitutional Treaty by the majority of voters in the referendums of 29 May and 2 June are produced, the only evidence available by which to gain an idea of the reasons for the rejection is an analysis of the campaign arguments put forward in favour of a 'no' vote. No objections appear to have been raised to the content of the Subsidiarity Protocol. On the contrary, in both France and the Netherlands the general tone of the campaigns was rather the insufficient account taken of national features and subsidiarity. If the European Council decided to adopt a set of declarations on implementing the content of the Subsidiarity Protocol, it would be difficult to raise objections in the name of the voters who voted against ratification of the Treaty. It should be noted in particular that the mechanism for monitoring subsidiarity and proportionality was intended to respond to the concerns of two sets of voters who could have voted against ratification, namely those who consider that the workings of the Union are not sufficiently democratic and those who consider that the Union interferes excessively in citizens' everyday lives.

(e) Provisions which can be Regarded as Concessions Granted by some Member States and Inseparable from Other Concessions Granted by Other Member States

The question of reciprocal concessions between States is quite different in relation to the Treaty establishing a Constitution for Europe from previous treaties simply because this time the draft was drawn up by the European Convention.

A number of amendments to the draft Convention were adopted within the framework of the IGC, and in particular during the conclave of foreign ministers in Naples on 28 and 29 November 2003 and during meetings in May and June 2004 at the level both of foreign ministers and of Heads of State and Government on 18 June. This is obviously the case as regards the composition of the Commission and the rules on majority voting in the Council. However, the problem of subsidiarity, and in particular the content of the Subsidiarity Protocol, clearly is not covered by such amendments.

The final wording of Protocol No 2, as annexed to the Treaty of

29 October 2004, differs from the wording of the Protocol as adopted by the Convention on 13 June 2003, presented to the Salonica European Council on 20 June, and submitted together with the full draft Treaty to the President of the European Council on 18 July 2003.[10]

However, the differences in the wording are purely formal. They were made by lawyers of the General Secretariat of the Council, in consultation with Member States' legal experts, and by the lawyer–linguists who finalized the wording of the Treaty and its annexes during the summer of 2004. The essential change lay in the structuring of the wording of the Protocol in the form of articles rather than the previous numbered paragraphs. Certain phrases were amended slightly for stylistic reasons, as had been done in relation to the entire draft Constitution before the IGC started its work.[11] Moreover, certain language versions were revised more thoroughly to ensure consistency between the texts. In any event, on this occasion there was no change to the substance of the wording of the Subsidiarity Protocol or the other provisions relevant to the monitoring of subsidiarity and proportionality.

Within the Convention, and in particular Working Group I on subsidiarity, chaired by Iñigo Mendez de Vigo, there were discussions and different positions which were subsequently reconciled. However, it does not appear possible to identify a particular feature of the Protocol as representing a concession by a Member State or group of Member States which was linked to other concessions. Quite to the contrary, the fact that the Protocol essentially incorporated the working group's ideas clearly demonstrates that the mechanism for monitoring subsidiarity should be considered independently.

The mechanism for monitoring the principles of subsidiarity and proportionality could therefore be implemented independently without the need for any reopening of negotiations between the Member States, with the exception of the possibility of an action being brought before the Court of Justice by the Committee of the Regions, which requires an explicit basis in the Treaty (Treaties).

In response to possible criticism of seeking to apply provisions of legislation which has not yet entered into force and, moreover, has been rejected by the voters of two countries, such application could be seen and presented as experimental. In that respect it could have a dual function:

- with a view to ratification which is still possible, to allow the drafting of interinstitutional agreements and possible acts to improve implementation of this mechanism;
- with a view to the drafting of a new constitution, and in particular a separation between Part III and the purely constitutional provisions, to amend the wording of Protocols Nos 1 and 2 and to insert them partially into the actual body of Part I.

Document 3.2: Reprinted with the permission of the publisher from Giuliano Amato, 'Will it be a New Europe after the Constitution?', in Christine Kaddous and Andreas Auer (eds), *Les Principes Fondamentaux de la Constitution Européene*, Collection des Dossiers de droit Européen, No 15, Helbing & Lichtenhahn, Geneva/Bâle/Munich 2006, pp. 3–12

My first aim with this lecture is to enhance the desire of Europe I sense in the air of this wonderful European country, Switzerland, despite her British self-image as an island in our continent. My second aim is to dig into the dilemma the European Constitution, as any other institutional innovation of some magnitude, opens before us: is it one of the several steps of incremental change, that have been typical of the European construction throughout the years, or is it a real turning point, due to which new and at the moment unpredictable developments might take place?

The distinction between these two kinds of changes is not at all easy. Economists speak of 'path dependence' to underline the tracks built by the past upon which future developments always run. And sooner or later also historians discover that the past always is part of the future. How could we say that the French Revolution was not an innovative event? Revolutions are innovative by definition. And yet already Toqueville discovered that there was a thick thread of continuity between the administrative power of the Ancien Régime and the post-revolutionary governance in France. And what about the communist revolution that was supposed to supersede the previous 'modes of production'? After some years of communism in the Soviet Union, the continuity between it and the Asiatic mode of production (whose authoritarian features Marx himself had described) became indisputably clear.

If path dependence exists for revolutions, do not expect Europe to be free of it. And the history of our common institutions is a long, long sequence of incremental changes, based on precedents. It is mostly in the early years that some bold moves can be found. Not by chance, we owe them to the Court of Justice, which could use the tranquilliser of legal interpretation ('I am just applying what is written here . . .'). But in 1963 it took courage to state in the *van Gend en Loos* case that European citizens have legal rights directly stemming from the articles of the Treaty of Rome, which they are entitled to exercise against their own States, when their States do not comply with obligations equally provided for in the Treaty. No tranquillizer could hide the fact that an international act was becoming the legal base not just of mutual obligations among States, but also of individual rights, independently of their specific recognition by domestic legislation. To put it differently, we teachers in Constitutional law smelled the perfume of new chairs for us in an area previously reserved to our colleagues in International law. And even more so in 1964 when the Court explicitly said in *Costa* v. *Enel* that the Treaty gives

Europe a constitutional order and has therefore to be considered as the source of constitutional principles in the legal system we have jointly created.

It is fair to say that the following steps forwards (perhaps even the direct election of the Parliament) were mostly based upon these initial moves and the Court itself was very careful in not challenging the existing frame. The principle establishing the primacy of Community law over national laws in areas where the Community has jurisdiction (which appears bold to many even today) was very modestly linked to the 'practical' argument of the *effet utile*, not to more exciting arguments such as the Constitution as a superior law. Should Community regulations not prevail upon conflicting national laws in areas where jurisdiction has been conferred on the Community (the Court said) such a conferral would simply be pointless.

Continuity became the main thread of European developments, more frequently interrupted by stops than by further steps. And yet, if one compares the European Community of the first years with the European Union we have nowadays, the differences are striking. Let us consider some examples, beginning with the Commission. Initially the Commission was, more than anything else, a technical agency with the mission to prepare proposals (exclusively based on the European interest), to be approved by a Council where the representatives (the Ministers) of a 'consortium' of States sat. This is the origin of the monopoly that the Commission still enjoys in legislative initiative, of its supposed neutrality and of the qualifications of its members, who should not be bound by political or by national interests. Nowadays the Commission is, to say the least, a very strange hermaphrodite. On the one side it has preserved – and it is expected to have – the initial features of the technical agency. On the other side it has become a quasi-political cabinet, quasi-politically responsible towards a Parliament. The Parliament has arrived in the meantime and for sure this has not been a minor change (I will move on to it shortly). However, the somehow paradoxical impact it has had upon the Commission has itself been incremental: the Commission has remained technical and neutral as it initially was, but its President is chosen on a political basis (even before the Constitution President Barroso has been selected on the basis of the European elections), the President and the members undergo a vote of confidence and they may also be subject to a vote of non-confidence. Not to speak of the Nice Treaty, that has added a clause according to which the Commission acts within the political guidelines of the President. One might argue that something inherently political already existed in the initial Commission and the case would not be groundless. Certainly such a political side has been growing over time, and, in almost 50 years, things have changed remarkably.

Let us pass on to the Parliament. As everybody knows, initially we had an indirectly elected assembly, conceived as a useful liaison between the Community and our national parliaments. Quite obviously, such assembly had no more than an advisory role. When the decision was taken to have a Parliament directly elected by the citizens (a decision that was more than consistent with the 'constitutional order' discovered by the Court in our initially international organization, but nonetheless quite innovative), its role necessarily changed. You cannot directly elect a parliament and expect it to be satisfied with advisory functions. To the contrary, the direct election will carry within itself the expectation that the newly elected body will enjoy the same functions as any Parliament in any parliamentary system of government, from legislation to political control. And so it has been in our case. On the one side the Commission was the target as 'the executive' upon which political control was built piece by piece. On the other side the advisory role on legislation has gradually been growing towards co-decision: initially as a limited exception, then as a wider and wider exception and now, on the basis of the Constitution, as a general principle with exceptions. And yet, if you read the article of the Treaty on the legislative procedure, you find in it the word 'opinion' to indicate the act that the Parliament adopts. Could we have a better example of both path dependence and innovative change?

The third case I want to illustrate rapidly before going on to the Constitution refers to the most astonishing and least understood development of recent years, namely the growing of a more and more complex cooperative Europe on the side of the communitarian one. The institutional setting in which a) the Commission has the monopoly of legislative proposals, b) the Council, with the ever growing co-decision of the Parliament, transforms such proposals into legislative acts and c) these legislative acts become binding in the Member States, refers to the construction of our economic market. With few exceptions, competencies have been transferred to the European level precisely to pursue this mission, which is the mission of the communitarian Europe. In the course of time, our Member States understood that their being together could be used also to pursue other goals, even more political than building a common market: foreign policy, justice and police cooperation and that cluster of objectives that fall under the so-called 'Lisbon strategy' (competitiviness to be fostered by intensifying research and development, improving our systems of education and adapting our welfare systems to the risks of the new century). However, in these areas they decided not to transfer new regulatory competencies to the communitarian Europe and to adopt different patterns, based on the coordinated exercise of their national competencies. These new patterns rely also on Community institutions, but giving them a different role. Therefore at least in some areas (not foreign policy) it is still the Commission that initiates the process, but it does so with a document, not with a legislative proposal. The document goes to the Council of Ministers (and ultimately to the European Council), but what the Council approves is not a binding act for the Member States, it is a set of 'recommendations' they should follow in the exercise of their domestic competencies. Also the coordination of budgetary policies, that is so crucial for the countries that have adopted the single currency, is carried out according to these patterns, strengthened, however, by sanctions that do not exist in other areas of coordinated policies.

Such growth of the cooperative Europe has been perceived by the advocates of the ever closer integration as a blow to communitarian Europe. It is a fact that, in the negotiation of the Maastricht Treaty, the proposal had been made to confer the new goals as new competencies on communitarian Europe. But the proposal was rejected. In legal terms, however, the victory of the 'intergovernmentalists' has not reduced the area and the powers of the communitarian Europe, it has added to this Europe a cooperative one, that is somehow parallel to it. For sure, this addition, which also is a partial overlapping, has deeply changed the overall machinery and its internal balances. The European Council, which did not even exist in the initial system of the European communities, first conceived as an informal gathering of the Heads of State and Government, has become the political strategist of both Europes. The tasks of the ministerial Councils have been doubled, they are both legislative bodies and policy makers and coordinators. There are areas where the borders between Community competencies and coordinated national competencies are very thin: take the case of foreign policy, where the High Representative of the coordinated Foreign Policy and the Commissioner for the External Relations of the Community have frequently intertwined jobs. Similar cases make life more difficult in Brussels: Europe has become double.

Step after step and incremental change after incremental change, the Europe we see today is profoundly different from the earlier one. Upon this Europe the moulding virtues of the Constitution should play their role. Will the Constitution be a turning point? Not surprisingly, nothing in it is entirely new, not even its own name, for having a Constitution was somehow already implicit in the constitutional order the Court of Justice proclaimed in 1964. I well know that 'Constitution' directly refers to a pact, not among States, but much more among citizens. Instead, we still speak of a Europe based on the will of its Member States and of its citizens. Furthermore we also speak of 'Constitution' and of 'Constitutional Treaty'. I may respond that Constitutional Treaty means a treaty the content of which is a constitution. But I understand that an ambivalence is undeniable. Well, this too is an incremental development: in 1964, a constitutional order was discovered in the legal framework of a treaty; now that framework is more and more a Constitution in a process that is continuing.

Turning to the contents, not even the most innovative change I can think of, namely the abolition of the so-called 'pillars' and the consequent merger of the European Union and of the Community into a single entity with legal personality, actually is entirely new. The Union was invented in Maastricht as a broad envelope into which both the communitarian Europe and the new cooperative one could be wrapped together and remain separate. Douglas Hurd, the British Foreign Minister, opposing any confusion between the two Europes, launched the image of the temple based upon three pillars, with the community as the first pillar, common foreign and security policy as the second one and justice and police cooperation as the third one. And the temple became the European Union, which was not given legal personality and the acts of which were consequently adopted on behalf of the Member States, as political or legal expressions of their cooperation. Since then, the two notions have been perceived as quite confusing. Many Europeans (and not just ordinary citizens) are unaware that there is a difference between European Union and European Community and where the difference lies. Furthermore, third parties with whom we negotiate agreements that are frequently mixed (in areas where both foreign and security policy and community external relations are involved), do not understand the reason for and express their surprise at the dual capacities that the Europeans have to exercise.

Having said this, it is a fact that the only two agreements that were signed by the Union on behalf of the Member States (one with the Republic of Yugoslavia, the other with the former Yugoslav Republic of Macedonia) were not ratified by any Member State and yet all of them consider them legally binding. This means that, despite the certainly innovative merger with the Community (a merger, however, that preserves the existing differences between the community method and the cooperative procedures), at least the legal personality of the Union had been anticipated by the facts. And the constitutional clause that explicitly declares such personality is based on these facts.

The role of path dependence or, if we prefer, of the precedents is even clearer in the Charter of Rights. The Charter itself is the outcome (not necessarily the final one) of a long process, that began with the already quoted *van Gend en Loos* case in 1963, when individual rights directly stemming from the Treaty were recognized by the Court of Justice. After that first case several rights were affirmed by drawing their contents not only from the Treaty, but also from the constitutional traditions and principles of the Member States. Later on these common constitutional traditions and principles were explicitly mentioned in the Treaties and eventually the Charter was written as if it were a sort of restatement of existing law (again, with some ambivalence, for some of its rights appear strikingly new). For sure, giving it legal force as part II of the Constitution (initially it had been approved by the European Council in 2000 as a 'political' document) does have innovative consequences. But the past undoubtedly has its mark on the future.

A preliminary conclusion can be reached on this basis: nothing in the

Constitution is free of path dependence and therefore without precedents. However, some of its innovations, despite the precedents they are based upon, have such a potentiality of new developments that in the years to come they might be considered as turning points. I will give three examples of such potentiality.

First example: the widening of the principle of subsidiarity. The principle was explicitly stated and strengthened by the European Council in 1992, at a time when the numerous directives promoted by the Delors Commission to complete the integration of the market were resented in several Member States as an overdose of Europe. Also firm supporters of the integration process such as Chancellor Helmut Kohl warned the Commission of the risks of too many and excessively detailed acts of harmonization. The procedure that was adopted by the European Council to give a stronger role to the principle of subsidiarity (substantially by imposing on the Commission the obligation to motivate its proposals accurately by demonstrating the need for a European act, whenever it adopted a new initiative) took it for granted that the issue to be resolved affected the relationship between Brussels and the Member States, without involving any other level of government. It was therefore a kind of subsidiarity adapted to the typical institutional framework of international organisations. Why were regional and local governments totally ignored, even though quite frequently community acts happen to affect competencies directly conferred on them (and not on national governments) by their national Constitutions? For the 'obvious' reason that States, not their internal partitions, are the only relevant legal subjects in international organizations.

This reason was openly set forth by representatives of national governments during the working of the Convention, to oppose my own proposal on behalf of a wider notion of subsidiarity, such as to also refer to subnational levels of government, whenever their competencies were at stake. These levels too were to be both informed by the Commission and entitled to interact with it on a case-by-case basis. Nor is it an intrusion in Member States' domestic affairs, I and others argued, for it is the Constitution of each of them that transparently allocates the competencies that are case-by-case relevant. Eventually we reached a compromise. On the one side the principle was stated in clear-cut terms as I wanted it to be: 'Under the principle of subsidiarity in areas which do not fall within its exclusive competence, the Union shall act only if, and insofar as, the objectives of the intended action cannot be sufficiently achieved by the Member States, either at central level or at regional and local level . . . .' On the other side the adopted procedure limits the interaction to the relationship between the Commission and national parliaments, leaving it to them to convey the Commission's communications to the subnational levels as well as the remarks of such levels to the Commission.

This is not exactly what I and others had in mind, but it is enough to pave the way to a very different future, in which further chairs in Constitutional law have a good chance of being introduced to the detriment of International law. Whatever the procedure, the new formulation of the principle abandons the International law framework, eliminates the diaphragm of the Member States and envisages a multi-level governance in which networking is both implied and feasible. I am not saying that it will happen. I am simply noticing that those few words that have been added to the definition of subsidiarity open a new scenario, whereby a constitutional future may be for the first time envisaged as to the vertical relationships among levels of government in Europe. Potentially this is exactly what we are looking for here, namely a profound change with unpredictable consequences.

Second example: individual rights and Union's role. We have already seen how and why the Charter of Rights is just the natural outcome of an incremental process. It is fair to add that, in itself, it does not push that process much further, for two main reasons: firstly because it is clearly addressed to Union institutions and agencies and to the Member States 'only when implementing Union law' (you may elaborate as much as you can on the borders of this 'implementation of Union law', but several legal actions and measures will remain outside them and therefore untouched by the Charter); secondly because the Charter itself says that it is not aimed at widening the competencies of the Union. And the competencies of the Union, as they have been up to now, do not include the promotion of human rights. The European Court of Justice has supported this view when asked for its advice. And its case law, even when asserting and defending the rights of the citizens, is firmly based on the principle that the Union cannot violate them (nor can the Member States do so, when implementing Union law), but has no power to promote them. The gate to a different future is somewhere else, in that Area of Freedom, Security and Justice, the clauses of which more and more appear to you, when you read them, as a sort of Pandora's box of the new Constitution (despite their being hidden in the cumbersome part III). In regulating asylum it says that European laws or framework laws shall lay down measures for a common European asylum system, comprising a uniform status of asylum for nationals of third countries. In regulating immigration, it says that the Union shall develop a common immigration policy, aiming at ensuring at all stages fair treatment of nationals of third countries, legally residing in our Member States. In regulating judicial cooperation in criminal matters, it says that European laws shall establish minimum rules, concerning, among others, the rights of individuals in criminal proceedings as well as the rights of the victims of crime. Furthermore, according to a widely supported interpretation, even the clauses on mutual recognition of judicial decisions presuppose minimum rules of harmonisation of substantive law. These rules, it is argued, might be necessary to establish the necessary mutual trust between the legal systems the decisions of which are mutually recognised.

Now, what is the common thread of these clauses? All of them confer on the Union a legislative competence that goes beyond the general obligation to regulate the sectors under its jurisdiction in such a way as not to violate human rights. To the contrary, it is extended to their promotion in specific areas. And promotion of rights is a totally new job for the Union, which can use these new legal bases both for giving, at least in some cases, new flesh to existing rights and for setting a common minimum denominator for others. How far the Union will go in exercising both options is unpredictable at the moment. Whatever it does, however, a new future may be on its way.

Third example: the future of the two Europes (the communitarian and the intergovernmental). Having to tackle their co-existence, the Constitution on the one side has strengthened both of them, aiming at making both of them efficient, on the other side it has built bridges between them. What are the foreseeable consequences of these two moves? Part of the strengthening has been the enhanced role of the European Council, in view of more continuity and more cohesion in the overall work of the European machinery. The European Council becomes an institution, whose main task is defining the 'Richtlinien' for all the policies to be carried out by the ministerial Councils both in the cooperative and in the communitarian areas (under the exclusive initiative of the Commission in the latter). This newly defined role both of the European Council and, consequentially, of the ministerial Councils clearly implies that more and more we have, in the very area of the cooperative Europe, policies that it would be hard not to define as European. Therefore Europe seems to have an executive power with a capital 'E', which does not execute legislative acts, but most of all defines political goals, political priorities and consequent policies. However this largely new executive power with the capital 'E' is bestowed upon institutions different from the one (the Commission) holding the executive power with a small 'e'. And while the Commission is responsible towards the European Parliament, there is no democratic European institution whom the executive power with the capital 'E' responds to.

National Governments do not see this as a problem. The members of the European Council and of the ministerial ones (they argue) respond to their respective national Parliaments. There is no reason for them to respond to the European Parliament and such responsibility would also be inadmissible, for it would profoundly change the institutional nature of Europe. Once more, the imprint of international organizations is transparent in this argument, but Europe has gone beyond the patterns of such organizations and, as matters stand now, relying on national Parliaments is not a solution at all. National Parliaments quite naturally care about the attention given to national interests at the European level, not about the European quality of the policies adopted at such a level. There is a democratic vacuum that only a liaison between the

Council and the European Parliament can fill. But filling that vacuum (national governments are right) profoundly changes the existing institutional setting.

Well, this is the direction the Constitution is taking and the cluster of relevant clauses constitute another gate opening the way to an unpredictable future. In the clauses of part III devoted to policies where the open method of coordination applies, we find a final sentence according to which 'the European Parliament will be kept fully informed' of the continuing coordination (and here we are speaking of national policies and measures to be coordinated on the basis of common guidelines and benchmarks). In the area of foreign and security policy, whatever the European Council and the double-hatted Foreign Minister do, they have to report to the European Parliament. Furthermore, in the article that defines the structure and the mission of Europol (again, a structured form of cooperation of our national police authorities) we read that 'European laws shall lay down the procedures for scrutiny of Europol's activities by the European Parliament, together with Member States' National Parliaments.' Not to speak of one of the implications of the new Union with legal personality, namely the extension of parliamentary scrutiny to the international agreements stipulated by the Union itself also in the area of Foreign and Security Policy.

It is not a full-fledged political responsibility of the Councils before the European Parliament, but a wall has fallen, that almost completely separated and defended intergovernmental activities from the scrutiny of the Parliament. Those who are familiar with the history of our national parliaments, specifically of the British one, well know how they have built upon initially limited and narrow prerogatives: from information to recommendations, from recommendations to political responsibility. Therefore, to predict a similar development also in our case is not at all unrealistic. And it would be quite an innovative development. It would point to the merger of the two Europes within the framework of the communitarian one and of the parliamentary system of government that has been growing in it.

Even more so, should the two executive powers of the Union be reduced to one, for at the moment they are still separate, with the European Council as the executive power with the capital 'E', the Commission as the executive power with the small 'e' and the ministerial Councils mostly sharing (at a secondary level) the former but still intruding into the latter. There is already a loose separation, for it is the Commission that submits the initial documents and the programmes that the European Council adopts as its own 'Richtlinien'. This initiative is not supported by the privileges that accompany legislative initiatives throughout the legislative process, but it does allow the Commission to take part in the production of the highest political acts, by making the first move.

This being so, the risk of confusion, overlapping and conflicts is even higher than it would be with a two-headed Europe in which the two do not communicate with each other. But a two-headed Europe remains a monster and the most desirable future of the two heads is for them to become one. Might this happen in the years to come?

The Convention discussed proposals going in this direction, namely the merging into one of the Presidency of the European Council and of the Presidency of the Commission. The proposals were rejected, but a small signal has remained: the two positions were initially defined as incompatible, while in the final text they are not incompatible any more. It is too small a sign, but it is better than nothing. I do not know when and how, but one day we might arrive at a unified European executive. To those who wonder whether it will be centred on the Commission or on the Council, I respond: if it ever exists, it will stem from both. And it will be the most innovative development coming from this Constitution.

My conclusion leads me back to where I started from: the Constitution is part of the incremental process that has been changing Europe over the years, but it is also a potential turning point. Why just 'potential'? Because future developments do not depend on its clauses, but mostly on those who will use them for pursuing the missions Europe is responsible for. We may hope that, in the difficult world that surrounds us, they will understand that these missions more and more demand that they be bold and farsighted, which means, to say the least, not to remain timidly caught up in the enduring shortcomings and limitations of the institutional tools at their disposal.

However, boldness and farsightedness are not abundant resources. The Constitution gives plenty of room to a good use of such resources, but does not make them mandatory. In a few weeks we might realise that they are already missing in the ratification process that the Constitution has to pass through before entering into force. In such a case, we could face quite a different future.

Document 3.3: Translated with the permission of *Droit Social* from Jacques Ziller, 'Social Europe in the Constitution for Europe', in *Droit Social*, no. 2, February 2005, pp. 188–99 (selected extracts) [translation]

Relevant Provisions of the Constitution in Social Matters: Far More than may Seem at First Glance

The provisions of the Constitution relevant to social matters can be found in all three parts of the text: the first contains fundamental principles of the constitutional order of the new European Union, and is the most important in political terms and in view of informing citizens. It represents the main work of the Convention and quite logically attracted most attention, all the more so as innovations appear most clearly in this part of the text. However, for a lawyer, the appreciation and understanding of the provisions of this first part are subordinated to the understanding of part III in all its detail. Part III indeed contains the indispensable legal basis to the Union's action, since not only does it provide for the scope of its competence, but also and most of all for the type of legal acts which can be used and the procedure to adopt such acts for the purpose of European intervention. Moreover, only the provisions contained in part III have, where applicable, the characteristics required (unconditional and sufficiently precise) to be considered directly applicable by the European Court of Justice.

Part III is the direct result of the decisions of the Convention, under whose control a group of six lawyers from the three institutions – Parliament, Council and Commission – worked between March and May 2003. The group summarised the contents of the current treaties (TUE and TEC) and adapted them to the innovations adopted by the Convention. From a drafting viewpoint it was a case of putting forward persons, whereas the EC Treaty is first concerned with goods and services. This development should lead the Court of Justice to give more weight to social considerations, as opposed to considerations pertaining to the functioning of the market. Experts also adapted these bases to the new decision-making procedures (increased powers of the Parliament) and to the new terminology designating acts (European laws, European framework laws, European regulations).

The understanding of part I is also subordinated to taking into account part II: the Charter of fundamental rights. This is not the result of the work of the European Convention on the future of Europe, but is the work of the 2000 Convention presided over by Roman Herzog. The 2000 Convention was restricted in its action, to a much greater extent than the Convention presided over by Valéry Giscard d'Estaing, and limited essentially to codifying written law, case law and general principles of law, from Union and Community law and from the Council of Europe, leaving substantive law unchanged. The main battlefront for the 2000 Convention was the choice of provisions worthy of featuring in the charter as fundamental rights, a battle which it won, against, on the one hand, those national governments who feared the imposition of growing constraints on the market – in particular the UK – and, on the other hand, against those who feared social harmonization in line with the lowest standard (mainly Nordic countries). But this victory was only possible because the Charter, for an unspecified period of time, was to have no obligatory effect. The 2002–03 Convention touched up some articles in order to adapt them to the institutional framework of the Constitution, but without affecting the substance of these articles. However, it decided not only to give the Charter obligatory effect, but also to include it in the Constitution itself, to avoid any doubts as to its value, and it is now on an equal footing with the other provisions of the Constitution.

In the sense that part III summarised the provisions of current treaties, part II, including its first articles which pertain to the values and objectives of the Union, must most of all be seen as a potential means of reorienting the current interpretation of treaties by the Court of Justice and by the European executive (Parliament, Council and Commission). The provisions of Part II enjoy, in a way, an intermediate status: they will most of all allow renewed interpretation and application of Union law, but they may also generate new initiatives, in particular from the European legislator, on the basis of the current competences of the Community and the Union.

Notes

1. See also Chapter 4 of this book.
2. Insofar as he replaces the Secretary-General of the Council, High Representative for Foreign and Security Policy, he is a member of the European Commission while still being responsible to the Council, and he presides over the Foreign Affairs Council although the Council is normally presided over by a Member State.
3. At present no provision having treaty status sets out the rules applicable to the presidency of the European Council.
4. Case 302/87 *Parliament* [1988] ECR 5615.
5. The technical legal problem that arises can be attributed to the fact that the institutions and bodies do not have legal personality – only the Community has this status – and therefore are unable to rely on the fourth paragraph of Article 230 EC under which 'Any natural or legal person may, under the same conditions, institute proceedings against a decision addressed to that person or against a decision which, although in the form of a regulation or a decision addressed to another person, is of direct and individual concern to the former.'
6. The situation is a little more complex for proposals by the Member States, that is to say in the rare cases where they have a right of initiative. Breach of their obligations could nevertheless lead to the annulment of the legislation finally adopted by the institutions, thus sanctioning this obligation.
7. On the basis of the EC Treaty, in conjunction with the Amsterdam Protocol on subsidiarity which establishes the category of legislative acts, it would certainly even be possible to adopt a regulation or an interinstitutional agreement in order to designate a number of present regulations 'European laws' and a number of directives 'European framework laws'. The matter of 'European regulation' is more difficult on account of the confusion which would arise between 'regulation' within the meaning of the treaty and 'regulation' in the new sense.
8. In most cases it is governed by the regulations of parliamentary assemblies. The case of France is exceptional because the 1958 constitution prohibited the adoption of resolutions by the chambers of parliament as they were considered to be a source of government instability in the Fourth Republic. The amendment of the constitution in 1992 to ratify the Treaty of Maastricht allowed resolutions to be adopted on 'draft or proposed acts of the European Communities and the European Union containing provisions of a legislative nature' (Article 88-4 of the Constitution). This could pose a problem in the early warning procedure because the scope of 'provisions of a legislative nature' in the French constitution is not identical to that of legislative acts in Community law. That is why the 2005 amendment for the purpose of ratifying the Treaty establishing a Constitution for Europe laid down a new Article (88-5) permitting the adoption of resolutions issuing reasoned opinions in the early warning procedure. The constitution provides that this Article is to apply only from the entry into

force of the Constitutional Treaty although in theory the French assemblies may be unable to draw up resolutions on all the draft legislative acts within the framework of the present Treaties. Nevertheless, the present wording of Article 88-4 provides that the government 'may also submit to them other draft or proposed acts and any document from a European institution', thereby opening up to them the possibility of adopting resolutions. If the Member States and the institutions decided to test the early warning mechanism on a voluntary basis, the governments would undertake automatically and immediately to communicate draft legislative acts to the parliamentary assemblies and the matter would be resolved in practice.

9. It is clearly necessary to check all the other protocols annexed to the Treaty of 29 October 2004, since some of them could have an unnoticed impact on the monitoring of subsidiarity and proportionality.
10. OJ No C 169/01, 18 July 2003.
11. Document No CIG 50/03. This related to the French version of the draft Convention. The amendments made to it included abolishing the Legislative Council, moving the Article on the principle of primacy, supplementing a number of legal bases to add acts (laws, regulations, decisions) which sometimes did not appear in the wording adopted by the Convention, grouping certain articles together, and changing the numbering system. These changes were also made to the English version during the work of the IGC, but the other language versions were not amended until the summer of 2004 during the drafting of the final text.

4. Primacy of EU law

Document summary

4.1 Article I-6 and Declaration on Article I-6, Treaty Establishing a Constitution for Europe
4.2 ECJ, Case 6/64, *Costa* v. *ENEL*, ECR 585 (selected extracts)
4.3 Paul Craig and Gráinne de Búrca, 'The Relationship between EC Law and National Law: Supremacy', *EU Law Text, Cases and Materials*, 3rd edn, Oxford University Press (2003), p. 275 (selected extracts)
4.4 Denys Simon, 'The theory of the primacy of community law', *Le Système Juridique Communautaire*, Paris: PUF, 1997), pp. 406–14 (selected extracts)
4.5 Spanish Constitutional Court, Declaration 1/2004 of 13 December 2004, Case 6603/2004, Treaty establishing a Constitution for Europe (selected extracts) [translation]
4.6 French Constitutional Council, Decision no. 2004-505 DC of 19 November 2004, The Treaty establishing a Constitution for Europe (selected extracts) and Decision no. 2004-496 DC, of 10 June 2004, Law on data protection in the electronic economy (selected extracts) [translation]
4.7 Polish Constitutional Court, Polish Constitutional Court from Judgment K 18/04, of 11 May 2005, Poland's Membership in The European Union (selected extracts)
4.8 German Basic Law of 23 May 1949, Article 31
4.9 Jacques Ziller, 'The Contribution of the European Constitution to a Theory of Federalism', *Revista d'Estudis Autonòmics i Federals*, no. **1**, 2005, 79–96 (selected extracts) [translation]
4.10 Constitution of the United States of America, Clause VI
4.11 Wikipedia on Article Six of the United States Constitution

See also in Chapter 6 Document 6.1: Conv 375/02, Final Report of the European Convention Working Group V on Complementary Competencies, 'Respecting the national identity of the Member States' at p. 149.

Introduction

According to Article I-6 of the Constitutional Treaty, EU law 'shall have primacy over the Law of the Member States' (Document 4.1). Perhaps at first glance this does not seem particularly significant. After all, has not any beginner in EC/EU law been taught for more than 40 years that the ECJ established the principle of primacy in the famous case of *Costa* v. *ENEL* (Document 4.2)? And is not the 'Declaration on Article I-6' annexed to the Constitutional Treaty' (Document 4.1) a mere redundancy? Upon closer examination, however, the merits of Article I-6 should not be underestimated.

First, by affirming in black letters this important principle of Community law, which in theory has been accepted by all Member States since the first enlargement – of 1973 – as being part of the acquis communautaire, the Constitutional Treaty may be considered as a formal acknowledgement of this acceptance, considering that each Member State signed it on 29 October 2004, thus giving a solid basis to the Member States' courts in applying it when needed. The mere fact that British members of the Convention reacted negatively to the fact that the draft Constitutional treaty expressly incorporated the principle of primacy, and the fact that the Declaration on Article I-6 was adopted by the IGC at the request of the British Government, show how essential this type of clarification was.

Second, the principle of primacy as stated in Article I-6 clearly applies to the entire law of the European Union, whereas it is not obvious that it would apply beyond the EC Treaty, to the second and third pillars set forth in the EU Treaty.

Third, the wording of Article I-6 is illuminating because it steers clear of the word 'supremacy', which is predominantly used in the English language literature (Document 4.3), and instead uses the word 'primacy', which corresponds more exactly to the nouns *primauté* and *primato* (in French and Italian), which have been used notably by the French literature on the subject (Document 4.4). These latter terms have been used in reference to the 'precedence' which appears in the English language translation of the *Costa* judgment (adopted ten years before English became an official EC language) and which corresponds to the words *préeminence* and *preminenza* in the judgment. The German version uses the word *Vorrang* (priority), which underlines the notion of priority embedded in precedence, *préeminence* and *preminenza,* and which is typically used in the German doctrine.

Using the word 'primacy' facilitates a distinction between the characteristics of EC law and those of most written constitutions which has always been familiar to the most astute EC law doctrine (Documents 4.3 and 4.4) and which was developed in detail by the Spanish Constitutional Court in its binding opinion on the ratification of the Constitutional Treaty (Document 4.5). According to this distinction, EC law takes precedence over national law in case of conflict with provisions which are embedded in the latter, whereas the Constitution of a State is the 'supreme law of the land'. The wording of Article I-6, as well as its vicinity to Article I-5, which states the principles applicable to the relations between the Union and its Member States, and the new clause of voluntary withdrawal from the Union (Article I-60) have all been referred to by the French and Spanish Constitutional Courts when asked to adjudicate on the possibility of ratifying the European Constitution (Documents 4.5 and 4.6). These considerations were clearly also in the minds of the judges sitting on the Polish Constitutional Court when they had to decide on the compatibility of the 2003 Accession Treaty with the Polish Constitution (Document 4.7), at a time when the ratification process had not yet come to a halt.

Article I-6 also reveals the closeness of the EC/EU principle of primacy to the German notion of *Bundesrecht bricht Landesrecht* (Documents 4.8 and 4.9), which does not have the same features as the classical US American notion of supremacy (Documents 4.10 and 4.11). Finally, besides its utility as a contribution to the theory of federalism (Document 4.9), the principle expressed in Article I-6 is also a typical illustration of the codification work accomplished by the European Convention and the IGC.

Document 4.1: Treaty Establishing a Constitution for Europe (Article I-6 and Declaration on Article I-6, Treaty Establishing a Constitution for Europe, annexed to the Treaty)

Article I-6 Union Law

The Constitution and law adopted by the institutions of the Union in exercising competences conferred on it shall have primacy over the law of the Member States.

Declaration on Article I-6

The Conference notes that Article I-6 reflects existing case law of the Court of Justice of the European Communities and of the Court of First Instance.

Document 4.2: European Court of Justice, Judgment of the Court of 15 July 1964. – *Flaminio Costa* v. *E.N.E.L.* – Reference for a preliminary ruling: Giudice conciliatore di Milano – Italy – Case 6/64, ECR 585 (selected extracts)

Grounds

On the submission that the court was obliged to apply the national law

The Italian government submits that the request of the Giudice Conciliatore is absolutely inadmissible, inasmuch as a national court which is obliged to apply a national law cannot avail itself of Article 177.

By contrast with ordinary international treaties, the EEC Treaty has created its own legal system which, on the entry into force of the treaty, became an integral part of the legal systems of the Member States and which their courts are bound to apply.

By creating a Community of unlimited duration, having its own institutions, its own personality, its own legal capacity and capacity of representation on the international plane and, more particularly, real powers stemming from a limitation of sovereignty or a transfer of powers from the States to the Community, the Member States have limited their sovereign rights, albeit within limited fields, and have thus created a body of law which binds both their nationals and themselves.

The integration into the laws of each Member State of provisions which derive from the Community, and more generally the terms and the spirit of the treaty, make it impossible for the States, as a corollary, to accord precedence to a unilateral and subsequent measure over a legal system accepted by them on a basis of reciprocity. Such a measure cannot therefore be inconsistent with that legal system. The executive force of Community law cannot vary from one State to another in deference to subsequent domestic laws, without jeopardizing the attainment of the objectives of the treaty set out in Article 5(2) and giving rise to the discrimination prohibited by Article 7.

The obligations undertaken under the Treaty establishing the Community would not be unconditional, but merely contingent, if they could be called in question by subsequent legislative acts of the signatories. Wherever the Treaty grants the States the right to act unilaterally, it does this by clear and precise provisions (for example Articles 15, 93(3), 223, 224 and 225). Applications, by Member States for authority to derogate from the Treaty are subject to a special authorization procedure (for example Articles 8(4), 17(4), 25, 26, 73, the third subparagraph of Article 93(2), and 226) which would lose their purpose if the Member States could renounce their obligations by means of an ordinary law.

The precedence of Community law is confirmed by Article 189, whereby a regulation 'shall be binding' and 'directly applicable in all Member States'. This provision, which is subject to no reservation, would be quite meaningless if a State could unilaterally nullify its effects by means of a legislative measure which could prevail over Community law.

It follows from all these observations that the law stemming from the Treaty, an independent source of law, could not, because of its special and original nature, be overridden by domestic legal provisions, however framed, without being deprived of its character as Community law and without the legal basis of the Community itself being called into question.

The transfer by the States from their domestic legal system to the

Community legal system of the rights and obligations arising under the Treaty carries with it a permanent limitation of their sovereign rights, against which a subsequent unilateral act incompatible with the concept of the Community cannot prevail. Consequently Article 177 is to be applied regardless of any domestic law, whenever questions relating to the interpretation of the Treaty arise.

Document 4.3: Reprinted with the permission of Oxford University Press, from Paul Craig and Gráinne de Búrca, *EU Law Text, Cases and Materials*, 3rd edn, Oxford University Press (2003), p. 275 (selected extracts)

The Relationship between EC Law and National Law: Supremacy

1. CENTRAL ISSUES

i. Like the doctrine of direct effect, the doctrine of supremacy of Community law[1] had no basis in the EC Treaty but was developed by the ECJ on the basis of its conception of how the 'new legal order' should operate. EC law was autonomous rather than derivative on the basis that Member States had voluntarily chosen to transfer their sovereignty.

ii. More pragmatically, the ECJ ruled that the aim of creating a uniform common market between the different States would be undermined if Community laws could be made subordinate to the national laws of the various States.[2]

iii. Accordingly, the validity of EC law can never be assessed by reference to national law. National courts are required to give immediate effect to the provisions of directly effective EC law (of whatever rank) in cases which arise before them, and to ignore or to set aside any national law (of whatever rank) which could impede the application of EC law.

iv. The requirement to 'set aside' conflicting national law does not entail an obligation to nullify national law, which may continue to apply in any situation which is not covered by a conflicting provision of Community law.

v. Most national courts do not accept the unconditionally monist view of the ECJ as regards the supremacy of EC law. While they accept the requirements of supremacy in practice, most regard this as flowing from their national constitutions rather than from the authority of the EC treaties of the ECJ, and they retain a power of ultimate constitutional review over measures of EC law.

Document 4.4: Reprinted with the permission of Presses Universitaires de France, from Denys Simon, 'The theory of the primacy of community law', in Denys Simon, *Le Système Juridique Communautaire* (Paris: PUF, 1997³), pp. 406–14 (selected extracts) [translation]

Section II The theory of the primacy of community law

I PRINCIPLES

BASIS AND AUTONOMY OF THE COMMUNITY LEGAL ORDER

In contrast to federal constitutions, the community constitution does not contain any provisions regarding conflict of laws and ensuring the supremacy of community law over national law;[4] correlatively, community jurisdictions have no power to eliminate national regulations incompatible with community regulation, akin to the jurisdiction of supreme courts of federal states to void such regulations. It would be tempting to consider that the links between the community legal order and the legal orders of member states are governed by international law. International law postulates the 'primacy of international law', that is the superiority of international rules over domestic legal orders;[5] however, domestic law has the responsibility of organizing 'internal primacy', that is the means of defining the penetration and hierarchical position of international law within the domestic legal order, in accordance with the monist or dualist rules favoured by the domestic constitutional legal order. This 'internationalist' point of view may have been held by certain national courts, in particular in states attached to a dualist system,[6] to apply to the relationship between national and community legal orders. Despite 'revisionist' suggestions on the part of some commentators,[7] the ECJ never sanctioned this approach. The firm and definitive position of the community judge is based on the idea that the relationship between community and national law cannot be defined by reference to the relationship between international law and domestic law, and can most certainly not be defined in reference to the varying solutions defined by national constitutions. This is the meaning of the vigorous assertion of the irreducible autonomy of the community legal order as outlined by the *Van Gend en Loos* case and further highlighted by the *Costa* v. *Enel* case.[8] There is indeed 'an intrinsic and essential link between the autonomy and the primacy of community law',[9] and as a consequence the basis for the primacy of community law is to be found only in the principle itself. This is indeed the meaning of the Court's ritual phrasing according to which:

> The law stemming from the treaty, an independent source of law, could not, because of its special and original nature, be overridden by domestic legal provisions, however framed, without being deprived of its character as community law and without the legal basis of the community itself being called into question.[10]

It has to be added that its 'special and original nature', according the court's wording, which is, significantly, tautological, justifies the assertion that the primacy of community law is an 'existential'[11] feature of community law.

JUSTIFICATION: THE UNIFORM APPLICATION OF COMMUNITY LAW

It is difficult to distinguish the crucial motives which necessarily imply the primacy of community law over national law without going beyond an analysis of the wording used in *Costa* v. *Enel*.[12] The irreversible transfer of competences from states to the community, the direct and immediate effect of community law, the prohibition of discriminations by reason of nationality, the safeguard clauses and the scope of article 249 (ex article 189) EC are successively called upon to justify, in a 'macro-legal' reasoning process, the proposition that the primacy of community law 'results from all these elements taken together'. In reality, the justification for the court's conclusion rather seems to proceed from an undeclared premise which inspires an overall conception of the nature of the community legal order. The intention of Member States to build a customs' union and a common market necessarily implies a unity in the application of common rules on the whole of the territory of the community, because any dent on the uniformity of the law is by its very nature, in the light of free movement principles, liable to produce distortions of competition and diversions of trade, if not artificial relocations of activities. The 'economic constitution' of the Community carries with it as a necessary legal implication the uniformity of community law, which the court describes as a 'fundamental requirement of the Community legal order'.[13] This in turn implies that the domestic laws of Member States cannot be allowed to obstruct the implementation of common rules. The uniformity of community law indeed requires that all laws, whether primary or secondary legislation, have the same meaning (*gleichbedeutend*) in all the Member States, the same mandatory force (*gleichbindend*) and the same invariable content (*gleichbleibend*).[14] This cannot be conceived without the absolute primacy of community law over national law. It brings a better understanding of the meaning and reach of the well-known passages of the *Costa* v. *Enel* decision:

> The integration into the laws of each member state of provisions which derive from the community, and more generally the terms and the spirit of the treaty, make it impossible for the states, as a corollary, to accord precedence to a unilateral and subsequent measure over a legal system accepted by them on a basis of reciprocity. Such a measure cannot therefore be inconsistent with that legal system.
>
> The executive force of community law cannot vary from one state to another in deference to subsequent domestic laws, without jeopardizing the attainment of the objectives of the treaty [. . .].
>
> The obligations undertaken under the treaty establishing the Community would not be unconditional, but merely contingent, if they could be called in question by subsequent legislative acts of the signatories.

> [. . .]
>
> The transfer by the states from their domestic legal system to the community legal system of the rights and obligations arising under the treaty carries with it a permanent limitation of their sovereign rights, against which a subsequent unilateral act incompatible with the concept of the community cannot prevail.

SCOPE: GENERAL AND ABSOLUTE PRIMACY

The basis and the justification we attach to the primacy of community law quite logically imply the unitary and undividable nature of this primacy. By asserting that 'the law stemming from the treaty [. . .] could not [. . .] be overridden by domestic legal provisions, however framed', the Court lays down the principle of the unconditional primacy of all community law over all national law.

Firstly, the whole of community law imposes itself upon national law. That is to say that this property attaches to all the sources of community law, whether primary or secondary legislation,[15] international obligations binding upon the community[16] or general principles of law.[17] That is to say, also, that the primacy of European law applies to rules with direct effect as well as to rules with no such effect. While this latter observation may have been overshadowed by the 'intimacy'[18] of the link between direct effect and primacy of international law resulting from the phrasing of some passages in rulings of the Court, both notions are at the same time theoretically distinct and autonomous in practice.

Secondly, the primacy of international law applies to the whole of national law. As a result, the primacy of community law is not affected by the classification of national laws within the national constitutional order: primacy applies to regulations emanating from central government as well as to regulations emanating from 'infra-state' local authorities. Similarly, the obligation that community law should prevail must be complied with not only by the government and the civil service, but also by the legislator and the courts.[19] The question of the relationship between community law and national constitutional law might appear more delicate.[20] However, the logic behind the primacy construct, based on the autonomy of community law and justified by its uniform application, necessarily implies the assertion of its primacy, including primacy over national constitutions. The principle, touched upon in the *Costa* v. *Enel* decision ('domestic legal provisions, however framed'), was confirmed by subsequent case law,[21] the Court holding that 'the validity of a community measure or its effect within a member state cannot be affected by allegations that it runs counter to either fundamental rights as formulated by the constitution of that state or the principles of a national constitutional structure'.[22]

As a result, a member state cannot avail itself of reasons pertaining to its constitutional order to derogate from liability for non-performance of its obligations under community law. However, it has to be said that the principle of primacy of community law over constitutional national law, although perfectly logical and coherent from the perspective of community law, is not so easily accepted by national courts.[23]

Finally, the primacy of community law over an internal text, whatever its nature, also requires that the superiority of community law over 'legal provisions, however framed' applies whatever the date of the laws in question: primacy operates in relation to an earlier national law as well as to a subsequent national law.[24]

Document 4.5: Spanish Constitutional Court, Declaration 1/2004 of 13 December 2004, Case 6603/2004 Treaty establishing a Constitution for Europe, available at http://www.tribunalconstitucional.es (selected extracts[25])

3. The first question refers to Article I-6 of the Treaty [. . .]

This clause of the Treaty, as has been formally pointed out by the Conference of Representatives of the Governments of the Member States by virtue of the Declaration [reflects existing case law of the Court of Justice of the European Communities and of the Court of First Instance] and in its express proclamation it sets forth the primacy of the Law of the Union in the scope of the exercise of the competences attributed to the European institutions. Said primacy is not set forth as a hierarchical superiority but as an 'existential requirement' of said Law, in order to achieve in practice the direct effect and equal application in all states. The consequent coordinates for the definition of the scope of force of said principle are, as we shall see, determining for its understanding in view of our own constitutional categories.

The first point to highlight for the correct interpretation of the proclaimed primacy and the framework in which it is developed is that the Treaty which lays down a Constitution for Europe is based on the respect for the identity of the states involved therein and their basic constitutional structures, and it is founded on the values that are to be found in the base of the constitutions of said states. [. . .]

Said precepts, among others, confirm the guarantee of the existence of the states and their basic structures, as well as their values, principles and fundamental rights, which under no circumstances may become unrecognizable after the phenomenon of the transfer of the exercise of competences to the supra-state organization, a guarantee whose absence or lack of explicit proclamation previously explained the reservations against the primacy of Community legislation with regard to the different constitutions by known decisions of the constitutional jurisdictions of certain states, in what has become known in the doctrine as the dialogue between the constitutional courts and the TJCE. In other words, the limits referred to by the reservations of said constitutional justifications now appear proclaimed unmistakeably by the Treaty under examination, which has adapted its provisions to the requirements of the constitutions of the member states.

Consequently, the primacy proclaimed in the Treaty which lays down a Constitution for Europe operates with regard to a legislation which is built on the common values of the constitutions of the states integrated into the Union and their constitutional traditions.

On the basis of said guarantees, it must also be pointed out that the primacy set forth for the Treaty and its resulting legislation in the questioned Art. I-6 is reduced expressly to the exercise of the competences attributed to the European Union. Therefore, it is not a primacy with a general scope, but one which refers exclusively to the competences of the Union. Said competences are set in accordance with the principle of attribution (Art. I-11.1 of the Treaty) [. . .] Therefore, the primacy operates with regard to the competences transferred to the Union by the sovereign will of the State and also sovereignly recoverable by means of the procedure of 'voluntary withdrawal' as set forth in Article I-60 of the Treaty.

At the same time, it must be pointed out that the Union must exercise its non-exclusive competences in accordance with the principles of subordination and proportionality (Art. I-11.3 and 4), in such a way that the phenomenon of the expansion of competences, which was previously caused by the functional and dynamic nature of Community legislation, is rationalized and limited, since, thereafter and by virtue of the 'flexibility clause' as presently set forth in Article I-18 of the Treaty, in the absence of specific powers for taking the necessary actions for obtaining its objectives, the Union may act only through measures adopted unanimously by the Cabinet of Ministers on the proposal of the Commission and after approval by the European Parliament, including the participation of the national parliaments in the framework of the procedure for controlling the principle of subordination set forth in Article I-11.3 of the Treaty.

And as a result of what it does to the way of distributing competences between the European Union and the member states, Articles I-12 to I-17 of the Treaty define the scope of competences of the Union in a more precise way. Consequently, the new Treaty does not alter the situation created after our adhesion to the Communities in any substantial way and, if anything, simplifies and reorders it in a way that provides greater precision to the scope of the transfer of the exercise of competences as verified by Spain. But above all, the competences whose exercise is transferred to the European Union could not, without a breakdown of the Treaty itself, act as a foundation for the production of Community regulations whose content was contrary to the values, principles or fundamental rights of our Constitution.

[. . .]

The fact that the Constitution is the supreme regulation of Spanish legislation is a matter which, even when it is not expressly proclaimed under whatsoever precept, undoubtedly results from the principle of many of them, including, among others, Arts. 1.2, 9.1, 95, 161, 163, 167, 168 and prov. of repeal, and it is consubstantial to its condition as a fundamental regulation; supremacy or superior rank of the Constitution with regard to whatsoever other regulation and, in particular, with regard to the international treaties, which we set forth in DTC 1/1992 (FJ 1). The proclamation of the primacy of Union legislation by Art. I-6 of the Treaty does not contradict the supremacy of the Constitution.

Supremacy and primacy are categories which are developed in differentiated orders. The former, in that of the application of valid regulations; the latter, in that of regulatory procedures. Supremacy is sustained in the higher hierarchical character of a regulation and, therefore, is a source of validity of the lower regulations, leading to the consequent invalidity of the latter if they contravene the provisions set forth imperatively in the former. Primacy, however, is not necessarily sustained on hierarchy, but rather on the distinction between the scopes of application of different regulations, principally valid, of which, however, one or more of them have the capacity for displacing others by virtue of their preferential or prevalent application due to various reasons. In principle, all supremacy implies primacy (which leads to its occasional equivalence, as in our DTC 1/1992, FJ 1), unless the same supreme regulation has set forth, in some scope, its own displacement or non-application. The supremacy of the Constitution is therefore compatible with application systems which award applicative preference to regulations of another legislation other than the national legislation as long as the Constitution itself has set forth said provision, which is what happens exactly with the provision set forth in Art. 93, which enables the transfer of competences resulting from the Constitution in favour of an international institution thus enabled constitutionally for the regulatory provision of matters until then reserved for constituted internal powers and the application thereto. In short, the Constitution has accepted, by virtue of Art. 93, the primacy of the Union legislation in the scope inherent to said Law, as now recognized expressly in Art. I-6 of the Treaty. [. . .]

In the unlikely case where, in the ulterior dynamics of the legislation of the European Union, said law is considered irreconcilable with the Spanish Constitution, without the hypothetical excesses of the European legislation with regard to the European Constitution itself being remedied by the ordinary channels set forth therein, in a final instance, the conservation of the sovereignty of the Spanish people and the given supremacy of the Constitution could lead this Court to approach the problems which, in such a case, would arise. Under current circumstances, said problems are considered inexistent through the corresponding constitutional procedures, apart from the fact that the safekeeping of the aforementioned sovereignty is always ultimately assured by Art. I-60 of the Treaty, the actual counterpoint of Art. I-6, which makes it possible to define, in its real dimension, the primacy set forth in the latter, incapable of overcoming the exercise of a waiver, which is reserved for the supreme, sovereign will of the member states.

[. . .]

6. The problems of configuration between the guarantee systems are characteristics of our system of fundamental rights, where this Constitutional Court is responsible for the function of setting forth the specific content of the rights and freedoms assured by the Spanish public power on the basis of the concurrence, in the definition thereof, of international regulations and strictly internal regulations, where the former are equipped with their own protection measures and, consequently, with an authorized definition of the content and scope thereof. The specific constitutional problems which may arise from the integration of the Treaty may not be the object of an anticipated and abstract opinion. As happens with those being proposed from the beginning by the integration of the Agreement of Rome, the solution may only be sought within the framework of the constitutional procedures attributed to the knowledge of this Court, that is weighting for each specific right and in the specific circumstances thereof the more relevant formulas for constitution and definition, in constant dialogue with authorized jurisdictional instances, where applicable, for the authentic interpretation of the international agreements that contain declarations of rights that coincide with those set forth by the Spanish Constitution.

Consequently, the doubt that can be examined here refers to the eventual contradiction with the Constitution of a Charter of Rights which, by virtue of the provisions set forth in Art. 10.2 CE, should stand, after its integration into Spanish legislation, as a model for the interpretation of 'the regulations related to the fundamental rights and to the freedoms which the Constitution recognizes'. This is, of course, without prejudice to their value regarding the legislation of the Union, integrated into our legislation ex Art 93 CE. This is the only possible meaning of the reference to Articles II-111 and II-112 of the Treaty, which, respectively, lay down the scope of application of the rights of the Charter, on the one hand, and the criteria that define the interpretation and scope thereof, on the other. With regard to the former, the Treaty identifies as addressees of the Charter the 'institutions, organs and bodies of the Union', as well as the member states thereof 'when they apply the legislation', with the express exception of the fact that the Charter does not alter, by extension, the scope of competence of the European Union. Said reduction of the scope of applicability of the Charter (and, consequently, of the criteria of interpretation set forth in Article II-112) could not prevent, should the consent for obligation by the Treaty be given, the fact that as an agreement of rights ratified by Spain, through the procedure set forth in Art. 93 CE, its interpretative efficiency regarding the rights and freedoms proclaimed by the Constitution has the general scope set forth in Art. 10.2 CE.

Consequently, the doubt is whether or not the unavoidable extension of the criteria for the interpretation of the Charter beyond the limits set forth in Article II-111 is compatible with the system of rights and freedoms guaranteed by the Constitution: in other words, whether or not the criteria set forth by the Treaty for the organs of the Union and for the member states when they apply European legislation can be reconciled with the fundamental rights of the Constitution and, to said extent, can also be applied to Spanish public powers when they act outside the scope of the legislation of the Union, namely, also in circumstances that do not offer whatsoever connection with said legislation. Finally, it must be remembered that it is perfectly evident that the application by the national judge, as by the European judge, of the fundamental rights of the Charter must imply, almost without exception, the simultaneous application of the correlative fundamental national right, a hypothesis which could be considered if the interpretation of the constitutional rights in view of the Charter (Art. 10.2 CE) can be reconciled, in turn, with the definition thereof resulting from our jurisprudence, which, as we have already said, always considers the corresponding treaties and agreements.

It is the reiterated doctrine of this Court that the international treaties and agreements referred to by Art. 10.2 of the Constitution 'constitute valuable interpretative criteria for the meaning and scope of the rights and freedoms recognized by the Constitution', in such a way that they must be considered 'in order to corroborate the meaning and scope of the specific fundamental right which [. . .] has been recognized by our Constitution [. . .].' (STC 292/2000, of 30 November, FJ 8, precisely with reference to the Charter of Nice; also STC 53/2002, of 27 February, FJ 3 b). The interpretative value which, with this scope, the Charter would have regarding fundamental rights would not cause more difficulties in our legislation than those currently resulting from the Agreement of Rome of 1950, simply because both our own constitutional doctrine (on the basis of Art. 10.2 CE) and Article II-112 (as shown by the 'explanations' which, as a means of interpretation, are incorporated into the Treaty by virtue of Paragraph 7 of the same Article) operate with a set of references to the European Agreement which give rise to the jurisprudence of the Court of Strasbourg as a common denominator for the establishment of shared elements of interpretation in the minimum content thereof. Even more so when Art. I-9.2 imperatively sets forth that 'the Union shall adhere to the European Agreement for the Protection of Human Rights and Fundamental Freedoms'.

Said reduction of the complexity inherent to the concurrence of criteria for interpretation says nothing new about the value the jurisprudence of the Courts of the European Union must have for the definition of each right. In other words, it does not represent a qualitative change for the relevance of said doctrine in the ultimate configuration of fundamental rights by this Constitutional Court. It simply means that the Treaty assumes as its own the jurisprudence of a court whose doctrine is already integrated into our legislation by virtue of Art. 10.2 CE, in such a way that there are no new or greater difficulties for the ordered constitution of our legislation. And the resulting difficulties, as has been said, may only be apprehended and solved by the constitutional processes with which we are familiar.

Furthermore, emphasis must be given to the fact that Article II-113 of the Treaty sets forth that none of the provisions in the Charter 'may be interpreted as limiting or detrimental to the human rights and fundamental freedoms recognized, in their respective scope of application, by the legislation of the Union, international law and the international agreements of which the Union and all the member states are a part, and in particular, the European Agreement for the Protection of Human Rights and Fundamental Freedoms, as well as by the constitutions of the member states'. Consequently, besides the bases of the Charter of Fundamental Rights in a community of values with the constitutions of the member states, it is clear that the Charter is conceived, in whatsoever case, as a guarantee of minimums on which the content of each right and freedom may be developed up to the density of content assured in each case by internal legislation.

The conclusion reached in answer to the second of the Government's questions must therefore be that there is no contradiction between the Spanish Constitution and Arts II-111 and II-112 of the Treaty which lays down a Constitution for Europe.

Document 4.6: French Constitutional Council, Decision no. 2004-505 DC of 19 November 2004, The Treaty establishing a Constitution for Europe, translation by the Conseil Constitutionnel available at http://www.conseil-constitutionnel.fr (selected extracts) and Decision no. 2004-496 DC Law on data protection in the electronic economy, of 10 June 2004, available at http://www.conseil-constitutionnel.fr (selected extracts) [translation]

Decision no. 2004-505 DC of 19 November 2004, The Treaty establishing a Constitution for Europe

[. . .]

Having regard to the decisions of the Constitutional Council nos 2004-496 DC dated 10 June 2004, 2004-497 DC dated 1 July 2004, 2004-498 DC and 2004-499 DC dated 29 July 2004;

[. . .]

With Respect to the Primacy of the Law of the European Union:

9. Firstly, the provisions of the 'Treaty establishing a Constitution for Europe', and in particular those pertaining to the entry into force and revision thereof and the possibility for signatories to withdraw therefrom, show that said instrument retains the nature of an international treaty entered into by the States signatory to the Treaty establishing the European Communities and the treaty on European Union;

10. The name given to this new Treaty does not require as such any ruling as to its constitutionality; Article l-5 thereof, pertaining to the relations between the European Union and the Member States thereof, shows that the title of said treaty has no effect upon the existence of the French Constitution and the place of the latter at the summit of the domestic legal order;

11. Secondly, pursuant to Article 88-1 of the Constitution: 'The Republic shall participate in the European Communities and in the European Union constituted by States that have freely chosen, by virtue of the Treaties that established them, to exercise some of their powers in common'; that the drafters of this provision thus formally acknowledged the existence of a Community legal order integrated into the domestic legal order and distinct from the international legal order;

12. Article 1-1 of the Treaty states that 'Reflecting the will of the citizens and States of Europe to build a common future, this Constitution establishes the European union, on which the Member states confer competences to attain objectives they have in common. The Union shall coordinate the policies by which the Member States aim to achieve these objectives, and shall exercise on a Community basis the competences they confer on it'; pursuant to article 1-5, the Union shall respect the national identities of Member States 'inherent in their fundamental structures, political and constitutional'; pursuant to Article 1-6 'The Constitution and law adopted by the institutions of the Union in exercising competences conferred on it shall have primacy over the law of the Member States'; a declaration annexed to the Treaty shows that this Article does not confer on the principle of primacy any greater scope than that which it previously had;

13. If Article 1-1 of the Treaty replaces the bodies established by previous treaties by a single institution, the European Union, upon which Article 1-7 confers legal personality, the provisions of this Treaty, particularly the close proximity of Articles 1-5 and 1-6 thereof, show that it in no way modifies the nature of the European Union, or the scope of the principle of the primacy of Union law as duly acknowledged by Article 88-1 of the Constitution, and confirmed by the Constitutional Council in its decisions referred to hereinabove; that hence Article 1-6 submitted for review by the Constitutional Council does not entail any revision of the Constitution.

Decision no. 2004-496 DC Law on data protection in the electronic economy

[. . .]

7. Whereas under the terms of article 88(1) of the Constitution: 'The Republic shall participate in the European Communities and in the European Union constituted by States that have freely chosen, by virtue of the treaties that established them, to exercise some of their powers in common'; whereas the transposition into internal law of a Community directive is mandated by a constitutional requirement which cannot be hindered on any grounds other than an express contrary provision of the Constitution; and whereas in the absence of any such provision, only the Community courts, seized of the case pursuant to a preliminary reference, have jurisdiction to examine the compatibility of a Community directive with the competences defined in the Treaties, and with the fundamental rights guaranteed by Article 6 of the Treaty on European Union;

8. Whereas under the terms of Article 14(1) of the aforementioned directive of 8 June 2000 which was implemented by the law under examination: 'Where an information society service is provided that consists of the storage of information provided by a recipient of the service, Member States shall ensure that the service provider is not liable for the information stored at the request of a recipient of the service, on condition that: – a) the provider does not have actual knowledge of illegal activity or information and, as regards claims for damages, is not aware of facts or circumstances from which the illegal activity or information is apparent; or (b) the provider, upon obtaining such knowledge or awareness, acts expeditiously to remove or to disable access to the information';

9. Whereas subsections 2 and 3 of article 6(1) of the law under examination only exclude civil and criminal responsibility for hosts in the two cases referred to by those provisions; and whereas these provisions do not have the effect of holding hosts liable for not having removed information alleged by a third party to be unlawful, unless such information is manifestly unlawful or its removal has been ordered by the courts; whereas, subject to this reservation, subsections 2 and 3 of article 6(1) are limited to drawing the necessary consequences of the unconditional and precise provisions of article 14(1) of the aforementioned directive in relation to which the Constitutional Council has no jurisdiction to pass judgment; and whereas in consequence the appellants pleas cannot be validly argued before it;

[. . .]

Document 4.7: Reprinted with the permission of the Polish Constitutional Court from Judgment K 18/04, of 11 May 2005, Poland's Membership in The European Union (The Accession Treaty) summary provided by the Court, available at http://www.trybunal.gov.pl (selected extracts)

Principal Reasons For The Ruling

1. The accession of Poland to the European Union did not undermine the supremacy of the Constitution over the whole legal order within the field of sovereignty of the Republic of Poland. The norms of the Constitution, being the supreme act which is an expression of the Nation's will, would not lose their binding force or change their content by the mere fact of an irreconcilable inconsistency between these norms and any Community provision. In such a situation, the autonomous decision as regards the appropriate manner of resolving that inconsistency, including the expediency of a revision of the Constitution, belongs to the Polish constitutional legislator.

2. The process of European integration, connected with the delegation of competences in relation to certain matters to Community (Union) organs, has its basis in the Constitution. The mechanism for Poland's accession to the European Union finds its express grounds in constitutional regulations and the validity and efficacy of the accession are dependent upon fulfilment of the constitutional elements of the integration procedure, including the procedure for delegating competences.

[. . .]

10. The regulation contained in Article 8(1) of the Constitution, which states that the Constitution is the 'supreme law of the Republic of Poland', is accompanied by the requirement to respect and be sympathetically predisposed towards appropriately shaped regulations of international law binding upon the Republic of Poland (Article 9). Accordingly, the Constitution assumes that, within the territory of the Republic of Poland – in addition to norms adopted by the national legislator – there operate regulations created outside the framework of national legislative organs.

11. Given its supreme legal force (Article 8(1)), the Constitution enjoys precedence of binding force and precedence of application within the territory of the Republic of Poland. The precedence over statutes of the application of international agreements which were ratified on the basis of a statutory authorization or consent granted (in accordance with Article 90(3)) via the procedure of a nation-wide referendum, as guaranteed by Article 91(2) of the Constitution, in no way signifies an analogous precedence of these agreements over the Constitution.

12. The concept and model of European law created a new situation, wherein, within each Member State, autonomous legal orders co-exist and are

simultaneously operative. Their interaction may not be completely described by the traditional concepts of monism and dualism regarding the relationship between domestic law and international law. The existence of the relative autonomy of both, national and Community, legal orders in no way signifies an absence of interaction between them. Furthermore, it does not exclude the possibility of a collision between regulations of Community law and the Constitution.

13. Such a collision would occur in the event that an irreconcilable inconsistency appeared between a constitutional norm and a Community norm, such as could not be eliminated by means of applying an interpretation which respects the mutual autonomy of European law and national law. Such a collision may in no event be resolved by assuming the supremacy of a Community norm over a constitutional norm. Furthermore, it may not lead to the situation whereby a constitutional norm loses its binding force and is substituted by a Community norm, nor may it lead to an application of the constitutional norm restricted to areas beyond the scope of Community law regulation. In such an event the Nation as the sovereign, or a State authority organ authorized by the Constitution to represent the Nation, would need to decide on: amending the Constitution; or causing modifications within Community provisions; or, ultimately, on Poland's withdrawal from the European Union.

14. The principle of interpreting domestic law in a manner 'sympathetic to European law', as formulated within the Constitutional Tribunal's jurisprudence, has its limits. In no event may it lead to results contradicting the explicit wording of constitutional norms or being irreconcilable with the minimum guarantee functions realized by the Constitution. In particular, the norms of the Constitution within the field of individual rights and freedoms indicate a minimum and unsurpassable threshold which may not be lowered or questioned as a result of the introduction of Community provisions.

Document 4.8: German Basic Law of 23 May 1949, Article 31

Artikel 31 Vorrang des Bundesrecht

BUNDESRECHT BRICHT LANDESRECHT

Article 31 Priority of Federal Law

FEDERAL LAW BREAKS COUNTRY [THAT IS STATE] LAW

Literal translation by Jacques Ziller. (NB most of the translations in the English language wrongly take over the vocabulary of US law 'supremacy' or that of EC law 'precedence or primacy').

Document 4.9: Translated with the permission of *Revista d'Estudis Autonòmics i Federals*, from Jacques Ziller, 'The Contribution of the European Constitution to a Theory of Federalism' (Les apports de la Constitution pour l'Europe à la théorie du fédéralisme) in *Revista d'Estudis Autonòmics i Federals*, no. 1, 2005, 79–96 (selected extracts) [translation]

2. The Relationships between the Various National Constitutions and the European Constitution

Coming immediately after the articles dedicated to the establishment of the Union (I-1), its values (I-2) and objectives (I-3) as well as its fundamental freedoms and the principle of non-discrimination on the grounds of nationality (I-4), articles I-5 'Relations between the Union and the Member States' and I-6 'Union Law' are clearly at the heart of the theory of federalism within the context of the European Union. It is remarkable that they were amended significantly between July 2003 and June 2004, without, however, many explanations being proffered for such changes.

A. THE RECOGNITION OF NATIONAL CONSTITUTIONAL STRUCTURES AND THE LOYALTY TOWARDS THE UNION

The Convention had attempted to produce as balanced a text as possible in article 5 of its draft 'Relations between the Union and the Member States'.

> 1. The Union shall respect the national identities of the Member States, inherent in their fundamental structures, political and constitutional, inclusive of regional and local self-government. It shall respect their essential State functions, including those for ensuring the territorial integrity of the State, and for maintaining law and order and safeguarding internal security.
>
> 2. Following the principle of loyal cooperation, the Union and the Member States shall, in full mutual respect, assist each other in carrying out tasks which flow from the Constitution.
>
> The Member States shall facilitate the achievement of the Union's tasks and refrain from any measure which could jeopardize the attainment of the Union's objectives.

The first paragraph enshrines respect of the Member States by the Union in relation to their national identity (also included in the preamble to the Charter of Fundamental Rights) and in particular concerning their political and constitutional structures 'inclusive of regional and local self-government'. This last phrase is particularly important in the German language version, which refers to the 'Grundsatz der Lokalen und Regionalen Selbstverwaltung', thereby evoking the principle of local self-government (literally self-management) enshrined in the German Basic Law as the 'Grundsatz der Kommunalen Selbstverwaltung'. The second phrase, known in Convention circles as the

'Christophersen clause', had been introduced at the request of the outgoing European Commission and former Danish minister Henning Christophersen who participated in the Praesidium of the Convention as a representative of the national parliaments. The clause is of particular interest in that it attempts to define the essential functions of the state; it is of interest to note that these concerned functions which fall under the competence of the states and not the federation under classical federal systems such as the United States and Federal Germany.

The second paragraph, echoing the first, proclaims the principle of federal loyalty, mirroring the principle at the heart of German federalism, drawing on a formulation already present in the Community treaties, regarding which article 5 of the draft Constitution displays a particular reverence.

The text of the Convention has been subject to two important amendments. In the first place, ICG experts saw fit, without giving any particular explanation, to move the contents of article 10(2) dedicated to 'Union Law' to title three on 'Union Competences', into article 5 after the first sub-section of paragraph 2. This results in a degree of repetition in paragraph 2 of article 5, which stresses the obligations of Member States towards the Union more than the text of the Convention did. Partly in response to this, the smaller Member States intervened in the IGC in an effort spearheaded by Portugal and its prime minister Barroso – who subsequently became president of the European Commission – to insert at the start of article 5 a clause stipulating that the Union respect the principle of equality between the Member States. This reference did not add anything new to the Union's institutional arrangements, though it did underscore the need to avoid an asymmetrical federalism. The definitive version of article 5 loses in elegance that which it gains in precision [. . .]

B. THE CHANGE IN POSITION OF THE ARTICLE DEDICATED TO THE PRIMACY OF EC LAW

Just as the experts had seen fit to move article 10(2) dedicated to 'Union Law' to title III on 'Union Competences', the IGC experts moved the first paragraph, inserting it right after article 5 in a new article 6 [. . .]

There was no official justification for the amendment, nor was it debated within the IGC. The officious draft drawn up by the Council Secretariat on the basis of the Convention text states simply that 'It is suggested that Article I-10(1) would be more appropriate here. It has therefore become a new Article I-5a.' However, there is in fact a legal justification for this change: as has clearly been the case in Community law since the renowned *Costa* v. *ENEL* case of 1964, the principle of primacy has not only applied to the institutions of the Union in the exercise of their competences, but also to the Member States in the exercise of their own competences, where such action might be in contradiction with the general principles of the Constitutional Charter. It could therefore be argued that the provision was incorrectly included under the title 'Union Competences'. But this reasoning cannot get beyond the fact that in the very same title the Constitution recognises in article 9 – which became article 11 of the Treaty – that 'competences not conferred upon the Union in the Constitution remain with the Member States'. This provision clearly evokes the 10th Amendment of the Constitution of the United States, the adoption of which Madison had to promise in order to secure the ratification of the text by the most important American States.

The system chosen by the Convention (the inclusion of the principle of primacy in title III) had numerous advantages for all those who had concerns about the equilibrium between the Union and its Member States. It followed in the footsteps of the German tradition, epitomised in the ephemeral Paulskirche Constitution of 1849, article 66 of which, under the heading *Reichsrecht bricht Landesrecht*, provided that the 'Laws of the Empire have primacy over the laws of the Länder, insofar as they have not been attributed subsidiary validity', the substance of which was repeated in a slightly different form in article 2 of the Constitution of the Empire of 1871. In the Weimar Constitution, article 13, again under the heading *Reichsrecht bricht Landesrecht*, came immediately after the provisions on the distribution of competences and provided that, 'where there is any doubt or dispute over whether the provisions of the law of a Land are compatible with the law of the Empire, the competent authorities of the Empire or the Land may seize the Supreme Court of the Empire according to a procedure to be regulated by a law of the Empire'. Article 30 of the Bonn Basic Law, which came immediately after the proclamation of the distribution of competences, is now termed 'Priority of Federal Law' (*Vorrang des Bundesrechts*) and simply provides that *Bundesrecht bricht Landesrecht*.

This logic turns up again in the draft Convention: the reference to the principle of primacy immediately after the principle of conferral and the restatement of the fact that residual competence in principle remains with the States and not the Union has the advantage of bringing to the fore the equilibrium between the Union and its Member States. Moreover, Article 10 had the advantage of specifying the consequences of the principle of primacy, the draft of which ran as follows:

> Article I-10: Union Law
> 1. The Constitution, and law adopted by the Union's Institutions in exercising competences conferred on it, shall have primacy over the law of the Member States.
> 2. Member States shall take all appropriate measures, general or particular, to ensure fulfilment of the obligations flowing from the Constitution or resulting from the Union Institutions' acts.

The insertion of the principle of primacy into the most general part of the Constitution, in isolation from the articles restating the principles of conferral, subsidiarity and proportionality, led more than one reader – especially during the French referendum debate – to misunderstand the scope of the principle, reading it from the perspective of a unitary super-state, rather than appreciating its more nuanced role.

Document 4.10: Constitution of the United States of America, Article VI

All Debts contracted and Engagements entered into, before the Adoption of this Constitution, shall be as valid against the United States under this Constitution, as under the Confederation.

This Constitution, and the Laws of the United States which shall be made in Pursuance thereof; and all Treaties made, or which shall be made, under the Authority of the United States, shall be the supreme Law of the Land; and the Judges in every State shall be bound thereby, any Thing in the Constitution or Laws of any state to the Contrary notwithstanding.

The Senators and Representatives before mentioned, and the Members of the several State Legislatures, and all executive and judicial Officers, both of the United States and of the several States, shall be bound by Oath or Affirmation, to support this Constitution; but no religious Test shall ever be required as a Qualification to any Office or public Trust under the United States.

Document 4.11: Reprinted from Wikipedia, the free encyclopedia, Article Six of the United States Constitution available at http://en.wikipedia.org/wiki/Article_Six_of_the_United_States_Constitution[26]

Debts

The first clause of the Article provides that debts contracted prior to the adoption of the Constitution remain valid, as they were under the Articles of Confederation.

Supremacy

Clause two provides that the Constitution, federal laws made pursuant to it and treaties made under its authority, constitute the supreme law of the land. It provides that state courts are bound by the supreme law; in case of conflict between federal and state law, the federal law must be upheld. Even state constitutions are subordinate to federal law.

The Supreme Court under John Marshall was influential in construing the supremacy clause. It first ruled that it had the power to review the decisions of state courts allegedly in conflict with the supreme law, claims of 'state sovereignty' notwithstanding. In *Martin* v. *Hunter's Lessee* (1816), the Supreme

Court confronted the Chief Justice of Virginia, Spencer Roane, who had previously declared a Supreme Court decision unconstitutional and refused to permit the state courts to abide by it. The Court upheld the Judiciary Act, which permitted it to hear appeals from state courts, on the grounds that Congress had passed it under the supremacy clause.

The Supreme Court has also struck down attempts by states to control or direct the affairs of federal institutions. *McCulloch* v. *Maryland* (1819) was a significant case in this regard. The state of Maryland had levied a tax on banks not chartered by the state; the tax applied, state judges ruled, to the Bank of the United States chartered by Congress in 1816. Marshall wrote that 'the States have no power, by taxation or otherwise, to retard, impede, burden, or in any manner control, the operations of the constitutional laws enacted by Congress to carry into execution the powers vested in the general government'. United States property is wholly immune to state taxation, as are government activities and institutions. Congress may explicitly provide immunity from taxation in certain cases, for instance by immunizing a federal contractor. Federal employees, however, may not be immunized from taxes, as the tax would not in any way impede government activities.

Gibbons v. *Ogden* (1824) was another influential case involving the supremacy clause. The state of New York had granted Aaron Ogden a monopoly over the steamboat business in the Hudson River. The other party, Thomas Gibbons, had obtained a federal permit under the Coastal Licensing Act to perform the same task. The Supreme Court upheld the federal permit. John Marshall wrote, 'The nullity of an act, inconsistent with the Constitution, is produced by the declaration, that the Constitution is the supreme law. The appropriate application of that part of the clause which confers the same supremacy on laws and treaties, is to such acts of the State legislatures as do not transcend their powers, but though enacted in the execution of acknowledged State powers, interfere with, or are contrary to the laws of Congress, made in pursuance of the Constitution, or some treaty made under the authority of the United States. In every such case, the act of Congress, or the treaty, is supreme; and the law of the State, though enacted in the exercise of powers not controverted, must yield to it.'

Reid v. *Covert* (1957) ruled that no branch of the United States Government can have powers conferred upon it by treaty that are free of the bounds of the United States Constitution.

Oaths

Federal and state legislators, executive officers and judges are, by the third clause of the article, bound by oath or affirmation to support the Constitution.

[. . .]

Reference

Irons, Peter (1999), *A People's History of the Supreme Court*, New York: Penguin.

Notes

1. The extent to which the principle of supremacy may apply to the second and third pillars of EU law remains to be seen, when the ECJ has the opportunity to rule on these questions.
2. See the statement in Case 44/79, *Hauer* v. *Land Rheinland-Pfalz* [1979] ECR 3727, para. 14, that this would 'lead inevitably to the destruction of the unity of the Common Market'.
3. The first edition of this handbook has been chosen rather than a more recent one in order to show, amongst other things, that references to the 'European Constitution' did not appear suddenly after the German Foreign Minister Joschka Fischer had launched political discussion in 2000 [note of the editors].
4. For this reason I think it is questionable to present the relationship between Community and national law in terms of hierarchy (see, for example, how J.C. Gautron refers to a 'second hierarchy', see J.C. Gautron, 'Un ordre juridique autonome et hierarchisé', in J. Rideau (ed.), *De la communauté de droit à l'union de droit, continuité et avatars européens* (Paris: LGDJ, 2000), 25s. especially para. II.2, p. 58).
5. See, amongst the abundance of international cases on the subject, *The factory at Chorzow (the merits)* PCIJ, 13 September 1928, Series A No 17, p. 32; advisory Case *Treatment of Polish nationals and other persons of Polish origin or speech in the Dantzig territory*, Series A/B No. 44, p. 24. See, amongst equally abundant commentaries, H. Kelsen, 'Les rapports de système entre le droit international et le droit interne', (1926) IV *RCADI* 14, 231; M.Virally, 'Sur un pont aux ânes, les rapports entre droit international et droits internes', in *Mélanges Rolin* (Paris: Pedone, 1964), p. 488.
6. See for example the positions of the Italian constitutional Court, in the cases of *Acciaierie San Michele*, 27 December 1965, (1966) I Foro italiano 8, commentary by P. Catalano; *Frontini*, 27 December 1973, (1975) CDE 127, observations by P. de Caterim; or even, in the *Granital* case, 18 June 1984 (1986) CDE 185, observations by J.V. Louis, and (1985) RTDE 313, note by A. Barav.
7. See, for example, B. de Witte, 'Retour a Costa, la primauté du droit communautaire à la lumière du droit international' (1984), *RTDE* 425; D. Wyatt, 'New Legal Order, or Old' (1982), *ELR* 147.
8. See also D. Simon, 'Les fondements de l'autonomie', in *Droit international et droit communautaire, perspectives actuelles* (Paris: Pedon, 2000).
9. In the words of R. Kovar, in 'La Contribution de la Cour de Justice à l'édification de l'ordre juridique communautaire', *Collected Courses of the Academy of European Law*, vol/ IV, Book 1, p. 49.
10. ECJ, 15 July 1964, Case 6/64 *Costa* v. *Enel*, ECR 1141, italics added.
11. P. Pescatore, *L'ordre juridique des Communautés européennes*, 2nd edn., (Liège: Presses Universitaires, 1973), esp. 227. See also R. Lecourt, 'Quel eut été le droit des Communautés Européennes sans les arrêts de 1963 et 1964?', in *Mélanges Boulouis* (Paris: Dalloz, 1991), p. 349.
12. In this sense, see De Witte, *supra*, note 7 (1984) *RTDE* 425, esp. at 436. *Contra*, see, inter alia, J.Boulouis and R.M. Chevallier, according to whom the court 'delivers a demonstration so clearly argued and so coherently conducted that its conclusion imposes itself upon the mind as obviously necessary' (GA/CJCE, vol. I, 6th edn, esp. 104).
13. ECJ, 21 February 1991, joined cases C-143/88 and C-92/89, *Zuckerfabrik Süderdithmarschen*, *ECR* I-415, esp. para. 26.
14. The German terms are borrowed from L.J. Constantinesco, 'Die Eigentumlichkeiten der Europäischen Gemeinschaftsrechts', *Juristische Schulung* (1965) fasc. 8 and 9, the subject of which is summarized in 'La spécificité du droit communautaire' (1966), *RTDE* 1.
15. Regarding regulations, see, inter alia, ECJ, 14 December 1971, Case 43/1971 *Politi*, ECR 1039 and ECJ, 7 March 1972, Case 84/71 *Marimex*, ECR 89. Regarding decisions, see ECJ,

8 March 1979, Case130/78 *Salumificio di Cornuda*, ECR 867; ECJ, 21 March 1987, Case 249/85 *Albako*, ECR 2345. Regarding directives, see ECJ, 7[h] July 1981, Case 158/80 *Rewe-Handelsgesellschaft Nord mbH et Rewe-Markt Steffen*, ECR 1805; 19[h] January 1982, Case 8/81 *Becker*, ECR 53.

16. ECJ, 19 November 1975, Case 38/75 *Nederlandse Spoorwegen*, ECR 1439 and 16 March 1976, Cases 267/81 to 269/81 *SPI* and *SAMI*, ECR 801.
17. ECJ, 13 July 1989, Case 5/88 *Wachauf.*
18. According to R.Kovar's expressive wording, in R. Kovar, 'La contribution de la Cour de Justice à l'édification de l'ordre juridique communautaire', *RCDA* IV-1, 15s., esp. 63.
19. These principles also apply in international law generally: see *Certain German interest in Polish Upper Silesia (the merits)* PCIJ, 13 September 1928, Series A No. 7, p. 19; *The factory at Chorzow (the merits)* PCIJ, 13 September 1928, Series A No. 17, p. 32, esp. pp. 13 and 19.
20. Even though under international law the principle of the primacy of international law over domestic constitutional law applies: according to the PCIJ, 'a state may not rely on its own constitution to derogate from the obligations imposed by international law or international treaties' (advisory Case *Treatment of polish nationals and other persons of Polish origin or speech in the Dantzig territory*, Series A/B No. 44, p. 24). On the issue of the relationship between community law and national constitutions, see bibliography provided further, para. 330.
21. See, inter alia, ECJ order, 22 June 1965, Case 9/65 *San Michele*, ECR 35.
22. ECJ, 17 December 1970, Case 11/70 *Internationale Handelsgesellschaft mbH*, ECR 533 (italics added).
23. See, on the position of the French Conseil d'Etat, C.E., Ass. 30 October 1998 *Sarran, Levacher et autres*, GAJA, No. 117, (1998) RFDA 1081, conclusions by Maugue and note by D. Alland (1999), *RFDA* 57, notes by Dubouis, Mathieu and Verpeaux, Gohin (1999), *RDP* 919 note by Flauss; *LPA* 23 July 1999 note by Aubin. See also D. Simon, 'L'arrêt Sarran, dualisme incompressible ou monisme renversé?', *Europe*, March 1999, chron. 3. On the position of the Cour de Cassation, see Cass. ass. plén., 2 June 2000, *Frausse*, and, on this decision, A. Rigaux and D.Simon, 'Droit communautaire et constitution française, une avancée significative de la Cour de Cassation', *Europe*, August–September 2000, chron. 8; B. Mathieu and M.Verpeaux, 'Traité international: le régime électoral de la Nouvelle Calédonie entre arrangements constitutionnels et exigences constitutionnelles', note under Cour Cass. *Frasse*, 2 June 2000, *Dalloz*, 2000, 865.
24. ECJ, 29 November 1978, Case 83/78 *Pigs Marketing Board c/Redmond*, ECR 533 (italics added).
25. Translation by the Spanish Constitutional Court.
26. Consulted on 11 October 2006. 'All text is available under the terms of the GNU Free Documentation Licence.'

5. The EU Charter of Fundamental Rights

Document summary

5.1 Final Report of the European Convention Working Group II 'Incorporation of the Charter/ accession to the ECHR', 22 October 2002 (selected extracts)

5.2 Declaration no. 12 concerning the explanations relating to the Charter of Fundamental Rights, annexed to the Treaty Establishing a Constitution for Europe (selected extracts)

5.3 Gráinne de Búrca, 'Fundamental Rights and Citizenship', in Bruno de Witte (ed.), *Ten Reflections on the Constitutional Treaty for Europe*, study by the Robert Schuman Centre of Advanced Studies and Academy of European Law, European University Institute, Florence, 2003, pp. 11–44 (selected extracts)

5.4 ECJ, 27 June 2006, Case C 540/03, *European Parliament* v. *Council of the European Union* (selected extracts)

Introduction

The EU Charter of Fundamental Rights has become Part II of the Constitutional Treaty, with minor amendments. This was not an easy decision, as some of the governments, who only accepted the wording of the Charter as drafted by the Convention of 2000 (that is, the forerunner of the Convention that prepared the draft Constitutional Treaty) because it would not be legally binding, persisted in their diffidence, as appears partly in the final report of the European Convention's working group on 'Incorporation of the Charter/ accession to the ECHR' (Document 5.1). With respect to the drafting of the original Charter, several options were available which would have had different consequences in terms of legal certainty and clarity (Document 5.3). However, very little of the Charter represented an innovation, as the Convention of 2000 kept to its mandate of a mere codification of existing law.

In several language versions other than those in English and French, there are differences between the text of the Charter as proclaimed in Nice in

December 2000 and the text of Part II of the Constitutional Treaty. These differences do not amount to amendments but are simply the result of a more thorough language revision which was completed by the General Secretariat of the Council during the summer of 2004 in view of the signature of the Treaty.

For instance, while the English and French versions of Article 51 of the original Charter on the right to good administration corresponded to each other in using the words 'every person' and 'toute personne', the Italian version used the expression 'ogni individuo' ('each individual'). This was probably due to the fact that, in the English text of the Charter, most articles use the expression 'everyone' in order not to restrict the rights to EU citizens, while in French the expression 'toute personne' is used because it would not be good legal French to write 'tout le monde'. In the case of the right to good administration, the use of the expression 'every person' was necessary in English in order to extend this right to legal persons rather than reserving it to human beings, a characteristic which was missing in the Italian version. Consequently, when reviewing the language versions of Part II it was decided to follow the French wording in Italian and to refer to 'ogni persona' instead of 'ogni individuo' each time the French version said 'toute personne'.

More importantly, the so-called 'horizontal clauses' (Document 5.2) have been redrafted, following the recommendations of the Convention's working group (Document 5.1), a move which has been criticized by the doctrine (Document 5.3). Even more fiercely criticized was the reference to 'the explanations relating to the Charter of Fundamental Rights', which was inserted in the Preamble of the Charter and in its Article 52 (in the Nice Charter's numbering) in order to respond to the remaining objections of some Member States against a legally binding Charter. These 'explanations' were drafted during the Convention of 2000 without attracting much attention, as they were merely intended as a guide for doctrinal interpretation. Beyond doubts about the status of these explanations, which are the main focus of the criticism that has surfaced, it is worthwhile to look at them in detail, as they give a good idea of the sources of the rights enshrined in the Charter and as their wording does not fundamentally limit the possibilities of interpretation of judges who would have to apply the Charter.[1]

The status of the Charter changed on 29 October 2004: whereas, in December 2000, the document had only been 'proclaimed' by the Presidents of the European Parliament, the Council of the European Union and the Commission, the signature of all Member States amounts to a recognition of the formulations of the Charter – in the version of the Constitutional Treaty – which might therefore be used in the Member States.

As a result of the 'proclamation' of 2000, the EU legislator has begun referring to the Charter in certain legislative instruments. This practice eventually led the ECJ to refer officially to the Charter as an authentic expression of fundamental rights in the EU in its decision of 27 June 2006, Case C-540/03, *European Parliament* v. *Council of the European Union* (Document 5.4), that is, just one week after the European Council had decided on an extension of the 'period of reflection' in the ratification process.[2] One might be tempted to see a link between these (judicial and political) decisions given that, in many prior instances, litigants had tried to invoke the Charter without being followed by the ECJ, in contrast to the Court of First Instance and to several Advocates General, who did not hesitate in citing the Charter. However, in Case C-540/03, it was the European Parliament who referred to the Charter (Document 5.4, paragraph 30), and the Council had responded by arguing that 'the Charter does not constitute a source of Community law' (Document 5.4, paragraph 34), thus giving the Court little choice but to address the issue, especially since, as noted above, the EU legislator had referred to the Charter in the recitals of the relevant directive. More relevant than the date of the Court's decision might be the fact that the action had been brought before the Court on 22 December 2003, ten days after the failed attempt to agree on the Constitutional Treaty at the European Council, as well as the fact that the parties developed their argumentation during the period which saw the conclusion of the drafting process by the IGC and the complication of the ratification process with the French and Dutch referendums. The oral hearing took place on 28 June 2005, and the Advocate General delivered her conclusions on 8 September 2005.

Now that the ECJ has shown itself to be willing to refer to the Charter, the question of the differences of wording between the original Charter and Part II of the Constitution might also become relevant to practice, even if a good deal of time elapses before the Charter formally enters into force as part of a treaty.

Document 5.1: Final Report of the European Convention Working Group II 'Incorporation of the Charter/ accession to the ECHR', 22 October 2002, Conv. 354/02, available at http://european-convention.eu.int (selected extracts)

[. . .]

Introduction

On the basis of its mandate (doc. CONV 72/02), the Group has, in the course of its seven meetings and having held hearings with several legal experts, examined two main complementary issues:

- the modalities and consequences of possible incorporation of the EU Charter of Fundamental Rights (hereinafter: 'the Charter') into the Treaties (Chapter A);

– the modalities and consequences of possible accession of the Community/ the Union to the European Convention on Human Rights (hereinafter: 'the ECHR') (Chapter B).

In addition, the Group has discussed the specific issue of access by individuals to the Court of Justice, which, as mentioned in the Group's mandate, arises independently of the questions of incorporation of the Charter and of accession to the ECHR but has a wider link to fundamental rights (Chapter C).

A. ON THE CHARTER

I. Recommendations as to the Form of Possible Incorporation of the Charter

1. GENERAL RECOMMENDATION

At the outset, the Group stresses that, in accordance with its mandate, the political decision about possible incorporation of the Charter into the Treaty Framework will be reserved for the Convention Plenary. The mandate of the Group has been to prepare for such a decision through examination of a series of specific questions relating to modalities and consequences of such incorporation.

Without prejudice to that political decision, and on the basis of the common understanding reached by the Group on all key issues related to the Charter as set out below, all members of the Group either support strongly an incorporation of the Charter in a form which would make the Charter legally binding and give it constitutional status or would not rule out giving favourable consideration to such incorporation. Different forms exist, in the Group's view, to achieve that result, as set out below; but in any event, a 'building block' as central as fundamental rights should find its place in the Union's constitutional framework. The Group is confident that, with its report, the necessary groundwork allowing the Plenary to take its political decision on incorporation has now been done; notably, this general recommendation of the Group has been facilitated by a common understanding, reached within the Group as set out below, on clarifications of certain legal and technical aspects of the Charter which are advisable in case of a legally binding Charter and of great significance for smooth incorporation ensuring legal certainty.

2. RECOMMENDATIONS AS TO THE CONCRETE FORM OF INCORPORATION

The Group is fully aware that the choice to make as to the concrete form of incorporation does not depend exclusively on considerations linked to the Charter or to fundamental rights in general, but also on the overall picture of the Treaty architecture which will emerge in future discussions of the Convention Plenary. For this reason, it would not be appropriate for this Group to restrict the Convention's further overall work by proposing only one technique for incorporation of the Charter. Rather, out of the various possibilities submitted to the Group at the outset of its work,[3] the Group recommends the Plenary to consider the following basic options:

a. insertion of the text of the Charter articles at the beginning of the Constitutional Treaty, in a Title or Chapter of that Treaty; or
b. insertion of an appropriate reference to the Charter in one article of the Constitutional Treaty; such a reference could be combined with annexing or attaching the Charter to the Constitutional Treaty, either as a specific part of the Constitutional Treaty containing only the Charter or as a separate legal text (for example, in the form of a Protocol).
c. According to one member of the Group, an 'indirect reference'[4] to the Charter could be used in order to make the Charter legally binding without giving it constitutional status.

Having considered the questions coming under the Group's mandate, a large majority of the Group would prefer the first option in the interest of a greater legibility of the Constitutional Treaty. The second option is favoured by certain other members, some of them emphasising the need to annex the Charter to the Treaty, as a specific part of that Treaty or as a Protocol. The Group as a whole underlines that both these basic options could serve to make the Charter a legally binding text of constitutional status.

II. Conclusions and Recommendations on Certain Legal and Technical Aspects of the Charter of Importance for the Smooth Incorporation of the Charter into the New Treaty Architecture

An important part of the Group's work has been to examine a number of legal and technical aspects of the Charter which, as has become clear during the Group's discussions, are important in the perspective of a smooth incorporation of the Charter, as a legally binding document, into the new Treaty architecture. The Group has found a common understanding on these questions and on ensuing recommendations which are proposed with large majority support, two of its members having reservations, as set out hereafter.

1. RESPECTING THE CONTENT OF THE CHARTER

The basic starting point underlying the Group's conclusions on the Charter is that the content of the Charter represented a consensus reached by the previous Convention, a body which had special expertise in fundamental rights and served as a model for the present Convention, and endorsed by the Nice European Council. The whole Charter, including its statements of rights and principles, its preamble and, as a crucial element, its 'general provisions', should be respected by this Convention and not be re-opened by it.

Accordingly, the Group has not considered any changes to the rights and principles contained in the Charter. The Group recognises, however, that certain technical drafting adjustments in the Charter's 'general provisions' are nonetheless possible and appropriate as explained below; the Group therefore proposes to the Plenary the drafting adjustments set out in the Annex to this report.[5] It is important to note that these adjustments proposed by the Group do not reflect modifications of substance. On the contrary, they would serve to confirm, and render absolutely clear and legally watertight, certain key elements of the overall consensus on the Charter on which the previous Convention had already agreed. They are prompted by the new perspective of a Constitutional Treaty which has arisen in the present Convention, but also by the concern of legal certainty in the field of fundamental rights, to which the Charter is designed to contribute. Thus, all drafting adjustments proposed herein fully respect the basic premise of the Group's work, that is, to leave intact the substance agreed by consensus within the previous Convention, and the Group urges the Plenary equally to respect this premise when considering the proposed drafting adjustments.

2. INCORPORATION OF THE CHARTER WILL NOT MODIFY THE ALLOCATION OF COMPETENCES BETWEEN THE UNION AND THE MEMBER STATES

The Group is able to confirm that incorporation of the Charter will in no way modify the allocation of competences between the Union and the Member States. This point, on which there was consensus already in the previous Convention, is currently reflected in Article 51 §2 of the Charter. The fact that certain Charter rights concern areas in which the Union has little or no competence to act is not in contradiction to it, given that, although the Union's competences are limited, it must respect all fundamental rights wherever it acts and therefore avoid indirect interference also with such fundamental rights on which it would not have the competence to legislate.

However, in order to render this point clear beyond any doubt, even in the perspective of a Charter forming part of a constitutional treaty, the Group recommends the drafting adjustments to Article 51 §§1 and 2 set out in the Annex. Moreover, the Group considers it useful to confirm expressly, in Article 51 §2, in light of established case law, that the protection of fundamental rights by Union law cannot have the effect of extending the scope of the Treaty provisions beyond the competences of the Union.[6]

Furthermore, the Group recalls in this context that the Charter was drafted with due regard to the principle of subsidiarity, as is clear from its Preamble, its Article 51 §1 and from those Charter Articles which make references to national laws and practices; it seems appropriate to the Group to include a clause in the general provisions of the Charter (see Article 52 §6 in the Annex) recalling these references. Likewise, it is in line with the principle of subsidiarity that the scope of application of the Charter is limited, in accordance with its Article 51 §1, to the institutions and bodies of the Union, and to Member States only when they are implementing Union law.[7]

3. FULL COMPATIBILITY BETWEEN THE FUNDAMENTAL RIGHTS OF THE EC TREATY AND THE CHARTER ARTICLES WHICH RESTATE THEM

As regards the specific case of those fundamental rights which are already expressly enshrined in the EC Treaty and merely 'restated' in the Charter (notably rights derived from Union citizenship),[8] there was already consensus in the previous Convention on the principle that the legal situation as defined by the EC Treaty should remain unaffected by the Charter; this is presently expressed in the 'referral clause' of Article 52 §2 of the Charter.[9]

Reconfirming that point, the Group has reached consensus on the need to have, as concerns these rights, a legally 'watertight' referral clause, such as presently included in Article 52 §2 of the Charter, ensuring complete compatibility between the statements of the rights in the Charter and their more detailed regulation as currently found in the EC Treaty. The Group stresses that this clause of Article 52 §2 will, if the Charter is to become a part of the constitutional treaty, logically need a slight drafting adjustment, so as to make it clear that the referral is made to other parts of Treaty law where the conditions and limits of the exercise of these rights are defined. The precise formulation of such a drafting adjustment, reflecting that principle of compatibility, cannot be undertaken at this stage as it will depend on the exact overall Treaty architecture.

Furthermore, the Group is of the view that, as regards these rights, 'replication' ('*dédoublements*') between the Charter and other parts of Treaty law might, to a limited extent, be inevitable for legal reasons and will not be harmful, given that, as is proposed, a referral clause will ensure compatibility.

The Group signals that if, as advocated by a large majority of the Group, incorporation is achieved by the insertion of the Charter text in the first part of the Constitutional Treaty, it would then become necessary to combine, in an appropriate manner, in that Treaty the Charter articles on citizens' rights and the provisions on citizenship of the EC Treaty having constitutional importance; this should be considered as a technical operation raising no political problems.

4. CORRESPONDENCE BETWEEN CHARTER RIGHTS AND RIGHTS GUARANTEED BY THE ECHR

The Group underlines and reconfirms the central importance of Article 52 §3 of the Charter, on those Charter rights which correspond to rights guaranteed by the ECHR; it recalls that this clause was a crucial element of the overall consensus in the previous Convention.[10] On the basis of the 'Explanations' on the Charter,[11] the Group confirms its common understanding on the meaning of this provision: the rights in the Charter which correspond to ECHR rights have the same scope and meaning as laid down in the ECHR; this includes notably the detailed provisions in the ECHR which permit limitations of these rights. The second sentence of Article 52 §3 of the Charter serves to clarify that this article does not prevent more extensive protection already achieved or which may subsequently be provided for (i) in Union legislation and (ii) in some articles of the Charter which, although based on the ECHR, go beyond the ECHR because Union law *acquis* had already reached a higher level of protection (for example, Article 47 on effective judicial protection, or Article 50 on the right not to be punished twice for the same offence). Thus, the guaranteed rights in the Charter reflect higher levels of protection in existing Union law.

5. AN INTERPRETATION IN HARMONY WITH COMMON CONSTITUTIONAL TRADITIONS
The Group stresses that the Charter has firm roots in the Member States' common constitutional traditions, which were brought together impressively in the previous Convention's work. The extensive case law on fundamental rights derived from the common constitutional traditions established by the Court of Justice, and confirmed by Article 6 §2 TEU, represents an important source for a number of rights recognised by the Charter. In order to emphasise the importance of these roots and in the interest of smooth incorporation of the Charter as a legally binding document, the large majority of the Group proposes to include a rule of interpretation in the general provisions (see Article 52 §4 in the Annex); two of its members have reservations against this proposal. The rule is based on the wording of the current Article 6 §2 TEU and takes due account of the approach to common constitutional traditions followed by the Court of Justice as explained by Judge Skouris at the hearing of 17 September. Under that rule, rather than following a rigid approach of 'a lowest common denominator', the Charter rights concerned should be interpreted in a way offering a high standard of protection which is adequate for the law of the Union and in harmony with the common constitutional traditions.

6. THE DISTINCTION BETWEEN 'RIGHTS' AND 'PRINCIPLES' IN THE CHARTER
The Group stresses the importance of the distinction between 'rights' and 'principles', which was an important element – already expressed in the Preamble and in Article 51 §1 of the Charter – of the consensus reached by the previous Convention. In order to confirm that distinction while increasing legal certainty in the perspective of a legally binding Charter with constitutional status, the large majority of the Group proposes an additional general provision (see Article 51 §5 in the Annex) encapsulating the understanding of the concept of 'principles' which marked the work of the previous Convention and has been recalled in the discussions of the Working Group by members of that Convention; two of

its members have reservations against this proposal. According to that understanding, principles are different from subjective rights. They shall be 'observed' (Article 51 §1) and may call for implementation through legislative or executive acts; accordingly, they become significant for the Courts when such acts are interpreted or reviewed. This is consistent both with case law of the Court of Justice[12] and with the approach of the Member States' constitutional systems to 'principles', particularly in the field of social law.

In addition, with the proposed clause the Group reconfirms the line followed by the previous Convention to express the character ('right' or 'principle') of individual Charter articles as clearly as possible in the wording of the respective articles, taking into account the important guidance provided by the 'Praesidium's Explanations', supplemented by explanations from the current Working Group (see section III.3. below), permitting future jurisprudence to rule on the exact attribution of articles to the two categories.

III. Recommendations Concerning Further Questions Arising in the Context of Possible Incorporation

1. PREAMBLE OF THE CHARTER

The Group considers the Charter Preamble as a crucial element of the overall consensus on the Charter reached by the previous Convention. The Group therefore recommends that this element should in any event be preserved in the future Constitutional Treaty framework. The Group also recalls that the Charter Preamble comprises language on the fundamental nature of the Union going well beyond the area of fundamental rights. As is the case with the Charter as a whole, the concrete form of an 'incorporation of the Charter Preamble' into the Treaty framework, as recommended by the Group, will equally depend on the overall Treaty structure to be defined by the Plenary. Thus, if the Charter articles were to be inserted directly in the Constitutional Treaty, the Charter Preamble should be used as the Preamble to the Constitutional Treaty. If in turn the Charter is incorporated as a specific part of the Constitutional Treaty or as a separate binding legal text (for example, in the form of a Protocol) within the Union's constitutional architecture, the Charter Preamble could remain attached to the text of the Charter without any changes; that would of course not preclude the Convention from using, for the drafting of the new Treaty preamble, the elements of general importance to be found in the Charter preamble.

2. CONTINUED REFERENCE TO EXTERNAL SOURCES (SUCH AS CURRENTLY FOUND IN ARTICLE 6 §2 TEU)

The Group discussed whether or not, in case of incorporation of the Charter, the Constitutional Treaty should also contain a reference to the two external sources of inspiration for fundamental rights, as is currently found in Article 6 §2 TEU, that is, the ECHR and the constitutional traditions common to the Member States. Valid arguments have been advanced both for and against this.

Some members have taken the view that maintaining such a reference would be redundant and create legal confusion, given that the Charter already includes rights derived from the ECHR and the common constitutional traditions and makes references to these sources. Others have argued that such a reference in the Constitutional Treaty could serve to complete the protection offered by the Charter and clarify that Union law is open for future evolutions in ECHR and Member States' human rights law.

In any event, the Group recognises that this question is closely related to the choice of the form of incorporation which the Convention will have to make. The Group therefore refrains from making a firm recommendation on this issue; instead, it limits itself to stating that such a reference, if appropriately drafted,[13] is not excluded by the prospect of a legally binding Charter, and signals the issue to the Plenary for consideration.

3. THE IMPORTANCE OF THE 'EXPLANATIONS'

The Group stresses the importance of the 'Explanations', drawn up at the instigation of the Praesidium of the previous Convention,[14] as one important tool of interpretation ensuring a correct understanding of the Charter.[15] It recognises that these Explanations are presently not sufficiently accessible for legal practitioners. To the extent that the Convention takes on board the drafting adjustments proposed by this Group, the corresponding explanations given in this report should be fully integrated with the original Explanations. Upon possible incorporation of the Charter, attention should then be drawn in an appropriate manner to the Explanations which, though they state that they have no legal value, are intended to clarify the provisions of the Charter. In particular, it would be important to publicise them more widely.

4. PROCEDURE FOR FUTURE AMENDMENT OF THE CHARTER

As a consequence of possible incorporation of the Charter into the Constitutional Treaty framework, the question will arise according to which procedure the Charter can be amended in the future. However, the Group has considered that this question goes beyond its mandate since it will have to be examined by the Plenary as part of the general question of amendment procedure(s) for the various building blocks of the future Treaty framework.

B. ON ACCESSION TO THE EUROPEAN CONVENTION ON HUMAN RIGHTS

[. . .]

C. ACCESS TO THE COURT OF JUSTICE

The Group discussed the Union's current system of remedies available to individuals, notably in the light of the fundamental right to effective judicial protection.

In this context, the Group has examined the idea of establishing a special procedure before the Court of Justice for the protection of fundamental rights. As a majority of members had reservations about this idea, the Group does not recommend it to the Convention. The Group underlines, however, the great benefit which citizens would gain from a possible incorporation of the Charter into the Constitutional Treaty architecture, thereby making the Union's present system of remedies available.

The Group wishes, however, to draw the Plenary's attention to a different issue, namely the question whether or not the conditions of direct access by individuals to the Court (Article 230 §4 TEC) need to be reformed in the interest of ensuring effective judicial protection. On this point, the Group's discussion has shown that a certain lacuna of protection might exist, given the current condition of 'direct and individual concern' in Article 230 §4 TEC and the case law interpreting it, in the specific case of 'self-executing' Community regulations which impose directly applicable prohibitions on individuals. On the other hand, a widely shared trend emerged in the group's discussion according to which the present overall system of remedies, and the 'division of work' between Community and national courts it entails, should not be profoundly altered by a possible reform of Article 230 §4 TEC. Some members have referred to the possibility of a provision in the Treaty on the obligation of Member States, as spelt out in recent case law,[16] to provide for effective remedies for rights derived from Union law.

In any event, while the issue of Article 230 §4 TEC certainly has a nexus with fundamental rights, it transcends the protection of those rights (as judicial protection must exist for all subjective rights), and it arises quite independently of the concrete questions of the incorporation of the Charter and accession to the ECHR. The Group considers that this issue and its institutional implications must be examined together with other topics such as the limits of Court jurisdiction in Justice and Home affairs[17] or judicial control of subsidiarity. The Group therefore refrains from making concrete recommendations and commends the question of possible reform in Article 230 §4 TEC, together with the valuable contributions submitted thereon,[18] for further examination by the Convention in an appropriate context.

Document 5.2: Declaration no. 12 concerning the explanations relating to the Charter of Fundamental Rights, annexed to the Treaty Establishing a Constitution for Europe (selected extracts)

The Conference takes note of the explanations relating to the Charter of Fundamental Rights prepared under the authority of the Praesidium of the Convention which drafted the Charter and updated under the responsibility of the Praesidium of the European Convention, as set out below.

Explanations Relating to the Charter of Fundamental Rights

These explanations were originally prepared under the authority of the Praesidium of the Convention which drafted the Charter of Fundamental Rights of the European Union. They have been updated under the responsibility of the Praesidium of the European Convention, in the light of the drafting adjustments made to the text of the Charter by that Convention (notably to Articles 51 and 52 (36) and of further developments of Union law. Although they do not as such have the status of law, they are a valuable tool of interpretation intended to clarify the provisions of the Charter.

[. . .]

Title VII General Provisions Governing the Interpretation and Application of the Charter

ARTICLE 51 FIELD OF APPLICATION

1. The provisions of this Charter are addressed to the institutions, bodies, offices and agencies of the Union with due regard for the principle of subsidiarity and to the Member States only when they are implementing Union law. They shall therefore respect the rights, observe the principles and promote the application thereof in accordance with their respective powers and respecting the limits of the powers of the Union as conferred on it in the other Parts of the Constitution.

2. This Charter does not extend the field of application of Union law beyond the powers of the Union or establish any new power or task for the Union, or modify powers and tasks defined in the other Parts of the Constitution.

EXPLANATION

The aim of Article 51 (115) is to determine the scope of the Charter. It seeks to establish clearly that the Charter applies primarily to the institutions and bodies of the Union, in compliance with the principle of subsidiarity. This provision was drafted in keeping with Article 6(2) of the Treaty on European Union, which required the Union to respect fundamental rights, and with the mandate issued by Cologne European Council. The term 'institutions' is enshrined in Part I of the Constitution. The expression 'bodies, offices and agencies' is commonly used in the Constitution to refer to all the authorities set up by the Constitution or by secondary legislation (see, for example, Articles I-50 or I-51 of the Constitution).

As regards the Member States, it follows unambiguously from the case law of the Court of Justice that the requirement to respect fundamental rights defined in a Union context is only binding on the Member States when they act in the scope of Union law (judgment of 13 July 1989, Case 5/88 *Wachauf* [1989] ECR 2609; judgment of 18 June 1991, ERT [1991] ECR I-2925); judgment of 18 December 1997

(C-309/96 *Annibaldi* [1997] ECR I-7493). The Court of Justice confirmed this case law in the following terms: 'In addition, it should be remembered that the requirements flowing from the protection of fundamental rights in the Community legal order are also binding on Member States when they implement Community rules . . .' (judgment of 13 April 2000, Case C-292/97, [2000] ECR 2737, paragraph 37 of the grounds). Of course this rule, as enshrined in this Charter, applies to the central authorities as well as to regional or local bodies, and to public organisations, when they are implementing Union law.

Paragraph 2, together with the second sentence of paragraph 1, confirms that the Charter may not have the effect of extending the competences and tasks which the other Parts of the Constitution confer on the Union. Explicit mention is made here of the logical consequences of the principle of subsidiarity and of the fact that the Union only has those powers which have been conferred upon it. The fundamental rights as guaranteed in the Union do not have any effect other than in the context of the powers determined by Parts I and III of the Constitution. Consequently, an obligation, pursuant to the second sentence of paragraph 1, for the Union's institutions to promote principles laid down in the Charter, may arise only within the limits of these same powers.

Paragraph 2 also confirms that the Charter may not have the effect of extending the field of application of Union law beyond the powers of the Union as established in the other Parts of the Constitution. The Court of Justice has already established this rule with respect to the fundamental rights recognised as part of Union law (judgment of 17 February 1998, C-249/96 *Grant*, 1998 ECR I-621, paragraph 45 of the grounds). In accordance with this rule, it goes without saying that the incorporation of the Charter into the Constitution cannot be understood as extending by itself the range of Member State action considered to be 'implementation of Union law' (within the meaning of paragraph 1 and the above-mentioned case law).

ARTICLE 52 SCOPE AND INTERPRETATION OF RIGHTS AND PRINCIPLES

1. Any limitation on the exercise of the rights and freedoms recognised by this Charter must be provided for by law and respect the essence of those rights and freedoms. Subject to the principle of proportionality, limitations may be made only if they are necessary and genuinely meet objectives of general interest recognised by the Union or the need to protect the rights and freedoms of others.

2. Rights recognised by this Charter for which provision is made in other Parts of the Constitution shall be exercised under the conditions and within the limits defined by these relevant Parts.

3. Insofar as this Charter contains rights which correspond to rights guaranteed by the Convention for the Protection of Human Rights and Fundamental Freedoms, the meaning and scope of those rights shall be the same as those laid down by the said Convention. This provision shall not prevent Union law providing more extensive protection.

4. Insofar as this Charter recognises fundamental rights as they result from the constitutional traditions common to the Member States, those rights shall be interpreted in harmony with those traditions.

5. The provisions of this Charter which contain principles may be implemented by legislative and executive acts taken by institutions, bodies, offices and agencies of the Union, and by acts of Member States when they are implementing Union law, in the exercise of their respective powers. They shall be judicially cognisable only in the interpretation of such acts and in the ruling on their legality.

6. Full account shall be taken of national laws and practices as specified in this Charter.

7. The explanations drawn up as a way of providing guidance in the interpretation of the Charter of Fundamental Rights shall be given due regard by the courts of the Union and of the Member States.

EXPLANATION

The purpose of Article 52 (117) is to set the scope of the rights and principles of the Charter, and to lay down rules for their interpretation. Paragraph 1 deals with the arrangements for the limitation of rights. The wording is based on the case law of the Court of Justice: 'it is well established in the case law of the Court that restrictions may be imposed on the exercise of fundamental rights, in particular in the context of a common organisation of the market, provided that those restrictions in fact correspond to objectives of general interest pursued by the Community and do not constitute, with regard to the aim pursued, disproportionate and unreasonable interference undermining the very substance of those rights' (judgment of 13 April 2000, Case C-292/97, paragraph 45 of the grounds). The reference to general interests recognised by the Union covers both the objectives mentioned in Article I-2 of the Constitution and other interests protected by specific provisions of the Constitution such as Articles I-5(1), III-133(3), III-154 and III-436.

Paragraph 2 refers to rights which were already expressly guaranteed in the Treaty establishing the European Community and have been recognised in the Charter, and which are now found in other Parts of the Constitution (notably the rights derived from Union citizenship). It clarifies that such rights remain subject to the conditions and limits applicable to the Union law on which they are based, and for which provision is now made in Parts I and III of the Constitution. The Charter does not alter the system of rights conferred by the EC Treaty and now taken over by Parts I and III of the Constitution.

Paragraph 3 is intended to ensure the necessary consistency between the Charter and the ECHR by establishing the rule that, insofar as the rights in the present Charter also correspond to rights guaranteed by the ECHR, the meaning and scope of those rights, including authorised limitations, are the same as those laid down by the ECHR. This means in particular that the legislator, in laying down limitations to those rights, must comply with the same standards as are fixed by the detailed limitation arrangements laid down in the ECHR, which are thus made applicable for the rights covered by this paragraph, without thereby adversely affecting the autonomy of Union law and of that of the Court of Justice of the European Union.

The reference to the ECHR covers both the Convention and the Protocols to it. The meaning and the scope of the guaranteed rights are determined not only by the text of those instruments, but also by the case law of the European Court of Human Rights and by the Court of Justice of the European Union. The last sentence of the paragraph is designed to allow the Union to guarantee more extensive protection. In any event, the level of protection afforded by the Charter may never be lower than that guaranteed by the ECHR.

The Charter does not affect the possibilities of Member States to avail themselves of Article 15 ECHR, allowing derogations from ECHR rights in the event of war or of other public dangers threatening the life of the nation, when they take action in the areas of national defence in the event of war and of the maintenance of law and order, in accordance with their responsibilities recognised in Articles I-5 (1), III-131, III-262 of the Constitution.

The list of rights which may at the present stage, without precluding developments in the law, legislation and the Treaties, be regarded as corresponding to rights in the ECHR within the meaning of the present paragraph is given hereafter. It does not include rights additional to those in the ECHR.

1. Articles of the Charter where both the meaning and the scope are the same as the corresponding Articles of the ECHR:

- Article 2 corresponds to Article 2 of the ECHR,
- Article 4 corresponds to Article 3 of the ECHR,
- Article 5(1) and (2) correspond to Article 4 of the ECHR,
- Article 6 corresponds to Article 5 of the ECHR,
- Article 7 corresponds to Article 8 of the ECHR,
- Article 10(1) corresponds to Article 9 of the ECHR,
- Article 11 corresponds to Article 10 of the ECHR without prejudice to any restrictions which Union law may impose on Member States' right to introduce the licensing arrangements referred to in the third sentence of Article 10(1) of the ECHR,
- Article 17 corresponds to Article 1 of the Protocol to the ECHR,
- Article 19(1) corresponds to Article 4 of Protocol No 4,
- Article 19(2) corresponds to Article 3 of the ECHR as interpreted by the European Court of Human Rights,
- Article 48 corresponds to Article 6(2) and(3) of the ECHR,
- Article 49(1) (with the exception of the last sentence) and (2) correspond to Article 7 of the ECHR.

2. Articles where the meaning is the same as the corresponding Articles of the ECHR, but where the scope is wider:

- Article 9 covers the same field as Article 12 of the ECHR, but its scope may be extended to other forms of marriage if these are established by national legislation,
- Article 12(1) corresponds to Article 11 of the ECHR, but its scope is extended to European Union level,
- Article 14(1) corresponds to Article 2 of the Protocol to the ECHR, but its scope is extended to cover access to vocational and continuing training,
- Article 14(3) corresponds to Article 2 of the Protocol to the ECHR as regards the rights of parents,
- Article 47(2) and (3) correspond to Article 6(1) of the ECHR, but the limitation to the determination of civil rights and obligations or criminal charges does not apply as regards Union law and its implementation,
- Article 50 corresponds to Article 4 of Protocol No 7 to the ECHR, but its scope is extended to European Union level between the Courts of the Member States,
- Finally, citizens of the European Union may not be considered as aliens in the scope of the application of Union law, because of the prohibition of any discrimination on grounds of nationality. The limitations provided for by Article 16 of the ECHR as regards the rights of aliens therefore do not apply to them in this context.

The rule of interpretation contained in paragraph 4 has been based on the wording of Article 6(2) of the Treaty on European Union (cf. now the wording of Article

I-9(3) of the Constitution) and takes due account of the approach to common constitutional traditions followed by the Court of Justice (for example, judgment of 13 December 1979, Case 44/79 *Hauer* [1979] ECR 3727; judgment of 18 May 1982, Case 155/79, *AM&S* [1982] ECR 1575). Under that rule, rather than following a rigid approach of 'a lowest common denominator', the Charter rights concerned should be interpreted in a way offering a high standard of protection which is adequate for the law of the Union and in harmony with the common constitutional traditions.

Paragraph 5 clarifies the distinction between 'rights' and 'principles' set out in the Charter. According to that distinction, subjective rights shall be respected, whereas principles shall be observed (Article 51 (1)). Principles may be implemented through legislative or executive acts (adopted by the Union in accordance with its powers, and by the Member States only when they implement Union law); accordingly, they become significant for the Courts only when such acts are interpreted or reviewed. They do not however give rise to direct claims for positive action by the Union's institutions or Member States authorities. This is consistent both with case law of the Court of Justice (Cf. notably case law on the 'precautionary principle' in Article 174 (2) TEC (replaced by Article III-233 of the Constitution): judgment of the CFI of 11 September 2002, T-13/99, *Pfizer* v. *Council*, with numerous references to earlier case law; and a series of judgments on Article 33 (ex 39) on the principles of agricultural law, for example judgment of the Court of Justice C-265/85, *Van den Berg*, 1987 ECR 1155: scrutiny of the principle of market stabilisation and of reasonable expectations) and with the approach of the Member States' constitutional systems to 'principles' particularly in the field of social law. For illustration, examples for principles recognised in the Charter include for example Articles 25, 26 and 37. In some cases, an Article of the Charter may contain both elements of a right and of a principle, for example Articles 23, 33 and 34.

Paragraph 6 refers to the various Articles in the Charter which, in the spirit of subsidiarity, make reference to national laws and practices.

ARTICLE 53 LEVEL OF PROTECTION

Nothing in this Charter shall be interpreted as restricting or adversely affecting human rights and fundamental freedoms as recognised, in their respective fields of application, by Union law and international law and by international agreements to which the Union or all the Member States are party, including the European Convention for the Protection of Human Rights and Fundamental Freedoms, and by the Member States' constitutions.

EXPLANATION

This provision is intended to maintain the level of protection currently afforded within their respective scope by Union law, national law and international law. Owing to its importance, mention is made of the ECHR.

ARTICLE 54 PROHIBITION OF ABUSE OF RIGHTS

Nothing in this Charter shall be interpreted as implying any right to engage in any activity or to perform any act aimed at the destruction of any of the rights and freedoms recognised in this Charter or at their limitation to a greater extent than is provided for herein.

EXPLANATION

This Article corresponds to Article 17 of the ECHR: 'Nothing in this Convention may be interpreted as implying for any State, group or person any right to engage in any activity or perform any act aimed at the destruction of any of the rights and freedoms set forth herein or at their limitation to a greater extent than is provided for in the Convention.'

Document 5.3: Reprinted with the permission of the European University Institute, Robert Schuman Centre of Advanced Studies, from Gráinne de Búrca, 'Fundamental Rights and Citizenship', in Bruno de Witte's *Ten Reflections on the Constitutional Treaty for Europe*, study by the Robert Schuman Centre of Advanced Studies and Academy of European Law, European University Institute, Florence, 2003, pp. 11–44 (selected extracts)

[. . .]

3. The Charter of Fundamental Rights

A. MAINTAINING THE FUNDAMENTAL RIGHTS ACQUIS

A first question to be addressed is whether the Charter will replace all other references to fundamental rights currently contained in the Treaties such as in Article 6 TEU, and whether it will 'crystallize' the fundamental rights jurisprudence of the Court of Justice for the future. While the Charter was drafted on the basis that it would be essentially declaratory of the existing legal situation, and that it would not reduce or restrict the fundamental rights acquis built up over the years, it must nevertheless be recognized that the relatively open-ended and non-exhaustive approach adopted by the ECJ could possibly be restricted by the constitutional enactment of the Charter, if the latter is henceforth to be taken as the definitive and closed list of EU rights and values.

On the one hand, the Preamble to the Charter declares that the Charter 'reaffirms . . . the rights as they result, in particular, from the constitutional traditions and international obligations common to the Member States', including specifically the ECHR and the two Social Charters (of the Council of Europe and the EC, respectively). However, this seems merely to suggest that the rights actually specified in the Charter are derived from national constitutions and from these common international obligations, rather than that the EU continues to hold itself bound or at least inspired by international human rights obligations and standards more broadly. Further, while Article 53 of the Charter makes mention of human rights derived from international law and international agreements to which the Member States are party, as well as national constitutions, this is done merely to affirm that the Charter should not be used in such a way as to restrict those rights within their proper sphere of application. What is missing, however, is any equivalent in the Charter or its preamble to the ECJ's often-repeated statement that 'fundamental rights form an integral part of the general principles of law . . . for that purpose, the Court draws inspiration from the constitutional traditions common to the Member States and from the guidelines supplied by international treaties for the protection of human rights on which the Member States have collaborated or to which they are signatories'. This assertion of a category of general principles of EU law inspired by international human rights treaties is more fluid and is non-exhaustive (take the example often cited of the rights of minorities, which are protected under the European Framework Convention on the Rights of Minorities and under the ICCPR, but not mentioned in the Charter, although the former are international agreements on which Member States have 'collaborated' in accordance with ECJ case law), by comparison with the enumerated rights approach of the Charter, even if the latter are themselves derived from international law and from ECJ case law.

It is possible, of course, that the ECJ will continue to adopt an open approach to human rights protection, and to make references to the general principles of law and to internationally protected rights which are not specifically mentioned in the Charter, even though the Charter will exist as a first and primary reference point. It was indeed an article of faith during the drafting of the Charter that it was not to change the existing state of the law, but rather was designed to showcase the fundamental rights acquis of the EU. Nonetheless, if the Charter as it stands is incorporated as one of the first articles in a new constitutional document, then there is a danger that it may become the authoritative reference point for EU fundamental rights, to the detriment of international human rights norms which are not specifically included.

For this reason, in order to make sure that the normatively open acquis is not 'closed' by the incorporation of the Charter in a basic constitutional treaty, it would be advisable to include in the new treaty (for example in Article 2 of the preliminary draft constitutional treaty) a clause affirming that openness, for example by mentioning the general principles of EU law which are inspired by international law.

B. FULL INCORPORATION OF THE TEXT OF THE CHARTER OR INCORPORATION BY REFERENCE?

The majority of the Working Group favoured the full incorporation of the text of the Charter articles into the constitutional treaty, rather than incorporating it by reference by one of the other suggested methods. However, the debate in the Convention plenary indicated a range of views and, in the preliminary draft constitutional text, the three main options are set out for consideration: (a) a reference to the Charter, (b) a statement of the fact that the Charter is an integral part of the Constitution with the articles of the Charter being set out elsewhere in the treaty or in an annexed protocol, (c) full incorporation of all articles of the Charter.

It seems likely that the Working Group favoured the 'full incorporation' option (c) primarily for symbolic purposes, in the sense of indicating the central place of these values and principles in the new constitutional text, rather as the Bill of Rights tends to be a central chapter in modern state constitutions. And while this option poses various difficulties due to the way in which the Charter was drafted as a separate and self-standing instrument, yet with complex overlaps and interactions with the existing EC Treaty, it seems nonetheless to be the best way forward for a number of reasons.

OPTION (a) INCORPORATION BY SIMPLE REFERENCE

Option (a), to include a reference to the Charter, would presumably be along the lines of the current Article 6 of the EU Treaty, indicating that the Union commits itself to respect fundamental rights as they result from the EU Charter of Fundamental Rights, along with the ECHR and national constitutional traditions. Such a reference would place the Charter outside the constitutional treaty, as a source of inspiration for the fundamental rights recognised by the EU, rather than as an integral part of the new constitutional text, and would identify the Charter as one of the sources of rights alongside others. This would maintain the value of openness of the current position, but it seems to be the option less favoured both within the Working Group and also within the Convention's plenary debate. Certainly it would not give the prominence or centrality to the EU's commitment to human rights which the actual incorporation of the Charter into a new constitutional treaty would do. Had the question of the Charter's incorporation into the Treaties arisen at a time when there was no serious discussion of an EU constitution, then the option of incorporation by an additional reference in Article 6 of the EU Treaty would possibly have been the best solution. However, the fact that the current process and the 2004 IGC is likely to produce a basic constitutional text for the EU introduces a fundamental symbolic and substantive change, which would make the omission of the Charter from the new constitution a much more significant exclusion.

For this reason, option (a) of incorporation by reference would not be the best solution in the current context.

OPTION (b) INCORPORATION BY REFERENCE AND BY INCLUSION OF THE CHARTER IN A PROTOCOL TO THE CONSTITUTIONAL TREATY

Option (b) provides an intermediate solution. On the one hand it would achieve the full incorporation of the Charter into the new constitutional text with equal legal status alongside all other provisions of the latter, rather than leaving it as an external source of inspiration only (as under option (a)). And on the other hand it would achieve this without the awkwardness of inserting a relatively lengthy and self-standing text such as the Charter, with its own preamble, into the first articles of a new constitutional treaty.

However, this solution has two disadvantages. The first and most important is that it would lack the symbolic commitment of placing the Charter centrally within a new constitutional text, and would seem to relegate it to the less pivotal status of a protocol or annex. Given the importance of the message conveyed by placing the Charter's commitment to human dignity, equality and solidarity at the heart of a new documentary constitution, this would be a very significant loss. Further, while one apparent advantage of the incorporation-by-reference option is that it would seem to avoid some of the problems of duplication and overlap between the provisions of the Charter and those of the existing EC Treaty, that advantage would in fact be one of appearance only. This is because, given the equal legal status of the Charter and the Treaties under option (b), the practical problem of actual legal overlap and duplication would remain, even if the location of the Charter as a separate integral document in an annex or protocol would superficially reduce the degree of textual and visual awkwardness.

For this reason, option (b) of incorporation by reference, combined with inclusion of the Charter in a protocol or annex to the Treaty, should not be the preferred solution.

OPTION (c) FULL INCORPORATION OF ALL OF THE CHARTER PROVISIONS

Option (c), which would incorporate the full text of the Charter into a constitutional treaty was the choice favoured by most of the Convention Working Group members, and has also been proposed in the 'Feasibility Study' draft Constitution recently prepared by the Lamoureux working group for the Commission (published 4 December 2002, and referred to, rather strangely, as Penelope).[19] The essential value and importance of this approach would be the visibility and symbolism of setting out, at an early point in the new constitutional text, what is effectively a constitutional bill of rights. While this approach presents certain practical and legal problems which will be discussed below, it is nonetheless, in my view, the option to be preferred. In particular, the solution proposed in the Penelope draft of having a separate Part II in the basic constitutional treaty containing the full Charter would be preferable to placing it in the middle of something like Part I of the Praesidium's October 2002 draft. The detailed policies and legal bases would then be contained in a separate Part III of the constitutional treaty.

A first problem, however – one which has animated most of the political discussion of a constitutional treaty or a constitution for the EU – is arguably that of simplicity and readability. From this perspective, one might doubt the wisdom of incorporating a document of 54 articles into a basic constitutional treaty, which, according to the Praesidium's preliminary draft, would contain no more than 46 articles. However, the prospect of simplifying by reducing the number of articles in the Charter and changing its text in any substantive way (other than by the purely cosmetic change of 'grouping' several current Charter articles together under a smaller number of umbrella articles of the new constitutional treaty, as was mooted during the Convention debate on the Working Group's final draft) would be ill-advised, given the almost unchallenged assumption so far that the substance of the Charter should remain unchanged, in deference to the procedure by which it was drafted and proclaimed in 2000.

Perhaps a more substantial problem in relation to the feasibility of option (c), however, is that the Charter was drafted as a complete and integral instrument with its own preamble, its own internal coherence and with a set of final horizontal clauses, rather than being designed as one part of a larger text. Further, as a consequence of its having been drafted as a separate and complete instrument by the first Convention, the Charter contains many provisions which either duplicate, partially overlap with, repeat in slightly different form, or are somewhat in tension with provisions of the existing EC Treaty. If all of the Charter's provisions are to be incorporated into the new constitutional treaty in their current form it is inevitable that consequential changes to the substance of the existing EC Treaty will need to be made, and it seems likely that some duplication will in any event persist.

On the basis of the Praesidium's preliminary draft, it seems that the fundamental provisions establishing the single market and all of the legislative bases for action would be contained in a separate part of the constitutional text, which obviously raises the question of the relationship between legal bases such as the current Articles 12, 13 and 141 of the EC Treaty and the 'corresponding' rights contained in provisions of the Charter such as Articles 21 and 23. It seems unlikely, despite the opinion of the Working Group to that effect, that the 'referral clause' in Article 52(2) of the Charter is sufficient to deal with the replications and overlaps which are likely to result from its incorporation into the constitutional Treaty containing much of what currently exists in the EC Treaty. It would seem, on the contrary, that a significant 'cleaning-up' job would need to be done on the remaining provisions of the EC Treaty which intersect or overlap with the provisions of the Charter and which are likely to be included in the new constitutional document.

As an initial step in the direction of this task, [annexed at the end of this chapter is a table illustrating the various articles of the Charter which correspond in different ways with – whether by overlapping with, repeating, or even potentially contradicting – provisions contained in the current EC Treaty].[20] In some of these instances, it is evident that versions of these EC Treaty provisions would have to be included in the remaining Part of the preliminary draft constitutional treaty. The comments [in the third column of the table] attempt to indicate those cases where it is possible to envisage the EC Treaty provisions being adapted so as to relate more directly to the corresponding provision in the Charter, for example to provide the legal basis and mechanism for implementing or fleshing out the right expressed in the Charter.

In other words, for provisions such as Articles 21 and 23 (discrimination and gender equality), or 27, 28, 30 and 31 (workers' rights), which would have corresponding legal bases in the relevant Part of the constitutional treaty, the latter provisions could make direct reference to the Articles of the Charter. These could be expressed in a form such as: 'the Council, acting under the [co-decision procedure] shall adopt legislation to combat discrimination in accordance with Article [21, 23 . . .] of the Charter of Rights'. A similar and careful coordination of the competence provisions of the constitutional treaty in the field of social policy with the declaration of workers' rights and other social rights contained in the Charter would need to be undertaken. In other instances, for example the exhortatory provisions concerning cultural diversity, consumer protection and health protection, these could be mentioned in the remaining part of the constitutional treaty by means of an express reference to the relevant Charter provision. In the case of the citizenship provisions, as argued above, it would be advisable for the current draft of Article 5 of the preliminary draft constitutional text only to introduce and assert the basic concept of EU citizenship, rather than listing all of the specific rights pertaining to it. Instead, what is now draft Article 5 should refer to the Charter for a listing of the specific rights and incidents of EU citizenship. Finally, a corresponding legal basis providing power to adopt legislation to implement the citizenship rights contained in the Charter would be needed in the remaining part of the constitutional treaty. Indeed, the Penelope draft included an additional article 57 in the text of the Charter itself conferring competence to adopt measures to implement and facilitate the citizenship rights contained therein. This, however, is not recommended, since there are no other competence provisions in the Charter itself, and corresponding competence provisions for many other Charter rights will in any case need to be contained in the remaining part of the constitutional treaty.

Therefore it is recommended that the Charter (complete with preamble) be incorporated, along the lines indicated in the Penelope draft, in Part II of a three-part Constitutional Treaty, before Part III which would contain the detailed policies and legal bases. It could, if considered necessary, be specified that Part III of the constitutional Treaty should be read in conformity with the more fundamental Parts I and II.

C. PROPOSED WORKING GROUP AMENDMENTS TO THE HORIZONTAL CLAUSES OF THE CHARTER

[. . .]

A number of commentators had earlier pointed out the tension between the obligation in Article 51(1) on the institutions of the EU to 'promote' the application of the rights contained in the Charter and the assertion in Article 51(2) that the Charter does not modify powers or tasks defined by the Treaty. As a consequence of this, the Working Group has proposed something of a 'belt and braces' approach, supplementing both paragraphs (1) and (2) with limiting clauses designed to further underscore the intention not to increase, change or extend any of the existing powers under the EC or EU treaties. Arguably, these additional clauses are superfluous, somewhat ugly to read, and they do not remove the tension in question. It seems simply inevitable (and from the point of view of at least some, desirable) that the existence and incorporation of the Charter will influence the nature and interpretation of EU tasks and powers, although in subtler ways than the bald notion of 'establishing new power' suggests. The explicit articulation for the first time in the basic EU constitutional treaty of an array of fundamental rights seems unlikely not to 'modify' the way other aspects of the EU's powers and tasks are construed, at least by the Court of Justice if not by other actors. The fiction that the Charter of Rights, whether fully legally incorporated or not, 'makes no difference' to anything in the EU legal and political order is not an easy one to maintain, and although no doubt there were strong interests to be appeased within the Working Group which led to the belt and braces approach as a way of maintaining this fiction, the amended Article 51 presents a curious picture. It is of course a feature typical of the way in which the EU operates – in particular at high constitutional moments such as these – that bold and powerful new developments such as the constitutional incorporation of a new Bill of Rights are accompanied by a series of countervailing safeguards and even contradictory limiting provisions. Nevertheless, it seems unlikely that there will be much political opposition to the newly proposed 'double padlock' provision, and on the contrary that there will be clear political support for it as an assertion of the limits of EU competence.

However, for the reasons just given, it is recommended that the amendments proposed by the Working Group to Article 51 of the Charter be rejected.

Article 52(4)

[. . .]

This proposal seems a useful one. It reads as a direction to the Court of Justice to interpret the rights contained in the Charter in harmony with national constitutional traditions, in so far as the rights in question are derived from those traditions. This direction to strive for 'soft harmony' between national constitutional rights and the expression of those rights contained in the Charter is a more promising constitutional means of addressing the tension between them rather than positing the supremacy of one over the other, quite apart from the fact that political agreement on such a supremacy clause (of either kind) would be virtually impossible to achieve. Like the provision already contained in Article 52(3) concerning the relationship between the Charter and corresponding provisions of the ECHR, this proposed amendment leaves many questions open, but that seems inevitable and appropriate to the complexity of Europe's legal pluralism.

It is recommended that the Working Group's proposed amendment to Article 52(4) of the Charter be accepted.

Article 52(5)

[. . .]

Article 52(5), like the proposed amendments to Article 51 discussed above, seems to be a legally superfluous and fuzzy political compromise. This is the one amendment proposed by the Working Group which seems to be an attempt – or perhaps better described as a compromise proposal in response to such an attempt – to revisit the substance and content of the Charter, despite the Group's assertion that it proceeded on the basis that the content of the Charter which had been proclaimed at the Nice European Council should not be re-opened. If the 'integrity' of the Charter as a whole, on account of the mechanism by which it was drafted and proclaimed is to be taken seriously, then this in itself provides a clear argument against including the proposed amendment in Article 52(5).

The amendment seems likely to have been pressed by one of the UK members of the Working Group, although a large majority of the Working Group supported it, in particular since the UK government's previous representative on the Convention which drafted the Charter in 2000, Tony Goldsmith, had fought hard for a distinction between rights and principles to be made in the text, but had been defeated in this attempt at an early stage of the Charter drafting process.[21] The main thrust behind this position seems to be the wish not to render many of the so-called 'economic and social rights' (which are considered to require positive action and social expenditure) justiciable, and therefore to reclassify them as 'principles', while maintaining the more traditional and often negatively framed civil and political rights (which are considered to require only non-interference) as justiciable individual rights. According to the proposed amendment, Charter provisions 'which contain principles . . . shall be judicially cognisable only in the interpretation of [acts which implement these principles] and in ruling on their legality'.

Without needing to engage in the longstanding academic and policy debate on the distinction between economic/social and civil/political rights, and on their alleged indivisibility under international law,[22] the likelihood of the proposed amendment rendering all 'social rights' contained in the Charter non-justiciable seems in any case extremely slight. This is partly because the distinction which the amendment introduces between 'principles' and 'subjective rights' (to use the language of the Working Group's explanatory note on the proposed amendment[23]) is extremely hazy, and partly because there is no clear division between economic/social and civil/political rights in the Charter. The latter division does not in any case map neatly onto a distinction between 'rights requiring positive action or expenditure' and rights which require only non-interference for their protection.

Further, the polarisation of the notions of justiciability and non-justiciability underlying the proposed amendment reflects a simplistic and legally unsophisticated understanding of the function and operation of a Charter of Rights such as this. It is unlikely that the rights and values set out in the Charter will be used in any significantly different way from the way in which fundamental rights and provisions of the ECHR have until now been used in litigation before the ECJ. The legal and constitutional culture within which the ECJ has operated over the past four decades, and the approach it has adopted to fundamental rights adjudication, has shown no indication of following the strong paradigm associated with the US legal system of rights as weapons used to 'trump' legislation. Indeed the complaint has more usually been that the ECJ does not 'take rights seriously' in the sense that it has only extremely rarely struck down any provision of EU law, other than individual administrative or staff actions, for violation of human rights.[24] Instead, the articulation of legal rights in a text such as the ECHR and now the EU Charter is much more likely to continue to function as a source of values and norms other than those set out in the other Treaties, to influence the interpretation of EU legislative and other measures, and to feed into policy making and into EU activities more generally. And it is unlikely that the ECJ's role and approach in relation to these values and norms will change very much from the approach it has demonstrated to date with other fundamental rights and norms derived from the ECHR and national constitutional law.

There is therefore a range of arguments in favour of abandoning the Working Group's proposed amendment to Article 52(5) (which, incidentally, was accepted in the Penelope draft). It represents an attempt to re-open the substance of the Charter as agreed by the previous Convention by consensus; it is premised on a very unclear distinction between 'principles' and everything else; it is based on a rather crude understanding of the notion of justiciability; and it reflects a lack of awareness of the role and approach which has over the years been adopted by the ECJ (and CFI) in cases raising fundamental rights issues. The best that can be said about the proposed amendment is that the ECJ can decide for itself what constitutes a 'principle', and that this language is unlikely to restrict it in drawing on the range of values and norms expressed in the Charter in its adjudicative role.

It is recommended that the Working Group's proposed amendment to Article 52(5) of the Charter be rejected.

Article 52(6)

[. . .]

This seems to be an exhortatory and fairly uncontroversial amendment encouraging those who apply and interpret the Charter to pay full account to national laws and practices when the Charter specifies this.

It is recommended that the Working Group's proposed amendment to Article 52(6) of the Charter be accepted.

Document 5.4: European Court of Justice, Decision of 27 June 2006, *European Parliament* v. *Council of the European Union*, Case C 540/03, available at http://curia.eu.int

Judgment of the Court (Grand Chamber) 27 June 2006[25] in Case C 540/03, action for annulment under Article 230 EC, brought on 22 December 2003, European Parliament, represented by H. Duintjer Tebbens and A. Caiola, acting as Agents, with an address for service in Luxembourg, *applicant* v. *Council of the European Union*, represented by O. Petersen and M. Simm, acting as Agents, defendant,

supported by Commission of the European Communities, represented by C. O'Reilly and C. Ladenburger, acting as Agents, with an address for service in Luxembourg, intervener, and by Federal Republic of Germany, represented by A. Tiemann, W.-D. Plessing and M. Lumma, acting as Agents, intervener,

The Court (Grand Chamber),

composed of V. Skouris, President, P. Jann, C.W.A. Timmermans, A. Rosas (Rapporteur) and K. Schiemann, Presidents of Chambers, J.-P. Puissochet, K. Lenaerts, P. Kūris, E. Juhász, E. Levits and A. Ó Caoimh, Judges, Advocate General: J. Kokott, Registrar: M. Ferreira, Principal Administrator,

having regard to the written procedure and further to the hearing on 28 June 2005, after hearing the Opinion of the Advocate General at the sitting on 8 September 2005, gives the following

Judgment 1 By its application, the European Parliament seeks the annulment of the final subparagraph of Article 4(1), Article 4(6) and Article 8 of Council Directive 2003/86/EC of 22 September 2003 on the right to family reunification (OJ 2003 L 251, p. 12; 'the Directive').

[. . .]

3 The Directive, founded on the EC Treaty and in particular Article 63(3)(a) thereof, determines the conditions for the exercise of the right to family reunification by third country nationals residing lawfully in the territory of the Member States.

4 The second recital in the preamble to the Directive is worded as follows:

> Measures concerning family reunification should be adopted in conformity with the obligation to protect the family and respect family life enshrined in many instruments of international law. This Directive respects the fundamental rights and observes the principles recognised in particular in Article 8 of the European Convention for the Protection of Human Rights and Fundamental Freedoms and in the Charter of Fundamental Rights of the European Union [OJ 2000 C 364, p. 1; 'the Charter'].

[. . .]

8 Article 4(1) of the Directive provides that the Member States are to authorise the entry and residence, pursuant to the Directive, of, in particular, the minor children, including adopted children, of the sponsor and his or her spouse, and those of the sponsor or of the sponsor's spouse where that parent has custody of the children and they are dependent on him or her. In accordance with the penultimate subparagraph of Article 4(1), the minor children referred to in this article must be below the age of majority set by the law of the Member State concerned and must not be married. The final subparagraph of Article 4(1) provides:

> By way of derogation, where a child is aged over 12 years and arrives independently from the rest of his/her family, the Member State may, before authorising entry and residence under this Directive, verify whether he or she meets a condition for integration provided for by its existing legislation on the date of implementation of this Directive.

9 Article 4(6) of the Directive is worded as follows:

> By way of derogation, Member States may request that the applications concerning family reunification of minor children have to be submitted before the age of 15, as provided for by its existing legislation on the date of the implementation of this Directive. If the application is submitted after the age of 15, the Member States which decide to apply this derogation shall authorise the entry and residence of such children on grounds other than family reunification.

10 Article 5(5) of the Directive requires the Member States to have due regard to the best interests of minor children when examining an application.

11 Article 8 of the Directive provides:

> Member States may require the sponsor to have stayed lawfully in their territory for a period not exceeding two years, before having his/her family members join him/her.
>
> By way of derogation, where the legislation of a Member State relating to family reunification in force on the date of adoption of this Directive takes into account its reception capacity, the Member State may provide for a waiting period of no more

than three years between submission of the application for family reunification and the issue of a residence permit to the family members.'

[. . .]

The Rules of Law in whose Light the Directive's Legality may be Reviewed
30 The Parliament contends that the contested provisions do not respect fundamental rights – in particular the right to family life and the right to non-discrimination – as guaranteed by the European Convention for the Protection of Human Rights and Fundamental Freedoms signed in Rome on 4 November 1950 ('the ECHR') and as they result from the constitutional traditions common to the Member States of the European Union, as general principles of Community law; the Union has a duty to respect them pursuant to Article 6(2) EU, to which Article 46(d) EU refers with regard to action of the institutions.

31 The Parliament invokes, first, the right to respect for family life, set out in Article 8 of the ECHR, which the Court has interpreted as also covering the right to family reunification (Carpenter, paragraph 42, and Case C-109/01 Akrich [2003] ECR I 9607, paragraph 59). This principle has been repeated in Article 7 of the Charter which, the Parliament observes, is relevant to interpretation of the ECHR in so far as it draws up a list of existing fundamental rights even though it does not have binding legal effect. The Parliament also cites Article 24 of the Charter, devoted to rights of the child, which provides, in paragraph 2, that 'in all actions relating to children, whether taken by public authorities or private institutions, the child's best interests must be a primary consideration' and, in paragraph 3, that 'every child shall have the right to maintain on a regular basis a personal relationship and direct contact with both his or her parents, unless that is contrary to his or her interests'.

32 The Parliament invokes, second, the principle of non-discrimination on grounds of age which, it submits, is taken into account by Article 14 of the ECHR and is expressly covered by Article 21(1) of the Charter.

[. . .]

34 The Council observes that the Community is not a party to the various instruments of public international law invoked by the Parliament. In any event, those norms require merely that the children's interests be respected and taken into account, and do not establish any absolute right regarding family reunification. Nor should the application be examined in light of the Charter, given that the Charter does not constitute a source of Community law.

Findings of the Court
35 Fundamental rights form an integral part of the general principles of law the observance of which the Court ensures. For that purpose, the Court draws

inspiration from the constitutional traditions common to the Member States and from the guidelines supplied by international instruments for the protection of human rights on which the Member States have collaborated or to which they are signatories. The ECHR has special significance in that respect (see, inter alia, Case C-260/89 ERT [1991] ECR I-2925, paragraph 41; Opinion 2/94 [1996] ECR I 1759, paragraph 33; Case C-274/99 *P Connolly* v. *Commission* [2001] ECR I 1611, paragraph 37; Case C-94/00 *Roquette Frères* [2002] ECR I-9011, paragraph 25; Case C-112/00 *Schmidberger* [2003] ECR I-5659, paragraph 71; and Case C-36/02 *Omega* [2004] ECR I-9609, paragraph 33).

36 In addition, Article 6(2) EU states that 'the Union shall respect fundamental rights, as guaranteed by the [ECHR] and as they result from the constitutional traditions common to the Member States, as general principles of Community law'.

37 The Court has already had occasion to point out that the International Covenant on Civil and Political Rights is one of the international instruments for the protection of human rights of which it takes account in applying the general principles of Community law (see, inter alia, Case 374/87 *Orkem* v. *Commission* [1989] ECR 3283, paragraph 31; Joined Cases C-297/88 and C-197/89 *Dzodzi* [1990] ECR I 3763, paragraph 68; and Case C-249/96 *Grant* [1998] ECR I-621, paragraph 44). That is also true of the Convention on the Rights of the Child referred to above which, like the Covenant, binds each of the Member States.

38 The Charter was solemnly proclaimed by the Parliament, the Council and the Commission in Nice on 7 December 2000. While the Charter is not a legally binding instrument, the Community legislature did, however, acknowledge its importance by stating, in the second recital in the preamble to the Directive, that the Directive observes the principles recognised not only by Article 8 of the ECHR but also in the Charter. Furthermore, the principal aim of the Charter, as is apparent from its preamble, is to reaffirm 'rights as they result, in particular, from the constitutional traditions and international obligations common to the Member States, the Treaty on European Union, the Community Treaties, the [ECHR], the Social Charters adopted by the Community and by the Council of Europe and the case law of the Court . . . and of the European Court of Human Rights'.

39 Subject to the European Social Charter which will be mentioned in paragraph 107 of this judgment, the remaining international instruments invoked by the Parliament do not in any event appear to contain provisions affording greater protection of rights of the child than those contained in the instruments already referred to.

The final subparagraph of Article 4(1) of the Directive

[. . .]

Findings of the Court

52 The right to respect for family life within the meaning of Article 8 of the ECHR is among the fundamental rights which, according to the Court's settled case law, are protected in Community law (Carpenter, paragraph 41, and Akrich, paragraphs 58 and 59). This right to live with one's close family results in obligations for the Member States which may be negative, when a Member State is required not to deport a person, or positive, when it is required to let a person enter and reside in its territory.

[. . .]

57 The Convention on the Rights of the Child also recognises the principle of respect for family life. [. . .]

58 The Charter recognises, in Article 7, the same right to respect for private or family life. This provision must be read in conjunction with the obligation to have regard to the child's best interests, which are recognised in Article 24(2) of the Charter, and taking account of the need, expressed in Article 24(3), for a child to maintain on a regular basis a personal relationship with both his or her parents.

59 These various instruments stress the importance to a child of family life and recommend that States have regard to the child's interests but they do not create for the members of a family an individual right to be allowed to enter the territory of a State and cannot be interpreted as denying Member States a certain margin of appreciation when they examine applications for family reunification.

60 Going beyond those provisions, Article 4(1) of the Directive imposes precise positive obligations, with corresponding clearly defined individual rights, on the Member States, since it requires them, in the cases determined by the Directive, to authorise family reunification of certain members of the sponsor's family, without being left a margin of appreciation.

[. . .]

76 It follows from all of the foregoing that the final subparagraph of Article 4(1) of the Directive cannot be regarded as running counter to the fundamental right to respect for family life, to the obligation to have regard to the best interests of children or to the principle of non-discrimination on grounds of age, either in itself or in that it expressly or impliedly authorises the Member States to act in such a way.

Article 4(6) of the Directive

[. . .]

Article 8 of the Directive

[. . .]

104 In the final analysis, while the Directive leaves the Member States a margin of appreciation, it is sufficiently wide to enable them to apply the

Directive's rules in a manner consistent with the requirements flowing from the protection of fundamental rights (see, to this effect, Case 5/88 *Wachauf* [1989] ECR 2609, paragraph 22).

105 It should be remembered that, in accordance with settled case law, the requirements flowing from the protection of general principles recognised in the Community legal order, which include fundamental rights, are also binding on Member States when they implement Community rules, and that consequently they are bound, as far as possible, to apply the rules in accordance with those requirements (see Case C-2/92 *Bostock* [1994] ECR I-955, paragraph 16; Case C 107/97 *Rombi and Arkopharma* [2000] ECR I-3367, paragraph 65; and, to this effect, ERT, paragraph 43).

106 Implementation of the Directive is subject to review by the national courts since, as provided in Article 18 thereof, 'the Member States shall ensure that the sponsor and/or the members of his/her family have the right to mount a legal challenge where an application for family reunification is rejected or a residence permit is either not renewed or is withdrawn or removal is ordered'. If those courts encounter difficulties relating to the interpretation or validity of the Directive, it is incumbent upon them to refer a question to the Court for a preliminary ruling in the circumstances set out in Articles 68 EC and 234 EC.

107 So far as concerns the Member States bound by these instruments, it is also to be remembered that the Directive provides, in Article 3(4), that it is without prejudice to more favourable provisions of the European Social Charter of 18 October 1961, the amended European Social Charter of 3 May 1987, the European Convention on the legal status of migrant workers of 24 November 1977 and bilateral and multilateral agreements between the Community or the Community and the Member States, on the one hand, and third countries, on the other.

108 Since the action is not well founded, there is no need to consider whether the contested provisions are severable from the rest of the Directive.

109 Consequently, the action must be dismissed.

[. . .]

Notes

1. See also in Chapter 4, the Decision of the French Constitutional Council on the Constitutional Treaty, Document 4.6, p. 102.
2. See Chapter 1.
3. See documents CONV 72/02 and 116/02, pp. 7–8.
4. See document CONV 116/02, p. 7.
5. In addition to the adjustments indicated in the Annex, it should be kept in mind that, depending on the future Treaty architecture, purely drafting adjustments may become necessary to the various references, made throughout the Charter, to 'the Treaties', 'the Community Treaties', 'the Treaty on the European Union', 'Community law', and so on; see doc. CONV 116/02, p. 7.
6. See Judgment of the Court of Justice C-249/96 Grant, 1998 ECR I-621, at para. 45.

7. It should be noted that, upon possible incorporation of the Charter into the Treaty, the current wording of Article 46(d) TEU would have to be brought in line with existing case law and Article 51 of the Charter on the (limited) application of fundamental rights to acts of Member States.
8. A list of those rights is to be found in WD No. 9 of the Chairman, page 3, fn. 2.
9. See also the 'Explanations' (Document CHARTE 4473/00 CONVENT 49 of 11 October 2000; see in detail below, section A III 3) under Article 52 §2: 'The Charter does not alter the system of rights conferred by the Treaties.'
10. Cf. on Article 52 §3 of the Charter also the concurrent statements made by Judge Fischbach of the European Court of Human Rights and Judge Skouris of the European Court of Justice at the hearing on 17 September, doc. CONV 295/02.
11. On the 'Explanations', see in detail below, section A III 3.
12. Cf. notably recent case law on the 'precautionary principle' in Article 174 §2 TEC: judgment of the CFI of 11 September 2002, T-13/99, *Pfizer* vs. *Council*, with numerous references to earlier case law; and a series of judgments on Article 33 (ex-39) on the principles of agricultural law, for example judgment of the Court of Justice C-265/85, *Van den Berg*, 1987 ECR 1155: scrutiny of the principle of market stabilization and of reasonable expectations; for further references see Comm. Megret, vol. 3, pp. 80 et seq.
13. See doc. CONV 116/02, page 9.
14. Document CHARTE 4473/00 CONVENT 49 of 11 October 2000.
15. The Group furthermore notes in this context that the previous Convention worked in public – as the present Convention does – and that its meeting records and working documents are publicly accessible (see http://ue.eu.int/df).
16. Judgment of the Court of Justice of 25 July 2002, C-50/00 P, UPA, at paras 41, 42. It should also be recalled that the Court noted in this judgment that, while it is possible to envisage a system of judicial review of the legality of Community measures of general application different from that established by the Treaty, it is for the Member States, if necessary, in accordance with Article 48 TEU, to reform the system currently in force.
17. In this connection, attention is drawn to expert testimony given to the Group reflecting concerns, from a perspective of protection of fundamental rights, about these limits as currently contained in Article 68 TEC and Article 35 TEU in an area as sensitive to fundamental rights as Justice and Home affairs, and on limits of judicial control over Union bodies such as Europol; see the hearing of Judge Skouris (WD No. 19) and of Mr Schoo of 23 July 2002 (WD No. 13), as well as WD No. 20 of Mr Ben Fayot presenting a note by Advocate-General Francis Jacobs.
18. See, comprehensively on judicial and non judicial remedies, doc. CONV 221/02 CONTRIB 76 of Mr Söderman; specifically on Art. 230: CONV 45/02 CONTRIB 25 by Mr Hannes Farnleitner; the Group's WD No. 17 by Mr Jürgen Meyer; WD No. 20 of Mr Ben Fayot presenting a note by Advocate-General Francis Jacobs; the hearing of Judge Skouris (WD No. 19); the hearing of Mr Schoo (WD No. 13); and an overview of the debate and options in WD No. 21 by the Group's Chairman.
19. See <http://europa.eu.int/futurum/documents/offtext/const051202_en.pdf>.
20. The table is not reproduced in this book for reasons of space (note of the eds).
21. For an account of the Charter from his perspective, see T. Goldsmith, 'A Charter of Rights, Freedoms and Principles' (2001) **38**, *Common Market Law Review*, 1201.
22. See H. Steiner and P. Alston, *International Human Rights in Context*, 2nd edn, OUP, 2000, Chap. 4; C. Fabre, 'Constitutionalising Social Rights' (1998) **6**, *Journal of Political Philosophy*, 263.
23. See WD 023.
24. See J. Coppel and A. O'Neill, 'The European Court of Justice: Taking Rights Seriously?' (1992) **29**, *Common Market Law*, 669, and the response in J. Weiler and N. Lockhart '"Taking Rights Seriously" seriously: the European Court and its Fundamental Rights Jurisprudence' (1995) **32**, *Common Market Law Review*, 51, 579.
25. Language of the Case: French.

6. Competences, legal bases and instruments in the constitution for Europe

Document summary

6.1 European Convention Working Group V on Complementary Competences, Final Report of 4 November 2002 (selected extracts)
6.2 European Convention Working Group IX on Simplification, Final Report of 29 November 2002 (selected extracts)
6.3 Articles I-11 to I-16, Treaty Establishing a Constitution for Europe
6.4 Article 308 Treaty Establishing the European Community and article I-18 Treaty Establishing a Constitution for Europe
6.5 Articles I-33–I-39, Treaty Establishing a Constitution for Europe
6.6 Article III-396, Treaty Establishing a Constitution for Europe
6.7 Paul Craig, 'Competence: Clarity, Conferral, Containment and Consideration', in European Law Review 2004, 29(3), pp. 323–344 (selected extracts)

Introduction

By reading the existing Treaties, drawing the line between the areas and sectors in which the Community legislates and those still under the jurisdiction of the Member States is not an easy task. The difficulty stems from the principles that have been adopted since the birth of the Community to give legal ground to its regulatory powers. On the one hand, for the caution of the Member States in conferring powers on their common institutions, and on the other hand for the administrative culture of the (French and German) officials who translated the European project into a legal construct, the Community is empowered to legislate by adopting specific measures whose scope and sphere of legal effects are defined by specific legal bases. Some legal bases are much broader than the average (for example, 'directives for the approximation of such laws, regulations or administrative provisions of the Member States as directly affect the establishment or functioning of the internal market': Article 94 TEC). However, all of the legal bases are conceived along the patterns used in our domestic legal systems to define and authorise administrative measures, not legislation. The names themselves of the European legislative acts (regulations and directives) remind us of administrative law.

Throughout the life of the Community, the peculiar structure of these legal bases has produced several consequences: on the one hand, it has prevented the expansion of Community regulations beyond the narrow borders of most of them (promoting however a sort of gerrymandering between Community regulations and national ones); on the other hand, it has frequently led the Community to avail itself to the utmost (and beyond) of the elasticity of the most 'transversal' legal bases, such as Article 94 TEC (see above), and to resort to the so-called 'flexibility clause' (Article 308 TEC Document 6.6), according to which appropriate measures may be adopted whenever an action proves necessary and the Treaty does not confer for it a corresponding legal basis. There is a third and overall consequence: the difficulty in discerning the existing allocation of legislative roles and an increasing demand to clarify 'who does what'.

That demand was high in the list of the Laeken Declaration, and responding to it was one of the priorities for the Convention. The response was given firstly by defining, in broad terms, the areas of European legislative 'competence', and secondly, by listing such areas on the basis of the nature (either exclusive, shared or complementary) of the competence to be exercised in them. The notion of competence is not foreign to the existing Treaties but it is used quite marginally and, again, in a confusing manner. Suffice it to say that Article 5 TEC speaks of 'exclusive' competences of the Community, but nowhere in the Treaty do we find which competences are exclusive.

The Constitution lists competences and groups them into categories (Articles I-11 to I-16 [Document 6.3]), making things remarkably clearer than they are under the EC and EU treaties. There are almost no new areas in the lists (except for very minor ones), but it is a fact that during the Convention some representatives of national governments expressed surprise at what they were reading and were disappointed to realise that we were simply reconnecting legal bases already conferred on the Community by the Member States.

The Final Report of the European Convention Working Group V on Complementary Competences (Document 6.1) (actually, the Group worked and reported on all categories of competences) is very helpful in analysing how clearer the system may turn out after the approval of the Constitution and the issues that lie underneath. However, a final point has to be added in relation to the limits of the innovations embodied in the Constitution. In principle, categorising and listing competences could lead to the abandonment of the existing (narrowly defined) legal bases and to the consequent reconstruction of the European legislative powers on the much broader basis of areas of competence, according to the same patterns of federal States. This issue was debated in the Convention, but caution prevailed even on the side of the Commission, fearful of losing the pre-existing certainties. Therefore, the list of competences has no more than a cognitive value, for Article I-12(6) clearly states: 'The scope and arrangements for exercising the Union's competences shall be determined by the provisions specific to each area in Part III.' And the provisions specific to each area are the pre-existing legal bases.

Therefore, it is quite predictable that, even with the Constitution in force, most of the previous tensions will remain, as well as the need to use the flexibility clause (Document 6.7). That provision is maintained in the Constitution, with certain notable innovations, namely the need for the consent, and no longer just the advice, of the European Parliament; mandatory consultation of national parliaments; and a prohibition on harmonisation if the contemplated measure falls within areas where harmonisation is explicitly excluded (compare Article I-18 with Article 308 TEC).

If, in the area of competences, the demand was for clarification, in the area of instruments the demand was for simplification (which by itself leads to more clarity). As the Final Report of the European Convention Working Group IX on Simplification (Document 6.2) explains, summing up the instruments currently used by the Community and by the Union (the 'Union' here meaning the second and third pillars), we reach the remarkable figure of 15. And some of the 15 instruments, despite their different names, produce the same legal effects. The work of simplification reflected in the Constitution (Articles I-33 to I-39 [Document 6.5]) was based on two main criteria. The first was to give the same names to instruments producing the same legal effects, which by itself reduced the total number from 15 to five. The second and more sophisticated goal was to introduce an order, which is also a hierarchy, among the acts and their sources, connected to the specific nature of their effects. Acts making new basic choices in an area of Community intervention require greater democratic legitimacy than acts that simply execute previous choices. Accordingly, institutions not enjoying such greater legitimacy should only be empowered to adopt either executive acts or acts that do not produce legal effects. This is the reasoning behind, firstly, making the co-decision procedure (involving the European Parliament, which expresses the will of the citizens, and the Council, which expresses the will of the States) the ordinary procedure for legislative acts (Document 6.6) (as legislative acts contain the 'basic choices'); secondly, limiting the Commission to the adoption of executive acts only; and finally, the distinction between acts producing legal effects and acts that only produce political effects.

The exercise was very similar to the one carried out more than two centuries ago, when the division of power was introduced into our national systems. Not only the inspiring principles but also the assessment of the relevant acts have been similar. In the Convention we went through a number of acts adopted by the Council in order to understand which of them were legislative (and therefore to be passed to co-decision or, exceptionally, to be maintained in the remaining unilateral Council's legislation), or executive (and therefore to be left to the Commission or exceptionally to the Council), or finally, 'governmental' (and therefore to be maintained for the Council as the political Government of the Community). Several acts adopted by royal decree in our 18th century legal systems were similarly processed afterwards.

This very analogy suggests how remarkable the impact would be if these articles of the Constitution entered into force. Simplifying the array of instruments is already innovative: unifying under the same name the directives of the Community method and the framework decisions of the third pillar necessarily means assuming that they already have the same legal effects. We will see in Chapter 8 that this assumption is disputed. However, as the Report of the Working Group demonstrates, there is much more than this kind of simplification in this part of the Constitution. Owing to the new boundaries among acts (and sources), the existing judicial control of the legality of Community acts would be correspondingly widened. Furthermore, a new category of act is introduced, namely delegated regulations. This has been one of the most disputed and least understood innovations. The purpose is very simple and clear: to concentrate legislation on policies and principles, avoiding parliamentary debates and votes on details and technicalities that take time and attention and that sometimes are not even understood by members of Parliament. However, in countries where delegated legislation does not exist, it seems very difficult to understand the sense and the usefulness of this device, and it is even difficult for some to comprehend that it is not inconsistent with the newly introduced demarcation between legislative and executive acts. The conditions to which delegation is subject according to Article I-35 only partially reflect such difficulty and the consequent reluctant doubts the innovation has met. The objections it keeps receiving demonstrate that the difficulty is still with us and may eventually sentence delegated regulations to an undeserved prenatal death.

Document 6.1: European Convention Working Group V on Complementary Competences, Final Report of 4 November 2002, Conv 375/02, available at http://european-convention.eu.int (selected extracts)

1. Introduction

Complementary competence in the TEC is a part of the general system of Union competence and covers national policy areas of significance for the identity of the Member States. While focusing on the issues of complementary competence and related areas the working group therefore had to devote considerable time to certain basic issues of competence. The recommendations reflect the general view of the group with respect to matters where many individual opinions were expressed. A small minority of the group is only to a limited extent supporting the recommendations.

2. Complementary Competence should be Renamed 'Supporting Measures'
The term 'complementary competence' is inadequate. It is too technical, and it does not transmit the essence of the relation between the Member States and the Union in areas of complementary competence. Several members of the working group found that it was in fact misleading to speak of complementary competence and preferred terms like 'Union measures in fields where Member States are fully competent'. The working group agreed that the need for a short and expressive name would make a term like 'supporting measures' appropriate.[1] This term is consequently used in the report.

RECOMMENDATION
- The term 'complementary competence' should be substituted by a term like 'supporting measures' which better denotes the essence of the relationship between the Member States and the Union and the limited intensity of the measures which the Union may adopt.

3. A Separate Title on Competence in a Future Treaty
Following the guiding principle of greater transparency and a higher level of clarity the working group took as its point of departure that a 'basic treaty of constitutional significance' should contain a separate title covering all issues of competence, and in particular:

(1) Provisions giving a basic delimitation of competence in each policy area;
(2) Definition of the three categories of Union competence;
(3) Conditions for the exercise of Union competence.

Each of these issues is further discussed below under point 4, 6, and 7, respectively, with separate recommendations.

On the assumption that the Convention will draft a Treaty signalling a constitutional consolidation of a Union with wide areas of competence, it was felt that the reference to 'an ever closer Union' in TEU Article 1 should be rephrased or clarified to avoid giving the impression that further transfer of competence to the Union is in itself an aim and objective of the Union.

RECOMMENDATION
- A future Treaty should comprise a separate title devoted to all issues of competence.

– Assuming that the Convention presents a draft Treaty signalling constitutional consolidation and covering wide areas of Union competence it is suggested for further consideration in appropriate Convention bodies that the reference to 'an ever closer Union' in TEU Article 1 should be rephrased or clarified in order to avoid the impression that future transfer of competence to the Union remains in itself an aim and objective of the Union.

4. Basic Delimitation of Competence in a Future Treaty

To meet the requirements of transparency and clarity a future Treaty should contain a short, crisp and easily understood delimitation of the competence granted to the Union in each sphere of action. The group was well aware that it is difficult to separate the policy provisions of the current Treaties from their competence provisions. A detailed definition of all Union competence would consequently make the Treaty less short and clear, thus not contributing to the overall objective of clarity and transparency.[2] However, that difficulty would be considerably reduced if only the basic delimitation of competence in each policy area is described, while leaving the precise and detailed definition of competence in the existing Treaties. A separate Article would make clear that the competence in each policy area should be exercised in accordance with the provisions of the relevant Treaty Articles for each policy area.

The overriding interest of providing the citizens with a short and clear picture of the distribution of competence as well as fundamental constitutional considerations led the working group to recommend to the Convention to opt for such basic delimitation of competence to be part of a future Treaty.

While recognising that procedures for amending the future Treaty fall outside the scope of the working group, several members stressed that Treaty amendments transferring new powers to the Union were unthinkable without ratification by all Member States.

RECOMMENDATION

– A basic delimitation of Union competence in each policy area should be part of a future Treaty. A separate Article should make clear that competence should be exercised in accordance with the provisions of the relevant Treaty Articles for each policy area.

5. Defining and Classifying Categories of Competence[3]

SUPPORTING MEASURES

Broad agreement existed in the working group that:

– Supporting measures cover Treaty provisions giving authority to the Union to adopt certain measures of low intensity with respect to policies which continue to be the responsibility of the Member States, and where Member States have not transferred their legislative competence to the Union;

- Supporting measures enable the Union to assist and supplement the national policies where there is a common Union and Member States interest to do so;
- Supporting measures may take the form of financial support, administrative cooperation, pilot projects, guidelines and many other forms, including the Open Method of Coordination.

A review of the acts adopted in the fields generally described as falling under supporting measures[4] shows that the overwhelming number of acts are resolutions, recommendations, action programmes, and other 'soft' instruments. However, legally binding decisions are also occasionally used. The most characteristic Treaty articles dealing with supporting measures expressly provide that the Council may not harmonise national legislation. In a general sense this implies that the Union cannot 'legislate' and corresponds well with the notion that Member States have retained their legislative competence. It would be logic to conclude that legally binding decisions may be adopted as supporting measures, whereas Union legislation (regulations and directives) to substitute or harmonise national law cannot be adopted as supporting measures.

However, before such conclusion can be reached it is necessary to consider whether the budgetary law of the Union might necessitate the adoption of regulations in certain instances. The Court of Justice[5] has made clear that 'implementation of Community expenditure in relation to any significant Community expenditure presupposes not only the entry of the relevant appropriation in the budget of the Community . . . but in addition the prior adoption of a basic act authorising that expenditure'. It is thus clear that supporting measures must necessarily allow the Council (and as the case may be the European Parliament) to adopt such basic act. But nothing in the judgement requires a basic act to have the form of a regulation. In the case before the Court the basic act authorising expenditure had the form of a decision *sui generis*.[6]

On this background the working group found that the requirements of clarity justified that a definition of supporting measures contained an element, that such measures may consist of legally binding decisions, but that Union legislation (regulations and directives) may not be used.[7]

To ensure legal precision each Article related to supporting measures should expressly ensure that only supporting measures could be adopted.[8]

The Treaty provisions on public health and trans-European networks allow as a general rule only the adoption of supporting measures. However, in both areas the Council may in very restricted, clearly defined fields adopt legislation (regulations or directives). The working group discussed if this required a modification of the definition of supporting measures to allow trans-European networks and public health (and other future similar cases) to be classified in toto as areas of supporting measures. The group felt that such a modification would be useful.

The determination of areas where supporting measures may be adopted in accordance with the definition proposed follows below under point 6.

RECOMMENDATION

- Supporting measures should be defined in the future Treaty on the basis of the following elements:
- Supporting measures apply to policy areas where the Member States have not transferred legislative competence to the Union, unless exceptionally and clearly specified in the relevant Treaty Article;
- Supporting measures allow the Union to assist and supplement national policies where this is in the common interest of the Union and the Member States;
- Supporting measures authorise the Union to adopt recommendations, resolutions, guidelines, programmes and other legally non-binding acts as well as legally binding decisions, to the extent specified in the relevant Articles of the 'secondary Treaties'. Union legislation (regulations and directives) may not be adopted as supporting measures, unless exceptionally and clearly specified in the relevant Treaty Article;
- Credits from the Union budget may be allocated under supporting measures.

EXCLUSIVE COMPETENCE/SHARED COMPETENCE

Having considered the definition of supporting measures, exclusive competence must be defined. Shared competence will comprise matters being neither supporting measures nor exclusive competence.

The essential feature of matters falling under exclusive competence of the Union is that Member States may only act in such fields if authorised by the Union. Based on this common point of departure two different views were expressed in the group with respect to the criteria to be applied for classification under exclusive competence.

According to one view, exclusive competence should be renamed 'Union competence' and the criteria for classification under 'Union competence' should primarily be political. All competence where the Union would have total or primary responsibility should be classified as 'Union competence'. According to this view the central objective should be to make clear to the Union citizens all the areas where the Union should play the leading or exclusive role.

According to another view, classification under exclusive competence must be based on purely legal considerations because it has far-reaching legal consequences. The criteria for classification should remain unchanged. Only matters where it is essential that the Member States do not act by themselves, even if no Union solution can be found, should be classified as exclusive competence.

In support of this other view it was further pointed out that it follows from the Treaty that the principle of subsidiarity does not apply where the Community has exclusive competence (it would make no sense to consider if Union action is more effective than national action in areas where Member States have no power to act on their own). It was also pointed out that enhanced cooperation does not apply to matters of exclusive competence. A broad political classification of policies as 'Union (exclusive) competence' would have serious negative consequences in these respects.

A full analysis of the merits of the two views makes them reconcilable. The first view may be met by a rewriting of the tasks and responsibilities of the Union currently described in TEC Articles 3 and 4. It would no doubt be helpful to the general public if the tasks and responsibilities of the Union were described in a manner so that policies that fully or primarily fell to the Union to pursue would be described in a way that made this distribution of responsibility clear.

The second view may be met by maintaining the existing definition and criteria for exclusive competence.

RECOMMENDATION

- It is suggested for further consideration in relevant bodies of the Convention that the tasks and responsibilities of the Union (currently described in TEC Articles 3 and 4) be rewritten in such a manner that policy areas where the Union shall be fully or primarily responsible are identified as Union responsibilities;
- Exclusive competence and shared competence should be defined in the future Treaty in accordance with existing jurisprudence of the Court of Justice, and areas of exclusive and shared competence respectively determined in accordance with the criteria developed by the Court.

THE OPEN METHOD OF COORDINATION

Some members of the working group requested that the Open Method of Coordination be codified in the Treaty as an additional instrument for the Union. They defined the method as 'a mutual feedback process of planning, examination, comparison and adjustment of the (social) policies of (EU) Member States, all of this on the basis of common objectives'. The working group noted that the Open Method of Coordination, as instituted by the European Council in Lisbon, March 2000, applies to areas of Union competence, of supporting measures as well as areas of Member States' competence. Broad agreement was found in the group to ask the working group on simplification (WG IX) to include the instrument of Open Method of Coordination in its work as a 'soft' instrument or method.

RECOMMENDATION

- The Open Method of Coordination should be considered in the working group on simplification as a 'soft' instrument or method.

6. Areas of Supporting Measures

Based on its working document 29 the working group discussed the Treaty provisions related to the following areas:[9]

- Employment (TEC Articles 125-30),
- Education and vocational training (TEC Articles 149 and 150),
- Culture (TEC Article 151),
- Industry (TEC Article 157),
- Research and development (TEC Articles 163–73),[10]
- Public health (TEC Article 152),
- Trans-European networks (TEC Articles 154–6),
- Customs cooperation (TEC Article 135),
- Consumer protection (TEC Article 153),
- Development cooperation (TEC Articles 177–81).

The working group's primary objective was to ensure that the definition and classification of 'supporting measures' would provide the maximum clarity without changing the legal competence of the Union in the areas concerned. In this context it was stressed by many members of the group that the classification of a subject matter as supporting measures could not and should not be equalled with an evaluation of the field of Union activity as being less important. The fundamental importance (f.i.) of the 'Erasmus programme' and the Union programmes on research and development, public health and trans-European networks was often referred to in this context.

Research and development was specifically discussed, due to its importance for the Union and its weight on the Union budget. It was noted that regulation of patents and other research-related intellectual property rights is covered elsewhere in the Treaty. A special recommendation in point 8 of the report recommends a separate legal basis for intellectual property rights. It was also noted that research and development of the Union is not limited to activities of direct interest for the economic life of the Union, but may have a wider scope. The group concluded that under the definition chosen research and development was an area of supporting measures.

The working group noted that legislation in the form of regulations and/or directives is clearly authorised with respect to consumer protection and development cooperation and probably also with respect to customs cooperation, not as a clearly defined exception, but as a main rule. These fields would therefore under the definitions chosen fall under shared competence. The group discussed if any inconveniences would arise out of this categorisation. It was observed that development cooperation has special features because Union activities in this field would never preempt the competence of the Member States to maintain their own national development policy. With respect to consumer protection the group noted that most legal acts adopted are in fact based on other Treaty provisions than Article 153. However, the fact that (minimum) directives could be adopted under Article 153 made it logical that consumer protection should be classified as shared competence.

The group also had a general discussion on the substance of the individual Articles dealing with supporting measures including some proposals for substantive amendments either enlarging or limiting the scope of some of the provisions. However, the group decided to concentrate on the abstract issue concerning supporting measures and did not wish to take any decision on detailed and substantive amendments to the present Treaty in this respect.

A proposal to establish the fight against narcotics as an area where supporting measures could be adopted was partly held to be already covered by TEC Article 152 (drugs-related health damage) and partly to belong to the working group on Freedom Security and Justice (WG X). A proposal providing for the adoption of supporting measures with respect to international sports was not broadly supported.

RECOMMENDATION

The following subject matters should be considered matters of supporting measures:

- Employment (TEC Articles 125–30),
- Education and vocational training (TEC Articles 149 and 150),
- Culture (TEC Article 151),
- Public health (TEC Article 152),
- Trans-European networks (TEC Articles 154–6),
- Industry (TEC Article 157),
- Research and development (TEC Articles 163–73).[11]

7. Principles on the Exercise of Union Competence

A Treaty title on competence must contain a chapter on the principles applicable to the exercise of Union competence. The point of departure for the working group was the general principles of the common interest and of solidarity.

In addition to these more abstract yet fundamental principles a number of legal principles were considered. Principles of direct relevance to the workings of the group are covered in some depth in this report. Others are covered cursorily thereafter.

THE PRINCIPLE OF ALLOCATED POWERS

The principle of allocated powers contained in the TEC Article 5(1) is a basic principle of Union law. In a narrow sense it establishes a fundamental condition for the exercise of any Union activity. In a wider sense the principle is a vital safeguard for the Member States ensuring that powers not allocated to the Union remain with the Member States. In the opinion of the working group the latter aspect of the principle of allocated powers ought to be expressly stated in the Treaty. Such an amendment would in itself establish an assumption in favour of national competence.

RECOMMENDATION

- An explicit text stating that all powers not conferred on the Union by the Treaty remain with the Member States should be inserted into a future Treaty.

RESPECTING THE NATIONAL IDENTITY OF THE MEMBER STATES

The Group discussed ways to clarify that the Union respects certain core responsibilities of the Member States. There was broad support for doing so by elaborating the fundamental principle, today enshrined in TEU Article 6(3), that the EU shall respect the national identities of its Member States. The purpose would be to provide added transparency of what constitutes essential elements of national identity, which the EU must respect in the exercise of its competence.

The discussion of the group related to two areas of core national responsibilities:

- Fundamental structures and essential functions of a Member State, for example (a) political and constitutional structure, including regional and local self-government; (b) national citizenship; (c) territory; (d) the legal status of churches and religious societies; (e) national defence and the organisation of armed forces; (g) choice of languages.
- Basic public policy choices and social values of a Member State, for example (a) policy for distribution of income; (b) imposition and collection of personal taxes; (c) system of social welfare benefits; (d) educational system; (e) public health care system; (f) cultural preservation and development; (g) compulsory military or community service.

By clarifying in TEU Article 6(3) what constitutes the national identity of a Member State, it seems possible to meet the main concerns expressed in the Working Group and elsewhere of safeguarding the role and importance of the Member States in the Treaty while at the same time allowing the necessary margin of flexibility. In the latter respect it was noted that the provision was not a derogation clause. The Member States will remain under a duty to respect the provisions of the Treaties. The article would therefore not constitute a definition of Member State competence, thereby wrongly conveying the message that it is the Union that grants competence to the Member States, or that Union action may never impact on these fields.

The purpose would be to render more visible and more operational the existing principle that the Union, in the exercise of its competence, is under an obligation to respect the national identities of the Member States. The clause would send an important message to the citizens as well as provide useful guidance for the Union institutions in the fulfilment of its tasks. Were the Court of Justice to be given power with respect to such article in a future 'basic treaty of constitutional significance', the Court could be the ultimate interpreter of the provision if the political institutions went beyond a reasonable margin of appreciation.

Taking into account the clear and precise recommendations of the working group on the definition of supporting measures, and on the use of TEC Articles 94/95 and 308 in fields covered by supporting measures, broad agreement was found that no specific mentioning of basic policy choices of the Member States in the identity clause would be required.

RECOMMENDATION

- The provisions contained in TEU Article 6(3) that the Union respects the national identity of the Member States should be made more transparent by clarifying that the essential elements of the national identity include, among others, fundamental structures and essential functions of the Member States, notably their political and constitutional structure, including regional and local self-government; their choices regarding language; national citizenship; territory; legal status of churches and religious societies; national defence and the organisation of armed forces.

SPECIAL PRINCIPLES GOVERNING THE RELATION BETWEEN INTERNAL MARKET COMPETENCE AND SUPPORTING MEASURES

The working group discussed the relationship between Articles 94 and 95 on the internal market and the policy areas where supporting measures may be adopted. The views expressed ranged from suggestions to abolish Article 94 and 95 to maintaining status quo. On the basis of the discussion it was possible to conclude that a measure should be based on the Article where the measure had its 'centre of gravity'. However, the term 'centre of gravity' was considered too technical and difficult to understand for ordinary citizens. In order to clarify the legal situation it should be specified in the Treaty that measures to harmonise legislation based on Treaty provisions on the internal market may apply only with respect to areas of supporting measures if the principal objectives, contents and intended effects of such measures relate to Treaty Articles on the internal market.

RECOMMENDATION

- It should be specified in the Treaty that measures to harmonise legislation based on Treaty provisions on the internal market may apply only to areas of supporting measures if the principal objectives, content and intended effects of such measures relate to Treaty Articles on the internal market.

SCHEME OF INTENSITY OF UNION ACTION

In addition to the principles referred to above, the working group discussed a scheme provided by the Commission representative setting out the following types of Community interventions according to intensity of the Community action.

LEGISLATIVE ACTION

- Uniform regulation (for example common customs tariff),
- Harmonisation (for example company law),
- Minimum harmonisation (for example consumer protection),
- Mutual recognition and 'interconnection' of the national legal systems (for example mutual recognition of qualifications; social security of migrant workers)

NON-LEGISLATIVE ACTION (WHERE MEMBER STATES IN PRINCIPLE HAVE THE LEGISLATIVE COMPETENCE)

- Joint action (for example police missions in the Balkans)
- Compulsory coordination of national policies (for example, broad economic policy guidelines)
- Financial support programmes (for example, programmes in relation to education and health)
- Non-binding coordination of national policies (for example, the fight against social exclusion)

Some members of the working group felt that such hierarchy of intensity should be inserted into the Treaty as a separate legal principle along with the principles of subsidiarity and proportionality. Others felt that this 'scale of intervention' would be a useful element in a further elaboration of the principles of subsidiarity and proportionality.

OTHER GENERAL PRINCIPLES GOVERNING THE EXERCISE OF COMPETENCE

In addition to the above principles the working group agreed without any detailed discussion that the following principles should also be included in a competence title in a future Treaty:

- The principle of subsidiarity,
- The principle of proportionality,
- The principle of primacy of Community law,
- The principle of national implementation and execution (except Commission implementation and execution where provided for in the Treaties),
- Statement of reasons for the adoption of an act, including information necessary to review compliance with requirements of all the general principles governing the exercise of competence,
- The principles of common interest and of solidarity.

RECOMMENDATION

- A chapter on conditions for the exercise of competence in a general title on competence in a future Treaty should, in addition to the three recommendations given above, contain separate clauses covering:
- The principle of subsidiarity,
- The principle of proportionality,
- The principle of primacy of Community law,
- The principle of national implementation and execution (except Commission implementation and execution where provided for in the Treaties),
- Statement of reasons for the adoption of an act, including information necessary to review compliance with requirements of the principles governing the exercise of competence,
- The principles of common interest and of solidarity.

8. TEC Article 308[12]

The large majority of the Group agreed that it was necessary to preserve a certain measure of flexibility in the Treaty system of competence so as to allow the Union to deal with unexpected developments and challenges. TEC Article 308 should therefore be maintained. Some members felt that Article 308 was inherently open to misuse and should therefore be deleted.

It was common ground that flexibility should not be founded on a lack of transparency or clarity regarding the allocation of competence to the Union. It was also common ground that a flexibility clause must never give the impression that the Union defines its own competence. The provision has been the cause of concern and controversy in several Member States, especially out of fear that it might undermine the principle of allocated powers. Most members therefore agreed on the necessity of clarifying and possibly tightening the conditions for its use.

The group noted that Article 308 may only be used if Community action is necessary, that is, if a satisfactory result may not be achieved through national action. However, nothing in the Treaty excludes the application of the principle of subsidiarity in relation to acts adopted under Article 308.

To avoid the current repeated recourse to Article 308 in certain areas, such as balance-of-payment aid to third countries, intellectual property rights, energy, civil protection and the establishment of agencies, the working group agreed on the need to recommend new specific legal bases in the Treaty for such policy areas if the Union wished to pursue policies in these fields. As regards tourism, which is mentioned in TEC Article 3(u) along with energy and civil protection, there was wide agreement in the group that no separate Treaty article was desirable. The group felt that it was an anomaly to have subject matters mentioned in TEC Article 3 without having any corresponding Treaty article setting out the policy objectives and the competence. The working group consequently found that TEC Article 3 (u) should be adapted.

The working group looked at two different ways to improve Article 308:

BETTER CRITERIA

General agreement prevailed that it should be specified that Article 308 can not serve

- 'as the basis for widening the scope of [Union] powers beyond the general [Treaty] framework' or 'be used as a basis for the adoption of provisions whose effect would, in substance, be to amend the Treaty',[13] or
- as the basis for harmonisation measures in policy areas where the Union rules out harmonisation.[14]

It was suggested that only measures aiming at 'the establishment and functioning of the internal market' should fall under Article 308. Several members of the working group felt that such limitation would be too narrow since most acts adopted under Article 308 have related to other subject matters. Furthermore matters related to the internal market were already covered under TEC Article 95.

Others suggested modernising the existing condition in Article 308 that a measure shall be 'within the framework of the common market'. To make that condition more operational, and thereby facilitating an effective control, they suggested that a measure adopted under Article 308 should be 'within the operation of the common market, the Economic and Monetary Union, or the implementation of common policies or activities referred to in Articles 3 and 4'.[15]

Some members of the group proposed to clarify that only measures to deal with unforeseen events could be adopted under that article. However, as time passes it becomes increasingly more difficult to establish what might have been foreseen at the time of the adoption of the Treaty.

NEW PROCEDURAL REQUIREMENTS

Wide agreement existed in the group that unanimity in the Council should continue to be required under Article 308. Considered in the light of the enlargement it was pointed out that unanimity requirement in a Union of, for example, 25 Member States might in itself entail a decreased use of Article 308. Assent or other substantial involvement of the European Parliament should be required.

Possible ex ante judicial control drawing inspiration from TEC Article 300(6) on the conclusion of international agreements or ECSC Article 95(3–4) was discussed in the group. The majority view was that, given the requirement of unanimity under Article 308, it might in fact be useful to open up the possibility for any Member State and the Commission to request an ex ante opinion from the Court of Justice. Such possibility might avoid deadlocks in the Council on the applicability of Article 308.

Several suggestions were made to allow for the adoption of legal acts under Article 308 to 'take back competence transferred to the Union' through the use of that Article. The majority of the working group agreed that such a clause could give the erroneous impression that Article 308 was in fact a 'competence-to-competence' provision. Furthermore all that is necessary to restore freedom of action to the Member States in a matter regulated under Article 308 is the repeal of such legal act. The majority therefore favoured a specific provision enabling a qualified majority to repeal acts adopted under Article 308.

As qualified majority would presumably be the general rule for adoption of legal acts under other provisions of a future Treaty such clause would in fact also simplify repeals of acts adopted jointly under Article 308 and other Treaty Articles.

It was the general feeling of the Working Group that Article 308 is an important provision of constitutional significance, which, depending on its final shape and scope, might best be placed in a general title on competence in a future Treaty.

RECOMMENDATION

- TEC Article 308 should be maintained to provide a necessary flexibility;
- Unanimity should continue to be required for adoptions under Article 308, and the assent or other substantial involvement by the European Parliament should be required;

- TEC Article 3(u) should be adapted. New specific legal bases in the Treaty should be adopted for subject matters that have been regulated primarily on the basis of Article 308, for example balance-of-payments loans to third countries, intellectual property rights, energy policy civil protection and the establishment of agencies, if the Union wishes to pursue policies in these fields.
- To allow for a better control with the application of Article 308, the material and procedural conditions for the application of the Article should be modernised and strengthened in the following ways:
  - o Article 308 cannot serve as the basis for widening the scope of Union powers beyond the general Treaty framework or be used as a basis for the adoption of provisions whose effect would, in substance, be to amend the Treaty, or as the basis for harmonisation measures in policy areas where the Union rules out harmonisation.
  - o A measure to be adopted under Article 308 shall be within the framework of the common market, the Economic and Monetary Union, or the implementation of common policies or activities referred to in TEC Article 3 or 4.
  - o Ex ante judicial control comparable to the provisions of TEC Article 300(6) should be available under Article 308.
- Article 308 should allow acts adopted under that Article to be repealed by qualified majority.

Document 6.2: European Convention Working Group IX on Simplification, Final Report of 29 November 2002, Conv 424/02, available at http://european-convention.eu.int (selected extracts)

Part I Simplification and Ranking of Union Acts

I. Simplification of Union Acts

(A) SIMPLIFICATION OF THE NUMBER OF UNION INSTRUMENTS

At present the Union has 15 different legal instruments. Some of these instruments, although bearing different names, have similar effects. The Working Group considers that the number of legal instruments available to the Union's Institutions should be significantly reduced, with the aim of reinforcing the democratic foundations of the Union's legal system by improving the comprehensibility of the system. However, this reduction must not compromise the flexibility and efficiency of those instruments. Nor must it prevent the introduction of particular specifications regarding the use of a given instrument in a given area. The Group proposes limiting the instruments of the Union to the following.

1. Binding Instruments

(a) Regulation (it is proposed that these should be called 'European Union laws' – 'EU laws' – in future).[16] This would be an act of general application, binding in its entirety and directly applicable in all Member States. Its definition would correspond to that currently existing in Article 249 TEC.

(b) Directive (it is proposed that these should be called 'European Union framework laws' – 'EU framework laws' – in future). The directive would be an act which is binding, as to the result to be achieved, upon Member States but which leaves to national authorities the choice of form and methods. Its definition would correspond to that of the directive referred to in Article 249 of the Treaty.

(c) Decision: The decision would be an act which was binding in its entirety. It might or might not designate specific addressees. If it had addressees, it would be binding upon them. The definition of the decision would therefore be broader than that currently set out in Article 249 of the Treaty, which stipulates that the decision is always specifically addressed.[17] It is not a legislative act.

2. Non-binding Instruments

(d) Recommendation: would be defined as an act without binding force (the same definition as that given in Article 249 TEC).

(e) Opinion: would also be defined as an act without binding force (so no change compared with the current Article 249).

The Group suggests that Part One of the constitutional treaty should contain an article listing and defining these five types of Union instrument. To these should be added regulations as defined below (see point C).

(B) THE SCOPE OF THE UNION'S LEGAL INSTRUMENTS

The Group suggests applying the new typology of instruments defined under (A) both to the areas currently covered by the EC Treaty and to the area currently covered by Title VI of the Treaty on European Union (judicial and police cooperation in criminal matters).

The 'framework decisions' and 'decisions' provided for in Title VI would thus respectively become 'directives' ('framework laws') and 'regulations' ('laws').

The only difference between the two types of act is that, at present, the former have no direct effect. Working Group X is to examine whether this type of act should have direct effect when adopted under Title VI. Nevertheless, the Group considers that it would always be possible to make provision in the new treaty for instruments adopted in the area of judicial and police cooperation in criminal matters to be characterised as not having direct effect, if that were to be the case.

With regard to the conventions under Title VI of the TEU (Article 34(2)(d)), they would be abolished and replaced by one of the instruments mentioned under (A), in most cases by regulations ('laws'). There are a number of reasons why they should be abolished: the convention is an instrument which has rarely been used since the Treaty of Amsterdam entered into force, most conventions have never entered into force and most have been replaced by regulations.

With regard to Title V of the Treaty on European Union, the Group is agreed on the need to retain the specific characteristics of the instruments in this field. However, a majority of the Group considers that it is not necessary to retain a specific name for these instruments (that is, 'common strategies', 'joint actions' and 'common positions'). The Group recommends that all three instruments should be replaced by a 'CFSP decision' as defined under (A) above, on condition that the content of decisions be further specified.

The Group recommends retaining the current mechanism whereby the Council adopts by qualified majority 'joint actions' and 'common positions' which implement a 'common strategy', as well as any 'decision' implementing a 'joint action' or a 'common position' (Article 23(2) of the TEU). Provision should therefore be made in the Treaty for what may be defined as 'CFSP implementing decisions' for a 'CFSP decision' adopted by the European Council or by the Council by unanimity to be adopted by the Council by a qualified majority.[18]

(C) CHANGE OF NAME

The Group suggests changing the name of the two legislative instruments par excellence, that is, replacing 'regulation' by 'European Union law' ('EU laws') and 'directive' by 'European Union framework law' ('EU framework law'). If the Group's suggestion that a hierarchy of legislation be introduced were to be adopted (see point II below), the name 'regulation' could be reserved for the adoption of 'delegated'[19] acts and implementing acts, that is generally for acts of a normative nature which are not legislative. The term 'decision' would also be reserved for non-legislative acts.

(D) NON-STANDARD ACTS

With regard to acts used by the Institutions but not provided for in the Treaty and in principle devoid of any binding legal force (resolutions, conclusions, declarations and so on), the Group considered that any simplification should be effected with caution in order to safeguard the flexibility required in the use of such acts.

The Group suggests including in the Treaty a rule whereby the legislator (Parliament/Council) should abstain from adopting non-standard acts on a subject when legislative proposals or initiatives on the same subject have been submitted to it. The use of non-standard acts in legislative areas may give the erroneous impression that the Union legislates through the adoption of non-standard instruments.

(E) HARMONISATION AND STANDARDISATION IN THE WORDING OF TREATY ARTICLES CONFERRING POWERS OF ACTION ON THE INSTITUTIONS

The Group suggests standardising and clarifying the terminology of the legal bases set out in the Treaty, for example by avoiding using the same term with different meanings, by only using the term 'measure' where the choice of instrument to be adopted is to be left to the Institutions, and by abolishing the generic uses of 'decision' or 'directive'. The Group recommends that the Convention agree that the necessary technical adjustments be made in the legal bases of the Treaty in order to standardise and clarify linguistically the terminology used. However, the Group considers that this work of standardisation and clarification should be effected with caution, on a case-by-case basis, and without affecting the institutional balance resulting from the political choices made by the Convention.

(F) THE OPEN METHOD OF COORDINATION

Constitutional status should be assigned to the open method of coordination, which involves concerted action by the Member States outside the competences attributed to the Union by the treaties. It should be emphasised that this should not be confused with the coordination competences conferred upon the Union by various legal bases, notably in the economic and employment fields.

II. Hierarchy of Union Legislation

Taking account of the special features of the Union's institutional system, it is difficult to make a crystal-clear distinction, as is done in national systems, between matters falling to the legislative arm and those falling to the executive. The Group thought that it was still, however, possible to make a clearer distinction than at present, based on the principles set out in the introduction above.

The Group proposes to clarify the hierarchy of Community legislation adopted on the basis of the Treaty by demarcating, as far as possible, matters falling within the legislative area and by adding a new category of legislation: delegated acts.

The excessive detail in Community legislation has often been criticised within the Convention. This excessive detail has been considered inappropriate, in particular in certain economic areas in which an ability to adapt to a changing environment is very important. The Community legislator is thus confronted with a dual requirement: that of producing legislation whose democratic legitimacy is beyond dispute, something which can only be guaranteed by legislative procedures, and that of responding rapidly and effectively to the challenges and demands of the real world and therefore retaining a degree of flexibility.

At present there is no mechanism which enables the legislator to delegate the technical aspects or details of legislation whilst retaining control over such delegation. As things stand, the legislator is obliged either to go into minute detail in the provisions it adopts, or to entrust to the Commission the more technical or detailed aspects of the legislation as if they were implementing measures, subject to the control of the Member States, in accordance with the provisions of Article 202 TEC.

To remedy this situation, the Group proposes a new type of 'delegated' act which, accompanied by strong control mechanisms, could encourage the legislator to look solely to the essential elements of an act and to delegate the more technical aspects to the executive, provided that it had the guarantee that it would be able to retrieve, as it were, its power to legislate.

The Group thus proposes to consider three levels with regard to the adoption of acts within the framework of the European Union:

1. Legislative acts: acts adopted on the basis of the Treaty and containing essential elements in a given field.
2. 'Delegated' acts: these acts would flesh out the detail or amend certain elements of a legislative act, under some form of authorisation defined by the legislator. This would be in cases where the legislator felt that essential elements in an area, as defined by it, necessitated legislative development which could be delegated, although such delegation would be subject to limits and to a control mechanism to be determined by the legislator itself in the legislative act.
3. Implementing acts: acts implementing legislative acts, 'delegated' acts or acts provided for in the treaty itself. With delegated acts, it would be for the legislator to determine whether and to what extent it was necessary to adopt at Union level acts implementing legislative acts and/or delegated acts, and, where appropriate, the committee procedure mechanism (Article 202 TEC) which should accompany the adoption of such acts.

It is the legislative act – and therefore the legislator – which would determine on a case-by-case basis whether and to what extent it was necessary to have recourse to 'delegated' acts and/or to implementing acts and what their scope would be.

(A) LEGISLATIVE ACTS

(a) Definition: legislative acts are adopted directly on the basis of the Treaty and contain the essential elements and the fundamental policy choices in a certain field. The scope of such a concept is to be determined on a case-by-case basis by the legislator. It is consequently for the legislator to determine the degree of detail of a legislative act in a given field and whether and to what extent certain elements of the act should be delegated by way of 'delegated' acts.

(b) Adoption procedure: co-decision should be the general rule for the adoption of legislative acts. Once this principle has been incorporated in the first part of the constitutional treaty, the legal bases of the second part should be reviewed accordingly, of course with the possibility of providing for exceptions.[20]

(c) Type of act: 'laws' and 'framework laws'.

(B) 'DELEGATED' ACTS

(a) Definition: legislative acts may provide for delegating to the Commission the power to adopt delegated acts. The powers delegated may range from rules on the technical and detailed elements which develop a legislative act, to the subsequent amendment of certain aspects of the legislative act itself.

The legislative act itself – and therefore the legislator – determines whether or not recourse should be had to a delegated act. It also formally lays down the objectives, content and scope of the delegated powers and establishes the control mechanisms at the legislator's disposal.

(b) Control mechanisms: through delegated acts the legislator delegates a power which is intrinsic to its own role. It must therefore be sure of being able to monitor its use. Effective control mechanisms must be made available to the legislator by the Treaty.

Examples of such mechanisms could be as follows:

- right of call-back: the ability to retrieve the power to legislate on the subject, should the delegated powers be exceeded (*ultra vires*), or where the issues are of major political sensitivity or have major financial implications;
- period of tacit approval: the provisions would enter into force if, after a certain period, the legislator had not expressed any objections;
- sunset clause: the provisions of the delegated act would have a limited duration; once this deadline has passed, the delegation of powers would have to be renewed by the legislator.

In any case, the Court of Justice would remain competent on the basis of Article 230 TEC to deal with any violation of the conditions established in the decision to delegate.

(c) Adoption procedure: by the Commission as a general rule and in particular and duly justified cases by the Council acting by a qualified majority.

(d) Type of act: delegated regulations.[21]

(C) IMPLEMENTING ACTS

(a) Definition: acts implementing legislative acts, 'delegated' acts, or acts provided for in the Treaty itself.

(b) Procedure: at present the basic principle of the Treaty is that it is for Member States to adopt implementing acts (Article 10 TEC). Where implementation by the Union is necessary, in accordance with the principle of subsidiarity, the procedure would remain the following: adoption by the Commission (the rule), with or without a mechanism for monitoring by Member States (committee procedure) or by the Council (the exception) in cases where it exercises executive functions. The Group broached the idea of introducing into the Treaty the possibility of assigning regulatory authorities the task of adopting certain implementing acts.

However, the Group thought that, if it were decided to create the new category of delegated acts, it might be possible to simplify certain committee procedures.[22] This being said, it must be pointed out that any change would not come under the Treaty directly but under secondary legislation, in this case the Decision laying down the procedures for the exercise of implementing powers conferred on the Commission, adopted on the basis of Article 202 TEC. This issue therefore goes beyond the Working Group's terms of reference.[23]

(c) Type of act: implementing regulation or implementing decision.

*

* *

Finally, the Group would draw attention to the fact that in certain cases the Institutions adopt directly on the basis of the Treaty acts which are not legislative acts. These include:

- internal organisation measures, for example the rules of procedure of the Institutions or the setting of the salaries, allowances and pensions of Members of the Commission and the Court of Justice or setting the conditions of employment, salaries, allowances and pensions of the Members of the Court of Auditors, and so on;
- appointments, such as for example the appointment of members of the Economic and Social Committee and the Committee of the Regions;
- cases where the Institutions act as technical authorities, for example measures adopted by the Commission in the area of competition and control of aids granted by States or certain tasks entrusted to the ECB;
- cases where the Institutions exercise executive functions and develop in detail the policy choices already expressed in the Treaty in a particular area.

The Group suggests that acts adopted on this basis by the Institutions should be in the form of decisions or regulations.

Part II Simplification of Procedures

(A) INTRODUCTION

The Group noted that the large number of different procedures in the Treaty (about 30) was explained by the variety of procedures for consulting various Institutions or bodies (Economic and Social Committee, Committee of the Regions, ECB and so on), and by the two main voting methods in the Council (unanimity or qualified majority). If these factors are left out of account and only the respective roles of the European Parliament and the Council are considered, there are basically five decision-making procedures: co-decision, cooperation, simple opinion and assent by the Parliament, and decision making by the Council alone. The Group concentrated its attention on these five procedures.

The Group recommends that the decision-making procedures should be listed and their key elements outlined in the first part of the constitutional treaty, and a detailed description of the way they operate should be given in the second part.

(B) CO-DECISION PROCEDURE (ARTICLE 251 TEC):

The Working Group considers that co-decision works well in general. However, it feels that certain improvements are possible and therefore recommends:

(a) Generalising qualified-majority voting in the Council to all cases where the co-decision procedure applies

Apart from three cases the Council acts by a qualified majority during the co-decision procedure. The Group agrees that the logic of the co-decision procedure requires qualified-majority voting in the Council in all cases.

(b) Making the composition of the Conciliation Committee more flexible

The composition of the Conciliation Committee is currently laid down by the Treaty (Article 251(4)): it is composed of 'the members of the Council or their representatives and an equal number of representatives of the European Parliament'. In an enlarged Union, the Conciliation Committee will grow from 30 to 50 members.

A large majority of the Group proposes that the composition of the Conciliation Committee should be made more flexible. The Treaty must enable the Council and the Parliament to decide on the number of their representatives on the Committee, whilst still preserving the principle of parity between the two Institutions.

(c) Changes of wording

As the 'co-decision' procedure is the principal legislative procedure, it is suggested to retain the designation 'legislative procedure' in the constitutional treaty. This designation might also replace the references in the Treaty to

Article 251. Nevertheless, certain members of the Group stated their preference for the designation 'co-decision procedure'.

Furthermore, some forms of words in the Treaty give the impression that the European Parliament and the Council are not on an equal footing. This is so in all cases where it is stated that it is the Council, acting in accordance with the procedure referred to in Article 251, which adopts the act in question. Article 251 itself, describing the procedure, implies that it is the Council which adopts acts.

The Group recommends amending the wording of Article 251 and of the various legal bases which refer to co-decision to make clear the parity between the Parliament and the Council as legislators in the context of that procedure.

(d) Generalising co-decision

In the light of the general principle set out in section II(A)(b), co-decision should become the general rule for the adoption of legislative acts. Exceptions to this rule would remain in areas where the special nature of the Union requires autonomous decision-making, or in areas of great political sensitivity for the Member States.

(C) COOPERATION PROCEDURE (ARTICLE 252 TEC)

A broad consensus has emerged, both during the debates in plenary session and in the Working Group, to abolish the cooperation procedure and replace it either with the co-decision procedure or by the consultation procedure (simple opinion of the European Parliament). The cooperation procedure still exists at present in four cases, all in the area of Economic and Monetary Union.

The Group suggests shifting to the co-decision procedure the provisions:

- for adopting the detailed rules for the multilateral surveillance system referred to in Article 99(3) and (4) TEC in the context of the coordination of economic policies (Article 99(5));
- to adopt measures to harmonise the denominations and technical specifications of all coins (Article 106(2));

And, owing to its eminently technical nature, to use the consultation procedure (simple opinion), for provisions:

- specifying definitions for the application of the principle of prohibition of privileged access by Community and national public authorities to financial institutions (Article 102(2));
- specifying definitions for the application of the principle that central banks are prohibited from granting overdraft facilities or any other type of credit facility to Community and national public authorities, and the principle that the Community and its Member States are prohibited from being

liable for or assuming commitments contracted by those public authorities (Article 103(2)).

(D) ASSENT PROCEDURE

The Treaty requires the assent of the European Parliament in certain cases.[24] A large majority of the members of the Working Group proposes that the assent procedure should be limited to the ratification of international agreements,[25] an area in which it should become the general rule when the agreement has repercussions for domestic legislation. Given their major political significance, most of the Group's members recommend a change to the co-decision procedure with qualified-majority voting in the Council for the other cases which are currently subject to the assent procedure, viz.:

- rules for the Structural Funds and the Cohesion Fund (Article 161);
- amendment of certain articles of the Protocol on the Statutes of the ESCB and of the ECB (Article 107(5));
- conferring of specific tasks on the ECB relating to the prudential supervision of credit institutions and other financial institutions (Article 105(6)).

As regards the uniform electoral procedure for the European Parliament, the Group takes note that this is a special procedure which also calls for ratification by national parliaments (Article 190(4)).[26]

(E) SIMPLE OPINION

Those legal bases which stipulate the simple opinion of the Parliament as the procedure for adoption should also be reviewed in the light of the general principle set out in II(A)(b) above.

(F) PROPOSALS COMMON TO ALL PROCEDURES

In a desire for transparency, the Group recommends that a rule should be established whereby legislative proposals for which the adoption procedures have not been completed within a time to be determined should be considered to have lapsed, unless reconfirmed by the Commission at the end of that period.

Articles 192 and 208, which respectively provide the European Parliament and the Council with the possibility of asking the Commission to present proposals for acts to them, should be strengthened. In particular, the Commission should have to substantiate a refusal in relation to any request supported by majorities to be determined by either Institution.

Moreover, the role of the European Parliament and of the Council with regard to legislative initiative can also be strengthened through their involvement in legislative planning.

(G) BUDGETARY PROCEDURE

In its examination of questions linked to simplification of the budgetary procedure, the Group noted that practice had rendered null and void the articles of the EC Treaty devoted to the budgetary procedure. It also took note of the fact that the distinction between compulsory and non-compulsory expenditure, which is one of the principal causes of the complexity of the budgetary procedure, no longer reflects a real difference in nature. Finally, the Group noted that the interinstitutional agreements on budgetary discipline and improvement of the budgetary procedure, including the financial perspective, have guaranteed budgetary peace and stability in the Union since 1989.

Taking these observations into account, the Group recommends:

A. That a separate article in the constitutional part of the treaty[27] should clearly enshrine the principles governing the budgetary provisions, particularly the principle of balance between revenue and expenditure (third paragraph of Article 268 TEC), the principle of the unity of the budget (first paragraph of Article 268 TEC), the principle of budgetary discipline (Article 270 TEC), the principle of necessary means (Article 6(4) TEU), the principle of an annual budget (Article 271 TEC), the principle by which the budget is wholly financed from own resources (first paragraph of Article 269 TEC) and the principle of the prior adoption of a basic act (as set out in paragraph 5 below).

B. Simplifying and updating the budgetary procedure on the basis of the following principles:

1. There must continue to be a dual budgetary authority: European Parliament and Council. Subject to the Council having the final say over resources and over the financial perspective ceilings, the European Parliament could have the final say on expenditure in the context of cooperation already consolidated by practice. The annual procedure would therefore take place within a framework of the financial perspective given legal force by the Treaty.[28]

2. The Council must maintain its dominant role as regards the definition of the regime for the Union's resources, which must subsequently be adopted by Member States.[29]

3. A single and unique procedure must be applied to both compulsory and non-compulsory expenditure. Both will be arranged within the various headings of the financial perspective which the annual budgetary procedure must in any case respect.

4. The annual budgetary procedure could consist of a simplified co-decision procedure, on the basis of the following outline:

- Initiative of the Commission, which submits a preliminary draft budget, first reading by the EP, which adopts a draft budget, position of the Council, which proposes amendments to the draft budget, and second reading by the European Parliament, which definitively adopts the budget (the positions of the Institutions must of necessity respect the expenditure ceilings laid down in the decision on the financial perspective – see below).
- Conciliation meetings should be provided for between the first reading by the Parliament and the adoption of the Council's position, and between then and the second reading by the Parliament. The rules concerning the Conciliation Committee would apply.
- The majorities should be those laid down at present for non-compulsory expenditure: majority of members of the EP for the first reading, qualified majority of the Council for adoption of its position. If the Council does not propose amendments within a certain deadline, the budget is deemed adopted; if the Parliament accepts all the amendments proposed by the Council, the budget could be adopted by a majority of votes. On the other hand, a majority of the members of the European Parliament and three-fifths of the votes cast in the Parliament would be required to amend or reject the Council's amendments.[30]
- The timetable consolidated by the practice of the Institutions should be incorporated into the treaty.

5. A new legal basis should be included in the Treaty so as to insert a medium-term financial planning mechanism which would incorporate the general principles of the agreements on budgetary discipline and improvement of the budgetary procedure, including the financial perspective, as follows:

- The planning mechanism would be adopted on the Commission's initiative by the two arms of the budgetary authority in accordance with the procedure involving adoption by the Council following the assent of the European Parliament.
- The duration of the financial planning mechanism should coincide with the term of office of the European Parliament and of the Commission.
- The planning mechanism would include a global resources ceiling and annual expenditure ceilings per heading. A procedure could be laid down to safeguard a margin of flexibility.
- It should constitute a binding framework for the annual budget.

6. The Treaty should also regulate the links between legislation and the budgetary procedure more fully. Article 270 should be amended to include the provision established by the Interinstitutional Agreement of 1998 that the

entry of appropriations in the budget for any Community action requires the prior adoption of a basic act, understood as an act of secondary legislation which provides a legal basis for the Community action and for the implementation of the corresponding expenditure entered in the budget. It could take the form of a 'law', a 'framework law', a 'decision' or a 'regulation'.

*

* *

TRANSPARENCY

The Group believes that, as already stated in the introduction, simplification should be seen as a factor promoting democracy. The Group has therefore at all times been concerned with clarity. Citizens must be able easily to understand not only the scope of an act, but also its legitimacy. In fine, they must know who does what within the Union.

It is indispensable, to guarantee democracy, that they should be able to distinguish the responsibilities of the different Institutions and of the various players on the European scene.

To reinforce clarity, it is not sufficient to simplify procedures or instruments; the Institutions must sit in public when they are exercising legislative functions, that is, when they are defining the fundamental policy choices of the Union's action.

The Group recommends that the Convention should look very closely at how to guarantee the transparency of the legislative procedure, when it examines institutional questions.

QUALITY OF LEGISLATION

During the Group's discussions, several questions were raised in this context which go beyond even the amendment of the Treaties, and which are addressed to the Institutions which participate in legislative tasks. The Group would draw the Convention's attention to the following questions in particular:

- The need to intensify consultation with interested circles, throughout the legislative process, including regional and local authorities, and the importance of the role of associations and organizations representing those circles as an 'interface' between citizens and political players. The role of the Economic and Social Committee and the Committee of the Regions should be highlighted.
- Legislative proposals should be accompanied by an impact assessment sheet, mentioning, inter alia, consultation with the sectors affected.
- The need to have more frequent recourse to 'self-regulation' by the sectors concerned themselves, or to 'co-regulation' by cooperation between those

sectors and public authorities, always in compliance with the law, so as to streamline the decision-making process in some areas.
- The need to intensify efforts to recast and codify Community law.
- The need to improve the drafting of legislation, in the sense of clarity of language and consistency with existing legislation.

Annex II
A number of proposals were made at the meetings of the Working Group. As they failed to receive sufficient support within the Group, they are not included in the recommendations of this report.

The proposals are as follows:

- One member suggested changing the type of majority expressed in the European Parliament during the co-decision procedure. Instead of an absolute majority of its Members, the Parliament should be able to act on a majority of votes cast.
- Some members called for setting mandatory deadlines during the first reading of the co-decision procedure, or a reference in the treaties to the informal meetings between the institutions ('trialogues'). These proposals did not win sufficient support as the Group considered that the first reading constituted an essential phase for aligning positions and that, as a result, such deadlines could cause a number of procedures to fail prematurely. The effectiveness of the institutional 'trialogues' lay in their flexibility and informal nature. They should therefore not be formalised in the treaty.
- Several members of the Group expressed their concern about the level of Member States representation in the Conciliation Committee. They wanted the Conciliation Committee to be composed of elected politicians and not officials.
- Some members of the Group would like majority voting in the Council to be applied without exception throughout the co-decision procedure, including in cases where the Council adopts a position on Parliament amendments on which the Commission has expressed a negative opinion.
- Some members proposed supplementing the provisions on subsidiarity in order to allow national or regional authorities responsible for implementing a Community measure sufficient leeway to ensure that objectives were attained taking account of local circumstances.
- Several members of the Group, including the European Commission, proposed applying the co-decision procedure to the adoption of the financial perspective.
- Two members of the Working Group expressed the view that some of the suggestions on the legislative and budgetary proceedings included in the

majority report would lead to a substantial power shift from the Council to the European Parliament.

Document 6.3: Article I-11 to I-16 Treaty Establishing a Constitution for Europe

Article I-11 Fundamental Principles

1. The limits of Union competences are governed by the principle of conferral. The use of Union competences is governed by the principles of subsidiarity and proportionality.

2. Under the principle of conferral, the Union shall act within the limits of the competences conferred upon it by the Member States in the Constitution to attain the objectives set out in the Constitution. Competences not conferred upon the Union in the Constitution remain with the Member States.

3. Under the principle of subsidiarity, in areas which do not fall within its exclusive competence, the Union shall act only if and insofar as the objectives of the proposed action cannot be sufficiently achieved by the Member States, either at central level or at regional and local level, but can rather, by reason of the scale or effects of the proposed action, be better achieved at Union level.

The institutions of the Union shall apply the principle of subsidiarity as laid down in the Protocol on the application of the principles of subsidiarity and proportionality. National Parliaments shall ensure compliance with that principle in accordance with the procedure set out in that Protocol.

4. Under the principle of proportionality, the content and form of Union action shall not exceed what is necessary to achieve the objectives of the Constitution.

The institutions of the Union shall apply the principle of proportionality as laid down in the Protocol on the application of the principles of subsidiarity and proportionality.

Article I-12 Categories of Competence

1. When the Constitution confers on the Union exclusive competence in a specific area, only the Union may legislate and adopt legally binding acts, the Member States being able to do so themselves only if so empowered by the Union or for the implementation of Union acts.

2. When the Constitution confers on the Union a competence shared with the Member States in a specific area, the Union and the Member States may legislate and adopt legally binding acts in that area. The Member States shall exercise their competence to the extent that the Union has not exercised, or has decided to cease exercising, its competence.

3. The Member States shall coordinate their economic and employment policies within arrangements as determined by Part III, which the Union shall have competence to provide.

4. The Union shall have competence to define and implement a common foreign and security policy, including the progressive framing of a common defence policy.

5. In certain areas and under the conditions laid down in the Constitution, the Union shall have competence to carry out actions to support, coordinate or supplement the actions of the Member States, without thereby superseding their competence in these areas.

Legally binding acts of the Union adopted on the basis of the provisions in Part III relating to these areas shall not entail harmonisation of Member States' laws or regulations.

6. The scope of and arrangements for exercising the Union's competences shall be determined by the provisions relating to each area in Part III.

Article I-13 Areas of exclusive competence

1. The Union shall have exclusive competence in the following areas:

(a) customs union;

(b) the establishing of the competition rules necessary for the functioning of the internal market;

(c) monetary policy for the Member States whose currency is the euro;

(d) the conservation of marine biological resources under the common fisheries policy;

(e) common commercial policy.

2. The Union shall also have exclusive competence for the conclusion of an international agreement when its conclusion is provided for in a legislative act of the Union or is necessary to enable the Union to exercise its internal competence, or insofar as its conclusion may affect common rules or alter their scope.

Article I-14 Areas of shared competence

1. The Union shall share competence with the Member States where the Constitution confers on it a competence which does not relate to the areas referred to in Articles I-13 and I-17.

2. Shared competence between the Union and the Member States applies in the following principal areas:

(a) internal market;

(b) social policy, for the aspects defined in Part III;

(c) economic, social and territorial cohesion;

(d) agriculture and fisheries, excluding the conservation of marine biological resources;

(e) environment;

(f) consumer protection;

(g) transport;

(h) trans-European networks;

(i) energy;

(j) area of freedom, security and justice;

(k) common safety concerns in public health matters, for the aspects defined in Part III.

3. In the areas of research, technological development and space, the Union shall have competence to carry out activities, in particular to define and implement programmes; however, the exercise of that competence shall not result in Member States being prevented from exercising theirs.

4. In the areas of development cooperation and humanitarian aid, the Union shall have competence to carry out activities and conduct a common policy; however, the exercise of that competence shall not result in Member States being prevented from exercising theirs.

Article I-15 The coordination of economic and employment policies

1. The Member States shall coordinate their economic policies within the Union. To this end, the Council of Ministers shall adopt measures, in particular broad guidelines for these policies.

Specific provisions shall apply to those Member States whose currency is the euro.

2. The Union shall take measures to ensure coordination of the employment policies of the Member States, in particular by defining guidelines for these policies.

3. The Union may take initiatives to ensure coordination of Member States' social policies.

Article I-16 The common foreign and security policy

1. The Union's competence in matters of common foreign and security policy shall cover all areas of foreign policy and all questions relating to the Union's security, including the progressive framing of a common defence policy that might lead to a common defence.

2. Member States shall actively and unreservedly support the Union's common foreign and security policy in a spirit of loyalty and mutual solidarity and shall comply with the Union's action in this area. They shall refrain from action contrary to the Union's interests or likely to impair its effectiveness.

Article I-17 Areas of supporting, coordinating or complementary action

The Union shall have competence to carry out supporting, coordinating or complementary action. The areas of such action shall, at European level, be:

(a) protection and improvement of human health;
(b) industry;
(c) culture;
(d) tourism;
(e) education, youth, sport and vocational training;
(f) civil protection;
(g) administrative cooperation.

Document 6.4: Article 308 Treaty Establishing the European Community and article I-18 Treaty Establishing a Constitution for Europe

Treaty Establishing the European Community

Article 308 (ex Article 235)

If action by the Community should prove necessary to attain, in the course of the operation of the common market, one of the objectives of the Community and this Treaty has not provided the necessary powers, the Council shall, acting unanimously on a proposal from the Commission and after consulting the European Parliament, take the appropriate measures.

Treaty Establishing a Constitution for Europe Article I-18
Flexibility clause

1. If action by the Union should prove necessary, within the framework of the policies defined in Part III, to attain one of the objectives set out in the Constitution, and the Constitution has not provided the necessary powers, the Council of Ministers, acting unanimously on a proposal from the European Commission and after obtaining the consent of the European Parliament, shall adopt the appropriate measures.

2. Using the procedure for monitoring the subsidiarity principle referred to in Article I-11(3), the European Commission shall draw national Parliaments' attention to proposals based on this Article.

3. Measures based on this Article shall not entail harmonisation of Member States' laws or regulations in cases where the Constitution excludes such harmonisation.

Document 6.5: Articles I-33–I-39, Treaty Establishing a Constitution for Europe

Treaty Establishing a Constitution for Europe
Title V Exercise Of Union Competence
Chapter I Common Provisions

Article I-33 The Legal Acts of the Union

1. To exercise the Union's competences the institutions shall use as legal instruments, in accordance with Part III, European laws, European framework laws, European regulations, European decisions, recommendations and opinions.

A European law shall be a legislative act of general application. It shall be binding in its entirety and directly applicable in all Member States.

A European framework law shall be a legislative act binding, as to the result to be achieved, upon each Member State to which it is addressed, but shall leave to the national authorities the choice of form and methods.

A European regulation shall be a non-legislative act of general application for the implementation of legislative acts and of certain provisions of the Constitution. It may either be binding in its entirety and directly applicable in all Member States, or be binding, as to the result to be achieved, upon each Member State to which it is addressed, but shall leave to the national authorities the choice of form and methods.

A European decision shall be a non-legislative act, binding in its entirety. A decision which specifies those to whom it is addressed shall be binding only on them. Recommendations and opinions shall have no binding force.

2. When considering draft legislative acts, the European Parliament and the Council shall refrain from adopting acts not provided for by the relevant legislative procedure in the area in question.

Article I-34 Legislative Acts

1. European laws and framework laws shall be adopted, on the basis of proposals from the Commission, jointly by the European Parliament and the Council under the ordinary legislative procedure as set out in Article III-396. If the two institutions cannot reach agreement on an act, it shall not be adopted.

2. In the specific cases provided for in the Constitution, European laws and framework laws shall be adopted by the European Parliament with the participation of the Council, or by the latter with the participation of the European Parliament, in accordance with special legislative procedures.

3. In the specific cases provided for in the Constitution, European laws and framework laws may be adopted at the initiative of a group of Member States or of the European Parliament, on a recommendation from the European Central Bank or at the request of the Court of Justice or the European Investment Bank.

Article I-35 Non-legislative Acts

1. The European Council shall adopt European decisions in the cases provided for in the Constitution.

2. The Council and the Commission, in particular in the cases referred to in articles I-36 and I-37, and the European Central Bank in the specific cases provided for in the constitution, shall adopt European regulations and decisions.

3. The Council shall adopt recommendations. It shall act on a proposal from the Commission in all cases where the Constitution provides that it shall adopt acts on a proposal from the Commission. It shall act unanimously in those areas in which unanimity is required for the adoption of a Union act. The Commission, and the European Central Bank in the specific cases provided for in the Constitution, shall adopt recommendations.

Article I-36 Delegated European Regulations

1. European laws and framework laws may delegate to the Commission the power to adopt delegated European regulations to supplement or amend certain non-essential elements of the law or framework law.

The objectives, content, scope and duration of the delegation of power shall be explicitly defined in the European laws and framework laws. The essential elements of an area shall be reserved for the European law or framework law and accordingly shall not be the subject of a delegation of power.

2. European laws and framework laws shall explicitly lay down the conditions to which the delegation is subject; these conditions may be as follows:

(a) the European Parliament or the Council may decide to revoke the delegation;

(b) the delegated European regulation may enter into force only if no objection has been expressed by the European Parliament or the Council within a period set by the European law or framework law.

For the purposes of (a) and (b), the European Parliament shall act by a majority of its component members, and the Council by a qualified majority.

Article I-37 Implementing Acts

1. Member States shall adopt all measures of national law necessary to implement legally binding Union acts.

2. Where uniform conditions for implementing legally binding Union acts are needed, those acts shall confer implementing powers on the Commission, or, in duly justified specific cases and in the cases provided for in Article I-40, on the Council.

3. For the purposes of paragraph 2, European laws shall lay down in advance the rules and general principles concerning mechanisms for control by Member States of the Commission's exercise of implementing powers.

4. Union implementing acts shall take the form of European implementing regulations or European implementing decisions.

Article I-38 Principles Common to the Union's Legal Acts

1. Where the Constitution does not specify the type of act to be adopted, the institutions shall select it on a case-by-case basis, in compliance with the applicable procedures and with the principle of proportionality referred to in Article I-11.

2. Legal acts shall state the reasons on which they are based and shall refer to any proposals, initiatives, recommendations, requests or opinions required by the Constitution.

Article I-39 Publication and Entry into Force

1. European laws and framework laws adopted under the ordinary legislative procedure shall be signed by the President of the European Parliament and by the President of the Council.

In other cases they shall be signed by the President of the institution which adopted them.

European laws and framework laws shall be published in the *Official Journal of the European Union* and shall enter into force on the date specified in them or, in the absence thereof, on the twentieth day following their publication.

2. European regulations, and European decisions which do not specify to whom they are addressed, shall be signed by the President of the institution which adopted them. European regulations, and European decisions when the latter do not specify to whom they are addressed, shall be published in the *Official Journal of the European Union* and shall enter into force on the date specified in them or, in the absence thereof, on the twentieth day following that of their publication.

3. European decisions other than those referred to in paragraph 2 shall be notified to those to whom they are addressed and shall take effect upon such notification.

Document 6.6: Article III-396, Treaty Establishing a Constitution for Europe

Article III-396

1. Where, pursuant to the Constitution, European laws or framework laws are adopted under the ordinary legislative procedure, the following provisions shall apply.

2. The Commission shall submit a proposal to the European Parliament and the Council.

FIRST READING

3. The European Parliament shall adopt its position at first reading and communicate it to the Council.

4. If the Council approves the European Parliament's position, the act concerned shall be adopted in the wording which corresponds to the position of the European Parliament.

5. If the Council does not approve the European Parliament's position, it shall adopt its position at first reading and communicate it to the European Parliament.

6. The Council shall inform the European Parliament fully of the reasons which led it to adopt its position at first reading. The Commission shall inform the European Parliament fully of its position.

SECOND READING

7. If, within three months of such communication, the European Parliament:

(a) approves the Council's position at first reading or has not taken a decision, the act concerned shall be deemed to have been adopted in the wording which corresponds to the position of the Council;

(b) rejects, by a majority of its component members, the Council's position at first reading, the proposed act shall be deemed not to have been adopted;

(c) proposes, by a majority of its component members, amendments to the Council's position at first reading, the text thus amended shall be forwarded to the Council and to the Commission, which shall deliver an opinion on those amendments.

8. If, within three months of receiving the European Parliament's amendments, the Council, acting by a qualified majority:

(a) approves all those amendments, the act in question shall be deemed to have been adopted;

(b) does not approve all the amendments, the President of the Council, in agreement with the President of the European Parliament, shall within six weeks convene a meeting of the Conciliation Committee.

9. The Council shall act unanimously on the amendments on which the Commission has delivered a negative opinion.

CONCILIATION

10. The Conciliation Committee, which shall be composed of the members of the Council or their representatives and an equal number of members representing the European Parliament, shall have the task of reaching agreement on a joint text, by a qualified majority of the members of the Council or their representatives and by a majority of the members representing the European Parliament within six weeks of its being convened, on the basis of the positions of the European Parliament and the Council at second reading.

11. The Commission shall take part in the Conciliation Committee's proceedings and shall take all necessary initiatives with a view to reconciling the positions of the European Parliament and the Council.

12. If, within six weeks of its being convened, the Conciliation Committee does not approve the joint text, the proposed act shall be deemed not to have been adopted.

THIRD READING

13. If, within that period, the Conciliation Committee approves a joint text, the European Parliament, acting by a majority of the votes cast, and the Council, acting by a qualified majority, shall each have a period of six weeks from that approval in which to adopt the act in question in accordance with the joint text. If they fail to do so, the proposed act shall be deemed not to have been adopted.

14. The periods of three months and six weeks referred to in this Article shall be extended by a maximum of one month and two weeks respectively at the initiative of the European Parliament or the Council.

SPECIAL PROVISIONS

15. Where, in the cases provided for in the Constitution, a law or framework law is submitted to the ordinary legislative procedure on the initiative of a group of Member States, on a recommendation by the European Central Bank, or at the request of the Court of Justice, paragraph 2, the second sentence of paragraph 6, and paragraph 9 shall not apply.

In such cases, the European Parliament and the Council shall communicate the proposed act to the Commission with their positions at first and second readings. The European Parliament or the Council may request the opinion of the Commission throughout the procedure, which the Commission may also deliver on its own initiative. It may also, if it deems it necessary, take part in the Conciliation Committee in accordance with paragraph 11.

Document 6.7: Reprinted with the permission of *European Law Review*, from Paul Craig, 'Competence: Clarity, Conferral, Containment and Consideration', *European Law Review*, 2004, 29(3), 323–44 (selected extracts)

Introduction

It has never been easy to specify with exactitude the division of competence between the EU and Member States.[31] Concerns about the scope of EU power had been voiced for some time, and it was therefore unsurprising that it was an issue identified for further inquiry after the Nice Treaty 2000. The draft Treaty establishing a Constitution addressed the issue, and the provisions will be analysed [below].

The discussion will begin with consideration of the nature of the competence problem, and the aims of the constitutional norms in this area. It is necessary to be clear about these background issues in order to assess the constitutional articles dealing with competence. This will be followed by analysis of the principal heads of EU competence set out in the Constitution. They will be considered against the criteria of clarity, conferral and containment, which bear the meanings described in the next section. The analysis throughout will include references to technical changes that were suggested by the legal experts attached to the IGC.[32]

It is well known that the Inter-Governmental Conference was unable to agree on the draft Constitution at the European Council meeting in December 2003 for reasons concerned with the allocation of voting rights within the Council. The fate of the constitutional project remains uncertain at the time of writing [beginning of 2004]. The differences may be resolved and the project will then move forward to the next stage of ratification by the Member States. This now seems more likely following the change of government in Spain which occurred immediately after the Madrid tragedy. The Member States hope to reach agreement on the constitution by June 2004. A detailed analysis of the competence provisions is therefore warranted, more especially because the IGC did not express any major misgivings about this aspect of the draft Constitution. These provisions are then likely to form the basis for any later discussions about competences even if the broader constitutional project fails.

THE NATURE OF THE 'COMPETENCE PROBLEM'

It is clear that the issue of competence is central to the relationship between the EU and the Member States in the new constitution. This was one of the key issues singled out for further investigation after the Nice Treaty in 2000.[33]

It is important at the outset to understand the 'nature of the competence problem'. The EU has always had attributed competence: it can only operate within the powers granted to it by the Member States. This is made clear by the first paragraph of Art.5 EC and is reflected also in Art.7(1) EC. Given that this is so, what then is the nature of the competence problem? A predominant concern was that Art.5 provided scant protection for state rights, and scant safeguards against an ever-increasing shift of power from the states to the EU, notwithstanding the strictures about subsidiarity and proportionality contained in the second paragraph of Art.5. This was the rationale for the inclusion of competence as one of the issues to be addressed after the Nice Treaty.

This view of the 'competence problem' is however based on implicit assumptions as to how the EU acquires competence over certain areas. The inarticulate premise is that the shift in power upward towards the EU is the result primarily of some unwarranted arrogation of power by the EU institutions to the detriment of states' rights, which Art.5 EC has been powerless to prevent. This is an oversimplistic view of how and why the EU has acquired its current range of power. The matter is more complex and more interesting.

The reality is that the EU's power has been expanded by a broad interpretation accorded to existing Treaty provisions, either legislatively or judicially, by a teleological view of Art.308 EC (ex 235), and by the attribution of new competences to the EU through successive Treaty amendments. There are nonetheless differences of view as to the relative importance of these factors.

For some, EU competence has been expanded primarily through the broad interpretation accorded to Treaty articles, both legislatively and judicially, and through the expansive interpretation of Art.308. Others acknowledge this, but place equal emphasis on the conscious decision by the Member States to grant the EU competence in areas such as the environment, culture, health, consumer protection, employment and vocational training. I fall into this latter camp. These decisions were reached after extensive discussion within Inter-Governmental Conferences leading to Treaty revisions. The fact that the EU wields competence in such areas can scarcely be regarded as illegitimate given that the Member States consciously consented to these grants of power.

It is of course possible to accept this, and to argue also that the legislative and judicial interpretation accorded to these heads of EU competence has, on occasion, been too expansive.

[. . .]

Conclusion

There will be no attempt to summarise the reasoning in the previous pages. A number of more general conclusions can however be posited.

First, it is clear from the preceding analysis that it is important to understand Pt III of the Constitution, as well as the provisions in Pt I, in order to evaluate the provisions on competence. It is only by doing so that one can draw conclusions about the reality of the divide between EU and Member State power.

Secondly, it is clear therefore that, leaving aside the domain of exclusive competence, much will depend on the precise degree of power accorded to the EU in the particular area in question, and on how the EU chooses to exercise its power in that area. This is especially true in relation to the default category of shared competence. The Member States will lose their competence to the extent that the EU decides to exercise its competence. The same is true, albeit to a lesser degree, in relation to the category of supporting etc action. The Constitution places boundaries on EU competence in these areas, through the proscription on harmonisation. We have seen however that the specific provisions in Pt III nonetheless allow 'persuasive soft law' and 'formal laws embodying incentives'. These may, depending on their content and specificity, serve to accord a significant measure of power on real terms to the EU.

Thirdly, the difficulty of dividing power between different levels of government is an endemic problem within any non-unitary polity. So too is the problem of ensuring that central power remains within bounds.[34] Experience from elsewhere is helpful. We should nonetheless be mindful of the distinctive features of the EU. The divide between EU and Member State power is not based on a general constitutional provision, such as an inter-state commerce clause, with the courts having the principal responsibility for determining its ramifications. The EU Constitution scheme is premised on categories of competence in Pt I, coupled with detailed provisions in Pt III, which elaborate the more specific nature and bounds of EU action in the many areas that comprise EU substantive law. It is German law that is probably closest to the categories of competence developed in the EU Constitution, and it may well be that the Court of Justice will draw on that domestic jurisprudence when adjudicating on difficult issues concerning competence within the EU.

Notes

1. Care should be taken to ensure satisfactory translations into other languages.
2. Reference is made to a similar position in CONV 250/02 from the Convention Secretariat.
3. The working group did not consider classification of subject matters currently falling under pillar 2 and 3, since any such classification would greatly depend on a number of policy choices belonging to other fora of the Convention.
4. See WD 1 of working group V.
5. Case C-106/96 (Judgement of 12 May 1998).
6. Regulations may of course be necessary to establish a binding regime for the financial control over credits allocated from the Union budget in a given sector, notably the fixing of a regime for control on the spot of sums paid to the recipients and so on. Such regulations may already now, and should certainly under a future Treaty, be based on the Treaty provisions relating to budgetary competence.
7. The conclusion is based on the present legal instruments of the Union.
8. For illustration the following example of the required technical adaptation is given relating to culture, TEC Article 151(5):

   'In order to contribute to the achievement of the objectives referred to in this Article, the Council:
   - Acting in accordance with the procedure referred to in Article 251 and after consulting the Committee on the Regions, shall adopt *supporting measures,* excluding harmonisation of the laws and regulations of the Member States. The Council shall act unanimously throughout the procedure referred to in Article 251;
   - Acting unanimously on a proposal from the Commission shall, as *supporting measures,* adopt recommendations.'

9. Economic coordination as a part of the Economic and Monetary Union was not considered as this subject matter falls under another working group. TEC Article 137 as amended by the Nice Treaty was not considered by the group.
10. The group did not consider the competence of the Union under the EURATOM Treaty, which is presumably shared competence.
11. The group did not consider the competence of the Union under the EURATOM Treaty, which is presumably shared competence.
12. The working group did not discuss the consequences for Article 308 of a possible merger of the TEU and TEC or of the pillar structure of the Union. This discussion would prejudge the outcome of the work in other fora of the Convention. However, the group noted that issues of major importance could arise with respect to TEC Article 308, particularly in the event of a merger of pillars 1 and 2.
13. See Opinion 2/94.
14. See the conclusions from the European Council in Edinburgh in 1992.
15. Thus limiting the use of TEC Article 308 to the general sphere of applicability of the TEC as described in TEC Article 2.
16. The 'law' would also cover certain matters currently the subject of *sui generis* decisions ('*Beschluss*' in German) which do not have addressees and which are currently used, amongst other things, for the adoption of financial programmes or action programmes in the context of complementary competences.
17. This decision as redefined could be especially useful for the CFSP, as explained under (B) below. It would be a flexible instrument which could be applied in numerous cases, for example for appointments, certain competition measures or State aids, and so on.
18. In any case, the Group stresses that the Working Groups on External Action and on Freedom, Justice and Security will need to consider the application of these principles to areas covered by Titles V and VI of EU Treaty.
19. The effects of the regulation could be different, depending on whether it were adopted on the basis of a 'law' or a 'framework law'.
20. See section II(B)(d) below.
21. The regulation could be adopted on the basis of a 'law', or 'framework law'.

22. It would, in particular, need to be examined whether the procedure of regulatory committees, which involves call-back, should be amended or abolished.
23. Article 202, together with Articles 10 and 211, raises the question of the exercise of executive functions at Union level; this issue lies beyond the Working Group's terms of reference and should be addressed by the Convention in the debate on the Institutions. (See Annex III.)
24. The Parliament gives its assent, according to the general rule, acting by an absolute majority of votes cast (Article 198 TEC). There is only one exception to this rule: the decision on the uniform electoral procedure, which requires a majority of the members of the Parliament.
25. This is already the case at present for certain international agreements, viz. association agreements, agreements establishing a specific institutional framework, agreements having important budgetary implications and agreements entailing amendment of an act adopted by the co-decision procedure (second subparagraph of Article 300(3) TEC).
26. The present Article 190(4) TEC lays down, apart from the assent procedure, that the Council must recommend provisions relating to the electoral procedure to Member States for adoption 'in accordance with their respective constitutional requirements'. The adoption of the financial perspective would constitute another special case (see under (G) B5 below).
27. See Articles 38, 39 and 40 of the preliminary draft constitutional treaty.
28. Naturally, the following text merely provides a broad outline of the budgetary procedures. Subsequent clarification will undoubtedly be required. Moreover, certain adjustments might also be useful to take account of substantive questions yet to be decided by the Convention in another context, for example the financing of the CFSP, the inclusion of the EDF in the budget and so on.
29. See Article 269 TEC.
30. The outcome of the co-decision procedure depends on agreement being obtained between the Parliament and the Council. Unlike legislative procedures, the budgetary procedure needs a definite outcome. This proposal guarantees that a decision will be taken at the end of the procedure by giving the Parliament the last word (as is already the case now for non-compulsory expenditure). The interplay of majorities should be able to guarantee institutional balance.

    If the option of giving the Parliament the last word is rejected, and the procedure is to be concluded by agreement between the two arms of the budgetary authority, provisional remedies should be stipulated for use if the procedure fails: for example, by a readjusted system of provisional twelfths or by the application of the Commission's proposal.
31. The Division of Competences in the European Union, Directorate-General for Research, Working Paper, Political Series W 26 (1997); A. von Bogdandy and J. Bast, 'The European Union's Vertical Order of Competences: The Current Law and Proposals for its Reform' (2002) 39 C.M.L.Rev. 227; G. de Búrca, 'Setting Limits to EU Competences' Francisco Lucas Pires Working paper 2001/2002, www.fd.unl.pt/je/wpflp02a.doc; Udo di Fabio, 'Some Remarks on the Allocation of Competences between the European Union and its Member States' (2002) 39 C.M.L.Rev. 1289.
32. CIG 50/03, 2003 IGC – Draft Treaty establishing a Constitution for Europe, Brussels, 25 November 2003. The working party of legal experts was mainly concerned to tidy up the draft produced by the Convention, but did make some more substantive recommendations relating especially to Pt IV, CIG 51/03, 2003 IGC: Editorial and Legal Adjustments to the Draft Treaty establishing a Constitution for Europe and to the Protocols, Brussels, 25 November 2003.
33. Treaty of Nice, Declaration 23 [2001] O.J. C80/1.
34. For a valuable analysis, see E. Young, 'Protecting Member State Autonomy in the European Union: Some Cautionary Tales from American Federalism' (2002) **77** *N.Y.U.L.Rev.*, 1612.

7. The role of national parliaments and the principles of subsidiarity and proportionality

Document summary

See also in Chapter 6, Document 6.1: Conv 375/02, Final Report of the European Convention Working Group V on Complementary Competences, '7. Principles on the exercise of Union competence' at p. 149.

Introduction

Far from establishing a Federal Europe, the Constitutional Treaty stresses the role of Member States' constitutions and institutions, going beyond the veil of the Member State as the sole public addressee of EU law.

It does so in the wording of several articles in Part I, amongst which the most prominent are Article I-5, Relations between the Union and the Member States (Document 7.1), according to which the Union must respect the national identities of its Member States 'inherent in their fundamental structures, political and constitutional, inclusive of regional and local self government', and Article I-11, which is a restatement of Article 5 Treaty establishing the European Community (TEC) (Document 7.2) in this new context. The text of the Constitutional Treaty is clearer than that of the TEC, as the principles of conferral, subsidiarity and proportionality are now specifically named. Furthermore, the reference to the regional and local level in the wording of the principle of subsidiarity reinforces the obligation established in Article I-5 to respect Member States' structures of regional and local self-government.

The role of Member States' institutions is particularly enhanced in the two protocols on the role of National Parliaments and on application of the principles of subsidiarity and proportionality (Documents 7.3 and 7.4). The latter protocols are also to a certain extent restatements of existing protocols on the same subjects, but they include the new 'early warning' procedure for the control of the principle of subsidiarity (Document 7.4, Article 6), which strengthens the role of national parliaments, together with the provision in Protocol 2 which acknowledges the possibility for Member States to bring actions before the ECJ in the name of their respective Parliaments (Document 7.4, Article 8). A detailed examination of both protocols, which has been carried out, for instance, by the British House of Lords (Document 7.7), could lead to the conclusion that the only innovation for which an amendment to the existing EC and EU treaties is indispensable is the standing granted to the Committee of the Regions by Protocol 2 to bring an action before the ECJ.

However, it is worth noting that the existence of these procedures in Protocols 1 and 2 has led to a constitutional amendment in France and to an Act of Parliament in Germany, in order to translate them into national law (Documents 7.5 and 7.6), and that in both cases these new provisions of national law will only take effect upon the entry into force of the Constitutional Treaty. Also noteworthy are the detailed provisions of both reforms in order to allow for the participation of both chambers of Parliament.[1] In the French case, the power given to the Senate in the early warning procedure and in bringing cases to the ECJ (Article 88-5 of French Constitution, which would enter force with the Constitutional Treaty

(Document 7.8)) is of particular interest, as the Senate may well have a majority different from that of the Government, which only needs the confidence of the National Assembly. It is also worthwhile to compare the German and French reforms with the detailed considerations of the House of Lords in its Report on the early warning mechanism (Document 7.7). In most Member States, studies have been undertaken by parliaments in order to examine the advantages and drawbacks of the new procedures (Document 7.8).

These studies are significant in that they concretely show that the innovations of the Constitution for Europe have been taken very seriously – and favourably – by national institutions, often even before the processes of ratification began. One of these studies has culminated in the Pilot project run by COSAC[2] on the early warning mechanism in May 2005 (Document 7.9).

Finally, it is worth highlighting the fact that the study of the practical implications of the Constitutional Treaty's innovations has not come to a standstill with the negative referendums in France and the Netherlands. There has also been debate within the EU institutions and between Member States regarding the possibility of implementing most of these reforms without waiting for the entry into force of the Treaty: the question is not so much a legal one (is a treaty amendment indispensable to such a reform?) as it is a political one: those in favour of the Treaty establishing a Constitutional Treaty as signed in Rome on 29 October 2004 strongly resist the option of so-called 'cherry picking', which could deprive the Constitutional Treaty of some of its more appealing features as seen from the perspective of national institutions and citizens.

Document 7.1: Article I-5, Treaty Establishing a Constitution for Europe

Article I-5 Relations between the Union and the Member States

1. The Union shall respect the equality of Member States before the Constitution as well as their national identities, inherent in their fundamental structures, political and constitutional, inclusive of regional and local self government. It shall respect their essential State functions, including ensuring the territorial integrity of the State, maintaining law and order and safeguarding national security.

2. Pursuant to the principle of sincere cooperation, the Union and the Member States shall, in full mutual respect, assist each other in carrying out tasks which flow from the Constitution.

The Member States shall take any appropriate measure, general or particular, to ensure fulfilment of the obligations arising out of the Constitution or resulting from the acts of the institutions of the Union.

The Member States shall facilitate the achievement of the Union's tasks and refrain from any measure which could jeopardise the attainment of the Union's objectives.

Document 7.2: Article I-11, Treaty Establishing a Constitution for Europe

Title III Union Competences

ARTICLE I-11 FUNDAMENTAL PRINCIPLES

1. The limits of Union competences are governed by the principle of conferral. The use of Union competences is governed by the principles of subsidiarity and proportionality.

2. Under the principle of conferral, the Union shall act within the limits of the competences conferred upon it by the Member States in the Constitution to attain the objectives set out in the Constitution. Competences not conferred upon the Union in the Constitution remain with the Member States.

3. Under the principle of subsidiarity, in areas which do not fall within its exclusive competence, the Union shall act only if and insofar as the objectives of the proposed action cannot be sufficiently achieved by the Member States, either at central level or at regional and local level, but can rather, by reason of the scale or effects of the proposed action, be better achieved at Union level.

The institutions of the Union shall apply the principle of subsidiarity as laid down in the Protocol on the application of the principles of subsidiarity and proportionality. National Parliaments shall ensure compliance with that principle in accordance with the procedure set out in that Protocol.

4. Under the principle of proportionality, the content and form of Union action shall not exceed what is necessary to achieve the objectives of the Constitution.

The institutions of the Union shall apply the principle of proportionality as laid down in the Protocol on the application of the principles of subsidiarity and proportionality.

Document 7.3: Protocol 1 on the Role of National Parliaments in the European Union, annexed to the Treaty Establishing a Constitution for Europe

The High Contracting Parties,

Recalling that the way in which national Parliaments scrutinise their governments in relation to the activities of the Union is a matter for the particular constitutional organisation and practice of each Member State;

Desiring to encourage greater involvement of national Parliaments in the activities of the European Union and to enhance their ability to express their views on draft European legislative acts as well as on other matters which may be of particular interest to them,

Have Agreed Upon the following provisions, which shall be annexed to the Treaty establishing a Constitution for Europe and to the Treaty establishing the European Atomic Energy Community:

Title I Information for National Parliaments

ARTICLE 1

Commission consultation documents (green and white papers and communications) shall be forwarded directly by the Commission to national Parliaments upon publication. The Commission shall also forward the annual legislative programme as well as any other instrument of legislative planning or policy to national Parliaments, at the same time as to the European Parliament and the Council.

ARTICLE 2

Draft European legislative acts sent to the European Parliament and to the Council shall be forwarded to national Parliaments.

For the purposes of this Protocol, 'draft European legislative acts' shall mean proposals from the Commission, initiatives from a group of Member States, initiatives from the European Parliament, requests from the Court of Justice, recommendations from the European Central Bank and requests from the European Investment Bank for the adoption of a European legislative act.

Draft European legislative acts originating from the Commission shall be forwarded to national Parliaments directly by the Commission, at the same time as to the European Parliament and the Council.

Draft European legislative acts originating from the European Parliament shall be forwarded to national Parliaments directly by the European Parliament.

Draft European legislative acts originating from a group of Member States, the Court of Justice, the European Central Bank or the European Investment Bank shall be forwarded to national Parliaments by the Council.

ARTICLE 3

National Parliaments may send to the Presidents of the European Parliament, the Council and the Commission a reasoned opinion on whether a draft European legislative act complies with the principle of subsidiarity, in accordance with the procedure laid down in the Protocol on the application of the principles of subsidiarity and proportionality.

If the draft European legislative act originates from a group of Member States, the President of the Council shall forward the reasoned opinion or opinions to the governments of those Member States.

If the draft European legislative act originates from the Court of Justice, the European Central Bank or the European Investment Bank, the President of the Council shall forward the reasoned opinion or opinions to the institution or body concerned.

ARTICLE 4

A six-week period shall elapse between a draft European legislative act being made available to national Parliaments in the official languages of the Union and the date when it is placed on a provisional agenda for the Council for its adoption or for adoption of a position under a legislative procedure. Exceptions shall be possible in cases of urgency, the reasons for which shall be stated in the act or position of the Council. Save in urgent cases for which due reasons have been given, no agreement may be reached on a draft European legislative act during those six weeks. Save in urgent cases for which due reasons have been given, a ten-day period shall elapse between the placing of a draft European legislative act on the provisional agenda for the Council and the adoption of a position.

ARTICLE 5

The agendas for and the outcome of meetings of the Council, including the minutes of meetings where the Council is deliberating on draft European legislative acts, shall be forwarded directly to national Parliaments, at the same time as to Member States' governments.

ARTICLE 6

When the European Council intends to make use of Article IV-444(1) or (2) of the Constitution, national Parliaments shall be informed of the initiative of the European Council at least six months before any European decision is adopted.

ARTICLE 7

The Court of Auditors shall forward its annual report to national Parliaments, for information, at the same time as to the European Parliament and to the Council.

ARTICLE 8

Where the national Parliamentary system is not unicameral, Articles 1 to 7 shall apply to the component chambers.

Title II Interparliamentary Cooperation

ARTICLE 9

The European Parliament and national Parliaments shall together determine the organisation and promotion of effective and regular interparliamentary cooperation within the Union.

ARTICLE 10

A conference of Parliamentary Committees for Union Affairs may submit any contribution it deems appropriate for the attention of the European Parliament, the Council and the Commission. That conference shall in addition promote the exchange of information and best practice between national Parliaments and the European Parliament, including their special committees. It may also organise inter-parliamentary conferences on specific topics, in particular to debate matters of common foreign and security policy, including common security and defence policy. Contributions from the conference shall not bind national Parliaments and shall not prejudge their positions.

Document 7.4: Protocol 2 on the Application of the Principles of Subsidiarity and Proportionality, annexed to Treaty Establishing a Constitution for Europe

The High Contracting Parties,

Wishing to ensure that decisions are taken as closely as possible to the citizens of the Union;

Resolved to establish the conditions for the application of the principles of subsidiarity and proportionality, as laid down in Article I-11 of the Constitution, and to establish a system for monitoring the application of those principles,

Have Agreed Upon the following provisions, which shall be annexed to the Treaty establishing a Constitution for Europe:

Article 1

Each institution shall ensure constant respect for the principles of subsidiarity and proportionality, as laid down in Article I-11 of the Constitution.

Article 2

Before proposing European legislative acts, the Commission shall consult widely. Such consultations shall, where appropriate, take into account the regional and local dimension of the action envisaged. In cases of exceptional urgency, the Commission shall not conduct such consultations. It shall give reasons for its decision in its proposal.

Article 3

For the purposes of this Protocol, 'draft European legislative acts' shall mean proposals from the Commission, initiatives from a group of Member States, initiatives from the European Parliament, requests from the Court of Justice, recommendations from the European Central Bank and requests from the European Investment Bank for the adoption of a European legislative act.

Article 4

The Commission shall forward its draft European legislative acts and its amended drafts to national Parliaments at the same time as to the Union legislator.

The European Parliament shall forward its draft European legislative acts and its amended drafts to national Parliaments.

The Council shall forward draft European legislative acts originating from a group of Member States, the Court of Justice, the European Central Bank or the European Investment Bank and amended drafts to national Parliaments.

Upon adoption, legislative resolutions of the European Parliament and positions of the Council shall be forwarded by them to national Parliaments.

Article 5

Draft European legislative acts shall be justified with regard to the principles of subsidiarity and proportionality. Any draft European legislative act should contain a detailed statement making it possible to appraise compliance with the principles of subsidiarity and proportionality. This statement should contain some assessment of the proposal's financial impact and, in the case of a European framework law, of its implications for the rules to be put in place by Member States, including, where necessary, the regional legislation. The reasons for concluding that a Union objective can be better achieved at Union level shall be substantiated by qualitative and, wherever possible, quantitative indicators. Draft European legislative acts shall take account of the need for any burden, whether financial or administrative, falling upon the Union, national governments, regional or local authorities, economic operators and citizens, to be minimised and commensurate with the objective to be achieved.

Article 6

Any national Parliament or any chamber of a national Parliament may, within six weeks from the date of transmission of a draft European legislative act, send to the Presidents of the European Parliament, the Council and the Commission a reasoned opinion stating why it considers that the draft in question does not comply with the principle of subsidiarity. It will be for each national Parliament or each chamber of a national Parliament to consult, where appropriate, regional parliaments with legislative powers.

If the draft European legislative act originates from a group of Member States, the President of the Council shall forward the opinion to the governments of those Member States.

If the draft European legislative act originates from the Court of Justice, the European Central Bank or the European Investment Bank, the President of the Council shall forward the opinion to the institution or body concerned.

Article 7

The European Parliament, the Council and the Commission, and, where appropriate, the group of Member States, the Court of Justice, the European Central Bank or the European Investment Bank, if the draft legislative act originates from them, shall take account of the reasoned opinions issued by national Parliaments or by a chamber of a national Parliament.

Each national Parliament shall have two votes, shared out on the basis of the national Parliamentary system. In the case of a bicameral Parliamentary system, each of the two chambers shall have one vote.

Where reasoned opinions on a draft European legislative act's non-compliance with the principle of subsidiarity represent at least one third of all the votes allocated to the national Parliaments in accordance with the second paragraph, the draft must be reviewed. This threshold shall be a quarter in the case of a draft European legislative act submitted on the basis of Article III-264 of the Constitution on the area of freedom, security and justice.

After such review, the Commission or, where appropriate, the group of Member States, the European Parliament, the Court of Justice, the European Central Bank or the European Investment Bank, if the draft European legislative act originates from them, may decide to maintain, amend or withdraw the draft. Reasons must be given for this decision.

Article 8

The Court of Justice of the European Union shall have jurisdiction in actions on grounds of infringement of the principle of subsidiarity by a European legislative act, brought in accordance with the rules laid down in Article III-365 of the Constitution by Member States, or notified by them in accordance with their legal order on behalf of their national Parliament or a chamber of it.

In accordance with the rules laid down in the said Article, the Committee of the Regions may also bring such actions against European legislative acts for the adoption of which the Constitution provides that it be consulted.

Article 9

The Commission shall submit each year to the European Council, the European Parliament, the Council and national Parliaments a report on the application of Article I-11 of the Constitution. This annual report shall also be forwarded to the Committee of the Regions and to the Economic and Social Committee.

Document 7.5: Amendments to the French Constitution, 28 February 2005: extracts from the French Constitution of 4 October 1958, available at http://www.assemblee-nationale.fr

French Constitution of 4 October 1958

(This English translation was prepared under the joint responsibility of the Press, Information and Communication Directorate of the Ministry of Foreign Affairs and the European Affairs Department of the National Assembly. The French original is the sole authentic text.)

TITLE XV – ON THE EUROPEAN COMMUNITIES AND THE EUROPEAN UNION

ARTICLE 88-1

The Republic shall participate in the European Communities and in the European Union constituted by States that have freely chosen, by virtue of the treaties that established them, to exercise some of their powers in common.

It shall participate in the European Union in the conditions provided for by the Treaty establishing a Constitution for Europe signed on 29 October 2004.

ARTICLE 88-2

Subject to reciprocity and in accordance with the terms of the Treaty on European Union signed on 7 February 1992, France agrees to the transfer of powers necessary for the establishment of European economic and monetary union.

Subject to the same reservation and in accordance with the terms of the Treaty establishing the European Community, as amended by the Treaty signed on 2 October 1997, the transfer of powers necessary for the determination of rules concerning freedom of movement for persons and related areas may be agreed.

Statutes shall determine the rules relating to the European arrest warrant pursuant to acts adopted under the Treaty on European Union.

ARTICLE 88-3

Subject to reciprocity and in accordance with the terms of the Treaty on European Union signed on 7 February 1992, the right to vote and stand as a candidate in municipal elections shall be granted only to citizens of the Union residing in France. Such citizens shall neither exercise the office of mayor or deputy mayor nor participate in the designation of Senate electors or in the election of senators. An institutional Act passed in identical terms by the two assemblies shall determine the manner of implementation of this article.

ARTICLE 88-4

The Government shall lay before the National Assembly and the Senate draft proposals for legislation of the European Union together with drafts of or proposals for acts of the European Communities or the European Union containing provisions which are matters for statute as soon as they have been transmitted to the Council of the European Union. It may also lay before them other drafts of or proposals for acts or any document issuing from a European Union institution.

In the manner laid down by the rules of procedure of each assembly, resolutions may be passed, even if Parliament is not in session, on the drafts, proposals or documents referred to in the preceding paragraph.

ARTICLE 88-5

Any legislative proposal authorizing the ratification of a Treaty pertaining to the accession of a State to the European Union and to the European Communities shall be submitted to referendum by the President of the Republic.

[1] TITLE XV – ON THE EUROPEAN UNION [AS APPLICABLE AFTER THE ENTRY INTO FORCE OF THE TREATY ESTABLISHING A CONSTITUTION FOR EUROPE]

Title XV shall apply after the coming into effect of the Treaty establishing a Constitution for Europe.

Art. 88-1. – The Republic shall, in the conditions laid down by the Treaty establishing a Constitution for Europe signed on 29 October 2004, participate in the European Union constituted by States that have freely chosen to exercise some of their powers in common.

Art. 88-2. – Statutes shall determine the rules relating to the European arrest warrant pursuant to acts adopted by the Institutions of the European Union.

Art. 88-3. – The right to vote and stand as a candidate in municipal elections may be granted to citizens of the Union residing in France. Such citizens shall neither exercise the office of mayor or deputy mayor nor participate in the designation of Senate electors or in the election of senators. An institutional Act passed in identical terms by the two assemblies shall determine the manner of implementation of this article.

Art. 88-4. – The Government shall lay before the National Assembly and the Senate, drafts of or proposals for Acts of the European Union containing provisions which are of a statutory nature as soon as they have been transmitted to the Council of the European Union. It may also lay before them other drafts of or proposals for Acts or any instrument issuing from a European Union Institution.

In the manner laid down by the rules of procedure of each assembly, resolutions may be passed, even if Parliament is not in session, on the drafts, proposals or instruments referred to in the preceding paragraph.

Art. 88-5. – The National Assembly or the Senate may issue a reasoned opinion as to the conformity of a draft proposal for a European Act with the principle of subsidiarity. Said opinion shall be addressed by the President of the Assembly involved, to the Presidents of the European Parliament, the Council of the European Union and the European Commission. The Government shall be informed of said opinion.

Each Assembly may institute proceedings before the Court of Justice of the European Communities against a European Act for non compliance with the principle of subsidiarity. Such proceedings shall be referred to the Court of Justice of the European Communities by the Government.

For the purpose of the foregoing, resolutions may be passed, even if Parliament is not in session, in the manner fixed by the rules of the National Assembly or the Senate for the tabling and discussion thereof.

Art. 88-6. – Parliament may, after a motion is passed in identical terms by the National Assembly and the Senate, oppose any modification of the rules governing the passing of Acts of the European Union under the simplified revision procedure as set forth in the Treaty establishing a Constitution for Europe.

Art. 88-7. – Any legislative proposal authorizing the ratification of a Treaty pertaining to the accession of a State to the European Union shall be submitted to referendum by the President of the Republic.

Document 7.6: German Act of Parliament of 17 November 2005 on the Expansion and Consolidation of the rights of the Bundestag and Bundesrat in European Union Matters, 3178 Federal Law Gazette 2005 Part I No. 71, published in Bonn on 25 November 2005 [selected extracts, translation]

[. . .]

The Bundestag has approved the following law in agreement with the Bundesrat:

Article 1

Law on the Exercise of the rights of the Bundestag and the Bundesrat under the Treaty of 29 October 2004 establishing a Constitution for Europe

§1 UNION DOCUMENTATION

The Bundestag and Bundesrat shall regulate in their standing orders how the documents which are to be forwarded to it pursuant to articles 1 and 2 of the Protocol to the Treaty establishing a Constitution for Europe on the Role of National Parliaments in the European Union (insert: date and location of the Law implementing the Treaty establishing a Constitution for Europe) are to be treated.

§2 SUBSIDIARITY OPINIONS

(1) The Federal Government shall send to the Bundestag and the Bundesrat comprehensive information concerning all such draft legislative acts of the European Union as are to be forwarded to the Bundestag and the Bundesrat pursuant to article 2 of the Protocol to the Treaty establishing a Constitution for Europe on the Role of National Parliaments in the European Union, as soon as possible after the commencement of the 6 week deadline under article 6(1) of the Protocol to the Treaty establishing a Constitution for Europe on the application of the principles of subsidiarity and proportionality and in any case no later than two weeks after its commencement. Such notifications shall contain the necessary information for evaluating the compatibility of the draft with the principle of subsidiarity in accordance with article I-11(2) of the Treaty establishing a Constitution for Europe. The Federal Government shall to this end send to the Bundestag and the Bundesrat the official documents of the European Union institutions which were drawn up in connection with the preparation of the draft bill and which are available to the Federal Government, as well as the official position of the Federal Government.

(2) The Bundestag and the Bundesrat shall make provision in their standing orders as to how a decision concerning the delivery of a reasoned opinion in accordance with Article 6 of the Protocol to the Treaty establishing a Constitution for Europe concerning the applicability of the principles of subsidiarity and proportionality is to be drawn up.

(3) Where the Bundestag or the Bundesrat has agreed upon a reasoned opinion, the relevant president shall send it to the presidents of the European Parliament, the

Council and the Commission and shall also bring the matter to the attention of the Federal Government.

§3 SUBSIDIARITY ACTIONS

(1) The Federal Government shall inform the Bundestag and the Bundesrat as early as possible of the conclusion of a legislative procedure of the European Union, and in any case no later than one week after the publication of the European legislative act. This notification shall also contain an evaluation as to whether the Federal Government deems the legislative act to be compatible with the principle of subsidiarity in accordance with article I-11(3) of the Treaty establishing a Constitution for Europe.

(2) At the request of one parliamentary group the Bundestag may decide whether to bring an action under article 8 of the Protocol to the Treaty establishing a Constitution for Europe concerning the principles of subsidiarity and proportionality, unless this is opposed by a majority of two-thirds of the members of the Bundestag. Such opinions are to be clearly noted in the petition where requested by one or more parliamentary groups which do not support the bringing of the action. This issue shall be regulated in further detail in the standing orders of the Bundestag.

(3) The Bundesrat may regulate in its standing orders how decisions of the Bundesrat relating to the bringing of an action under Article 8 of the Protocol to the Treaty establishing a Constitution for Europe on the principles of subsidiarity and proportionality are to be reached.

(4) The Federal Government shall without delay send the action to the Court of Justice of the European Union in the name of the house which has decided to make a challenge under sub-section 2 or sub-section 3.

(5) In actions brought under article 8 of the Protocol to the Treaty establishing a Constitution for Europe concerning the principles of subsidiarity and proportionality the house which decides to make the challenge is responsible for the conduct of the action before the European Court of Justice.

(6) If a request for the bringing of an action is placed before the Bundestag or the Bundesrat, the other house may give its own opinion.

§4 BRIDGING CLAUSES

(1) The Federal Government shall inform the Bundestag and the Bundesrat whenever the Council is engaged in the preparation of an initiative (*Federal Law Gazette*, 2005 Part I No. 71, published in Bonn on 25 November 2005 p. 3179) of the European Council pursuant to article IV-444 of the Treaty establishing a Constitution for Europe.

(2) The Federal Government shall inform the Bundestag and the Bundesrat whenever the European Council takes an initiative pursuant to article IV-444 of the Treaty establishing a Constitution for Europe.

(3) The following provisions apply in relation to the opposition to initiatives of the European Council concerning the transition from unanimity to qualified majority voting for acts of the Council in accordance with article IV-444(1) of the Treaty establishing a Constitution for Europe or the transition from the special legislative procedure to the ordinary legislative procedure in accordance with article IV-444(2) of the Treaty establishing a Constitution for Europe:

1. Where an initiative essentially concerns the exclusive legislative competence of the Federation, the initiative may be opposed by a majority of the votes cast in the Bundestag.

2. Where an initiative essentially concerns the exclusive legislative competence of the Länder, the initiative may be opposed by a majority of the votes of the Bundesrat.

3. In all other cases the Bundestag or the Bundesrat may resolve to oppose such an initiative within four months of the notification of the initiative of the European Council. In these cases the initiative may only be opposed where such a decision is also rejected by the other house no later than two weeks prior to the expiry of the deadline of six months contained in article IV-444(3) of the Treaty establishing a Constitution for Europe. An initiative shall not be opposed when one house rejects the decision of the other house within this time limit, provided that it is of the opinion that the issue does not fall under points 1 or 2. If the Bundestag reaches a decision to oppose the initiative with a majority of two-thirds, the Bundesrat may in turn only reject this decision with a majority of two-thirds of its votes. If the Bundesrat reaches a decision to oppose the initiative with a majority of at least two-thirds of its votes, the Bundestag may reject this decision with a majority of two-thirds, and the majority must include at least a majority of the members of the Bundestag. The Bundestag and the Bundesrat shall make more detailed provision in their standing orders.

(4) The Presidents of the Bundestag and Bundesrat shall jointly send any resolution made pursuant to sub-section 3 to the Presidents of the European Parliament and of the European Council and shall bring the matter to the attention of the Federal Government.

(5) The Federal Government shall inform the Bundestag and Bundesrat whenever the European Parliament has agreed to an initiative taken under sub-section 2 and also whenever it receives notice of a decision of the European Council.

§5 BUNDESTAG COMMITTEE ON EUROPEAN UNION MATTERS

The Bundestag may authorize the Committee on European Union Matters appointed by it pursuant to article 45 of the Basic Law to safeguard the rights of the Bundestag according to this law.

§6 AGREEMENTS CONCERNING NOTIFICATION

The details of agreements reached pursuant to this law shall be stipulated in an agreement to be concluded between the Bundestag and the Federal Government in accordance with §6 of the Law on Cooperation between the Federal Government and the German Bundestag in European Union matters, and in an agreement to be concluded between the Federal Government and the Länder in accordance with §9 of the Law on Cooperation between the Federation and the Länder in European Union matters.

Article 2 Amendments to Other Laws

(1) The Law on Cooperation between the Federation and the Länder in European Union Matters of 12 March 1993 (BGBl. I S. 311, 1780) shall be amended as follows:

[. . .]

Article 3 Entry into Force

This law shall enter into force on the day in which the Treaty establishing a Constitution for Europe enters into force in respect of the Federal Republic in accordance with article IV-447(2) of that Treaty. This date shall be notified in the *Federal Law Gazette*. Notwithstanding sub-section 1, article 2(1)(2) shall enter into force on the day after publication.

Document 7.7 House of Lords, European Union Committee Strengthening national parliamentary scrutiny of the EU – the Constitution's subsidiarity early warning mechanism, 14th Report of Session 2004–05, Ordered to be printed 5 April 2005 and published 14 April 2005, available at http://www.parliament.uk (selected extracts)

Chapter 7: Summary of Recommendations

WHY ARE WE REPORTING ON SUBSIDIARITY NOW?

279. We believe that it is now important to focus both Parliamentary and public attention on, and to raise the profile of, subsidiarity monitoring by national parliaments (para. 22).

280. In view of the delay in establishing Parliamentary scrutiny mechanisms in the United Kingdom when the United Kingdom joined the European Community on 1 January 1973 we hope the House will ensure that this time preparations are made well in advance (para. 24).

281. We are of the view that, even if the Constitutional Treaty does not enter into force, the provisions relating to national parliaments and to subsidiarity can and should provide a stimulus to greater and more effective scrutiny by all national parliaments in the EU (para. 25).

282. In view of the significance of the proposed new mechanism for monitoring subsidiarity and of the issues arising for the House which we set out in this report we make this report to the House for debate (para. 44).

APPLYING THE SUBSIDIARITY PRINCIPLE

283. We believe that the application of the existing subsidiarity Protocol needs to be more rigorous if it is to be effective. We support the Constitutional Treaty's proposed strengthening of the principle of subsidiarity and its enhanced role in the EU lawmaking process. We in particular welcome the Constitutional Treaty's emphasis on the role of national parliaments (para. 59).

284. National parliaments and EU institutions will have to be stringent in ensuring that the principle is adhered to and that the objective of subsidiarity, to ensure that action is taken at the appropriate level, is met. In particular the Council of Ministers, which represents the interests of Member States, has a particular duty to ensure that the principle of subsidiarity is adhered to in

practice. National parliaments have a responsibility to hold their Ministers to account in this regard (para. 73).

285. The clear statement in the Protocol as to what the Commission's reasoning should encompass as regards subsidiarity is welcome and underlines the need for the Commission to research fully the factual circumstances and to consult widely before bringing forward legislative proposals. Identifying the transnational/cross-border element or genuine Union dimension should continue to be an important criterion (para. 88).

THE BENEFITS AND DRAWBACKS OF THE NEW PROTOCOL

286. We hope that the new Protocol, if enacted, will provide a vehicle for highlighting and invigorating subsidiarity compliance across the Union (para. 84).

287. We believe that improved communication is an important aim of the Protocol. A clear benefit of the new Protocol would be that the early warning mechanism would encourage and reward effective communication between national parliaments and EU institutions and amongst national parliaments themselves (para. 86).

288. Whatever their thoughts on the practicability of the early warning mechanism, parliaments are enthused by the hope that enhanced subsidiarity monitoring would lead to greater involvement of national parliaments in European lawmaking (para. 250).

289. We agree that effective scrutiny measures for EU legislation in general are necessary and will vastly improve subsidiarity monitoring across Europe (para. 258).

290. The innovation providing for draft European legislative acts to be transmitted directly to national parliaments is to be warmly welcomed (para. 132).

291. The protocols laid out in the Constitutional Treaty specify that national parliaments can only trigger the early warning mechanism if they object to the proposal on grounds of subsidiarity, not on grounds of proportionality. We regret this (para. 76).

MAKING THE MECHANISM WORK – PROCEDURE IN THE HOUSE

292. In view of the political significance of the exercise of a vote under the early warning mechanism, we recommend that the House itself should cast the vote (subject to our conclusion in paragraph 99) (para. 95).

293. We recommend that in this House the trigger for a debate and decision on whether to cast a vote under the early warning mechanism should be a report from our Committee (para. 96).

294. The House could agree that the exercise of its vote on any legislative proposal would be delegated to the EU Select Committee in the event of a six week period expiring during a recess, unless the House had already come to a decision on the proposal in question (para. 99).

295. We recommend to the House that the operation of the early warning mechanism should be kept separate from the House's current Scrutiny Reserve under which we currently operate (para. 100).

296. We recommend that the Government should not support a proposal in Council which has been the subject of a subsidiarity yellow card in either House of Parliament without first further explaining to Parliament its reasons for doing so (para. 101).

297. We disagree with the suggestion that the two Houses must coordinate their response in individual cases. However, we recognise that although each chamber has its own vote it will be desirable for the House to work with the Commons on subsidiarity issues and, where possible, for the two Houses to support each other when submitting reasoned opinions. In spite of this, it is important to note that if the two Houses do reach a different view on whether a yellow card should be raised in a particular case their votes would not cancel each other out – it will just be that the threshold is not one step closer to being reached (paras 107–8).

WORKING WITHIN THE SIX-WEEK PERIOD PROVIDED BY THE TREATY

298. As the six-week timeframe is short we fully expect the EU institutions to ensure that proposals reach national parliaments at the same time as they reach national governments to give parliaments the opportunity to scrutinize them fully and do so in the light of each other's deliberations. We warmly welcome this new system as it will strengthen the process of parliamentary scrutiny and prompt national parliaments to investigate and act on breaches of the principle of subsidiarity in good time (paras 113–14).

299. We recommend that the Commission should inform national parliaments when consultation on a legislative act is launched (para. 115).

300. We welcome the commitment by the Government to assist Parliament during the six-week period. We expect the Government to assist Parliament as early as possible in the six-week period and to provide a detailed analysis in each case of the application of the subsidiarity principle. Such an analysis should take the form of the quantitative and qualitative analysis the Commission would be required to produce by Article 5 of the Protocol (para. 134).

301. Whilst we recognise that an analysis of subsidiarity issues upstream would be beneficial, the full subsidiarity implications of EU action in a particular field would not be clear until a draft legislative proposal has been tabled (para. 145).

THE EARLY WARNING MECHANISM AND THE EU INSTITUTIONS

302. Although we recognise that the Commission has previously carried out checks on their proposals to ensure compliance with subsidiarity, the new

protocol is to be warmly welcomed as it will once again highlight this responsibility (para. 117).

303. Even below the one-third threshold, the higher the number of objections from parliaments, the greater the political pressure would be on the Institutions concerned to review the draft. However we would warn against too much tactical manoeuvring at this stage. National parliaments should examine each case on its own merits and not just act on a speculative calculation as to whether or not the threshold will be reached. If national parliaments do not act responsibly, the process will be devalued (paras 120–21).

304. We share the view that the raising of a yellow card would have a significant impact on the EU institutions. We consider that if national parliaments operate the mechanism effectively it would be hard for the Commission and the Council to resist such sustained political pressure (para. 126).

305. We conclude that the Treaty does not clearly provide whether or not the early warning mechanism applies again in the case of a legislative proposal amended during negotiations in the Council and the Parliament, and we would welcome clarification from the Government on this point (para. 141).

COLLABORATION AND COORDINATION BETWEEN NATIONAL PARLIAMENTS

306. Exchange of information between national parliaments would in our view be highly desirable to ensure the effective operation of the Protocol. Although the Commission may listen to solitary objections to placate the Member State involved, coordinated objections are likely to carry more weight. We hope, too, that the new Protocol will encourage cooperation between national parliaments for wider informative and constructive purposes (para. 155).

307. The House should continue its work of ensuring the national parliaments influence the European legislative process at all stages and should in particular continue to develop links with MEPs from all Member States (para. 260).

308. We continue to support the development of the IPEX project. When the website is ready for use it will be an invaluable tool in achieving close collaboration between national parliaments with the aim of improving subsidiarity scrutiny (para. 163).

MONITORING THE MECHANISM

309. It is unclear whether the Constitutional Treaty intends subsidiarity monitoring to be a legal or simply a political obligation for each Member State and national parliament. In practice it would be up to each parliament to decide the extent to which they would become involved in scrutinizing subsidiarity compliance. While there may be no enforceable legal obligation upon them to do so, in our view the political pressure would be such that they ought to feel obliged to carry out this scrutiny fully (para. 170).

310. It is clear that the Commission and other EU institutions would intensify their subsidiarity checks in order to preempt the raising of yellow cards by national parliaments. We welcome this (para. 176).

311. The Commission's annual report on subsidiarity is to be welcomed and will be received with interest (para. 178).

312. Subsidiarity checks by the Government, and the assessments promised under Clause 3 of the European Union Bill, should be rigorous and detailed whether or not the Protocol comes into force. The Government's subsidiarity assessment should, as now, be part of the explanatory memoranda furnished by the government on each legislative proposal (para. 180).

313. We expect, given the short time frame allowed, that the Government's subsidiarity assessment will be received by Parliament no later than two weeks after submission of the draft legislative proposal. This is the timetable to which the Government currently works. In the event of a delay in preparation of an Explanatory Memorandum, the subsidiarity analysis should if necessary be presented separately to avoid delay (para. 181).

314. The new procedures will enhance openness and accountability, by subjecting the Government's assessments to public scrutiny by Parliament, which is all for the good. In addition, we will begin our analysis of draft legislative proposals as soon as they are received (para. 182).

THE ROLE OF REGIONAL ASSEMBLIES

315. The Federal Trust suggest that 'Regional parliaments and regional authorities ought to be made aware of forthcoming legislation at the time of the presentation of the Commission's Annual Programme, and to monitor the gradual emergence of policy proposals.' We agree and recommend that the Government sets the necessary mechanisms in place (para. 199).

316. The views of regional assemblies can best be presented to Parliament through a sustained dialogue between the two authorities. Effective communication would help to ensure the smooth operation of the early warning mechanism (para. 202).

317. The two Houses should ensure that the views of regional assemblies with legislative powers submitted to one House are available to both (para. 204).

318. The potential for problems to arise from clashes of opinion between Parliament and Regional Assemblies with legislative powers should be a topic for consideration before such problems materialise. A system will have to be constructed for dealing with such differences of opinion fairly and efficiently (para. 209).

319. It is for regional and local authorities themselves to decide how best to work with their European counterparts. We recognise the potential benefits of such cooperation and would urge regional and local authorities to continue making progress in this field (para. 213).

Article 8

320. A number of questions in relation to Article 8, not least the extent to which it would impose any obligation on the executive to bring an action on behalf of the national parliament or a chamber of it (para. 215).

321. The ability of a national parliament, or a chamber of a national parliament, to trigger proceedings under Article 8 is not subject to any precondition that that parliament, or chamber of it, should have sent a reasoned opinion under Article 6. Nor is any challenge under Article 8 limited to the reasons set out in any reasoned opinion given under Article 6. Nonetheless the failure to raise the yellow card might cast doubts on the merits of a challenge where the substance of the act in question has not changed and thus have a prejudicial effect on the chances of success of a challenge (para. 221).

322. We ask the Government to clarify whether Article III-365 would apply to an action notified under Article 8 by a Member State on behalf of a national parliament (or a chamber thereof) (para. 227).

323. We do not accept that it is in accordance with the letter and the spirit of Article 8 that 'careful consideration' by the executive of a request from our Parliament (or a chamber of our Parliament) would suffice. We are also not clear what the legal or political justification of the Government's interpretation is (para. 234).

324. We ask the Government to clarify first what the position would be in the United Kingdom. Given our national 'legal order' would the executive be required to act if either House of our parliament resolved that a challenge be notified under Article 8? If not why not and is this interpretation in accordance with the provisions of Article 8? We also ask the Government to set out in full to Parliament how other Member States interpret the effect of this provision (paras 235–6).

325. In particular we ask the Government what their interpretation is of the changes recently made to the French Constitution (para. 237).

326. We ask the Government to confirm that the national parliament (or chamber) should remain in control of any application (para. 239).

327. The Protocol reaffirms that application of the principle of subsidiarity must be properly substantiated in each case. National parliaments can be expected to look closely at this and can reasonably expect the Court to do likewise (para. 243).

328. It is to be hoped that the Court will take a more critical approach to subsidiarity, particularly in ensuring that the justification for action at Union level is adequate (para. 244).

329. We recommend that the Government make it their practice, if the Constitutional Treaty comes into force, to keep Parliament fully informed of any changes to a European legislative act during its passage that might give rise to a subsidiarity objection after adoption (para. 247).

330. In this chapter 5 we have raised a number of complex but in our view highly significant questions about the meaning and effect of Article 8. We will await the answers, and the House's debate on the matters raised, with considerable interest. We will in due course return to the question whether any of these issues are matters needing to be dealt with by way of amendments to the European Union Bill (para. 248).

Document 7.8: Reprinted with the permission of the Committee of the Regions, from Charlie Jeffery, 'Subsidiarity and Proportionality: the Role of National Parliaments' in Jacques Ziller and Charlie Jeffery, *The Committee of the Regions and the Implementation and Monitoring of the Principles of Subsidiarity and Proportionality in the Light of the Constitution for Europe*, study by the European University Institute for the Committee of the Regions, Brussels, Committee of the Regions, 2006, pp. 197–214 (selected extracts)

Section 2 Provisions for Regional Parliaments with Legislative Powers in the Early Warning System

Parliaments of regions with legislative power are explicitly envisaged in the Subsidiarity Protocol (Article 6) as contributors to the early warning process, assuming the national parliaments concerned establish procedures for involving them: 'It will be for each national Parliament or each chamber of a national Parliament to consult, where appropriate, regional parliaments with legislative powers.'

There are eight member states with regions with legislative power: Austria, Belgium, Finland, Germany, Italy, Portugal, Spain and the UK, though in Finland, Portugal and the UK only special status regions qualify for the description. As with national parliaments it is in some cases unclear how the involvement of regional parliaments in the early warning system would work, though in Spain, Portugal and in Italy no direct involvement of the regional parliaments is foreseen. In all the other cases regional parliaments individually will have some form of access to the early warning process, though in two – Austria and Germany – there will also be collective rights of access via national second chambers which represent the elected authorities of legislative regions at the national level. The following provides a summary of discussions and proposals hitherto.

I. SUMMARY OF PROPOSALS IN MEMBER STATES

Austria:[3] In Austria the second chamber of the national parliament, the Bundesrat, is a regional chamber, consisting of representatives of the regional parliaments (Landtage). Since Austria's accession to the EU the Bundesrat has had a role in Austrian EU policy formulation modelled on, but less extensive than, the Bundesrat in Germany.[4] As a national parliamentary chamber it has direct access to the early warning system (and ex-post appeal) as described above. Consideration is also being given as to how individual Landtage might have their concerns represented through the Bundesrat. There is recognition that many of the Landtage lack the resources and capacity to carry out effective scrutiny of legislative proposals in the six-week early warning period (not least since they will need to be in the position to feed their opinion into the national parliamentary review process some time before the conclusion of the six-week period if they are to influence the national parliamentary position). They will therefore need to work closely with, and be guided by their regional governments, which do have fuller administrative capacities. They will also need to have early access to emerging views in the national parliament. The collective Liaison Office of the Länder, with branches in Vienna and Brussels, would play a significant role in flagging the key issues on which to concentrate subsidiarity review, though particular areas of legislation will be reviewed, according to established procedures, by a 'lead Land'. It is not considered feasible for any individual Landtag to require the Bundesrat to issue a reasoned opinion (or indeed, an ex-post appeal to the Court of Justice). The Länder are likely to establish a procedure for 'applying' to the Bundesrat to issue a reasoned opinion in the early warning process or an ex-post appeal to the Court of Justice. Given the time pressure of the six-week period, this application process would need to be delegated to the President of any Landtag acting on behalf of that Landtag.

Belgium: Belgium is a special case in which federal and regional/community governments have equality of status in EU matters. That status has produced a complex coordination system which gives the lead role in defining the Member State's position in some fields to the federal governments, in others to the regional/community governments, though in practice it involves all governments in a process of mutual accommodation in all areas of EU policy.[5] This Belgian specificity has been transformed to the new terminology of national parliaments in the Subsidiarity Protocol in a Declaration on the Constitution which clarifies that.[6]

Not only the Chamber of Representatives and Senate of the Federal Parliament but also the parliamentary assemblies of the Communities and Regions act, in terms of competences exercised by the Union, as components of the national parliamentary system or chambers of the national parliament.

A number of working groups are now engaged in developing a cooperation agreement to implement the Declaration.[7] This will confirm that references in the Constitution to 'national parliaments' apply in Belgium also and equally to regional/community parliaments, that EU information flows to regional/community parliaments are improved and guaranteed, and that all

Belgian parliaments can act autonomously in issuing reasoned opinions. The agreement will be concluded whether or not the Constitution is ratified as the regional/community parliaments are keen to develop their subsidiarity monitoring roles, for example through better information flows, come what may.

Finland:[8] The Province of Åland has a far-reaching autonomy in many fields of legislative and administrative competence, and defines Finnish EU policy in areas falling under that competence. The Åland regional parliament, like the Finnish Eduskunta, can mandate its government in EU matters. In that sense the Subsidiarity Protocol does not imply additional powers, but merely adjustments in administrative procedure. Consequently Åland regional parliament will be informed of EU legislative matters on the same basis and at the same time as the Eduskunta, will contribute to the subsidiarity review of the Grand Committee of the Eduskunta, and will be able to insist that its concerns are represented by the Grand Committee in decisions to issue reasoned opinions.

Germany: In Germany the second chamber of the national parliament, the Bundesrat, is a regional chamber, consisting of representatives of regional governments. It already possesses extensive rights of input into German EU policy formulation, including the right to define the German position in a number of policy fields. As a national parliamentary chamber it has direct access to the early warning system (and ex-post appeal) as described above. Additional consideration has been given as to how individual Landtage might initiate action by the Bundesrat in the early warning process and in ex-post appeal. In line with earlier legal research commissioned by the Land government of Baden-Württemberg the Länder have made a 'gentleman's agreement' that the Bundesrat will respond to the initiative of any individual Land on early warning or ex-post appeal, unless any other Land opposes that initiative on grounds that its 'own, fundamental interests' would be affected.[9] In principle this agreement gives all 16 German regional parliaments individually the ability to take action under the Subsidiarity Protocol. However, it should be noted that this agreement was made by regional governments and does not mention the phrase 'regional parliament' or 'Landtag'; one can expect the subsidiarity process to be absorbed into Germany's characteristic intergovernmental coordination on EU affairs, with regional parliaments limited to a subordinate role.

Italy: Italy remains in the process of introducing far-reaching constitutional reforms whose outcome will in principle significantly strengthen subnational tiers of government. Those reforms are not complete, and make it rather difficult to draw out clear implications for the role of regional parliaments in subsidiarity review. An indication is given in a note of a meeting convened in November 2004 on the coordination of national and regional parliaments in EU affairs.[10] This note suggests a steep learning curve: one of its recommendations was for regional parliaments to establish European Affairs Committees where they do not yet exist. Other recommendations of potential relevance to the Subsidiarity Protocol were at a level of generality which suggests at best an indirect and non-systematic access of Italian regional parliaments to national parliament EU scrutiny:

a. An annual meeting of national and regional parliaments on EU legislation;
b. Incorporation of regional concerns in national European Affairs Committee work;
c. Access of regional parliaments to IPEX and support for a regional-level equivalent to IPEX to facilitate exchange.

None of these recommendations suggests direct engagement with early warning. They might best be seen as a starting point from which to develop more focused procedures. Separate provisions specify that regions may request that the national government appeals to the Court of Justice on subsidiarity grounds, and that a majority of regions can require such an appeal, though these provisions are not consequent on the Subsidiarity Protocol.

Portugal: The Azores and Madeira have regional parliaments with legislative power. Their governments are included in a national coordination system on EU affairs alongside national government departments (the Interministerial Commission for Community Affairs). No specific provisions apply for this system to extend to the early warning process or to include regional parliaments in that process.

Spain: The Spanish Autonomous Communities have traditionally had only restricted rights of access to Spain's EU decision-making process, with a number of consultative mechanisms but none of the possibilities available in Austria, Belgium, Finland or Germany for regions to determine the Member State's position in specified fields. Following agreement in the national–regional Conference of Ministers for European Matters, new provisions were published in February 2005 which establish for the Autonomous Communities the right to establish the position of the Spanish Member State in a number of fields, including their representation in the Council, and to delegate officials to the Permanent Representation in Brussels. This is a long-awaited breakthrough, but appears to make no separate provisions for regional involvement in the early warning system, and remains in any case government-dominated.

The United Kingdom: The UK has three regions with legislative power: Scotland, Wales and Northern Ireland (though the regional parliament in the latter has been out of operation since October 2002). The UK has a flexible constitutional system which has very quickly established significant roles for the Scottish and Welsh governments in UK EU policy formulation, including de facto shared control of the Member State's position in some policy fields. In addition, the Scottish Parliament in particular has established perhaps the most effective parliamentary scrutiny of regional government policy of any legislative region in the EU.[11] The relative openness of the UK's EU policy processes was confirmed in the pioneering statement by the UK government at the European Convention in January 2003 that it would include UK regional parliaments with legislative power in the early warning system. Accordingly the proposals discussed above on UK national parliament preparations for the early warning process make specific reference to the consultation of regional parliaments.[12] Indeed, the Scottish and Welsh regional parliaments were the only regional parliaments consulted by the respective national parliaments in COSAC's test run of the early warning system in spring 2005.[13] There is however no sense that the UK's regional parliaments can require the national parliament to represent their views, in particular if the regional parliament view should differ from that of the national parliament.

The Scottish Parliament, reflecting its activist role in EU matters, has considered how it could operationalise the early warning system:[14]

a. It is clear that it lacks the resources to conduct in-house assessment of all EU legislative proposals, so proposes that the Scottish Government presents a check-list assessing the subsidiarity implications of proposals, with the Parliament, through its European and External Relations Committee scrutinizing the Government's assessments.
b. The Scottish Government would be expected to grade that check-list on a traffic light system, with 'green' items raising no concerns, 'amber' items for review by the Parliament's European and External Relations Committee, and 'red' items matters that clearly raise subsidiarity concerns with the Scottish Government, and on which the Scottish Parliament is likely to seek the issuing of a reasoned opinion by the UK parliament.
c. Bearing in mind the time pressures of the six-week review period, the European and External Relations Committee held out the prospect of the Committee itself conducting subsidiarity review, and taking decisions on reasoned opinions (though leaving open options for subject committee involvement and debate in plenary). Confirming the point, the Welsh Assembly noted that it had one week in which to respond to the national parliament in the COSAC test run, and also foresaw a need for special procedures, including decision 'out of Committee', that is, under the delegated authority of the Committee Convenor.[15]

II. ANALYSIS

A number of issues emerge from this review.

1) The scope of regional parliaments' input to the provisions set out in the subsidiarity protocol is patchy. Only in Belgium, the Province of Åland and

the German Länder do individual regional parliaments have the possibility that their reasoned opinions (and/or ex-post appeals) are forwarded direct to the European legislator. In Austria and the UK access of regional parliaments is indirect, described by terminology of 'consultation' and 'request' and is not guaranteed. In Italy, Spain and the Portuguese special status regions there are no provisions for such access.

2) It is clear that the six-week timescale creates serious difficulties for individual regional parliaments to organise their review procedures in a way which fits with the national parliamentary timetable. As much or more investment needs to be made in pre-legislative monitoring and consultation as in the early warning process which starts after proposals have been published, and their key provisions set firm. Pre-legislative monitoring needs to work both as a preventive measure (addressing problematic issues before they get set firm) and as a prerequisite for hitting the ground running in the early warning phase (having established views on the issue which can be fed quickly into the early warning process). As the Welsh European and External Affairs Committee put it: 'The lack of time highlights the need to identify early on issues that might breach the subsidiarity principle. This will make it easier for the complex issues to be addressed early on and maybe eliminate the need to invoke the formal procedure. But if not, it will help Members [of the Committee] come quickly to a view in the limited time available.'[16]

Two examples of good practice recommend themselves:

i. The role of the Austrian Länder Liaison Office in Brussels in identifying potentially problematic issues in the annual Work Programme of the European Commission, and thereby prompting follow-up work by the nominated 'lead Land' in the policy field concerned, including active participation in consultation processes and hearings and exchange of views with national authorities.[17]
ii. The establishment of a Brussels Office by the Scottish Parliament (that is separate from the Scottish Government office) to ensure 'that any thoughts on the problems of proposed EU legislation are addressed earlier by the European Commission through effective and direct pre-legislative consultation.[18]

3) Regional parliaments and their European Union scrutiny committees are generally poorly resourced and lack the infrastructure for comprehensive subsidiarity monitoring. In most of the cases discussed above regional parliaments will be reliant on or subordinate to their regional governments in subsidiarity review. There follows a concern that characteristically intergovernmental – and often non-transparent and poorly accountable – processes of regional engagement in EU decision making will get replicated in the early

warning system. It was not the intention of the Subsidiarity Protocol to strengthen the role of governments and intergovernmentalism. Regional parliaments need to take steps to underpin the roles the Subsidiarity Protocol opens up, including: a) establishing a division of labour between parliament and government and ensuring each understands the other's role; and b) boosting their capacities to engage in subsidiarity review which reduce their dependence on regional governments. One means of doing the latter is to improve the structures and resourcing for European Affairs Committees within regional parliaments. Another is to build new sources of expertise, for example by establishing an independent intelligence presence in Brussels, or by working more systematically in cooperation with other regional parliaments. We address this latter possibility in the next section.

Document 7.9: COSAC, Report on the Results of COSAC's Pilot Project on the 3rd Railway Package to test the 'Subsidiarity early warning mechanism', Prepared by the COSAC Secretariat and presented to the XXXIII Conference of Community and European Affairs Committees of Parliaments of the European Union 17–18 May 2005, Luxembourg, available at http://www.cosac.eu (selected extracts)

Introduction

COSAC agreed at its XXXII meeting in the Hague on 23 November 2004 to conduct a 'pilot project' in order to assess how the subsidiarity early warning mechanism provided for in the Constitutional Treaty might work in practice. COSAC chose the Commission's 3rd Railway Package as the subject for this initiative, and the pilot project was launched on 1 March 2005 and completed by national parliaments on 12 April.

All participating parliaments sent a report to the COSAC secretariat summarizing how they conducted the pilot project and setting out any lessons learnt during the experiment. As requested, the COSAC secretariat has, on the basis of these replies from the national parliaments, made this report to facilitate an exchange of views and best practices between national delegations at the XXXIII COSAC on 17–18 May in Luxembourg. The replies of the participating parliaments and the reasoned opinions are compiled in two Annexes, which are printed in a separate document.

[. . .]

2. DID ANYONE FIND A BREACH OF THE PRINCIPLE OF SUBSIDIARITY?

In total 14 parliamentary chambers indicated that they found that one or more of the legislative proposals in the 3rd Railway Package breached the principle of subsidiarity. (And 11 of these chambers adopted a reasoned opinion: see

Appendix II.) In addition, a further three national parliaments expressed doubts as to whether one or more of the four proposals conformed to the principle of subsidiarity.

The national parliaments did not, however, identify problems with the same legislative proposals.

The Voting System under the Constitutional Treaty

Each Member State national parliament has two votes in the 'early warning system'. In a unicameral parliamentary system the national parliament has two votes; in a bicameral system each parliamentary chamber has one vote. There are a total of 50 votes in the EU 25.

The Commission will 'review' a draft legislative act, if at least one-third of the national parliaments within six weeks submit a reasoned opinion that states that a proposal does not comply with the principle of subsidiarity.

This means that at least 17 of the 50 votes are needed to initiate a review of a proposal. Ten parliamentary chambers (representing ten votes) found that the proposal for a Regulation on 'compensation in cases of non-compliance with contractual quality requirements for rail freight services' (Com(2004)144) breached the principle of subsidiarity. And a further two parliaments (representing four votes) expressed doubts about the proposal's conformity with subsidiarity, but did not adopt reasoned opinions. Furthermore, one parliament (two votes) considered that the objectives of the proposal would be better achieved by Member States through existing international agreements (COTIF), but it did not say that this constituted a breach of the principle of subsidiarity. And one parliament (two votes) considered that the proposal breached the principle of proportionality, although the Protocol in the Constitutional Treaty only provides for national parliaments to send reasoned opinions on the principle of subsidiarity. [For more on the distinction between subsidiarity and proportionality, see the separate section below.]

Five parliamentary chambers (representing six votes) concluded that the proposal for a Directive on the 'certification of train crews operating locomotives and trains on the Community's rail network' (Com(2004)142) did not adhere to the principle of subsidiarity. Also, a further parliament (representing two votes) expressed doubts about the proposal's conformity with subsidiarity, but did not adopt a reasoned opinion. And one parliament (two votes) considered that the proposal breached the principle of proportionality.

Four parliamentary chambers (representing four votes) expressed doubts about the conformity with the principle of subsidiarity of the proposal for a Regulation on 'International Rail Passengers' Rights and Obligations' (Com(2004)143). Furthermore, one parliament (two votes) found that the objectives of this proposal would be better achieved through existing international agreements. And one further parliament (two votes) considered that the proposal breached the principle of proportionality.

Finally, three parliamentary chambers (representing four votes) found that the proposal for a Directive amending Council Directive 91/440/EEC 'on the development of the Community's railways' (Com(2004)139) breached the principle of subsidiarity.

[. . .]

3. WHAT WERE THE MAIN DIFFICULTIES ENCOUNTERED BY NATIONAL PARLIAMENTS?

THE LACK OF SUFFICIENT ARGUMENTS JUSTIFYING THE PROPOSALS IN TERMS OF SUBSIDIARITY

As a number of national parliaments pointed out, because the Constitutional Treaty is not in force, and the four legislative proposals examined in the pilot project were adopted by the Commission in March 2004, the Commission did not justify its proposals with regard to the principles of subsidiarity and proportionality in accordance with Article 5 of the Protocol on the application of the principles of subsidiarity and proportionality annexed to the new Treaty.

However, the concept of subsidiarity is not, of course, a new principle introduced by the Constitutional Treaty. And, as some national parliaments mentioned in their reports, there are a number of existing Treaty provisions that mean the Commission already has to justify the relevance of its proposals with regard to the principle of subsidiarity.

Despite these provisions, a large number of parliaments commented on the difficulty of reaching a decision on whether the proposals in the 3rd Railway Package complied with the principle of subsidiarity on the basis of the Commission's justifications. The justifications put forward by the Commission in the four legislative proposals examined in the pilot project were criticized as insufficient by a large number of parliaments who felt that the Commission will have to make a greater effort in this area and produce more substantial arguments. In total, 20 of the 31 participating parliamentary chambers mentioned in their reports that the Commission's justifications regarding subsidiarity and proportionality were less than satisfactory for one or more proposal.

The Belgian Senate said that the Commission's justifications regarding subsidiarity and proportionality must be systematic and explicit, demonstrating why the Commission judges that the action taken by Member States is insufficient, and, where the action of the Member States is judged to be insufficient, why it considers that the Union can better achieve the goals. The Irish Oireachtas asked the Commission to include more detailed background to its conclusions on subsidiarity and proportionality. And the Swedish Riksdag was concerned with 'the lack of proper analysis and argumentation by the Commission with regard to the subsidiarity principle' and called for the justifications to be presented 'in such a way as foreseen in the new Treaty'.

Difficulties with the Six-Week Period

A number of national parliaments reported that a six-week period (as provided for in the Constitutional Treaty) was a relatively short period of time to carry out the whole process of examining proposals and preparing reasoned opinions. In particular, parliaments raised concerns about how the timetable limited their ability to make consultations. The Parliament of Cyprus mentioned that the short amount of time available made it difficult to consult interested parties. The two Houses of the French Parliament pointed out the difficulty of consulting sectoral committees within the timeframe. And the House of Commons in the UK noted that the timetable was particularly tight if national parliaments were to consult regional parliaments with legislative powers.

The national parliaments of Slovakia and Sweden reported that the timetable could be a particular problem if parliament were not in session. The Riksdag concluded that this emphasised the need for national parliaments to follow EU proposals from an early stage and suggested that this could be done through examining the Commission's work programme and by using national parliament representatives in Brussels.

The Finnish Eduskunta pointed out that there was potential for uncertainty regarding the date from which the six-week period would start: if the six-week period starts when the last of the different language versions becomes available, by what mechanism will national parliaments be made aware of this date?

The Difficulty of Distinguishing between Subsidiarity and Proportionality

The Protocol to the Constitutional Treaty covers the application of the principles of subsidiarity and proportionality. And two national parliaments concluded that proposals in the 3rd Railway Package breached the principle of proportionality: the Luxembourg Parliament found that Com. 142 breached the principle of proportionality; and the Finnish Eduskunta found that Com. 144 breached the principle of proportionality. However, the Protocol only provides for national parliaments to send reasoned opinions on the principle of subsidiarity.

A number of parliaments (such as the French Sénat and the Hungarian Parliament) reported that it was difficult to make a distinction between the principle of subsidiarity and the principle of proportionality.

The Swedish Riksdag concluded that more work needed to be done to define the principle of subsidiarity and the criteria to be used when assessing it.

The Parliament of Cyprus questioned whether national parliaments could indeed examine legislative proposals to see whether they conform to the principle of proportionality and considered that this issue should be clarified.

Some national parliaments (such as the French Assemblée Nationale) raised a related issue, reporting that it was difficult to distinguish between opinions on the content of a proposal and opinions on whether the proposal complied with the principle of subsidiarity.

In addition, four chambers (the Czech Senate, the Estonian Parliament, the German Bundesrat and the Luxembourg Parliament) questioned what happens when a Commission proposal deals with a subject that is already regulated by existing international agreements (such as COTIF), which raises the issue of what the consequences of such an overlap are when judging a proposal against the principles of subsidiarity and proportionality.

The Difficulty of Knowing about the Results in other National Parliaments

A number of national parliaments (including the French Sénat and the German Bundesrat) reported that it was difficult for the committee considering the proposals in their parliament to know at the time of their consideration the position adopted by other national parliaments. This was because the information from other national parliaments was often not available until the end of the six-week period. The French Assemblée Nationale considered that this could lead to chambers considering proposals as late as possible within the six-week period in order to first be able to know the positions of other parliaments. The Assemblée Nationale concluded that in order to avoid this situation national parliaments would need an informal network for exchanging information within the six weeks.

The Irish Oireachtas also considered that 'encouragement be given to the development of a practical and efficient means of communicating between the national parliaments'. The Swedish Riksdag reported that several of its members 'wanted more information on what other parliaments did'. It suggested that in the future IPEX would 'facilitate the exchange of information', but it stressed that 'personal contacts/networks' would also be 'necessary'.

Notes

1. In German Constitutional Law, the Bundesrat is not strictly speaking a chamber of Parliament but a Federal Institution involved in the adoption of both legislative and regulatory norms.
2. COSAC is the French acronym for Conférence des organes spécialisés dans les affaires communautaires, that is, the 'Conference of the Community and European Affairs Committees of EU Member States' Parliaments', established by the Treaty of Amsterdam.
3. This information is derived from http://www.calre.net/documents/Working%20groups/subsidiarity/National%20docs/Austria/UnterlageBarcelona.doc and Andreas Kiefer, 'Die

regionale Dimension des Vertrags über eine Verfassung für Europa', *SIR-Mitteilungen und Berichte*, Vol. 31 (2004–5), pp. 35–7.

4. Michael Morass, 'Austria: The Case of a Federal Newcomer in European Union Politics', *Regional and Federal Studies*, Vol. 6 (1996).
5. Bart Kerremans and Jan Beyers, 'The Belgian Sub-National Entities in the European Union: Second or Third Level Players', *Regional and Federal Studies*, Vol. 6 (1996).
6. http://www.calre.net/documents/Working%20groups/subsidiarity/National%20docs/Belgium/Finalact_declBelg.doc.
7. Information supplied by officials in the Flemish government.
8. http://www.cosac.org/upload/application/pdf/f51d6748/Finnish%20model.pdf, pp. 27–8, 40.
9. http://www.berlin.de/rbmskzl/mpk/ergebnisse050414.html.
10. http://www.calre.net/documents/Working%20groups/subsidiarity/National%20docs/Italy/seminar%20nov%2004%20Italy%20EN.doc.
11. Charlie Jeffery, 'Devolution and the European Union: Trajectories and Futures', in Alan Trench (ed.), *The Dynamics of Devolution. The State of the Nations 2005* (Thorverton: Imprint Academic, 2005), pp. 189–90.
12. House of Commons Select Committee on the Modernisation of the House of Commons, *Scrutiny of European Business*, Second Report of Session 2004–05, HC 465-I, at http://www.publications.parliament.uk/pa/cm200405/cmselect/cmmodern/465/465i.pdf, p. 44; House of Lords, European Union Committee, 14th Report of Session 2004–05, *Strengthening national parliamentary scrutiny of the EU – the Constitution's subsidiarity early warning mechanism*, HL Paper 101 at http://www.publications.parliament.uk/pa/ld200405/ldselect/ldeucom/101/101.pdf, pp. 37–40.
13. *Reports from national parliaments on Pilot project*, at http://www.cosac.org/en/info/earlywarning/pilotproject/dannex/, p. 49.
14. Convenor's Report, Annex C, Briefing Paper on the Subsidiarity Early Warning System, in http://www.scottish.parliament.uk/business/committees/europe/papers-04/eup04-14.pdf, pp. 40–44.
15. http://www.wales.gov.uk.
16. Ibid.
17. Andreas Kiefer, 'Die regionale Dimension des Vertrags über eine Verfassung für Europa', *SIR-Mitteilungen und Berichte*, Vol. 31 (2004–5), p. 36.
18. Convenor's Report, Annex C, Briefing Paper on the Subsidiarity Early Warning System, in http://www.scottish.parliament.uk/business/committees/europe/papers-04/eup04-14.pdf, p. 44.

8. The area of freedom, security and justice

Document summary

Introduction

The Area of Freedom, Security and Justice demonstrates how the demand for European action may successfully mould the response far beyond the initial caution of our Member States. In the late 1980s and early 1990s, all of them were convinced that new missions should be added to the integration of our economic markets, but the great majority of them opposed the extension of the

Community method with regard to the attainment of such missions. Common goals and policies seemed to be increasingly necessary in foreign affairs, in making our industries more competitive, in education and research, in the social field and in fighting cross-border criminal activities. After a long debate on how to deal with these new missions, the Treaty of Maastricht organised all of them along the patterns of intergovernmental cooperation, which meant no transfer of regulatory powers from the State to the European level, but common standards and principles to be implemented by the Member States under their own responsibility.

Throughout the years, doubts have been increasingly raised as to the efficacy of such patterns, even in their most sophisticated instrument, the open method of coordination, which is applied to the common economic strategy named after Lisbon. It is a fact that, where the need for common action (and effective results) has been most compelling, and where the European response has not met significant opposition from the citizens, there has been a continuous change. And piece by piece, there has been a gradual extension of Community principles and instruments to areas originally reserved to intergovernmental cooperation. This is the case for the Area of Freedom, Security and Justice.

The Treaty of Maastricht more modestly referred to 'judicial and police cooperation' and consequently provided for cooperative action in the fields of immigration, police activities and judicial investigations into crimes of common interest. In a few years, firstly with the Treaty of Amsterdam in 1996 and secondly with the Treaty of Nice of 2001, this area of cooperation became the Area of Freedom, Security and Justice. Some of its elements (asylum and visa policy among them) passed under the Community's sphere of competence and new items were added by opening the door not only to crimes defined at European level but also to judicial cooperation in civil matters having cross-border implications.

However, until Nice, the transfer of such matters to the Community and hence the Community method has been partial, and the intergovernmental mechanisms have remained. Article 34 TEU (Document 8.2) is quite telling: it still provides for 'conventions' to be recommended to the Member States for adoption in accordance with their constitutional requirements, and when empowering the Council to adopt 'framework decisions for the purpose of approximation of the laws and regulations of the Member States', it is explicit in limiting their binding effect to the result to be achieved and in excluding the possibility that they may 'entail direct effect'. Furthermore, the European Court of Justice is given jurisdiction as to the legal acts of the Area of Freedom, Security and Justice, but only upon ad hoc declarations of the Member States who explicitly accept it (Article 35 TEU).

This limited (but undeniable) hybridisation has undergone several judicial tests, which on the one hand have accentuated the Community features of the Area, and on the other hand have underlined their own limits. Our documents here (Documents 8.3 to 8.7) provide evidence concerning both aspects. For the Pupino case ([Document 8.3] we give selected excerpts, but we suggest reading it in its entirety, also because it is quite intriguing) demonstrates how it happens that thin walls erected by the words of a Treaty may easily fall under the strength of the principles of that very Treaty. Frameworks decisions adopted under Article 34 are not supposed to entail direct effect. But no national judge – the Court says – can implement national laws contrary to the principles set forth in such decisions (which gives these principles an effect that it is difficult not to call 'direct').

By a framework decision, the European arrest warrant has been adopted and consequently introduced into our national systems through national legislative acts. The European warrant is an enormous step forward in fighting crime, and several citizens are ready to admit that the usefulness of Europe is mostly here. However, Europe as it is, and therefore with the existing level of hybridisation in its institutions, cannot give satisfactory answers with respect to all important criminal matters. For States whose constitutions prohibit the extradition of national citizens, is surrendering an accused citizen to another Member State something different from extraditing him/her (Document 8.5)?[1] This is the focus of some of the judicial decisions collected in this Chapter, and it is here that Europe, as it is, appears to be an open dilemma. To be sure, the relationships between its Member States are quite different from those falling under the general principles of international law, and yet they are still quite far from those of an institutional organisation, where the same constitutional principles and rules apply whenever individual rights are at stake. And this is even more the case if those principles do not entirely apply at the highest level where the 'framework' decisions are taken. In none of our national systems would regulatory decisions directly affecting fundamental rights be acceptable if such decisions were taken by the Executive and not by our Parliaments. At the European level, 'framework decisions' are adopted by the Council, and the requirement of unanimity does not change the nature of the institution: 25 Ministers representing 25 cabinets make the Council a super-Executive, not a Parliament.

This is the concern that can be read in the decision of the German Constitutional Court, formally focused upon the German statute on the European warrant (Document 8.6). It is the same concern initially expressed by that court in its famous decision on the Treaty of Maastricht. In several cases, transferring competencies to Brussels is essential for the Union to deliver what it promises. However, if the rights of citizens are affected, the democratic dimension of the European level becomes a crucial factor and those rights are adequately protected only when that dimension is comparable to our own. As long as regulatory decisions on fundamental rights remain within the jurisdiction of the Council, the level of protection is not adequate and instruments such as the European warrant raise unpleasant objections (to be remedied, whenever possible, at the national level).

Reading the Constitutional Treaty (Document 8.1) against this background gives the sense both of its continuity in pursuing the process of communitarization of the Area of Freedom, Security and Justice and, at the same time, of its rate of innovation in doing so. The remarks of Dora Kostakopoulou (Document 8.10) are illuminating from both standpoints. Framework decisions become European framework laws (on the same footing as directives), further items are to be governed by Community regulations (the Area itself becomes an area of shared competence between the Union and the Member States; see Article I-14 CT) and the range of the Council's regulations is restricted to the benefit of bicameral legislation, which satisfies the basic Maastricht standard of the German Federal Constitutional Court. There are other innovations that deserve to be noticed, first of all the clauses empowering the Union to set the threshold for individual rights in criminal proceedings: might a new European competence to promote, and not just to respect, individual rights be built on this in the future? It is an open question but it is enough to understand how far we could go, should the Constitution be approved.

The overall lesson that comes from the Area of Freedom, Security and Justice is clear and has a value that goes beyond its borders. The need for better 'delivery' is frequently portrayed as being in contrast to the need for a new Constitution. However, we are forced to realise that the two needs frequently coincide with each other, for in several respects, no improvement in delivery is feasible with the existing rules. In conclusion: if you happen to be British, and therefore pragmatic by definition, rely on a realistic analysis of the facts more than on your prejudices.

Document 8.1: Articles III-257–III-264, Treaty Establishing a Constitution for Europe

Chapter IV Area of Freedom, Security and Justice

SECTION 1 GENERAL PROVISIONS

ARTICLE III-257

1. The Union shall constitute an area of freedom, security and justice with respect for fundamental rights and the different legal systems and traditions of the Member States.

2. It shall ensure the absence of internal border controls for persons and shall frame a common policy on asylum, immigration and external border control, based on solidarity between Member States, which is fair towards third-country nationals. For the purpose of this Chapter, stateless persons shall be treated as third-country nationals.

3. The Union shall endeavour to ensure a high level of security through measures to prevent and combat crime, racism and xenophobia, and through measures for coordination and cooperation between police and judicial authorities and other competent authorities, as well as through the mutual recognition of judgments in criminal matters and, if necessary, through the approximation of criminal laws.

4. The Union shall facilitate access to justice, in particular through the principle of mutual recognition of judicial and extrajudicial decisions in civil matters.

ARTICLE III-258

The European Council shall define the strategic guidelines for legislative and operational planning within the area of freedom, security and justice.

ARTICLE III-259

National Parliaments shall ensure that the proposals and legislative initiatives submitted under Sections 4 and 5 of this Chapter comply with the principle of subsidiarity, in accordance with the arrangements laid down by the Protocol on the application of the principles of subsidiarity and proportionality.

ARTICLE III-260

Without prejudice to Articles III-360 to III-362, the Council may, on a proposal from the Commission, adopt European regulations or decisions laying down the arrangements whereby Member States, in collaboration with the Commission, conduct objective and impartial evaluation of the implementation of the Union policies referred to in this Chapter by Member States' authorities, in particular in order to facilitate full application of the principle of mutual recognition. The European Parliament and national Parliaments shall be informed of the content and results of the evaluation.

ARTICLE III-261

A standing committee shall be set up within the Council in order to ensure that operational cooperation on internal security is promoted and strengthened within the Union. Without prejudice to Article III-344, it shall facilitate coordination of the action of Member States' competent authorities. Representatives of the Union bodies, offices and agencies concerned may be involved in the proceedings of this committee. The European Parliament and national Parliaments shall be kept informed of the proceedings.

ARTICLE III-262

This Chapter shall not affect the exercise of the responsibilities incumbent upon Member States with regard to the maintenance of law and order and the safeguarding of internal security.

ARTICLE III-263

The Council shall adopt European regulations to ensure administrative cooperation between the relevant departments of the Member States in the areas covered by this Chapter, as well as between those departments and the Commission. It shall act on a Commission proposal, subject to Article III-264, and after consulting the European Parliament.

ARTICLE III-264

The acts referred to in Sections 4 and 5, together with the European regulations referred to in Article III-263 which ensure administrative cooperation in the areas covered by these Sections, shall be adopted:

(a) on a proposal from the Commission, or

(b) on the initiative of a quarter of the Member States.

Document 8.2: Articles 34–5, Treaty on European Union

Title VI Provisions on Police and Judicial Cooperation in Criminal Matters

[. . .]

ARTICLE 34 (EX ARTICLE K.6)

1. In the areas referred to in this Title, Member States shall inform and consult one another within the Council with a view to coordinating their action. To that end, they shall establish collaboration between the relevant departments of their administrations.

2. The Council shall take measures and promote cooperation, using the appropriate form and procedures as set out in this Title, contributing to the pursuit of the objectives of the Union. To that end, acting unanimously on the initiative of any Member State or of the Commission, the Council may:

(a) adopt common positions defining the approach of the Union to a particular matter;

(b) adopt framework decisions for the purpose of approximation of the laws and regulations of the Member States. Framework decisions shall be binding upon the Member States as to the result to be achieved but shall leave to the national authorities the choice of form and methods. They shall not entail direct effect;

(c) adopt decisions for any other purpose consistent with the objectives of this Title, excluding any approximation of the laws and regulations of the Member States. These decisions shall be binding and shall not entail direct effect; the Council, acting by a qualified majority, shall adopt measures necessary to implement those decisions at the level of the Union;

(d) establish conventions which it shall recommend to the Member States for adoption in accordance with their respective constitutional requirements. Member States shall begin the procedures applicable within a time limit to be set by the Council.

Unless they provide otherwise, conventions shall, once adopted by at least half of the Member States, enter into force for those Member States. Measures implementing conventions shall be adopted within the Council by a majority of two-thirds of the Contracting Parties.

3. Where the Council is required to act by a qualified majority, the votes of its members shall be weighted as laid down in Article 205(2) of the Treaty establishing

the European Community, and for their adoption acts of the Council shall require at least 62 votes in favour, cast by at least 10 members.

4. For procedural questions, the Council shall act by a majority of its members.

ARTICLE 35 (EX ARTICLE K.7)

1. The Court of Justice of the European Communities shall have jurisdiction, subject to the conditions laid down in this Article, to give preliminary rulings on the validity and interpretation of framework decisions and decisions, on the interpretation of conventions established under this Title and on the validity and interpretation of the measures implementing them.

2. By a declaration made at the time of signature of the Treaty of Amsterdam or at any time thereafter, any Member State shall be able to accept the jurisdiction of the Court of Justice to give preliminary rulings as specified in paragraph 1.

3. A Member State making a declaration pursuant to paragraph 2 shall specify that either:

(a) any court or tribunal of that State against whose decisions there is no judicial remedy under national law may request the Court of Justice to give a preliminary ruling on a question raised in a case pending before it and concerning the validity or interpretation of an act referred to in paragraph 1 if that court or tribunal considers that a decision on the question is necessary to enable it to give judgment, or

(b) any court or tribunal of that State may request the Court of Justice to give a preliminary ruling on a question raised in a case pending before it and concerning the validity or interpretation of an act referred to in paragraph 1 if that court or tribunal considers that a decision on the question is necessary to enable it to give judgment.

4. Any Member State, whether or not it has made a declaration pursuant to paragraph 2, shall be entitled to submit statements of case or written observations to the Court in cases which arise under paragraph 1.

5. The Court of Justice shall have no jurisdiction to review the validity or proportionality of operations carried out by the police or other law enforcement services of a Member State or the exercise of the responsibilities incumbent upon Member States with regard to the maintenance of law and order and the safeguarding of internal security.

6. The Court of Justice shall have jurisdiction to review the legality of framework decisions and decisions in actions brought by a Member State or the Commission on grounds of lack of competence, infringement of an essential procedural requirement, infringement of this Treaty or of any rule of law relating to its application, or misuse of powers. The proceedings provided for in this paragraph shall be instituted within two months of the publication of the measure.

7. The Court of Justice shall have jurisdiction to rule on any dispute between Member States regarding the interpretation or the application of acts adopted under Article 34(2) whenever such dispute cannot be settled by the Council within six months of its being referred to the Council by one of its members. The Court shall also have jurisdiction to rule on any dispute between Member States and the Commission regarding the interpretation or the application of conventions established under Article 34(2)(d).

Document 8.3: European Court of Justice, Decision of 16 June 2005, Pupino C-105-03, ECR I-5285 (selected extracts)

[. . .]

Jurisdiction of the Court of Justice

19. Under Article 46(b) EU, the provisions of the EC, EAEC and ECSC Treaties concerning the powers of the Court of Justice and the exercise of those powers, including the provisions of Article 234 EC, apply to the provisions of Title VI of the Treaty on European Union under the conditions laid down by Article 35 EU. It follows that the system under Article 234 EC is capable of being applied to the Court's jurisdiction to give preliminary rulings by virtue of Article 35 EU, subject to the conditions laid down by that provision.

[. . .]

33. It should be noted at the outset that the wording of Article 34(2)(b) EU is very closely inspired by that of the third paragraph of Article 249 EC. Article 34(2)(b) EU confers a binding character on framework decisions in the sense that they 'bind' the Member States 'as to the result to be achieved but shall leave to the national authorities the choice of form and methods'.

34. The binding character of framework decisions, formulated in terms identical to those of the third paragraph of Article 249 EC, places on national authorities, and particularly national courts, an obligation to interpret national law in conformity.

35. The fact that, by virtue of Article 35 EU, the jurisdiction of the Court of Justice is less extensive under Title VI of the Treaty on European Union than it is under the EC Treaty, and the fact that there is no complete system of actions and procedures designed to ensure the legality of the acts of the institutions in the context of Title VI, does nothing to invalidate that conclusion.

36. Irrespective of the degree of integration envisaged by the Treaty of Amsterdam in the process of creating an ever closer union among the peoples of Europe within the meaning of the second paragraph of Article 1 EU, it is perfectly comprehensible that the authors of the Treaty on European Union should have considered it useful to make provision, in the context of Title VI of that treaty, for recourse to legal instruments with effects similar to those provided for by the EC Treaty, in order to contribute effectively to the pursuit of the Union's objectives.

37. The importance of the Court's jurisdiction to give preliminary rulings under Article 35 EU is confirmed by the fact that, under Article 35(4), any Member State, whether or not it has made a declaration pursuant to Article 35(2), is entitled to submit statements of case or written observations to the Court in cases which arise under Article 35(1).

38. That jurisdiction would be deprived of most of its useful effect if individuals were not entitled to invoke framework decisions in order to obtain a

conforming interpretation of national law before the courts of the Member States.

39. In support of their position, the Italian and United Kingdom Governments argue that, unlike the EC Treaty, the Treaty on European Union contains no obligation similar to that laid down in Article 10 EC, on which the case law of the Court of Justice partially relied in order to justify the obligation to interpret national law in conformity with Community law.

40. That argument must be rejected.

41. The second and third paragraphs of Article 1 of the Treaty on European Union provide that that treaty marks a new stage in the process of creating an ever closer union among the peoples of Europe and that the task of the Union, which is founded on the European Communities, supplemented by the policies and forms of cooperation established by that treaty, shall be to organise, in a manner demonstrating consistency and solidarity, relations between the Member States and between their peoples.

42. It would be difficult for the Union to carry out its task effectively if the principle of loyal cooperation, requiring in particular that Member States take all appropriate measures, whether general or particular, to ensure fulfilment of their obligations under European Union law, were not also binding in the area of police and judicial cooperation in criminal matters, which is moreover entirely based on cooperation between the Member States and the institutions, as the Advocate General has rightly pointed out in paragraph 26 of her Opinion.

43. In the light of all the above considerations, the Court concludes that the principle of conforming interpretation is binding in relation to framework decisions adopted in the context of Title VI of the Treaty on European Union. When applying national law, the national court that is called upon to interpret it must do so as far as possible in the light of the wording and purpose of the framework decision in order to attain the result which it pursues and thus comply with Article 34(2)(b) EU.

44. It should be noted, however, that the obligation on the national court to refer to the content of a framework decision when interpreting the relevant rules of its national law is limited by general principles of law, particularly those of legal certainty and non-retroactivity.

45. In particular, those principles prevent that obligation from leading to the criminal liability of persons who contravene the provisions of a framework decision from being determined or aggravated on the basis of such a decision alone, independently of an implementing law (see for example, in relation to Community directives, Joined Cases C-74/95 and C-129/95 X [1996] ECR I-6609, paragraph 24, and Joined Cases C-387/02, C-391/02 and C-403/02 Berlusconi and Others [2005] ECR I-0000, paragraph 74).

46. However, the provisions which form the subject-matter of this reference for a preliminary ruling do not concern the extent of the criminal liability of

the person concerned but the conduct of the proceedings and the means of taking evidence.

47. The obligation on the national court to refer to the content of a framework decision when interpreting the relevant rules of its national law ceases when the latter cannot receive an application which would lead to a result compatible with that envisaged by that framework decision. In other words, the principle of conforming interpretation cannot serve as the basis for an interpretation of national law *contra legem*. That principle does, however, require that, where necessary, the national court consider the whole of national law in order to assess how far it can be applied in such a way as not to produce a result contrary to that envisaged by the framework decision.

Document 8.4: European Court of Justice, Decision of 15 March 2005, *Spain* v. *Commission* [Eurojust] C-160-03, ECR I-2077 (selected extracts)

[. . .]

Findings of the Court

35. First of all, it must be pointed out that it is for the applicant to choose the legal basis of its action and not for the Community judicature itself to choose the most appropriate legal basis (see, to that effect, Case 175/73 *Union syndicale and Others* v. *Council* [1974] ECR 917, and the order of the Court of First Instance in Case T-148/97 *Keeling* v. *OHIM* [1998] ECR II2217). It is clear from the examination of the action that the applicant brought it under Article 230 EC. The admissibility of that action must therefore be examined in the light of that provision.

36. As is clear from Article 230 EC, the Court shall review the legality of acts adopted jointly by the European Parliament and the Council, of acts of the Council, of the Commission and of the ECB, other than recommendations and opinions, and of acts of the European Parliament intended to produce legal effects vis-à-vis third parties.

37. Clearly, the acts contested in the present action are not included in the list of acts the legality of which the Court may review under that article.

38. Moreover, Article 41 EU does not provide that Article 230 EC is to apply to the provisions on police and judicial cooperation in criminal matters in Title VI of the Treaty on European Union, the jurisdiction of the Court in such matters being defined in Article 35 EU, to which Article 46(b) EU refers.

39. In any event, the Kingdom of Spain has not denied that the contested calls for applications are to be regarded as acts adopted under Title VI of the Treaty on European Union.

40. It follows that the action brought under Article 230 EC cannot be declared admissible.

41. As regards the right to effective judicial protection in a community based on the rule of law which, in the view of the Kingdom of Spain, requires that all decisions of a body with legal personality subject to Community law be amenable to judicial review, it must be observed that the acts contested in this case are not exempt from judicial review.

42. As is clear from Article 30 of the Decision, Eurojust staff are to be subject to the rules and regulations applicable to officials and other servants of the European Communities. It follows that, in accordance with the consistent case law, the main parties concerned, namely the candidates for the various positions in the contested calls for applications, had access to the Community Courts under the conditions laid down in Article 91 of the Staff Regulations (to that effect, see *Vandevyvere* v. *European Parliament* [. . .]).

43. In the event of such an action, Member States would be entitled to intervene in the proceedings in accordance with Article 40 of the Statute of the Court of Justice and could, where appropriate, as is clear from the second and third paragraphs of Article 56 of that Statute, appeal against the judgment of the Court of First Instance.

44. It follows from all those considerations that the application is inadmissible.

Document 8.5: Polish Constitutional Court, Decision P 1/05 of 27 April 2005, Application of The European Arrest Warrant to Polish Citizens, Summary in English, available at http://www.trybunal.gov.pl (selected extracts)

[. . .]

On 13 June 2002, the Council of the European Union issued a Framework Decision on the European arrest warrant and the surrender procedures between Member States (2002/584/JHA).

[. . .]

When Poland acceded to the European Union on 1 May 2004, it accepted the obligation to implement in full the Framework Decision of 13 June 2002. For the purpose of executing this obligation, it was primarily necessary to transpose the content of the Framework Decision into Polish legislation (framework decisions issued within the EU's Third Pillar, just as Directives issued within the First Pillar, are not directly applicable).

A divergence of opinions arose within judicial circles regarding Poland's ability to execute an EAW against its own citizens, given the prohibition on 'extraditing' Polish citizens contained in Article 55(1) of the 1997 Constitution. Alongside views expressing the opinion that an appropriate amendment of the Constitution was required, other commentators suggested that the 'surrendering' of a citizen on the basis of an EAW is a concept distinct from the notion of 'extradition' within international law, which is mirrored (in these commentators' opinions) in Article 55(1) of the Constitution. The Marshal of the Sejm and the Prosecutor General referred to the latter views in proceedings before the Constitutional Tribunal.

The Polish legislator decided to transpose the Framework Decision of 13 June 2002 by way of amendment to the Criminal Procedure Code 1997, without any accompanying alteration of the Constitution. The aforementioned amendment took place on the basis of a 2004 Act amending several criminal statutes. Two new chapters were introduced into the Criminal Procedure Code (CPC): Chapter 65a, regulating situations when a Polish court issues an EAW, and Chapter 65b, regulating situations when an EAW issued by a court of another EU Member State concerns a person present in Poland. Concomitantly, the legislator created a terminological distinction between extradition and the surrendering of a person on the basis of an EAW: in the amended Article 602 of the CPC, located in Chapter 65 (entitled 'Extradition and transport of prosecuted or convicted persons, or the delivery of material objects upon the request of foreign states'), 'extradition' is defined in a manner so as to exclude the surrendering of a person on the basis of the EAW, pursuant to the procedure regulated in Chapter 65b.

No provision in the Code expressly states that the surrendering of a person from Polish territory, on the basis of an EAW, may also apply to a Polish citizen. Such a conclusion stems, however, from certain regulations contained in Chapter 65b, as interpreted in conjunction with the Framework Decision of 13 June 2002. Namely, Article 607p of the CPC, specifying the compulsory prerequisites for refusing to execute an EAW, fails to envisage that the possession of Polish citizenship by the person to whom the warrant relates could constitute a basis for refusal to execute such a warrant (in comparison, Article 604 of the CPC, concerning extradition, states that extradition is not permissible where the person to whom the extradition relates is a Polish citizen or enjoys the right of asylum in Poland). Articles 607s and 607t successively institute certain restrictions for executing an EAW in respect of Polish citizens and persons enjoying the right of asylum in Poland, who are treated in the same way as Polish citizens.

These latter two articles of the Criminal Procedure Code differentiate the application of an EAW in respect of Polish citizens on the basis of whether an EAW was issued for the purpose of executing a previously imposed custodial sentence (or detention order), or rather for the purpose of prosecuting the person for a criminal offence. Article 607s §1 governs the first situation and states that an EAW may not be executed against a Polish citizen in the absence of their consent to the surrender. In the absence of such consent, the carrying out of the penalty takes place in Poland (Article 607s §3–5). Article 607t §1, challenged in the present case, concerns the second situation: 'Where a

European arrest warrant has been issued for the purposes of prosecuting a person holding Polish citizenship or enjoying the right of asylum in the Republic of Poland, the surrender of such a person may only take place upon the condition that such person will be returned to the territory of the Republic of Poland following the valid finalisation of proceedings in the State where the warrant was issued.'

In the present case, proceedings before the Constitutional Tribunal were initiated by the Regional Court for Gdańsk, which considered the public prosecutor's application concerning the issuance of a procedural decision on surrendering a Polish citizen (Maria D.) on the basis of an EAW, for the purpose of conducting a criminal prosecution against her in the Kingdom of the Netherlands.

The delay of loss of binding force of the unconstitutional provision, determined in part II of the ruling, runs from the date on which the judgment was announced in the *Journal of Laws* (this took place on 4 May 2005). It follows from the reasoning for the judgment that the legislator may avoid the effects of failing to adjust Polish law to the requirements of the Framework Decision by way of an appropriate amendment of the Constitution and, subsequently, the re-introduction of the statutory norm found unconstitutional in the judgment summarised herein [. . .].

The Tribunal's Ruling

I Article 607t §1 of the Criminal Procedure Code, insofar as it permits the surrendering of a Polish citizen to another Member State of the European Union on the basis of the European Arrest Warrant, does not conform to Article 55(1) of the Constitution.

II The Tribunal ruled that the loss of binding force of the challenged provision shall be delayed for 18 months following the day on which this judgment was published in the *Journal of Laws*.

Principal Reasons for The Ruling

[. . .]

7. Whilst the obligation to implement secondary European Union law, including framework decisions adopted within the Union's Third Pillar (cf. Article 32 of the Treaty on the European Union, as amended by the Amsterdam Treaty), has its basis in Article 9 of the Constitution of the Republic of Poland, the fact that a domestic statute was enacted for the purpose of implementing secondary EU law does not per se guarantee the substantive conformity of this statute with the norms of the Constitution.

8. The obligation to interpret domestic law in a manner sympathetic to EU law (so as to comply with EU law) has its limits. In particular, it stems from the jurisprudence of the Court of Justice of the European Communities (ECJ)

that EU secondary legislation may not independently (in the absence of appropriate amendments in domestic legislation) worsen an individual's situation, especially as regards the sphere of criminal liability. It is beyond doubt that the surrender of a person prosecuted on the basis of an EAW, in order to conduct a criminal prosecution against them in respect of an act which, according to Polish law, does not constitute a criminal offence, must worsen the situation of the suspect.

9. The basic function of the Constitutional Tribunal within the Polish constitutional system is to review the conformity of normative acts with the Constitution. The Tribunal is not relieved of this obligation where the allegation of non-conformity with the Constitution concerns the scope of a statute implementing European Union law.

10. Given the content of Article 9 of the Constitution, and the obligations stemming from Poland's membership of the European Union, an amendment of the currently operative law is inevitable, enabling a full and, concomitantly, constitutionally compatible implementation of the Framework Decision of 13 June 2002. In order to enable fulfilment of this task, an appropriate amendment of Article 55(1) of the Constitution may not be excluded so that this provision will envisage an exception to the prohibition on extraditing Polish citizens, so as to permit their surrender to other Member States of the European Union on the basis of an EAW.

[. . .]

15. Taking into account the complexity and more stringent requirements (also regarding the relevant time periods) governing the procedure for amending the law, as well as the fact that Poland's obligation to implement the Framework Decision of 13 June 2002 only exists from the date of Poland's accession to the EU, that is, from 1 May 2004, the Tribunal decided (in part II of the ruling) that the loss of binding force of the unconstitutional provision shall be delayed for 18 months, that is, for the maximum period of delay, as envisaged in Article 190(3) of the Constitution.

16. If, as a consequence of the present judgment, an amendment of the Constitution is introduced, it will be necessary, in order to ensure the compatibility of domestic law with EU law, to re-introduce legal provisions concerning the EAW which were found unconstitutional on the grounds of the hitherto constitutional provision.

17. The institution of the EAW has crucial significance for the functioning of the administration of justice and, primarily – as a form of cooperation between Member States assisting in the fight against crime – for improving security. Accordingly, the Polish legislator should give the highest priority to ensuring its functioning. The absence of appropriate legislative actions undertaken within the time period specified in part II of the judgment summarised herein will not only amount to an infringement of the constitutional obligation

for Poland to observe binding international law but could also lead to serious consequences on the basis of European Union law.

Document 8.6: German Constitutional Court, Decision of 18 July 2005 on the European Arrest Warrant, 2 BvR 2236/04, available at http://www.bundesverfassungsgericht.de (selected extracts) [translation]

[. . .]

62 The Law on the European Arrest Warrant breaches Article 16(2)(1) of the Basic Law because in implementing the framework decision on the European Arrest Warrant the legislature has not satisfied the constitutional requirements laid down by the qualified reservation of statutory powers contained in article 16(2)(2) of the Basic Law (1.). In removing all means of legal redress against extradition orders to a Member State of the European Union, the Law on the European Arrest Warrant breaches Article 19(4) of the Basic Law (2.).

[. . .]

69 b) Incursions into the field of protection of the basic rights contained in Article 16(2)(1) of the Basic Law are justified only where they satisfy the requirements contained in Article 16(2)(2) of the Basic Law. Since the entry into force of Article 1 of the 47th law amending the Basic Law of 29 November 2000 (BGBl I S. 1633), the Basic Law permits the extradition of German citizens to a Member State of the European Union or to an international court, subject to the fulfilment of particular requirements. It thereby opens up the internal legal order to European and international law, as well as international cooperation in the form of a controlled linkage, with a view to increasing respect for international organisations dedicated to the defence of peace and freedom as well as for international law, while also promoting the integration of the European peoples within a European Union (Article 23(1), Basic Law).

[. . .]

74 cc) The possibility of a limitation on the hitherto absolute prohibition on extradition of Germans does not entail a denationalisation of the legal order established by the Basic Law, which would be precluded by virtue of the inviolable principles contained in article 20 of the Basic Law relating to the legislative freedom in constitutional amendments (cf. Federal Constitutional Court, 89, 155, 182 et seq.).

[. . .]

75 Owing to the sectoral limitation imposed by the European prohibition on discrimination on the grounds of nationality, there is no unlawful denationalisation within the meaning of the provisions of the Basic Law as far as the extradition of Germans to other Member States of the European Union is

concerned. It is not only the case that the state retains functions of substantial importance; in addition the curtailment of the protection against extradition does not imply any renunciation of functions that are already in themselves essential state functions. The cooperation carried out under the 'third pillar' of the European Union consisting of limited reciprocal recognition, which does not entail any general harmonisation of the criminal legal systems of the Member States, is a means of protecting national identity and sovereignty in a single European legal order, in particular in view of the principle of subsidiarity (Article 23(1), Basic Law).

76 c) The legislature cannot without limitation set aside the prohibition on the extradition of Germans.

[. . .]

89 d) The Law on the European Arrest Warrant falls foul of this constitutional requirement. The approach adopted by the law enacted to realise the goals of the framework decision constitutes a disproportionate encroachment on the freedom from extradition under Article 16(2) of the Basic Law.

[. . .]

96 cc) The implementation of the framework decision into national law had to take full advantage of this leeway in order to avoid a breach by the Law on the European Arrest Warrant of the basic right to protection against extradition and any other applicable principles of the rule of law. The legislature was not at liberty to set aside in this manner the requirement to take advantage of this margin which was necessary for the protection of the relevant basic rights, not even in the light of the principle of legislative freedom. The legislature has failed to conduct the mandatory balancing operation between the cross-border European law enforcement interests and the claim to protection of Germans flowing from their status as such, incumbent on it pursuant to article 16(2) of the Basic Law and the general principle of the rule of law. It has already overlooked the requirement to strike a balance imposed by the specific reservation of statutory powers contained in Article 16(2) of the Basic Law, and has in any case not satisfied it by guaranteeing a sufficient level of protection against extradition.

[. . .]

116 The Law on the European Arrest Warrant is void (§95(3)(2), Law on the Federal Constitutional Court); it is not possible to interpret it in a manner which conforms to the constitution, or to declare partial nullity, because the German legislature must once again be able reach a freely informed legislative decision, giving consideration to constitutional standards concerning the exercise of the qualified reservation of statutory powers contained in Article 16(2)(1) of the Basic Law. Insofar as the legislature does not pass any new law implementing Article 16(2)(2) of the Basic Law, the extradition of German citizens to Member States of the European Union is unlawful.

[. . .]

Document 8.7: Italian Supreme Court [Corte Suprema Di Cassazione], Decision no. 33642/2005 on the European Arrest Warrant, available at http://www.cortedicassazione.it (selected extracts) [translation]

[. . .]

Findings of Fact and of Law

In a judgment of 17 August 2005 the Court of Appeal of Rome ordered the surrender to the judicial authorities of the United Kingdom of H.O., born in Eritrea or in Somalia on 23/7/1978, alias I.A.H., born in Ethiopia in 1978, against whom 'The Commission of the peace for England and Wales Bow Street Magistrates Court' had issued a European arrest warrant dated 29/7/2005. The trial court also deferred the surrender until a deadline of 35 days after the date of the sentence, in order to allow the Italian judicial authorities to complete investigations in progress concerning the offences falling under articles 270-bis and 497-bis of the Criminal Code in relation to which the investigating judge (GIP) of the criminal court of Rome had remanded the appellant in custody on 1 August 2005.

On 30 July 2005 the Rome police provisionally arrested O.H. alias I.A.H., because he was wanted internationally by the authorities of the United Kingdom in connection with the events which occurred in London on 21 July 2005, immediately after which the said person absconded from the city and travelled to Italy where he had already lived in the past.

[. . .]

It should at the outset be noted that the Framework Decision of the Council of the European Union of 13 June 2002 n. 2002/584/GAI, adopted pursuant to the Treaty on European Union and in particular to article 31(a) and (b) and article 34(2)(b) therein, with a view to facilitating extradition between Member States and to avoid jurisdictional conflicts, acknowledges that the mechanism of the European arrest warrant is based on a high level of confidence between the Member States and is intended to abolish extradition and replace it with a system of surrender of requested persons (according to a procedure which is more simple than that previously applicable) in the context of the implementation of the principle of mutual recognition of foreign judicial decisions in a common space founded on the shared principles of the rule of law.

The Italian law no. 69 of 2005 which makes reference to and incorporates the Framework Decision which it implements, provides that any additional information that is necessary to reach a decision may be requested from the issuing authority, in order to ensure full cooperation between the Member States (Article 16, clearly linked with Article 6(2) and the corresponding Article 15 of the Framework Decision) is to be understood in this context.

[. . .]

Besides, the tradition of the rule of law in the requesting state, whose legislation outlaws subjection to acts of persecution or discrimination, and which, with the passing of the Human Rights Act 1998, has given priority to the Convention on Human Rights of 4 November 1950 over ordinary legislation and the case law of the upper courts, provides an ample guarantee of the absence of any prejudice to the position of the appellant in the United Kingdom on account of his personal characteristics and the potential impact on the decisions of the courts of a public opinion inflamed by the terrorist attacks. Neither is it possible to interpret as a prejudicial act the failure by the United Kingdom to transmit an immediate report on the materials seized, as requested by the defence counsel of the appellant during the course of the hearing in camera before the Court of Appeal of Rome, because it was impossible to transmit a report which did not exist, and therefore the allegation of discriminatory conduct on the basis of the failure to transmit a non-existent report is purely speculative.

[. . .]

Therefore the appeal of H.O. alias I.A.H. is unfounded in respect of all heads of claim and must be rejected.

[. . .]

For these reasons

The Appeal is dismissed.

Document 8.8: Belgian Court of Arbitration [Cour d'Arbitrage], Decision 124/2005 of 13 July 2005 on the European Arrest Warrant (selected extracts) [translation]

[. . .]

Re: application for total or partial annulment of the law of 19 December 2003 concerning the European arrest warrant, presented by the non-profit association 'Advocaten voor de Wereld' [Lawyers for the World].

[. . .]

On the admissibility of the application

B.1.4. By virtue of Article 3 of its articles of association, the principal objective of the association is cooperation and development and it pursues in particular the goal of establishing, supporting and protecting throughout the world, both on a national and international level, the rule of law and procedural fairness, generally promoting human rights and, within this context, assisting accused persons, lawyers or organisations which defend human rights, carrying on the fight against poverty and defending the rights of the poor in the broadest sense.

Although it is important not to understand such a definition of the social object of a non-profit association in a literal sense as a means for allowing this association to challenge absolutely any law under the pretext that any law impinges on the rights of somebody, the court accepts that a law which regulates the means of implementation of European arrest warrants is of such a nature as to have an unfavourable impact on the social objective of the association.

[. . .]

B.3.1. The applicant claims that the framework decision is not valid because the issue of the European arrest warrant should have been implemented by a treaty and not by a framework decision, since by virtue of Article 34(2)(b) of the EU Treaty, framework decisions may only be adopted for the 'approximation of the laws and regulations of the Member States', which was not the issue in this case. The applicant requests the court to ask the Court of Justice for a preliminary ruling concerning the validity of the framework decision.

B.3.2. The contested law is the direct consequence of the decision of the Council of the European Union to use a framework decision to regulate the issue of the European arrest warrant. By virtue of Article 35(1) of the EU Treaty, the Court of Justice is the only competent organ to rule, pursuant to a preliminary ruling, on the validity of framework decisions. In accordance with Article 35(2) of the Treaty, Belgium has accepted the jurisdiction of the Court of Justice in this area.

B.3.3. Before examining the first submission, the court finds that it is necessary to refer to the Court of Justice the first question mentioned in the ruling below.

B.4. Should the Cour d'arbitrage find that the first submission is unfounded, the applicant provides, in the alternative, four submissions in support of his application for annulment.

[. . .]

B.6. The applicant's pleas against the law also apply indirectly against the framework decision of 13 June 2002, of which the law constitutes the mandatory implementation into internal law.

B.7.1. In its fourth submission, the applicant argues that Article 5(2) of the law violates the principle of equality and non-discrimination on the grounds that, in respect of the offences mentioned in this provision, there is a derogation from the requirement of double criminality which is neither reasonable nor objectively justified in the case of the implementation of European arrest warrants, whilst this requirement is maintained for other offences.

B.7.2. There is certainly a difference between the framework decision and the law, since in accordance with Article 2(4) of the framework decision, the requirement of double criminality may be maintained for offences other than those mentioned in article 2(1), whilst, according to Article 5(1) of the law, the requirement of double criminality must be maintained for offences other than those mentioned in Article 5(1).

B.7.3. The foregoing does not however prevent the framework decision or the law from containing a specific rule for a range of offences for which the assessment of the requirement of double criminality is dropped.

B.8. In its fifth submission, the applicant claims that the contested provision does not satisfy the conditions of the principle of legality in criminal matters, insofar as it does not provide a list of offences with a sufficiently clear and precise normative content, but rather only vague categories of undesirable behaviour. The judicial authorities which must decide on the execution of a European arrest warrant will, in the opinion of the applicant, have insufficient information at their disposal to allow for an effective control over whether the offences for which the requested person is being prosecuted, or in respect of which a sentence has already been passed, fall under one of the categories mentioned in Article 5(2) of the law.

The absence of a clear and precise definition of the offences provided for in Article 5(2) will, in the opinion of the appellant, result in a non-uniform application by the various authorities which are responsible for the execution of European arrest warrants and for this reason also breaches the principle of equality and non-discrimination.

B.9.1. Article 6(2) of the EU Treaty provides that:

'The Union shall respect fundamental rights, as guaranteed by the European Convention for the Protection of Human Rights and Fundamental Freedoms signed in Rome on 4 November 1950 and as they result from the constitutional traditions common to the Member States, as general principles of Community law.'

B.9.2. The principle of legality in criminal matters and the principle of equality and non-discrimination, which the applicant claims has been violated, must both be respected by the Union in accordance with Article 6(2) of the EU Treaty.

B.10. The applicant's pleas concerning the contested law apply in the same manner to the framework decision. Any differences of interpretation between the national courts concerning the validity of Community acts and the validity of the legislation which implements them in internal law would compromise the unity of the Community legal order and would undermine the general Community law principle of legal certainty.

B.11. Since, according to Articles 35 and 46 of the Treaty, the assessment of the validity of a framework decision taken under Article 34(2)(b) of the EU Treaty falls within the jurisdiction of the Court of Justice of the European Communities, whose jurisdiction in this area Belgium has recognized, the Court finds that it is necessary, before examining the fourth and fifth submissions, to refer, as a subsidiary matter, the second question mentioned in the ruling below.

For these reasons, the Court, before reaching a decision, refers to the Court of Justice of the European Communities the following questions:

1. 'Is Framework Decision 2002/584/JHA (1) of the Council of the European Union of 13 June 2002 on the European arrest warrant and the surrender procedures between Member States compatible with Article 34(2)(b) of the Treaty on European Union, under which framework decisions may be adopted only for the purpose of approximation of the laws and regulations of the Member States?'

2. 'Is Article 2(2) of Framework Decision 2002/584/JHA of the Council of the European Union of 13 June 2002 on the European arrest warrant and the surrender procedures between Member States, in so far as it sets aside verification of the requirement of double criminality for the offences listed therein, compatible with Article 6(2) of the Treaty on European Union and, more specifically, with the principle of legality in criminal proceedings guaranteed by that provision and with the principle of equality and non-discrimination?'

Document 8.9: Spanish Audiencia Nacional, Decision of 21 September 2005 on the European Arrest Warrant, available at http://www.justicia.es (selected extracts) [translation]

Full Session of the Penal Division of the Spanish Audiencia Nacional convened in accordance with art. 264 of the Law of the Judiciary to unify the criteria regarding the European Arrest Warrant in relation to the Federal Republic of Germany following the judgment of the Bundesverfassungsgericht on 18 July 2005, BVefG 18.07.2005 (2 BvR 2236/04), to go together with the Decision of the Full Session of 21 July 2005, presided by the President of the Court,

Holds:

1. In paragraph 4 of the Full Session's non jurisdictional judgment of 21 July 2005 it was held that 'once the official communication regarding the scope and effects of the German Federal Court's sentence is received, the Penal Division in Full Session will reconvene in its non-jurisdictional guise to study and revise, if necessary, this judgment which only regulates the temporary situation until the receipt of said official communication'.

No official communication has been received regarding the scope and effects of the German Federal Court's judgment different from that deriving from the proceedings started by the Central Court of Investigation in Criminal Matters (Juzgado Central de Instrucción) no. 6 for the extradition of the German national Darkazanli.

2. From this it is to be concluded that Germany has remained outside the system of cooperation mandated by the Council Framework Decision of 13 June 2002 on the European arrest warrant and the surrender procedures between Member States, as long as new internal German legislation is passed.

3. In accordance with paragraph 2 of the Full Session of 21 June's Judgment, European Arrest Warrants in force shall be considered international

arrest warrants with a view to extradition in accordance with art. 16 of The European Convention on Extradition (ECE) in conjunction with art. 8 of the Spanish Law on Passive Extradition (LEP), this fact must be made known to the German authorities, requesting of them that they, within 40 days from the date of detention (art. 10 LEP), present through diplomatic channels the documentation required in art. 12 of the ECE.

If the documentation is not presented on time the subject of the arrest warrant must be declared free, and the proceedings archived.

If it is presented on time, governmental authorization to continue the proceedings, as required by in art. 9 and 11 of the Spanish LEP, is necessary.

If this is obtained, the proceedings should continue according to the general rules regarding extradition.

The Full Session of this Court considers this to be the most appropriate interpretation for the sake of ensuring international judicial cooperation, with attention to art. 12 of the Council Framework Decision on the European Arrest Warrant and the doctrine laid down by the ECJ (Grand Chamber) on 16 June 2005 (case C-105/03, the Pupino Judgment) according to which a national judge must bear in mind the content of a Framework Decision when interpreting the corresponding norms of his/her domestic law (the principle of Conforming Interpretation).

4. The procedures laid down by Law 3/2003, of 14 March, on the European arrest warrant, shall not apply to European Arrest Warrant proceedings when the State which puts out the warrant is Germany (temporary provision according to point 3 of the Law and the principle of reciprocity contained in art. 13.3 of the Constitution).

Document 8.10: Reprinted with the permission of the Academy of European Law, from Dora Kostakopoulou, 'The Area of Freedom, Security and Justice and the European Union's Constitutional Dialogue', Academy of European Law lectures, summer school 2005, European University Institute (selected extracts)

[. . .]

Lacking a robust institutional framework and the clearly defined goals that characterise other EU policy fields, JHA cooperation has always been in transition in some form or another.

The Convention's deliberations concerning the area of freedom, security and justice and the Constitutional Treaty that sprung from the Convention's work are good cases in point.[2] The Constitutional Treaty completed the process of transition from intergovernmentalism to supranationalism and opened up the possibility for better and more efficient law making in JHA matters and for a more open and accountable EU. The infrastructure has also been laid down for a more proactive and better coordinated JHA cooperation, and the principle of mutual recognition clearly enhances the array of policy options at the Union's disposal. Although the ratification crisis prompted by the French and Dutch referenda has stalled progress and has sparked lively debates, such as whether the Treaty is 'dead' or 'in a coma',[3] simply relying on the Nice settlement is unlikely to be a viable option for the Area of Freedom, Security and Justice. Nor can it be argued that the key reforms in the institutional framework and procedures in this area introduced by the Constitutional Treaty can be adopted by a series of interinstitutional agreements.[4]

But irrespective of whether one concedes that the Constitutional Treaty is unlikely to be salvaged in its current form and that some kind of Treaty amendment will be needed in the near future, both the evolution of JHA and the present debate about the constitutional future of the EU are poignant reminders of the fact that EU constitutionalism is, essentially, an ongoing discursive engagement with the principles and terms of European governance and with institutional design.[5] In this respect, old and new debates, such as whether the Constitutional Treaty was a treaty or a constitution; or whether it represented 'a critical moment' for shaking off the institutional past[6] or constituted an exercise in simplification and consolidation;[7] or whether the Constitutional Treaty could be salvaged as a whole or in parts (Part I and II), and the merits and demerits of a second referendum in France and the Netherlands, all make important contributions to the European constitutional dialogue.

More importantly, irrespective of the form that institutional reform takes and of whether the constitutional language and symbolism are retained in the future,[8] it is important to bear in mind that any future revision of the provisions concerning the AFSJ, as indeed any other revision that has preceded it, will be both a consolidating and a transformative project. Provisions that preserve, conserve, confirm the institutional balance and consolidate existing relations will thus be interwoven with provisions that destabilize and generate new openings. For institutional change in the EU is neither a process of simple iteration nor the result of radical breaks. It is, instead, incremental–transformative, that is, the product of a complex mix of consolidation and transformation, of a vision and a compromise. European integration has been a journey in institutional experimentation, reflection and critique, and gradients, be they ascending or descending, by and large, make journeys interesting.

The discussion in this chapter maps the evolution of justice and home affairs cooperation since 1975. In this 'constitutional odyssey',[9] attention will be paid to the process of incremental–transformative change culminating in the provisions of the Constitutional Treaty. By bringing JHA cooperation in line with the Community method, the Constitutional Treaty brought about the most significant institutional innovations in this area. And although it is true that JHA cooperation will not be marked by stagnation in the absence of the Constitutional Treaty, it is equally true that the Constitutional Treaty's provisions are bound to be the point of departure for any future discussion about institutional reform and Treaty amendment in this area.

[. . .]

3. Recasting the Institutional Design: the Constitutional Treaty

The Convention and the ensuing Constitutional Treaty initiated a 'deeper and wider debate' about European governance; they addressed issues that strike at the heart of the EU's constitutional framework, including the pillared architecture of the Union. Introduced by the Treaty on European Union (1992), the pillared structure has resulted in unnecessarily complex institutional configurations, has hindered effective policy making and the implementation of law, has preserved executive domination at the expense of democratic accountability and judicial scrutiny, and has given rise to jurisdictional conflicts owing to divergent positions about the correct legal base for an act.[10]

The Convention's Working Group on Justice and Home Affairs (Working Group X 'Freedom, Security and Justice') produced its final report on 28 November 2002.[11] The report was followed by a lively plenary debate and, following various amendments, it culminated in a revised draft. The latter entailed a number of reforms based on two 'golden rules'; namely, a) the formal abolition of the pillared structure and the unification of the legal framework in justice and home affairs matters, and b) the separation between 'legislative' and 'operational' tasks within the Union and reinforced coordination of operational collaboration at Union level. The latter could be achieved by the creation of a more efficient structure for the coordination of operational cooperation at high technical level within the Council; namely, a new standing Committee which would coordinate the activities of the various bodies dealing with (broadly defined) 'internal security'. The report also suggested the standardisation of co-decision and qualified majority voting in JHA matters, that is, its application to all areas in Title IV EC, with the exception of measures concerning family law with cross-border implications, and to most areas of the revised third pillar.[12] Following the Tampere 'milestones', the Report also recommended the inclusion of the principle of mutual recognition of judicial and extrajudicial decisions in the Constitutional Treaty and suggested further progress in the field of the approximation of certain elements of criminal procedure and substantive criminal law.

The Brussels European Council managed to secure agreement on the Constitutional Treaty on 18 June 2004, which was then signed on 29 October 2004 in Rome. The Constitutional Treaty abolishes the pillared structure, thereby placing all justice and home affairs matters under a single institutional framework. The unification of law making will result in a simpler institutional configuration. The distinctive third pillar instruments (that is, common positions, framework decisions, decisions and conventions) will be replaced by European laws (directly applicable regulations) and framework laws (directives). Co-decision will be standardised, and unanimity will be replaced by qualified majority voting at least in those areas where there are not divergent national positions. The Commission's exclusive right of initiative is strengthened and the European Court of Justice assumes full jurisdiction to all JHA matters, with the exception of the validity and proportionality of policing actions.

One of the objectives of the Union is to offer its citizens 'an area of freedom, security and justice without internal frontiers, and a single market where competition is free and undistorted' (I-3(2)). Although the specific objectives of this policy area are defined in greater detail in Part III of the Treaty and in Article I-42 which states that 'the Union shall constitute an area of freedom, security and justice', Article I-3(2) will, nevertheless, function as an interpretational aid to the definition and implementation of AFSJ. According to Article I-42, the AFSJ will be achieved by combining positive and negative integration and by enhancing the operational cooperation among the competent authorities of the MS, including the police, customs and other authorities specialising in the prevention and detection of criminal offences (Article I-42). It may be observed, here, that the above means are not novel; legislative harmonisation and operational cooperation were envisaged by the Treaty of Amsterdam (Articles 29, 34(2) and 30(1)(a) EU), while mutual recognition, which was first included in the Presidency Conclusions of the Cardiff European Council in June 1998, was explicitly endorsed by the Tampere European Council (October 1999).[13] Interestingly, the Treaty does not envisage the creation of federal agencies endowed with executive power. It relies, instead, on the horizontal cooperation of law enforcement authorities. In addition, the AFSJ is expressly stated to be an area of shared competence, while new legal bases have been created concerning the integrated management of external borders (Article III-265), criminal procedure (III-270(2)) and the establishment of a European Public Prosecutor's Office (Article III-274).

The Constitutional Treaty strengthens the Commission's right of initiative by giving it exclusive power to propose legislation in migration and asylum related matters.[14] This will shield the Community interest against possible resurgence of intergovernmentalism. However, the Constitutional Treaty also preserves the MS's right to bring forward legislative initiatives in the fields of police and criminal judicial cooperation (Article I-42(3)). While at present any MS can propose legislation in this area, Working Group X had suggested the introduction of a threshold of either one-third or one-quarter or even one-fifth of the Member States for a MS initiative to be admissible. Following this suggestion, the Treaty (Article III-264) states that a quarter of MS can bring forward legislative initiatives in criminal matters including the operational cooperation between administrative and police bodies of the MS. The imposition of this threshold will prevent governments from taking politically expedient decisions reflecting national political situations and the perceptions or interests of national elites. The exercise of a MS initiative would thus have to reflect a wider European interest and to promote the development of the Union.

The Constitutional Treaty increased the EP's powers. Co-decision is stated to be the 'ordinary legislative procedure'; the traditional consultation and consent procedures are 'special legislative procedures'. The reach of the co-decision procedure has also been extended to cover more areas than hitherto (from 37 to 80 to 90 domains), thereby enhancing the democratic credentials of European legislation. What is important is the extension of co-decision to police and criminal judicial cooperation matters where the EP has currently only a consultative role. Making the EP a genuine co-legislator will bring about greater accountability in this policy field and will facilitate effective scrutiny.

The scope of QMV has also been extended from about 35 to 70 policy areas. Police and criminal judicial cooperation have, generally speaking, been removed from the domain of unanimity. The areas that still require unanimity are family law (Article III-269(3)); Article III-270(2)(d) on the establishment of minimum rules on specific aspects of criminal procedure; Article III-271(1) on the identification of new areas of serious crime for which minimum rules concerning the definition of criminal offences may be introduced; Article II-274(1) concerning the adoption of a European law on the establishment of a European public prosecutor; Article III-275(3) on the adoption of legislative measures regarding operational cooperation between law enforcement officers; and Article III-277 concerning the adoption of legislative measures laying down the conditions and limitations under which law enforcement authorities may operate in the territory of another MS. From 1 November 2009, QMV will require the support of 55 per cent of the MS representing at least three-fifths of the population of the Union. When the constitution does not require the European Council or the Council of Ministers to act on the basis of a proposal of the Commission, the required qualified majority consists of two-thirds of the MS representing at least three-fifths of the population of the Union (Article III-25(2)). It may be noted, here, that the President of the European Council and the President of the Commission are not voting members.

The Treaty also formalises the institutional role of the European Council; the latter shall 'define the strategic guidelines for legislative and operational planning within the area of freedom, security and justice' (Article III-258). Reflecting on and institutionalizing the Council's leadership role since the

Treaty of Amsterdam, the Treaty opens to us the opportunity for the European Council to continue to provide special impetus in the institutionalisation of the AFSJ by defining its general political direction and strategic priorities. The election of a Council President for a period of two and half years, renewable once, will aid this process by ensuring policy continuity and by bridging legislative and operational programmes. The European Council could also contribute to enhancing the effectiveness of JHA cooperation by influencing the Council to adopt legislative instruments. Although the Treaty is silent on the issue of judicial review of the European Council's acts (except for the case of the suspension of voting rights of the MS), it is plausible to argue that the provisions concerning the capacity to bring an action for failure to act and preliminary rulings apply to it. Likewise, the provisions concerning access to documents and the jurisdiction of the Ombudsman apply to the European Council.

The Constitutional Treaty also envisages the establishment of a new standing committee on 'internal security', the Article III-261 standing committee, which replaces the Article 36 Committee. The new committee will be endowed with the task of coordinating the action of national police, customs and civil protection authorities. Although the reinforced coordination of operational collaboration might enhance the effectiveness of EU action in this area, and the Committee does not appear to have powers of directing the actions of national police and other authorities in relation to specific actions, the all-embracing concept of 'internal security', coupled with the fact that the committee will not be accountable to parliaments, be they European or national, give rise to concern.[15]

The Constitutional Treaty foresees greater transparency in JHA matters. Article I-50 reaffirms the link between transparency and participatory democracy by stating that 'in order to promote good governance and ensure the participation of civil society, the Union's institutions, bodies and agencies shall conduct their work as openly as possible'. To this end, the updated and amended text of Article 255 extends the right of access to documents to the Union's institutions, bodies and agencies. Although each institution, body or agency shall determine in its own rules of procedure specific provisions regarding access to documents, Article 50(3), which is specified in Article III-399, encapsulates the centrality of the principle of transparency in the new constitutional order. In addition to the constitutional guarantee of openness, that is, the obligation on the part of the Union to act as openly as possible, a European law will lay down the general principles and limits which govern the right of access and, finally, the institutions' own rules of procedure will entail the specific provisions for public access to documents in accordance with the relevant European law (Article I-50(4) and (5)). Given the chronic lack of democratic control and oversight in JHA, the promise of increased transparency and the constitutionalisation of the openness of legislative proceedings in the Council are welcome reforms. More specifically, Article I-50 on 'transparency in the proceedings of Union institutions, bodies, offices and agencies' states that all the above bodies shall work as openly as possible and that the European Parliament and the Council (when it considers and votes on a draft legislative act) shall meet in public. And under Article III-399(2), 'the European Parliament and the Council of Ministers shall ensure publication of the documents relating to the legislative procedures'.[16]

The general extension of the European Court of Justice's jurisdiction is a welcome reform.[17] The restrictions in the Court's jurisdiction under Titles IV EC and VI EU, including the intergovernmentalist modifications of the preliminary ruling reference procedure in Article 68(1) EC and 35 EU have not found their way into the European Constitution. This means that any national court or tribunal will be able to activate the preliminary ruling reference procedure. The only limitation in the Court's jurisdiction that has been preserved is Article 35(5) EU in relation to police and criminal judicial cooperation; that is, the exclusion of the Court from reviewing 'the validity or proportionality of operations carried out by national police or other law enforcement authorities or the exercise of responsibilities incumbent upon MS with regard to the maintenance of law and order and the safeguarding of internal security, where such action is a matter of national law' (Article III-377).

Crucial for the AFSJ and the judicial protection of individuals is also Article III-365(5) which expands the scope of judicial review to acts of bodies and agencies that produce legal effects; 'acts setting up bodies and agencies of the Union may lay down specific conditions and arrangements concerning actions brought by natural or legal persons against acts of these bodies or agencies intended to produce legal effects'. By so doing, Article III-365(5) grafts flesh onto the principle of judicial protection enshrined in Article II-107 of the EU Charter. The need for ensuring adequate protection for individuals in this area has been made apparent by the reasoning of the Constitutional courts in Germany and Poland concerning the European Arrest Warrant, which found that national implementing legislation does not conform to the constitutional guarantee of recourse to a court (Articles 19(4) and 55(1) of the German and Polish Constitutions, respectively).[18]

Concerning the restrictive *locus standi* under Article 230(4) EC, the Discussion Circle on the European Court of Justice addressed the issue in detail without reaching a decision on the appropriate reform. Some members did not favour a reformulation of Article 230 on the grounds that private litigants were afforded effective judicial protection by activating the preliminary ruling reference procedure at national courts. Critics of the strict interpretation of direct and individual concern requirements argued for a liberalization of the conditions by allowing private litigants to challenge at least some acts of direct concern to them and which do not entail implementing measures without the need to prove individual concern would enhance access to justice. The compromise solution put forward by the Chairman, Antonio Vittorino, found its way into the Constitution; namely, according to Article III-365(4), any natural or legal person can challenge legislative and regulatory acts which are of direct and individual concern to him/her and regulatory acts which do not entail implementing measures if he/she is able to prove direct concern. True, such a modest liberalization of standing rules for non-privileged applicants does not address in depth the problems raised by the restrictive rules of standing and the need for providing sufficient legal protection for individuals as highlighted by Advocate General Jacobs in the *UPA* case (21 March 2002) and may be seen to contradict the principle of effective judicial protection underpinning Article I-29.

[. . .]

D. THE EVOLVING AREA OF FREEDOM, SECURITY AND JUSTICE

Article III-257, which replaces Articles 29 EU and 61 EC, states that 'the Union shall constitute an area of freedom, security and justice with respect for fundamental rights and the different legal traditions and systems of the Member States'. Although it was suggested during the Convention's deliberations that the AFSJ should apply to 'everyone within its jurisdiction irrespective of nationality legal status and the place they are' this suggestion did not find its way into the text. Article III-257, nevertheless, contains explicit references to the need to respect fundamental rights, an acknowledgement of the different legal traditions and systems of the MS, the application of the mutual recognition principle to both civil and criminal judicial cooperation and the framing of 'a common policy on asylum, immigration and external border control, based on solidarity between the MS, which is fair towards third country nationals'. Article III-257(3) strengthens the legal basis for taking action concerning crime prevention.

Concerning migration-related matters (Articles III-265 to III-268), the Treaty establishes a legal basis for the gradual introduction of an integrated management system for external borders without explicitly referring to the establishment of a European Border Guard which featured in the Conclusions of the Seville and Thessaloniki European Council meetings in June 2002 and 2003, respectively. Although the provision concerning the integrated management system for external borders builds on the momentum created by the incorporation of the Schengen acquis into the EC/EU and the Tampere conclusions, the suggestion that any measure in this area must give 'due regard to the necessary safeguards for democratic control and the rights of individuals' was not adopted. Reflecting national executives' anxieties, the third paragraph of Article III-265 states that the Community's competence in this area shall not impinge upon MS's sovereign powers concerning the geographical demarcation of their borders, in accordance with international law.

A welcome development in the field of asylum is the reference to a uniform status of subsidiary protection for nationals of third countries requiring international protection. A provision that has given rise to many concerns, however, is Article III-266(2)(g) which refers to measures concerning partnership and cooperation with third countries with a view to managing inflows of asylum seekers – a provision that was not included in the Working Group's report and was especially supported by the British Government. NGOs have criticised this provision for legitimising attempts to 'sub-contract' the MS asylum obligations to third countries via the establishment of reception centres or even resettlement schemes. Explicit references have been added concerning the combating of trafficking in persons and readmission agreements, thereby delineating the key aspects of the Union's policy in this area.[19] In addition, the EU has now express power to act against unauthorised residence, in addition to illegal immigration, including removal and repatriation of persons residing without authorisation. However, the Tampere commitment to the equal treatment of long-term resident third country nationals has not found its way into the Treaty. In addition, Article III-267(4) establishes a legal basis for 'measures to provide incentives and support for the action of MS with a view to promoting the integration of third country nationals residing legally in their territories, excluding any harmonisation of the laws and regulations of the MS'. Article III-267(5), nevertheless, limits the Community's competence in the field of migration by stating that 'this article shall not affect the right of the MS to determine volumes of admission of third country nationals coming from third countries to their territory to seek work, whether employed or self-employed'.

The enshrinement of the principle of solidarity and fair sharing of responsibility (including its financial implications) between the MS in the areas of immigration, asylum and border controls into the Treaty creates a specific legal basis for the adoption of appropriate measures in this area (III-268), thereby replacing the existing Community competence to adopt measures on burden sharing related to asylum (Article 63(2)(b)).

Section 3 of the chapter on the AFSJ deals with civil judicial cooperation. Building upon the existing acquis in this area, the Treaty amends Article 65 EC by deleting the sentence 'insofar as necessary for the proper functioning of the internal market' contained in Article 65 EC, thereby laying the foundation for the extension of the Union's competence to non-economic matters. The enshrining of the principle of mutual recognition of judgements and decisions in extrajudicial cases, the development of measures of preventive justice and alternative methods of dispute settlement, support for the training of the judiciary and judicial staff and the application of the co-decision procedure for measures concerning parental authority, the only sector of family law governed by unanimity, are noteworthy provisions. Finally, in line with the Tampere conclusions, the treaty envisages the adoption of measures designed to ensure a high level of access to justice. This cannot but have implications for the future establishment of minimum standards guaranteeing an appropriate level of legal aid for cross-border cases throughout the Union and special common procedural rules in order to simplify and speed up the settlement of cross-border disputes concerning small commercial claims under consumer legislation or to establish minimum common standards for multilingual forms or documents in cross-border proceedings.

Section 4 of Chapter IV deals with criminal judicial cooperation while section 5 deals with police cooperation. More specifically, Article III-270 formalises the close link between negative and positive integration. As regards the former, the principle of mutual recognition of judgements and decisions, which was proclaimed to be 'the cornerstone for judicial cooperation' at Tampere receives explicit reference in Article III-270(1). As regards the latter, mutual recognition is accompanied by the approximation of substantive and procedural criminal laws. According to Article III-270(2), European framework laws may establish minimum rules on a) the mutual admissibility of evidence among the MS, b) the rights of individuals in criminal procedure, c) the rights of victims of crime and d) any other specific aspects of a criminal procedure identified by the Council in advance. The important criteria for the approximation of legislation in procedural criminal law are the facilitation of the mutual recognition of judgements and judicial decisions, and police and criminal cooperation in criminal matters having a cross-border dimension. The explicit acknowledgement of the need for such provisions echoes previous commitments made at Tampere. In addition to the principle of mutual recognition, certain MS, such as the UK and Ireland, insisted on the inclusion of an explicit reference to the principle of respect for the diversity of the MS's legal systems, thereby alleviating concerns about the implications of the harmonisation of criminal procedural law. In addition, an emergency brake mechanism is envisaged in the case where an MS believes that harmonisation of certain elements of criminal procedure 'would affect fundamental aspects of its criminal justice system'. Under Article III-270(3), an MS can request the referral of the draft framework law to the European Council, which has the obligation either to refer the draft back to the Council or to request the submission of a new draft. As noted earlier, a failure to take action on the part of the European Council can always activate the enhanced cooperation procedures.

The extension of the Union's competence regarding criminal procedural law also applies to substantive criminal law (Article III-271). As regards the approximation of substantive criminal law, European framework laws can be used in two instances. First, European framework laws may establish the minimum rules concerning the definition of offences and sanctions in 12 listed areas of serious crime with a cross-border direction, ranging from terrorism and trafficking in human beings to tackling computer crime and organised crime (Article III-172(1)). It has been suggested that organised crime should be deleted from this list, since there is no common understanding of this category of criminal offence within the EU. Secondly, the second paragraph of Article III-271 refers to the minimum harmonisation of criminal legislation in order to ensure the effective implementation of a Union policy in an area which has been subject to harmonisation measures, such as fraud affecting the financial interests of the Union, counterfeiting of the euro, facilitation of unauthorised entry and residence, counterfeiting and piracy of products, environmental crime and also racism and xenophobia. What is noteworthy, here, is that the Union may define minimum rules with regard to the definition of criminal offences and sanctions, irrespective of whether or not they are of a cross border nature. Article III-271(3) *et seq* also entails an emergency brake mechanism and the referral of a legislative measure to the European Council, thereby providing a safeguard of last resort. In addition, the new clause III-272 gives specific legal basis for measures concerning crime prevention.[20] Community action in this area, however, can only promote and support the action of MS and excludes the approximation of legislation.

The remaining two articles of section 4, namely, Articles III-273 and III-274, deal with Eurojust and the creation of a European Public Prosecutor respectively. The former article outlines Eurojust's mission and expands its powers, which now include the initiation of criminal investigations and proposing the initiation of prosecutions to be conducted by the competent national authorities, particularly those relating to offences against the financial interests of the Union, and the resolution of conflicts of jurisdiction. According to Article III-273(2), 'European laws shall determine Eurojust's structures, workings, scope of action and tasks' and 'European laws shall determine arrangements for involving the European Parliament and Member States' national parliaments in the evaluation of Eurojust's activities'. It remains to be seen whether Eurojust will be endowed with supervisory powers over Europol, thereby subordinating the latter to the former. It has also been suggested that Eurojust should not have the open-ended brief provided for under Article III-273. Instead, it would have been preferable to define Eurojust's mandate on the basis of specifically enumerated offences.

The Constitutional Treaty has extended further the Union's JHA acquis by establishing a legal basis for a European Public Prosecutor's Office within Eurojust. Drawing on the Commission's green paper on the establishment of a European Public Prosecutor in the field of the Community financial interests,[21] the Constitutional Treaty stipulates that the EPP shall be responsible for investigating, prosecuting and bringing to judgement, the perpetrators of and accomplices in offences against the financial interests of the Union. The establishment of an EPP requires a unanimous Council decision after obtaining the consent of the EP. The powers of the EPP may be extended to include serious crime having a cross-border dimension by the European Council acting by unanimity after obtaining the consent of the European Parliament. Although the structural and functional relations between the EPP and Eurojust are unclear, as indeed are the details concerning its modus operandi, it nevertheless remains the case that the extension of judicial criminal cooperation into the field of law enforcement has generated anxieties about the Union's creeping competence or federalising tendencies.

The EU's powers concerning police cooperation remain broadly unchanged. European laws and/or framework laws could be used to establish rules concerning a) the collection, storage, analysis and exchange of relevant information, b) support for the training of staff, and cooperation on the exchange of staff, on equipment and on research into crime detection, and c) common investigative techniques in relation to the detection of serious forms of organised crime (Article III-275). Concerning Europol the Constitutional Treaty extended its powers to carry out investigations and to participate in operational actions carried out jointly with the MS's competent authorities or in the context of joint investigative teams where appropriate in liaison with Eurojust. According to Article III-276(3), any operational action by Europol must be carried out in liaison and in agreement with the authorities of the MS whose territory is concerned. The application of coercive measures would remain the exclusive responsibility of the competent national authorities. And although Article III-276 delineates Europol's broad areas of action, rather than providing an exhaustive list of Europol's tasks, the last indent of this paragraph ensures the accountability of Europol by stating that European laws shall also lay down the procedures for scrutiny of Europol's activities by the European Parliament, together with the MS's national parliaments. Finally, Article III-277 on operations on the territory of another MS does not make any substantive amendments to Article 32 EU.

Taking an overall view, it may be said that the Constitutional Treaty entails significant innovations.[22] It has redesigned Justice and Home Affairs, boosted the efficiency and effectiveness of cooperation and has addressed important deficits with regard to democracy, judicial supervision, transparency, coherence and complexity. Although the ratification of the Constitutional Treaty has stalled, it is, nevertheless, the case that its provisions have made an important contribution to the constitutional dialogue surrounding the area of freedom, security and justice. It is certainly true to say that preserving these institutional innovations will not be easy. Nor could possible activation of Article 42 EU provide a comprehensive and viable solution.[23] And although it would be wrong to assume that the absence of a Constitutional Treaty will lead to either stagnation or inaction in this area,[24] its provisions are bound to exert a deep influence on the continuing conversation about institutional reform in the area of freedom, security and justice. By setting up a pattern of institutional reform within the bounds of possibility, the Constitutional Treaty is very likely to prompt a close reflection on the procedural, institutional and substantive weaknesses of AFSJ, thereby making the retention of the Treaty of Nice framework a problematic option. Whether these ideas and institutional reforms will find their fullest and lasting expression in a treaty amendment or a constitutional treaty in the future remains to be seen.

Document 8.11: Council and Commission Action Plan implementing the Hague Programme on strengthening freedom, security and justice in the European Union, 9778/2/05, 10 June 2005, available at register.consilium.eu.int (selected extracts)

[. . .]

1. In response to the request from the European Council, the Council and the Commission have adopted on 2/3 June 2005 the appended Action Plan translating the Hague Programme into specific measures. By adopting it, the Council and the Commission reiterate the importance which they attach to the correct and timely transposition of legislative acts adopted, to the effective implementation of measures agreed, and to their evaluation in practice. In that connection, the European Council has invited the Commission to provide it with an annual report on the implementation of the Action Plan.

2. The programme is based on the Commission communication (8922/05), which the Council welcomes and has studied with the greatest interest.

3. The Council invites the European Council to take note of the appended Action Plan.

1. General Orientations

The Council and the Commission intend this Action Plan to be the frame of reference for their work over the next five years, it being understood that it:

- is to be supplemented by the Drugs Action Plan submitted to the Council/European Council for approval (8652/1/05 REV 1 + COR 1), by the Plan of Action on Combating Terrorism adopted by the European Council at its meeting on 17 and 18 June 2004 (10586/04) and by the strategy on the external aspects of the area of freedom, security and justice which will be submitted to the European Council in December 2005;
- must retain a degree of flexibility, for example in order to take the greatest possible account of the demands of current events;

- will be updated at the end of 2006, so that the European Council can establish the Union's legislative and operational priorities in the field of justice and home affairs;
- sets out the list of legislative (in italics) and non-legislative measures which the Council and the Commission consider necessary to put into practice the guidelines set in the Hague Programme. Adoption of the list is without prejudice to the scope or content of the proposals for measures which will be negotiated in compliance with the provisions of the Treaties. Except where otherwise indicated, the plan specifies the date by which it is expected that the Commission or a Member State will take an initiative;
- will be implemented in strict compliance with the legal bases laid down in the Treaties and the principles of solidarity, subsidiarity and proportionality;
- will seek to ensure a better coherence among legal instruments;
- does not interfere with the Commission's right of initiative in the matters dealt with in Title IV of the TEC or with the Commission's and the Member States' rights of initiative in those dealt with in Title VI of the TEU;
- takes due account of the debates which have taken place within the European Parliament with a view to and following the presentation by the Commission of its communication (8922/05) and is without prejudice to the institutional prerogatives of the European Parliament.

1.1. EVALUATION

- Setting up of a system for objective and impartial evaluation of the implementation of EU measures in the field of Freedom, Security and Justice–Communication on and Proposal for the creation of an evaluation mechanism, as envisaged by Article III-260 of the Constitutional Treaty (2006).

Notes

1. In a similar way, the Supreme Court of Cyprus ruled on 7 November 2005 that issuing European Arrest Warrants to extradite Cypriots was unconstitutional.
2. On the Convention on the Future of Europe and the Constitutional Treaty, see K. Lenaerts and M. Desomer, 'Bricks for a Constitutional Treaty of the European Union: values, objectives and means', *European Law Review* (2002), 377; P. Magnette and C. Nicolaïdes, 'The European Convention: Bargaining in the shadow of rhetoric', **27** *West European Politics* (2004), 381; J. Temple Lang, 'The main issues after the Convention on the Constitutional Treaty for Europe', **27** *Fordham International Law Journal* (2004), 544; P. Craig, 'Constitutional Process and Reform in the EU: Nice, Laeken, the Convention and the IGC', **10**(4) *European Public Law* (2004), 653; M. Dougan, 'The Convention's Draft Constitutional Treaty: A "Tidying-Up Exercise" That Needs Some Tidying-Up Of Its Own', *Federal Trust Online Constitutional Essay*, 27/2003; A. Dashwood, 'The Draft EU Constitution – First Impressions', **5** *Cambridge Yearbook of European Legal Studies* (2002/2003), 419; G. de Burca, 'The Constitutional Challenge of New Governance in the European Union', **28** *European Law Review* (2003); B. de Witte, 'Simplification and Reorganisation of the European Union', **39** *Common Market Law Review* (2002), 1244; *Ten Reflections on the*

Constitutional Treaty for Europe (2003); M. Dougan, 'The Convention's draft Constitutional Treaty: bringing Europe closer to its lawyers?', **28** *European Law Review* (2003), 763; A. Arnull, 'Member States of the European Union and Giscard's Blueprint for its Future', **27** *Fordham International Law Journal* (2004), 503; P. Birkinshaw, 'A Constitution for the European Union? – A Letter from Home', **10** *European Public Law* (2004), 57.

3. See the briefing papers for the European Parliament Committee on Constitutional Affairs on the occasion of the Symposium 13/14 October 2005 (http://www.europarl.eu.int/meetdocs/2004_2009/organes/afco).
4. Such interinstitutional agreements could ensure the implementation of other institutional innovations of the Constitutional Treaty, such as, for example, the provisions concerning the increased input from national parliaments in relation to the subsidiarity principle; see Jo Shaw's contribution to the symposium on 13/14 October 2005.
5. Compare Bruno de Witte, 'The Closest Thing to a Constitutional Conversation in Europe: The Semi-Permanent Treaty Revision Process', in P. Beaumont, C. Lyons and N. Walker (eds), *Convergence and Divergence in European Law* (Oxford: Hart Publishing, 2002); N. Walker, 'Constitutionalising Enlargement, Enlarging Constitutionalism', **9** *European Law Journal* (2003), 365; P. Craig, 'Constitutions, Constitutionalism and the European Union', **7**(2) *European Law Journal* (2001), 125; J. Weiler, 'A Constitution for Europe? Some Hard Choices', **40**(4) *Journal of Common Market Studies* (2002), 563; J. Shaw, *The Legal and Political sources of the Treaty establishing a Constitution for Europe*, working paper, Manchester University.
6. Critical moments represent opportunities for significant change and complete departure from previously established patterns. The retention of the existing institutional balance in the legislative process, the making of the co-decision procedure as the ordinary legislative procedure, the extension of the EU's competence to new areas, the abolition of the pillared structure, the incorporation of the EU Charter into the Treaty and the enhanced role of national parliaments in the EU decision-making process, all could be taken to be reforms endowed with deep transformative effects.
7. According to the minimalist view, the Constitutional treaty does not substantially alter the constitutional balance between the MS and the EU. Nor does it signal a new supranational direction for the Union. Adherents of this perspective would pinpoint the attribution of formal institutional status to the European Council and the strategic role it enjoys in JHA issues, the provisions on the double Presidency, that is, the Chair of the European Council, elected by qualified majority, and the President of the Commission, who is chosen by the European Council and elected by the European Parliament by majority voting, the appointment of the Foreign Affairs Minister by the European Council by qualified majority with the agreement of the Commission President, the omission of references to 'an ever closer Union' and 'the acquis communitaire being an express objective of the Union' and the explicit reference to the possibility of states' withdrawal from the Union.
8. This refers to the possibility of giving the next European Parliament the explicit mandate to draft the European constitution. On the importance of constitutional symbolism, see N. Walker 'After the Constitutional Moment', Federal Trust Online Constitutional Essay (2003).
9. The term is borrowed from Walker, *supra*, n. 8.
10. In Case C-176/03 *Commission* v. *Council* (Judgement of 13 September 2005), the Grand Chamber annulled Council Framework Decision 2003/80/JHA on the protection of the environment through criminal law (OJ L 29, 55) on the ground that it was established law that acts adopted under Title VI were not to encroach on powers conferred by the EC Treaty on the Community, and there was such encroachment in the present case as Articles 1 to 7 of the Framework Decision had as their main purpose the protection of the environment and so could properly have been adopted on the basis of Article 175 EC. On the implications of this judgement, see Commission Communication COM (2005) 583 final/2, Brussels, 24.11.2005.
11. CONV 426/02, Brussels, 2 December 2002.
12. The exceptions were legislation on the establishment of a European Public Prosecutor's office; cross-border actions by police; operational police measures; the establishment of

minimum rules concerning not explicitly mentioned aspects of criminal procedure; and the identification of new areas of serious crime for which minimum rules concerning the definition of criminal offences may be introduced.

13. The importance of this principle has also been reaffirmed by the ECJ in *Gozutok and Brugge*; Joint Cases C-187/01 and C-385/01, [2003] ECR I-1345 at para. 33.
14. The Commission already had an exclusive right of initiative in judicial cooperation in civil matters under the Treaty of Nice.
15. In light of the Praesidium's note that the Committee would coordinate operational cooperation in the 'event of a major catastrophe, attacks and events and demonstrations on a European scale', it is plausible to argue that 'internal security' was not confined to police matters.
16. The Amsterdam Treaty required the Council, when acting as legislator, to publish the results of its votes, but not its deliberations (Article 207 (3) EC). The Seville European Council (June 2002) obliged the Council to open its legislative meetings to the public. Implementing the conclusions of the Seville European Council, the new rules of procedure for the Council state deliberations on acts to be adopted in accordance with the co-decision procedure shall be open to the public.
17. Compare also the novel provision of Article I-29(1) which reinforces the dialogic and decentralized pattern of enforcement of Community law; 'the MS shall provide rights of appeal sufficient to ensure effective legal protection in the field of Union law'.
18. Judgement of 18 July 2005, 2 BvR 2236/04, Bundesverfassungsgericht and Judgement of the Polish Constitutional Tribunal, 27 April 2005, p1/05.
19. The Hague Programme envisages the appointment of a Special Representative for a common readmission policy.
20. Notably, crime prevention was mentioned in Article 29 EU, but it was not included in the specific legal bases of Articles 30 and 31 EU.
21. COM(2001) 715 final.
22. Compare S. Peers, 'The EU Constitution and Justice and Home Affairs: the Accountability Gap', Statewatch (2004); S. White, 'European Constitution: What is New in the Area of Judicial Cooperation in Criminal Matters and Police Cooperation', Federal Trust Online Constitutional Essay, 27/2003.
23. On this see E. Guild and S. Carrera, *No Constitutional Treaty? Implications for the Area of Freedom, Security and Justice*, CEPS Working Document, No. 231 (2005).
24. On 4 November 2004, the European Council adopted the Hague Programme which set the objectives to be implemented in the area of freedom, security and justice for the period 2005–10. This was followed by the Commission's Action Plan (May 2005) which outlined ten priorities for action, a set of implementing measures and a timetable for their adoption. The priorities cover fundamental rights and citizenship, counter-terrorism, a common asylum area, migration management, integration, internal borders, external borders and visas, privacy and security, organized crime, civil and criminal justice, sharing responsibility and solidarity. The Commission's effort to strike a better balance between freedom and security is evident in the Action Plan, which was approved by the Council on 2 June 2005. See European Commission Communication to the Council and the European Parliament, *The Hague Programme: Ten Priorities for the next five years – the Partnership for European Renewal in the field of Freedom, Security and Justice*, COM(2005), 184 final, Brussels 10.5.2005.

9. Developments under the Common Foreign and Security and Defence Policies

Document summary

Introduction

The Common Foreign and Security Policy corresponds to a common need our Member States already perceived several years ago. Nevertheless, it is one of the areas where their sovereign prerogatives are mostly rooted, with the consequence that all of them proclaim the need for unity, but that need is only satisfied when the agreement of the Member States is unanimous, and then only by means remaining under their own control. It is therefore an intergovernmental area, but it does have a peculiar feature: if there is no agreement on the policy to be adopted, no action follows. If there is agreement, the Member States force the intergovernmental limits of the consequent action, penetrate into the Community area and, sitting in Council, adopt measures provided for by the Treaty exclusively for Community actions (and sometimes they go even beyond, as we will see by reading the documents in this chapter).

This apparent inconsistency once more demonstrates (and it does so beyond any reasonable doubt) the hybrid nature of our common architecture. It is a nature that has increasingly emerged throughout the years, but it has always been so in the area of foreign policy. The first decision to cooperate in this area goes back to the late 1960s, when the so-called 'European Political Cooperation' was established upon a purely political basis. But even before the Single Act gave it a formal recognition, when, in 1981, a common declaration was adopted condemning the Soviet Union for its support of General Jaruzelski in Poland, the declaration itself was strengthened by asking the Commission to introduce trade sanctions against Moscow. The same happened in 1986 against South Africa for its apartheid policy. Such use of Community sanctions was considered legitimate, and several arguments could be used to demonstrate that it was. It is a fact that our Member States would never have allowed their common foreign policy to become communitarian and therefore to be pursued by using Community decision making and Community acts. But they have always been ready to use such acts as complements to their own intergovernmental decisions.

Things have not changed after the Treaty of Maastricht formalized this area as the Common Foreign and Security Policy. The CFSP became the so-called 'second pillar', to be distinguished and separate from the communitarian pillar, that is, the first one. On that basis, and with the Treaty of Amsterdam of 1996, the High Representative entered the scene as the single voice of the Common Policy. But the High Representative depended on the Council, and could thus only reflect the common views of the Member States sitting in that capacity. Eventually he also became the Secretary General of the Council, and turned out to be more of a *politische beamte* than a Minister for Foreign Affairs. It has also to be noted that Maastricht provided for international agreements to be concluded within the second pillar, which, although signed at the common level, were supposed to be ratified by each of the Member States.

This kind of setting could only add to the confusing features of the ensemble. International agreements signed within the first pillar had direct legal effect, as the Community had legal personality. Agreements signed under the second pillar could not have direct legal effect, because the Union did not have legal personality. Consequently, mixed agreements were a mess for our foreign counterparts. Not to mention our daily external relationships, divided between the High Representative, under the direct control of the Council, and the Commissioner for External Relations, bound by the collegiality of the Commission.

Once more the need for bridges and hybrid solutions became paramount. The only two international agreements adopted under the second pillar were de facto considered to enter into force independently of ratification (actually, they have not been ratified by anybody). And whenever there was a strong agreement on sensitive issues, Community measures were added to give the agreement the necessary strength.

The first three documents published in this chapter (Documents 9.1, 9.2 and 9.3) provide impressive evidence on this point. They refer to the implementation to be given after 11 September to the UN Security Council Resolutions against the Taliban regime and Osama bin Laden, aiming at preventing any financial support to them from any source whatsoever. Financial sanctions, such as freezing the assets and funds of both groups and named individuals, clearly fall under the jurisdiction of our Member States, and not of the Community, which is empowered by the Treaties to adopt economic sanctions only against States. Furthermore, implementing UN resolutions corresponds to an obligation of the members of the UN and therefore of national States, not of the European Community, which is not a member of the UN, nor of the European Union (which, as noted above, does not even enjoy legal personality). Nevertheless, thanks to their firm support for the fight against terrorism after 11 September in the context of our Common Foreign and Security Policy, our Member States decided to implement the UN resolutions not individually, but by a Community Regulation adopted upon the legal basis of the EC Treaty. And Member States generally very restrictive in allowing any expansion of Community powers, such as the United Kingdom, were among the most resolute supporters of this unusual and very bold move.

The Regulation was challenged before the Court of First Instance and, by reading the judgment of the court, it is easy to understand how difficult it was for our judges not to strike down the measures. Eventually they relied upon a cocktail of legal bases, and mostly on Article 308 TEC, the flexibility clause, which empowers the Community to adopt measures not otherwise justifiable.

The case is an extreme demonstration of the inherent inconsistency of our Common Foreign and Security Policy: by jealously and carefully defending its intergovernmental nature, our Member States deprive it of the necessary strength. When they agree on a specific issue, they also feel the need to supply their agreement with the teeth the CFSP lacks, and at that point they trespass upon all jurisdictional divides, not only between intergovernmental responsibilities and Community competencies, but also between Community and national prerogatives.

The Constitution is not revolutionary in this area and does not go beyond its usual 'bridging and merging' of the two sides of the existing setting. However, it is undeniable that it would both introduce more clarity and pave the way for a badly needed consolidation of instruments (Document 9.4). First of all, by merging the Union and the Community into a single entity with legal personality, it does not eliminate the intergovernmental nature of the procedures leading to CFSP decisions, but the international agreements concluded within the framework of the CFSP would necessarily have immediate and direct effects. This very fact is, by itself, a partial merger between the first and second pillars, for thanks to it the CFSP is no longer an intergovernmental area completely separate from the Community area; rather, it becomes an intergovernmental procedure inside a single legal framework. The consequences might be manifold, and the expansion of judicial control would be one of them.

Beyond this first and crucial change and inside the new framework due to it, the double-hatted Foreign Minister would be the most symbolic novelty of the Constitution in this area (Document 9.5). As the nickname 'double-hatted' suggests, this new figure would stem not from a merger but from a sort of structural joining of the High Representative and the Commissioner for External Relations. The Constitution is both admirable and somehow comical for the delicate surgical ability by which it keeps the terminals of the two hats separate from each other. The Minister will be double-hatted, but for the CFSP missions he/she will only depend on the Council, while his/her loyalty to the collegiality of the Commission will be limited to the Community's External Relations. However, one way or another, we would have one single voice, one single figure representing us in foreign relations and one single portfolio of the tools to be used in such relations. It could be quite a new beginning.

The unified diplomatic service (Document 9.6) would be a crucial part of this new beginning, as putting two hats on the same head also requires putting the existing services (of the High Representative and of the Commissioner for External Relations) under the same head. And this innovation would satisfy not only a standard of more functional and efficient organisation but also the need for geopolitical analysis and doctrines gradually unifying those of the too many actors who currently play an international role in Europe.

The Constitution devotes special attention to the new diplomatic service, even though unifying the existing ones does not necessarily require an amendment procedure. But overcoming oppositions and vested interests is so hard as to make it quite unlikely that the necessary decisions would be taken on a purely political basis. Already during the Convention and the Intergovernmental Conference, entering into the organisational details proved to be impossible (where should the unified service go? Under the Council, under the Commission or somewhere else?) and any decision on them was postponed to a future interinstitutional agreement. A further illustration of such difficulties can be seen in what happened more recently when the High Representative Javier Solana and the President of the Commission José Barroso were urged by the Member States to prepare a joint report on the scope and structure of the future diplomatic service. The joint report was presented in March 2005, but after the French and the Dutch referendums the European Council decided not to consider it (our last document in this Chapter is devoted to all of these developments).

Now, making an effort to better organise our external services has nothing to do with the reasons for the French and Dutch 'Nos' to the Constitution. But these negative votes were enough for our Member States to fall back into their ever-more irrational defence of the status quo. They know that the CFSP cannot work as it is, for it is less efficient than it could be from our standpoint, while it is confusing and less effective than it could be from the standpoint of our interlocutors. Because of their awareness of this miserable state of affairs, the Member States are ready to supply the CFSP with Community and even national resources whenever they feel it necessary. But changing is too costly for them. The sovereign prerogatives they so stubbornly defend are increasingly symbolic, while their actual standing and power of influence in the international arena are increasingly reduced. Sooner or later they will be forced to understand it. The sooner, of course, the better. And the better – they will be forced to realise – coincides with the Constitution, or at least with most of it.

We have already underlined that opposing the Constitution on behalf of a better delivery, as if constitutional innovations had nothing to do with improving delivery at the European level, is a typical form of ideological disinformation. This concluding chapter, no less than the previous ones, offers good arguments to make it clear.

Document 9.1: Court of First Instance, Judgement of 21 September 2005, Ahmed Ali Yusuf and Al Barakaat International Foundation, Case T-306/01, available at http://curia.europa.eu (selected extracts)

[. . .]

Findings of the Court

112 With regard, first, to the kind of measures that the Council is empowered to take under Articles 60 EC and 301 EC, the Court considers that nothing in the wording of those provisions makes it possible to exclude the adoption of restrictive measures directly affecting individuals or organisations, whether or not established in the Community, in so far as such measures actually seek to reduce, in part or completely, economic relations with one or more third countries.

113 As the Council has correctly observed, the measures at issue in this case were among what are conventionally known as 'smart sanctions', which appeared in United Nations practice during the 1990s. Those sanctions replace classic general trade embargos aimed at a country with more targeted and selective measures, such as economic and financial sanctions, prohibition of travel, embargos on arms or specific goods, so as to reduce the suffering endured by the civilian population of the country concerned, while none the less imposing genuine sanctions on the target regime and those in charge of it.

114 The practice of the institutions has developed in the same way, the Council having successively considered that Articles 60 EC and 301 EC allowed it to take restrictive measures against entities which or persons who physically controlled part of the territory of a third country (see, for example, Council Regulation (EC) No 1705/98 of 28 July 1998 concerning the interruption of certain economic relations with Angola in order to induce the 'União Nacional para. a Independência Total de Angola' (UNITA) to fulfil its obligations in the peace process, and repealing Council Regulation (EC) No 2229/97 (OJ 1998 L 215, p. 1)) and against entities which or persons who effectively controlled the government apparatus of a third country and also against persons and entities associated with them and who or which provided them with financial support (see, for example, Council Regulation (EC) No 1294/1999 of 15 June 1999 concerning a freeze of funds and a ban on investment in relation to the Federal Republic of Yugoslavia (FRY) and repealing Regulations (EC) No 1295/98 and (EC) No 1607/98 (OJ 1999 L 153, p. 63), and Council Regulation (EC) No 2488/2000 of 10 November 2000 maintaining a freeze of funds in relation to Mr Milosevic and those persons associated with him and repealing Regulations (EC) Nos 1294/1999 and 607/2000 and Article 2 of Regulation (EC) No 926/98 (OJ 2000 L 287, p. 19)). That development is fully compatible with the measures provided for in Articles 60 EC and 301 EC.

115 In fact, just as economic or financial sanctions may legitimately be directed specifically at the rulers of a third country, rather than at the country as such, they may be directed at the persons or entities associated with those rulers or directly or indirectly controlled by them, wherever they may be. As the Commission has rightly pointed out, Articles 60 EC and 301 EC would not provide an efficient means of applying pressure to the rulers with influence over the policy of a third country if the Community could not, on the basis of those provisions, adopt measures against individuals who, although not resident in the third country in question, are sufficiently connected to the regime against which the sanctions are directed. Furthermore, as the Council has emphasised, the fact that some of those individuals so targeted happen to be nationals of a Member State is irrelevant, for, if they are to be effective in the context of the free movement of capital, financial sanctions cannot be confined solely to nationals of the third country concerned.

116 That interpretation, which is not contrary to the letter of Article 60 EC or Article 301 EC, is justified both by considerations of effectiveness and by humanitarian concerns.

117 With regard, second, to the objective pursued by Regulation No 467/2001, the Council has argued, referring to Security Council Resolutions 1267 (1999) and 1333 (2000), Common Position 2001/154 and to the first and second recitals in the preamble to that regulation and to its actual title, that the

measures at issue were directed essentially against the Taliban regime which, at the time, effectively controlled 80 per cent of Afghan territory and called itself the 'Islamic Emirate of Afghanistan' and, incidentally, against persons who and entities which, by means of economic or financial transactions, assisted that regime by providing sanctuary and training for international terrorists and their organisations, thus in fact acting as agents of that regime or being closely connected to it.

118 In so far as the applicants complained that Regulation No 467/2001 was directed at Usama bin Laden and not the Taliban regime, the Council has added that Usama bin Laden was in fact the head and 'éminence grise' of the Taliban and that he wielded the real power in Afghanistan. His temporal and spiritual titles of 'Sheikh' (head) and 'Emir' (prince, governor or commander) and the rank he held beside the other Taliban religious dignitaries can leave little doubt on that score. Moreover, even before 11 September 2001, Usama bin Laden had sworn an oath of allegiance ('Bay'a') making a formal religious bond between him and the Taliban theocracy. He was thus in a situation comparable to that of Mr Milosevic and the members of the Yugoslav Government at the time of the economic and financial sanctions taken by the Council against the Federal Republic of Yugoslavia (see paragraph 114 above). With regard to Al-Qaeda, the Council has observed that it was common knowledge that it had many military training camps in Afghanistan and that thousands of its members had fought beside the Taliban between October 2001 and January 2002, during the intervention of the international coalition.

119 There are no grounds for challenging the validity of those considerations as to which there exists, within the international community, a broad consensus expressed, inter alia, by the several resolutions adopted unanimously by the Security Council and which have not been specifically rebutted or even challenged by the applicants.

120 More particularly, the chief object of the sanctions at issue in this case was to prevent the Taliban regime from obtaining financial support from any source whatsoever, as is apparent from Paragraph 4(b) of Resolution 1287 (1999). The sanctions might have been circumvented if the individuals who were thought to maintain that regime had not been affected by them. As regards the relations between the former Taliban regime and Usama bin Laden, the Security Council considered that the latter, during the period in question, received assistance, at this point crucial, from the regime of which he could be regarded as forming part. Thus it is that, in the 10th recital in the preamble to Resolution 1333 (2000), the Security Council deplored the fact that the Taliban continued to provide safe haven to Usama bin Laden and to allow him and others associated with him to operate a network of terrorist training camps from Taliban-controlled territory and to use Afghanistan as a

base from which to sponsor international terrorist operations. Furthermore, in the seventh recital in the preamble to Resolution 1333 (2000), the Security Council reaffirmed its conviction that the suppression of international terrorism was essential for the maintenance of international peace and security.

121 Thus, contrary to what the applicants maintained, the measures at issue were indeed intended to interrupt or reduce economic relations with a third country, in connection with the international community's fight against international terrorism and, more specifically, against Usama bin Laden and the Al-Qaeda network.

122 With regard, third, to the proportionality of the measures at issue, that must be assessed in the light of the purpose of Regulation No 467/2001. As has been explained above, the imposing of 'smart' sanctions is intended precisely to exert effective pressure on the rulers of the country concerned, while restricting as far as possible the impact of those measures on the population of that country, in particular by confining their personal ambit to a certain number of individuals referred to by name. Now, in the circumstances of this case, Regulation No 467/2001 tended to increase the pressure on the Taliban regime, inter alia by freezing the funds and other financial assets of Usama bin Laden and the individuals and entities associated with him, as identified by the Sanctions Committee. Such measures are in keeping with the principle of proportionality, according to which sanctions may not go beyond what is appropriate and necessary to the attainment of the objective pursued by the Community legislation imposing them.

123 By contrast, the fact that the measures at issue also affected transactions having no cross-border element is not relevant. If it was the legitimate object of those measures to cause the sources of funding for the Taliban and international terrorism operating out of Afghanistan to dry up, they necessarily had to affect both international and purely internal transactions, given that the latter were just as likely as the former to supply such funding, having regard in particular to the free movement of persons and capital and the lack of transparency in international financial channels.

124 It follows from the foregoing that, contrary to what the applicants claimed, the Council was indeed competent to adopt Regulation No 467/2001 on the basis of Articles 60 EC and 301 EC.

CONCERNING THE LEGAL BASIS OF THE CONTESTED REGULATION

125 Unlike Regulation No 467/2001, the contested regulation has for its legal basis not only Articles 60 EC and 301 EC but also Article 308 EC. That reflects the development of the international situation of which the sanctions decreed by the Security Council and implemented by the Community successively form part.

[. . .]

133 It follows that on any view Articles 60 EC and 301 EC did not constitute in themselves a sufficient legal basis for the contested regulation.

134 Moreover, contrary to the view expressed by the Commission in the proposal for a Council regulation which is the source of the contested regulation [see paragraph 129], the Council considered that Article 308 EC did not on its own constitute an adequate legal basis for the adoption of the regulation either. Those considerations must also be approved.

[. . .]

152 It follows from all the foregoing that the fight against international terrorism, more particularly the imposition of economic and financial sanctions, such as the freezing of funds, in respect of individuals and entities suspected of contributing to the funding of terrorism, cannot be made to refer to one of the objects which Articles 2 EC and 3 EC expressly entrust to the Community.

[. . .]

157 It must therefore be concluded that Article 308 EC does not, any more than Article 60 EC or Article 301 EC taken in isolation, constitute of itself a sufficient legal basis for the contested regulation.

158 However, both in the recitals in the preamble to the contested regulation and in its pleadings, the Council has argued that Article 308 EC, in conjunction with Articles 60 EC and 301 EC, gives it the power to adopt a Community regulation relating to the battle against the financing of international terrorism conducted by the Union and its Member States under the CFSP and imposing, to that end, economic and financial sanctions on individuals, without establishing any connection whatsoever with the territory or governing regime of a third country. Those considerations must be accepted.

159 In the circumstances, account has to be taken of the bridge explicitly established at the time of the Maastricht revision between Community actions imposing economic sanctions under Articles 60 EC and 301 EC and the objectives of the Treaty on European Union in the sphere of external relations.

160 It must be held that Articles 60 EC and 301 EC are quite special provisions of the EC Treaty, in that they expressly contemplate situations in which action by the Community may be proved to be necessary in order to achieve, not one of the objects of the Community as fixed by the EC Treaty but rather one of the objectives specifically assigned to the Union by Article 2 of the Treaty on European Union, viz., the implementation of a common foreign and security policy.

161 Under Articles 60 EC and 301 EC, action by the Community is therefore in actual fact action by the Union, the implementation of which finds its footing on the Community pillar after the Council has adopted a common position or a joint action under the CFSP.

162 According to Article 3 EU, the Union is to be served by a single institutional framework which is to ensure the consistency and the continuity of the activities carried out in order to attain its objectives while respecting and building upon the acquis communautaire. The Union is in particular to ensure the consistency of its external activities as a whole in the context of its external relations, security, economic and development policies. The Council and the Commission are to be responsible for ensuring such consistency and are to cooperate to this end. They are to ensure the implementation of these policies, each in accordance with its respective powers.

163 Now, just as the powers provided for by the EC Treaty may be proved to be insufficient to allow the institutions to act in order to attain, in the operation of the common market, one of the objectives of the Community, so the powers to impose economic and financial sanctions provided for by Articles 60 EC and 301 EC, namely, the interruption or reduction of economic relations with one or more third countries, especially in respect of movements of capital and payments, may be proved insufficient to allow the institutions to attain the objective of the CFSP, under the Treaty on European Union, in view of which those provisions were specifically introduced into the EC Treaty.

164 There are therefore good grounds for accepting that, in the specific context contemplated by Articles 60 EC and 301 EC, recourse to the additional legal basis of Article 308 EC is justified for the sake of the requirement of consistency laid down in Article 3 of the Treaty on European Union, when those provisions do not give the Community institutions the power necessary, in the field of economic and financial sanctions, to act for the purpose of attaining the objective pursued by the Union and its Member States under the CFSP.

165 Thus it is possible that a common position or joint action, adopted under the CFSP, should demand of the Community measures for economic and financial sanctions going beyond those expressly provided for by Articles 60 EC and 301 EC, which consist of the interruption or reduction of economic relations with one or more third countries, especially with regard to movements of capital and payments.

166 In such a situation, recourse to the cumulative legal bases of Articles 60 EC, 301 EC and 308 EC makes it possible to attain, in the sphere of economic and financial sanctions, the objective pursued under the CFSP by the Union and its Member States, as it is expressed in a common position or joint action, despite the lack of any express attribution to the Community of powers to impose economic and financial sanctions on individuals or entities with no sufficient connection to a given third country.

167 In this instance, the fight against international terrorism and its funding is unarguably one of the Union's objectives under the CFSP, as they are defined in Article 11 EU, even where it does not apply specifically to third countries or their rulers.

168 Furthermore, it is not disputed that Common Position 2002/402 was adopted by the Council acting unanimously in relation to that fight and that it prescribes the imposition by the Community of economic and financial sanctions in respect of individuals suspected of contributing to the funding of terrorism, where no connection whatsoever has been established with the territory or governing regime of a third country.

169 Against that background, recourse to Article 308 EC, in order to supplement the powers to impose economic and financial sanctions conferred on the Community by Articles 60 EC and 301 EC, is justified by the consideration that, as the world now stands, States can no longer be regarded as the only source of threats to international peace and security. Like the international community, the Union and its Community pillar are not to be prevented from adapting to those new threats by imposing economic and financial sanctions not only on third countries, but also on associated persons, groups, undertakings or entities developing international terrorist activity or in any other way striking a blow at international peace and security.

170 The institutions and the United Kingdom are therefore right to maintain that the Council was competent to adopt the contested regulation which sets in motion the economic and financial sanctions provided for by Common Position 2002/402, on the joint basis of Articles 60 EC, 301 EC and 308 EC.

[. . .]

3. Concerning the third ground of annulment, alleging breach of the applicants' fundamental rights

[. . .]

Findings of the Court

PRELIMINARY OBSERVATIONS

226 The Court can properly rule on the plea alleging breach of the applicants' fundamental rights only in so far as it falls within the scope of its judicial review and as it is capable, if proved, of leading to annulment of the contested regulation.

227 In this instance, the institutions and the United Kingdom maintain, in essence, that neither of those two conditions is satisfied, because the obligations imposed on the Community and its Member States by the Charter of the United Nations prevail over every other obligation of international, Community or domestic law. Consideration of those parties' arguments thus appears to be a precondition to any discussion of the applicants' arguments.

228 The Court considers it appropriate to consider, in the first place, the relationship between the international legal order under the United Nations and the domestic or Community legal order, and also the extent to which the exercise by the Community and its Member States of their powers is bound by

resolutions of the Security Council adopted under Chapter VII of the Charter of the United Nations.

229 This consideration will effectively determine the scope of the review of lawfulness, particularly having regard to fundamental rights, which the Court will carry out in the second place in respect of the Community acts giving effect to such resolutions.

230 Thirdly and finally, if it should find that it falls within the scope of its judicial review and that it is capable of leading to annulment of the contested regulation, the Court will rule on the alleged breach of the applicants' fundamental rights.

CONCERNING THE RELATIONSHIP BETWEEN THE INTERNATIONAL LEGAL ORDER UNDER THE UNITED NATIONS AND THE DOMESTIC OR COMMUNITY LEGAL ORDER

231 From the standpoint of international law, the obligations of the Member States of the United Nations under the Charter of the United Nations clearly prevail over every other obligation of domestic law or of international treaty law including, for those of them that are members of the Council of Europe, their obligations under the ECHR and, for those that are also members of the Community, their obligations under the EC Treaty.

232 As regards, first, the relationship between the Charter of the United Nations and the domestic law of the Member States of the United Nations, that rule of primacy is derived from the principles of customary international law. Under Article 27 of the Vienna Convention on the Law of Treaties, which consolidates those principles (and Article 5 of which provides that it is to apply to 'any treaty which is the constituent instrument of an international organisation and to any treaty adopted within an international organisation'), a party may not invoke the provisions of its internal law as justification for its failure to perform a treaty.

233 As regards, second, the relationship between the Charter of the United Nations and international treaty law, that rule of primacy is expressly laid down in Article 103 of the Charter which provides that, '[i]n the event of a conflict between the obligations of the Members of the United Nations under the present Charter and their obligations under any other international agreement, their obligations under the present Charter shall prevail'. In accordance with Article 30 of the Vienna Convention on the Law of Treaties, and contrary to the rules usually applicable to successive treaties, that rule holds good in respect of Treaties made earlier as well as later than the Charter of the United Nations. According to the International Court of Justice, all regional, bilateral, and even multilateral, arrangements that the parties may have made must be made always subject to the provisions of Article 103 of the Charter of the United Nations (judgment of 26 November 1984, delivered in the case concerning military and paramilitary activities in and against Nicaragua

(*Nicaragua* v. *United States of America*), ICJ Reports, 1984, p. 392, paragraph 107).

234 That primacy extends to decisions contained in a resolution of the Security Council, in accordance with Article 25 of the Charter of the United Nations, under which the Members of the United Nations agree to accept and carry out the decisions of the Security Council. According to the International Court of Justice, in accordance with Article 103 of the Charter, the obligations of the Parties in that respect prevail over their obligations under any other international agreement (Order of 14 April 1992 (provisional measures), Questions of Interpretation and Application of the 1971 Montreal Convention arising from the Aerial Incident at Lockerbie (*Libyan Arab Jamahiriya* v. *United States of America*), ICJ Reports, 1992, p. 16, paragraph 42, and Order of 14 April 1992 (provisional measures), Questions of Interpretation and Application of the 1971 Montreal Convention arising from the Aerial Incident at Lockerbie (*Libyan Arab Jamahiriya* v. *United Kingdom*), ICJ Reports, 1992, p. 113, paragraph 39).

[. . .]

240 It also follows from the foregoing that, pursuant both to the rules of general international law and to the specific provisions of the Treaty, Member States may, and indeed must, leave unapplied any provision of Community law, whether a provision of primary law or a general principle of that law, that raises any impediment to the proper performance of their obligations under the Charter of the United Nations.

241 Thus, in *Centro-Com*, [cited in paragraph 236], the Court of Justice specifically held that national measures contrary to Article 113 of the EC Treaty could be justified under Article 234 of the EC Treaty (now, after amendment, Article 307 EC) if they were necessary to ensure that the Member State concerned performed its obligations under the Charter of the United Nations and a resolution of the Security Council.

242 However, it follows from the case law (*Dorsch Consult* v. *Council and Commission*, [paragraph 82], paragraph 74) that, unlike its Member States, the Community as such is not directly bound by the Charter of the United Nations and that it is not therefore required, as an obligation of general public international law, to accept and carry out the decisions of the Security Council in accordance with Article 25 of that Charter. The reason is that the Community is not a member of the United Nations, or an addressee of the resolutions of the Security Council, or the successor to the rights and obligations of the Member States for the purposes of public international law.

243 Nevertheless, the Community must be considered to be bound by the obligations under the Charter of the United Nations in the same way as its Member States, by virtue of the Treaty establishing it.

[. . .]

CONCERNING THE SCOPE OF THE REVIEW OF LEGALITY THAT THE COURT MUST CARRY OUT

260 As a preliminary point, it is to be borne in mind that the European Community is based on the rule of law, inasmuch as neither its Member States nor its institutions can avoid review of the question whether their acts are in conformity with the basic constitutional charter, the Treaty, which established a complete system of legal remedies and procedures designed to enable the Court of Justice to review the legality of acts of the institutions (Case 294/83 *Les Verts* v. *Parliament* [1986] ECR 1339, paragraph 23; Case 314/85 *Foto-Frost* [1987] ECR 4199, paragraph 16; Case C-314/91 *Weber* v. *Parliament* [1993] ECR I-1093, paragraph 8; Joined Cases T-222/99, T-327/99 and T-329/99 *Martinez and Others* v. *Parliament* [2001] ECR II-2823, paragraph 48; see also Opinion 1/91 of the Court of Justice of 14 December 1991, ECR I-6079, paragraph 21).

261 As the Court has repeatedly held (Case 222/84 *Johnston* [1986] ECR 1651, paragraph 18; Case C-97/91 *Oleificio Borelli* v. *Commission* [1992] ECR I-6313, paragraph 14, Case C-1/99 *Kofisa Italia* [2001] ECR I-207, paragraph 46; Case C424/99 *Commission* v. *Austria* [2001] ECR I-9285, paragraph 45, and Case C50/00 *P Unión de Pequeños Agricultores* v. *Council* [2002] ECR I-6677, paragraph 39), 'judicial control . . . reflects a general principle of law which underlies the constitutional traditions common to the Member States . . . and which is also laid down in Articles 6 and 13 of the [ECHR]'.

262 In the case in point, that principle finds expression in the right, conferred on the applicants by the fourth paragraph of Article 230 EC, to submit the lawfulness of the contested regulation to the Court of First Instance, provided that the act is of direct and individual concern to him, and to rely in support of his action on any plea alleging lack of competence, infringement of an essential procedural requirement, infringement of the EC Treaty or of any rule of law relating to its application, or misuse of powers.

263 The question that arises in this instance is, however, whether there exist any structural limits, imposed by general international law or by the EC Treaty itself, on the judicial review which it falls to the Court of First Instance to carry out with regard to that regulation.

264 It must be recalled that the contested regulation, adopted in the light of Common Position 2002/402, constitutes the implementation at Community level of the obligation placed on the Member States of the Community, as Members of the United Nations, to give effect, if appropriate by means of a Community act, to the sanctions against Usama bin Laden, members of the Al-Qaeda network and the Taliban and other associated individuals, groups, undertakings and entities, which have been decided and later strengthened by several resolutions of the Security Council adopted under Chapter VII of the Charter of the United Nations. The recitals of the preamble to that regulation refer expressly to Resolutions 1267 (1999), 1333 (2000) and 1390 (2002).

265 In that situation, as the institutions have rightly claimed, they acted under circumscribed powers, with the result that they had no autonomous discretion. In particular, they could neither directly alter the content of the resolutions at issue nor set up any mechanism capable of giving rise to such alteration.

266 Any review of the internal lawfulness of the contested regulation, especially having regard to the provisions or general principles of Community law relating to the protection of fundamental rights, would therefore imply that the Court is to consider, indirectly, the lawfulness of those resolutions. In that hypothetical situation, in fact, the origin of the illegality alleged by the applicant would have to be sought, not in the adoption of the contested regulation but in the resolutions of the Security Council which imposed the sanctions (see, by analogy, *Dorsch Consult* v. *Council and Commission*, [paragraph 82], paragraph 74).

267 In particular, if the Court were to annul the contested regulation, as the applicants claim it should, although that regulation seems to be imposed by international law, on the ground that that act infringes their fundamental rights which are protected by the Community legal order, such annulment would indirectly mean that the resolutions of the Security Council concerned themselves infringe those fundamental rights. In other words, the applicants ask the Court to declare by implication that the provision of international law at issue infringes the fundamental rights of individuals, as protected by the Community legal order.

268 The institutions and the United Kingdom ask the Court as a matter of principle to decline all jurisdiction to undertake such indirect review of the lawfulness of those resolutions which, as rules of international law binding on the Member States of the Community, are mandatory for the Court as they are for all the Community institutions. Those parties are of the view, essentially, that the Court's review ought to be confined, on the one hand, to ascertaining whether the rules on formal and procedural requirements and jurisdiction imposed in this case on the Community institutions were observed and, on the other hand, to ascertaining whether the Community measures at issue were appropriate and proportionate in relation to the resolutions of the Security Council which they put into effect.

269 It must be recognised that such a limitation of jurisdiction is necessary as a corollary to the principles identified above, in the Court's examination of the relationship between the international legal order under the United Nations and the Community legal order.

[. . .]

277 None the less, the Court is empowered to check, indirectly, the lawfulness of the resolutions of the Security Council in question with regard to *jus cogens*, understood as a body of higher rules of public international law binding

on all subjects of international law, including the bodies of the United Nations, and from which no derogation is possible.

278 In this connection, it must be noted that the Vienna Convention on the Law of Treaties, which consolidates the customary international law and Article 5 of which provides that it is to apply 'to any treaty which is the constituent instrument of an international organisation and to any treaty adopted within an international organisation', provides in Article 53 for a treaty to be void if it conflicts with a peremptory norm of general international law (jus cogens), defined as 'a norm accepted and recognised by the international community of States as a whole as a norm from which no derogation is permitted and which can be modified only by a subsequent norm of general international law having the same character'. Similarly, Article 64 of the Vienna Convention provides that 'If a new peremptory norm of general international law emerges, any existing treaty which is in conflict with that norm becomes void and terminates.'

279 Furthermore, the Charter of the United Nations itself presupposes the existence of mandatory principles of international law, in particular, the protection of the fundamental rights of the human person. In the preamble to the Charter, the peoples of the United Nations declared themselves determined to 'reaffirm faith in fundamental human rights, in the dignity and worth of the human person'. In addition, it is apparent from Chapter I of the Charter, headed 'Purposes and Principles', that one of the purposes of the United Nations is to encourage respect for human rights and for fundamental freedoms.

280 Those principles are binding on the Members of the United Nations as well as on its bodies. Thus, under Article 24(2) of the Charter of the United Nations, the Security Council, in discharging its duties under its primary responsibility for the maintenance of international peace and security, is to act 'in accordance with the Purposes and Principles of the United Nations'. The Security Council's powers of sanction in the exercise of that responsibility must therefore be wielded in compliance with international law, particularly with the purposes and principles of the United Nations.

281 International law thus permits the inference that there exists one limit to the principle that resolutions of the Security Council have binding effect: namely, that they must observe the fundamental peremptory provisions of jus cogens. If they fail to do so, however improbable that may be, they would bind neither the Member States of the United Nations nor, in consequence, the Community.

282 The indirect judicial review carried out by the Court in connection with an action for annulment of a Community act adopted, where no discretion whatsoever may be exercised, with a view to putting into effect a resolution of the Security Council may therefore, in some circumstances, extend to determining

whether the superior rules of international law falling within the ambit of jus cogens have been observed, in particular, the mandatory provisions concerning the universal protection of human rights, from which neither the Member States nor the bodies of the United Nations may derogate because they constitute 'intransgressible principles of international customary law' (Advisory Opinion of the International Court of Justice of 8 July 1996, The Legality of the Threat or Use of Nuclear Weapons, Reports 1996, p. 226, paragraph 79; see also, to that effect, Advocate General Jacobs's Opinion in Bosphorus [paragraph 239], paragraph 65).

283 It is in the light of those considerations that the pleas alleging breach of the applicants' fundamental rights must be examined.

CONCERNING THE ALLEGED BREACH OF THE APPLICANTS' FUNDAMENTAL RIGHTS

284 The arguments put forward by the applicants in relation to the alleged breach of their fundamental rights may be grouped under three headings: breach of their right to make use of their property, breach of the right to a fair hearing and breach of their right to an effective judicial remedy.

CONCERNING THE ALLEGED BREACH OF THE APPLICANTS' RIGHT TO MAKE USE OF THEIR PROPERTY

[. . .]

293 Thus, in so far as respect for the right to property must be regarded as forming part of the mandatory rules of general international law, it is only an arbitrary deprivation of that right that might, in any case, be regarded as contrary to jus cogens.

302 Having regard to those facts, the freezing of the funds of persons and entities suspected, on the basis of information communicated by the Member States of the United Nations and checked by the Security Council, of being linked to Usama bin Laden, the Al-Qaeda network or the Taliban and of having participated in the financing, planning, preparation or perpetration of terrorist acts cannot be held to constitute an arbitrary, inappropriate or disproportionate interference with the fundamental rights of the persons concerned.

303 It follows from the foregoing that the applicants' arguments alleging breach of their right to make use of their property must be rejected.

THE ALLEGED BREACH OF THE RIGHT TO A FAIR HEARING

328 In this instance, as is apparent from the preliminary observations above on the relationship between the international legal order under the United Nations and the Community legal order, the Community institutions were required to transpose into the Community legal order resolutions of the Security Council and decisions of the Sanctions Committee that in no way authorised them, at

the time of actual implementation, to provide for any Community mechanism whatsoever for the examination or re-examination of individual situations, since both the substance of the measures in question and the mechanisms for re-examination [see paragraphs 309 et seq.] fell wholly within the purview of the Security Council and its Sanctions Committee. As a result, the Community institutions had no power of investigation, no opportunity to check the matters taken to be facts by the Security Council and the Sanctions Committee, no discretion with regard to those matters and no discretion either as to whether it was appropriate to adopt sanctions vis-à-vis the applicants. The principle of Community law relating to the right to be heard cannot apply in such circumstances, where to hear the person concerned could not in any case lead the institution to review its position.

329 It follows that the Community institutions were not obliged to hear the applicants before the contested regulation was adopted.

330 The applicants' arguments based on the alleged infringement of their right to be heard by the Community institutions before the contested regulation was adopted must therefore be rejected.

331 It follows that the applicants' arguments alleging breach of the right to a fair hearing must be rejected.

CONCERNING THE ALLEGED BREACH OF THE RIGHT TO AN EFFECTIVE JUDICIAL REMEDY

345 Last, the Court considers that, in the absence of an international court having jurisdiction to ascertain whether acts of the Security Council are lawful, the setting-up of a body such as the Sanctions Committee and the opportunity, provided for by the legislation, of applying at any time to that committee in order to have any individual case re-examined, by means of a procedure involving both the 'petitioned government' and the 'designating government' (see paragraphs 310 and 311 above), constitute another reasonable method of affording adequate protection of the applicants' fundamental rights as recognised by jus cogens.

346 It follows that the applicants' arguments alleging breach of their right to an effective judicial remedy must be rejected.

347 None of the applicants' pleas in law or arguments having been successful, and the Court considering that it has sufficient information available to it from the documents in the file and the statements made by the parties at the hearing, the action must be dismissed, and there is no need to allow the application for the first applicant and Sir Jeremy Greenstock, former Chairman of the Sanctions Committee, to be heard.

Document 9.2: Translated with the permission of LexisNexis JurisClasseur from Denys Simon et Flavien Mariatte, 'The EC Court of First Instance: a Professor of International Law?' [Le Tribunal de première instance des Communautés: Professeur de droit international]', in *Europe*, December 2005, pp. 6–10 (selected extracts) [translation]

[. . .]

B. A Debatable Relativisation of the Principle of Immunity in the Light of Jus Cogens and Fundamental Rights

18. On the other hand, this line of reasoning raises without doubt far more delicate questions concerning the assessment of lawfulness which the Tribunal is obliged to carry out. It cannot be contested, and it was without doubt superfluous to discuss the matter at such length,[1] that in a Community governed by the rule of law which grants the courts the right to review legislation, the appeal against the disputed regulation was mandatory, especially since the appellants were manifestly, directly and individually concerned by virtue of the regulatory character of the contested act, even though the Tribunal did not expressly consider this question of admissibility. The difficultly lay elsewhere.

19. It was accepted that the contested regulation implemented at Community level the obligation incumbent on the Member States in their capacity as member of the United Nations to give effect, in this case by means of a Community act, to sanctions imposed and subsequently consolidated by various resolutions of the Security Council adopted on the basis of Chapter VII of the Charter. It was clear in this context that the institutions only enjoyed a circumscribed power which excluded any power directly or indirectly to amend the specific contents of the said resolutions. Whilst such a finding was evidently not incompatible with an assessment of the external legality of the regulation,[2] on the other hand an assessment of its internal legality, in particular in the light of the general principles of Community law relating to the protection of fundamental rights, logically and necessarily implied the Tribunal 'indirectly' examining the legality of the Security Council's resolutions themselves. This was justified on the grounds that:

> if the Court were to annul the contested regulation, as the applicants claim it should, although that regulation seems to be imposed by international law, on the ground that that act infringes their fundamental rights which are protected by the Community legal order, such annulment would indirectly mean that the resolutions of the Security Council concerned themselves infringe those fundamental rights. In other words, the applicants ask the Court to declare by implication that the provision of international law at issue infringes the fundamental rights of individuals, as protected by the Community legal order.[3]

20. This was a priori the settled position of the institutions and of the United Kingdom which requested the CFI to decline on principal any competence to undertake an indirect assessment of the legality of the resolutions of the Security Council. Initially, in a move which can only be approved, the CFI appeared to accept this argument. In the context of resolutions adopted under Chapter VII, it is hard to conceive of a regional court, let alone a national court, attempting to determine the existence of a threat to international peace and security within the meaning of Article 39 of the Charter, as well as any non-coercive or coercive measures necessary to maintain or restore peace within the meaning of Articles 41 and 42 of the Charter. It is the Security Council alone which, pursuant to a decision imposed on the members of the United Nations by virtue of article 48(2) of the said Charter,[4] decides to freeze the funds of particular individuals or entities, acting through the Sanctions Committee. Jurisdiction of the CFI could be justified on the basis neither of international law nor of Community law,[5] as the court concluded with reference to an impressive array of legal provisions. Such jurisdiction would in fact run contrary to Articles 5, 10, 297 and 307 of the EC Treaty, Article 5 of the EU Treaty and Articles 25, 48 and 103 of the UN Charter. The Court moreover did not hesitate to apply by analogy the argument proposed by the ECJ concerning the invocation of fundamental rights before the courts of the Member States which undermined the universal application of Community regulations.[6] The CFI therefore reached the following conclusion, which appeared to be definitive:

> It must therefore be considered that the resolutions of the Security Council at issue fall, in principle, outside the ambit of the Court's judicial review and that the Court has no authority to call in question, even indirectly, their lawfulness in the light of Community law. On the contrary, the Court is bound, so far as possible, to interpret and apply that law in a manner compatible with the obligations of the Member States under the Charter of the United Nation.[7]

21. The continuation of the argument is however infinitely less convincing. In actual fact the court curiously found itself to have jurisdiction to assess in an incidental manner the legality of the relevant Security Council resolutions 'with regard to jus cogens, understood as a body of higher rules of public international law binding on all subjects of international law, including the bodies of the United Nations, and from which no derogation is possible'.[8] Bearing in mind the uncertainty in public international law over the existence, content, nature and scope of general peremptory norms, this reference appeared somewhat extravagant. On the one hand it was founded on a logical contradiction: either the CFI has, as it itself confirmed, no jurisdiction within the sphere of its competence to rule on the legality of resolutions of the Security Council, which means that this lack of jurisdiction applies as a matter

of principle irrespective of the relevant norm invoked by the Security Council, whether it concerned respect for jus cogens or the conformity of the resolutions with the Charter itself; or alternatively the CFI thereby accepts that it can assess the validity of the resolutions of the Security Council, in which case one might ask on what authority it could base a self-proclaimed mission which is rejected on principle by the principal judicial organ of the United Nations. On the other hand, the justifications invoked as a basis for such an assessment are themselves particularly questionable. The CFI first invoked articles 53 and 64 of the Vienna Convention on the Law of Treaties, which do not provide in any way for any control over the resolutions of the Security Council, but which exclusively concern the question of the absolute nullity of treaties. It should also be noted that not all Member States are bound by the Vienna Convention, having neglected either to sign or ratify it, and that the Community is not a party to the Vienna Convention of 1969 or the Vienna Convention of 1986. It is clear that the CFI deems it expedient to give the impression that such effects flow from customary law as codified in the Vienna Convention. More specifically, the provisions concerning jus cogens by no means have their origin in the legal codification of the treaties, but in 'progressive development', and therefore are not mandatory beyond the extent of their conventional recognition. Then, by a curious anachronism, the CFI found that the 'Charter of the United Nations' itself presupposed the existence of peremptory norms of international law, since the preamble to the Charter proclaims the 'faith' of the peoples of the United Nations 'in fundamental human rights and the worth of the human person'. Avoiding the need to look further into the scope of the preamble to the Charter, it is clear for any international lawyer that the affirmation of a principle in a convention, even a universal convention, cannot have the effect of transforming by some obscure alchemy a conventional rule into a norm of jus cogens. As far as the conclusion that 'international law thus permits the inference that there exists one limit to the principle that resolutions of the Security Council have binding effect' is concerned, it probably confirms the veracity of the celebrated remark of Hector to Busiris: 'law is the most powerful school of the imagination'.[9] Recourse to the notion, which is incidentally an Anglicism, of 'fundamental peremptory provisions of jus cogens' appears in the context of positive international law difficult to justify the view that resolutions incompatible with the latter 'would bind neither the Member States of the United Nations nor, in consequence, the Community'.[10] The terminological variations invoking 'the superior rules of international law' or 'the mandatory provisions concerning the universal protection of human rights' are hardly more convincing than the invocation of 'intransgressible principles of international customary law' referred to in international jurisprudence,[11] which has never acknowledged their status as norms of jus cogens. The (perfectly legitimate) concern of the CFI to grant a maximum level of protection to fundamental rights should not justify pronouncements of this nature which are not only far from unanimously endorsed in international law, but also risk being counter-productive, in particular owing to their blurring of the difference between peremptory norms of general international law and the violation of fundamental rights.

22. An assessment of eventual violations of fundamental rights in fact bears out a semantic and conceptual discrepancy with the recognition of the existence of peremptory rules of general international law which have never been enshrined as such in international case law or international practice. Nevertheless the approach of the CFI is interesting insofar as it deals systematically with the claims made by the appellants.

23. In the first place, it criticised the contested regulations for their failure to respect private property rights, as guaranteed in Article 1 of the first additional protocol to the ECHR. Following the logic of the above findings, 'it is in principle by the sole criterion of the standard of universal protection of the fundamental rights of the human person falling within the ambit of jus cogens' that it is necessary to examine them. Although the relevance of the guarantee of private property rights was not fully clear, the CFI reached the undoubtedly justified conclusion that the imposition of sanctions as provided for in the resolutions of the Security Council did not subject the persons affected by the freezing of funds to inhuman and degrading treatment (para. 240, Kadi). The Court went on to find, deploying an array of ambiguous formulae the precise workings of which are best known to itself, that 'in so far as respect for the right to property must be regarded as forming part of the mandatory rules of general international law,[12] it is only an arbitrary deprivation of that right that might, in any case, be regarded as contrary to jus cogens,' which was clearly not the case in the dispute before the Court, according to the CFI's findings of the necessity and interim nature of the sanctions, reached after an in-depth analysis of the justifications.[13]

24. The second head of the appeal invoked by the appellants concerning the violation of fundamental rights concerned the failure to respect the right to be heard. Whilst such a principle may indeed be a general principle of Community law,[14] this by no means implies that it is a recognised rule of jus cogens – a fact which the CFI appeared to 'forget' in the enthusiasm of its argumentation. The eventual requirement to observe the rule *audi alteram partem* in its Community meaning and before the Community institutions responsible for the relevant act, the legality of which is disputed, thus appears to be somewhat beside the point. As far as any obligation incumbent upon the Sanctions Committee of the United Nations to respect such a rule is concerned, the Court found pursuant to an in-depth assessment of the operational procedures of the Sanctions Committee that the fact that the defence of the interests of persons involved was necessarily implemented through the

exercise by state to which they were attached of their rights of diplomatic immunity was not irrelevant for the rules of jus cogens. In this context, the right allowed under British law, according to the representations made by the United Kingdom before the Court, to make an application for judicial review under domestic law against an unjustified refusal by the national authorities to lay the matter before the Sanctions Committee was quite surprisingly invoked. Even if this possibility had any importance in the context of the dispute before the Court, it is in any case still true however that no international or Community rule could oblige a Member State to lodge an appeal against the refusal of its national authorities to exercise their diplomatic protection on behalf of its own nationals, or indeed to make a complaint to the Sanctions Committee on behalf of the nationals of third countries. In any case, even if the interested parties had not had the opportunity to discuss the facts of the case and evidence held against them, this fact did not for the CFI amount to a violation of their fundamental rights. Finally the appeal against the violation of a right to effective access to the courts was in turn dismissed: the appellant in fact enjoyed under Community law the right to appeal against the contested regulation; moreover, the absence of a judicial remedy against individual decisions taken by the Sanctions Committee, while constituting a 'lacuna in the judicial protection available to the applicant' was not however 'in itself contrary to jus cogens' (para. 286, *Kadi*) – though the court did not really say why this was the case. The CFI therefore accepted the immunity from jurisdiction of the resolutions of the Security Council adopted on the basis of Chapter VII (para. 289, *Kadi*).

In the light of these findings all heads of the appeal lodged by the appellants were dismissed.

25. To conclude, one cannot therefore help but wonder, after a gentle analysis of the Court's line of argumentation, whether we are bearing witness to a Community resurrection of the 'Solange I' method, despite the fact that it was vigorously opposed in its time by the Community courts: everything happens as if the Court, at the cost of some legal acrobatics, had solemnly intended to stake out its importance by declaring itself competent to assess the application in Community law of the resolutions of the Security Council in the light of a jus cogens in relation to which it is about the only court[15] which claims to have control over its content and scope, going on to find that since the Security Council had on the facts respected fundamental rights – which were supposed to be the archetype of peremptory norms – there were no good reasons to accept the claim of a violation of these rights by the Community regulation which implemented the decisions taken under Chapter VII of the United Nations Charter. Unfortunately, the dynamic tone of the Court's approach did not make up for the blatant ignorance of international law which characterised the lesson in international law it tried to give.

Document 9.3: Reprinted with the permission of Europa Law Publishing from Piet Eeckhout, 'Does Europe's Constitution Stop at the Water's Edge? Law and Policy of External Relations', Fifth Walter van Gerven Lecture, 2005

[. . .]

I am referring to *Yusuf* v. *Council and Commission* and *Kadi* v. *Council and Commission*. Those cases were brought by alleged terrorists listed, not only in an EU Common Position, but also in EC Regulations freezing their assets.[16] The Common Position and the Regulations reflected UN Security Council resolutions. The names of the persons involved were listed by the Sanctions Committee set up by those resolutions. The EC Regulations faithfully (or perhaps rudderlessly) followed the ebb and flow of the listing of persons and entities by the UN Committee. The Regulations were adopted on the basis, not only of Articles 301 and 60 EC, which provide for sanctions, but also of Article 308 EC. The apparent reason for the recourse to the latter provision is that Articles 301 and 60 only speak of reducing economic relations with third countries, and do not mention sanctions against individuals.

The applicants sought the annulment of those regulations on grounds of lack of competence and of breach of fundamental rights. The judgments are groundbreaking in all respects. I will not however focus on the competence issue here, even if here too the Court's analysis calls for substantial comment. Instead I would like to limit the analysis to those parts of the judgments where the Court looks into the applicants' human rights arguments. I will not set out the Court's full argument, which is lengthy, but will concentrate on some of the crucial elements in the reasoning.

It is perhaps best to start with the CFI's conclusion on the question of judicial review on grounds of violation of fundamental rights. The Court considers that the challenged regulations fall outside the ambit of its judicial review powers, and that it has no authority to call in question, even indirectly, their lawfulness in the light of Community law.[17] This is remarkable, of course, since we are dealing, not with EU common positions, but with EC regulations, clearly acts of the institutions in the sense of Article 230 EC. That is indeed not the issue. The issue is rather, in the Court's conception, that the regulations implement and apply, in a Community context, resolutions of the Security Council.

In order to come to this remarkable conclusion the Court starts off by considering the relationship between the international legal order under the United Nations and the domestic or Community legal order. It opens that analysis by stating that, from the standpoint of international law, the obligations of the EU Member States under the UN Charter clearly prevail over every other obligation of domestic law or of international treaty law, including their obligations under the EC Treaty.[18] The Member States will surely be interested to hear this. That the Charter prevails over other international treaties is of course spelled out by the Charter itself (Article 103), but I think it is relatively new to learn that it also prevails over domestic law. The CFI explains why this is the case: it simply follows from Article 27 Vienna Convention on the Law of Treaties (VCLT), according to which a party may not invoke the provisions of its internal law as justification for its failure to perform a treaty. This is customary international law, but it clearly does not mean, and has never been interpreted as meaning, that international treaties automatically prevail over domestic law, at least not as a matter of domestic law. As a matter of international law it is of course uncontested that *pacta sunt servanda*, but surely not every EU Member State is monist in the sense that as a matter of domestic law international treaties automatically prevail.

The CFI then points out that this 'primacy' as it calls it extends to Security Council resolutions. It subsequently draws attention to Articles 307 EC and 224 EC. Under the first Member States are permitted to give precedence to pre-EC treaty obligations; the second recognises that a Member State may be called upon to take measures in order to carry out obligations it has accepted for the purpose of maintaining peace and international security. The Court concludes that, pursuant both to the rules of general international law and to the specific provisions of the Treaty, Member States may, and indeed must, leave unapplied any provision of Community law that raises any impediment to the proper performance of their obligations under the UN Charter.[19]

Again the CFI is really focusing on the obligations of the EU Member States, rather than those of the EC. I do not agree with the statement that the specific provisions of the EC Treaty require the Member States to give effect to their obligations under the UN Charter. Articles 307 and 224 EC permit the Member States to derogate from Community law obligations, but they do not in express terms state that Member States are required to do so.

The CFI then admits that the Community, not being a member of the UN, is not directly bound by the Charter as a matter of international law. However, the Court does hold that the Community is bound, in the same way as its Member States, by virtue of the EC Treaty. It develops a sophisticated reasoning, referring to the analogy with the *International Fruit Company* judgment where the ECJ held that GATT was binding on the EEC,[20] to come to the conclusion that the Charter is binding. This is groundbreaking, but the arguments have merit. The conclusion is that, first, the Community may not infringe the obligations imposed on its Member States by the Charter or impede their performance and, second, that in the exercise of its powers it is bound to adopt all the measures necessary to enable its Member States to fulfil those obligations. This conclusion is again heavily directed towards avoiding Community interference with the Member States' UN obligations.

Let us pause here for a moment. As we will see, all these points lead up to the conclusion that the CFI is not allowed to review the EC sanctions regulations. But if the Court were to strike down those regulations, why would that impede the performance by the Member States of their UN obligations? Those obligations would remain intact, and surely every Member State could itself decide to take the action (freezing of assets) which is required by the relevant resolutions. The freezing measures are in place anyway, one assumes, and every Member State could under its domestic law take the action it considers is required. Surely there might be some Member States where it would be possible to have a review of the domestic measures on human rights grounds in domestic constitutional law. But that cannot be of concern to the CFI.

And yet the CFI considers that it results from all the preceding that there are structural limits on its judicial review capacity. It considers that the institutions, when adopting the regulations, acted under 'circumscribed powers', with the result that they had no autonomous discretion. Now come the vital paragraphs (276–7).

This the CFI is not willing to do. It does not have the jurisdiction to review the regulations on grounds of general principles of Community law. However, the Court does appear to realise that, if it were to leave it at that, there would be no remedy whatsoever. And it does find some room for judicial review. 'None the less', it states, 'the Court is empowered to check, indirectly, the lawfulness of the resolutions of the Security Council in question with regard to jus cogens, understood as a body of higher rules of public international law binding on all subjects of international law, including the bodies of the United Nations, and from which no derogation is possible.'[21] What is the basis for this jurisdictional competence? Simply the nature of jus cogens or peremptory norms under international law. If Security Council resolutions failed to respect jus cogens, however improbable that may be, they would bind neither the Member States of the UN nor, in consequence, the Community. The CFI then reviews the applicants' arguments concerning the right to property, the right to be heard, and the right to an effective remedy. I will not analyse this section of the judgments. The conclusion from the review is that there is no violation of jus cogens, but it has to be said that the CFI carefully examines the various arguments. This somewhat sweetens the pill of denial of jurisdiction. It is however obvious that jus cogens does not offer the same standard of review as do general principles of Community law.[22]

Notwithstanding the review on grounds of jus cogens the judgments in *Yusuf* and *Kadi* amount in my opinion to judicial abdication.

[. . .]

Conclusions

In this lecture I have attempted to review a sample of issues and developments relating to the boundary between law and policy in the conduct of the EU's external relations. The review reveals cause for concern. Despite the EU's attempts at profiling itself as a champion of democracy, human rights and the rule of law, its own internal processes fail some basic constitutionalism tests. The lecture has focused on judicial intervention and the rule of law. The ECJ has on the whole struck an appropriate balance between law and policy, and has located the boundary between them in such a way that a core constitutional territory is judicially maintained and protected. There is clearly no overarching political question doctrine. There are however border areas which should be revisited, such as the denial of all effect to WTO dispute decisions. But it is in CFSP-related matters that no such constitutional territory is safeguarded. The lack of jurisdiction of the EU courts is wholly unjustified in the light of the developing content of the Union's foreign policy. It constitutes a substantial breach in the rule of law. Unfortunately, both the ECtHR and the CFI are compounding the breach, the former by refusing to review EU measures branding individuals and groups as terrorists, and the latter by declining to review the legality of EC regulations on the ground of their origin in UN resolutions and CFSP decisions. The *Yusuf* and *Kadi* decisions are particularly worrying. Here judicial abdication is cloaked in respect for international law. The CFI's coronation of the Security Council as the world's supreme legislature constitutes a dangerous development. The Member States of the EU accept the primacy of EC law in light of the constitutional guarantees which EC law offers. But this type of primacy cannot as a matter of course be extended to the international level. No such guarantees are present at the UN level. Respect for international law cannot mean that core precepts of constitutionalism are abandoned. The approach by the CFI confirms the worrying rise of executive dominance, and risks further contributing to fundamental doubts about the legitimacy of international organisations. What appears to be based on respect for those organisations effectively does them a disfavour.

Document 9.4: Reprinted with the permission of Aspen Publishers from Marise Cremona, 'The Draft Constitutional Treaty: External relations and external action', *Common Market Law Review* (2004), volume 40, issue 6, 1347–66 (selected extracts)

[. . .]

2. The Principles and Objectives of External Policy

One way in which the draft Treaty seeks to integrate the Community and the Union and their differing policies is by establishing a framework of principles, values and objectives, on which the Union is based. The statement of values in particular, perhaps, is also designed to establish an identity for the Union; a defining identity which will be promoted both to its citizens and to the outside world. Thus, the external objectives of the Union, stated in Article I-3(4), are couched in terms of the Union's values:[23]

[. . .]

3. Legal Personality and the Delimitation of Union Competence

The express grant of legal personality to the Union is a logical consequence of the decision to merge the existing Treaties and the Union and Community into one.[24] It is likely to be seen by many as a welcome simplification and essentially a reflection of the existing position.

[. . .]

Article I-12(2) states: 'The Union shall have exclusive competence for the conclusion of an international agreement when its conclusion is provided for in a legislative act of the Union, is necessary to enable it to exercise its internal competence, or affects an internal Union act.'

This is, clearly, an attempt to codify the very complex case law of the Court of Justice on exclusivity in external Community competence.[25]

[. . .]

This brings us to the more general question of the extent to which the CFSP has been integrated into the 'EC pillar' – the 'Community way' – and the extent to which its own characteristics have been preserved.

4. The Common Foreign and Security Policy

4.1. PRINCIPLE CHANGES

Perhaps inevitably, the proposals for the Common Foreign and Security Policy have attracted a great deal of attention, in particular the creation of a Minister for Foreign Affairs. On the one hand, the conduct of foreign policy is still (rightly) seen as a powerful symbol of sovereignty and statehood, and on the other it has been easy, especially during the last 12 months, to point to common positions which appeared merely to cover over fundamental differences, and conspicuous failures in the attempt to forge a truly common policy. Here, it appears, we have yet another attempt to create an institutional structure in the hope that unity will emerge and foreign policy 'weight' in the world increase. The key changes are

- the bringing of the CFSP and Common Security and Defence Policy ('CSDP') under the umbrella of 'Union External Action', alongside the common commercial policy, development policy, and other external policies of Community origin;
- the merging of the roles of High Representative for the CFSP and the Commissioner for External Relations into one office, the Minister for Foreign Affairs, who will be both Chair of the Foreign Affairs Council and a Vice-President of the Commission;

- the removal of the current CFSP policy instruments (common strategies, common positions, joint actions) in favour of one type of instrument, the European decision, which is a binding but non-legislative act;
- some extension of qualified majority voting, but not in CSDP matters;
- the extended provisions on the common security and defence policy, including provision for enhanced cooperation in various forms.

The first of these is potentially the most fundamental. Eileen Denza has referred to the 'line in the sand' between a common foreign policy under which sovereign states may bind themselves to each other, and a single foreign policy which signifies a fusion of states into a single state (in a way that a single external trade policy, for example, does not).[26] Commentators have frequently pointed to the inter-governmental nature of the CFSP, by which it is meant that the CFSP creates 'traditional' international law obligations and operates under a less communautaire institutional structure, in particular as regards the roles of the European Parliament, Commission and the Court of Justice. The Convention appears to have attempted to bring the CFSP into the same Treaty as Community-origin competences, under the same institutional framework and with some integration of legal instruments, but at the same time to preserve to some extent the differentiated character of the CFSP competence. Unfortunately, the position of the CFSP in the draft Treaty is ambiguous. Article I-11 details the different categories of Union competence; there are three general categories: exclusive (including the CCP and the customs union), shared (including the internal market, environment and development cooperation and humanitarian aid) and competence to support, coordinate or supplement action by the Member States (including health, education and culture). In addition, Article I-11 includes in a separate paragraph 'competence to define and implement a common foreign and security policy, including the progressive framing of a common defence policy'. The implication is thus that the CFSP does not fall within any of the three other categories of competence (exclusive, shared or supporting and supplementary),[27] but it is a little difficult to see what kind of competence it could be, if not one of these.

The definition of shared competence in Article I-11(2) contains the concept of preemption: 'The Member States shall exercise their competence to the extent that the Union has not exercised, or has decided to cease exercising, its competence.' The Convention did not want to incorporate that Community law concept into the CFSP, although the example of development cooperation illustrates that it is possible, if not logical, to categorize a competence as shared but at the same time to exclude preemption.[28] The concept of supporting, coordinating or supplementary action might have been suited to the CFSP, especially as such action is not to 'supersede' Member States' competence in those areas, but would not perhaps reflect the desire that the Union should develop its own common foreign and security (and defence) policy which goes beyond supplementing or coordinating Member State action. Thus we are left with something 'special' or *sui generis*.

4.2. INSTITUTIONAL DESIGN

Clearly the desire was to set the CFSP apart, especially from types of competence which had been carried out by the European Community, and to signal that a complete integration was not desired. Title V of Part I on the Exercise of Union Competence follows that through with a specific chapter of 'special provisions' for the CFSP, the CSDP and the area of freedom, security and justice, alongside the 'general provisions' applicable to Union competence generally. The separation between the CFSP and other areas of Union competence is emphasized by Article III-209, which provides that the implementation of the CFSP 'shall not affect' the Union's exclusive, shared or supplementary competences, and vice versa. All external policies are intended to be consistent (Article III-193(3)) and as we have seen all are governed by shared objectives and principles. This provision is not concerned with the substantive effect of policies; rather, 'shall not affect' appears to carry the same meaning as Article 47 TEU (nothing in this Treaty shall affect the EC Treaty): to prevent encroachment between the different competences. The difficulty is that the special nature of CFSP competence is not then spelled out clearly. Instead, it is necessary to examine specific characteristics of CFSP decision making and the legal instruments available, in order to determine what the differences, if any, are.

Certainly, the reduced role of the European Parliament and the Court of Justice are maintained in the new CFSP provisions. The Parliament, as now, is to be regularly consulted and kept informed,[29] but does not participate in formal decision making. The CFSP is the only field of activity where the Parliament does not even have to be consulted upon the conclusion of an international agreement.[30] The Court's jurisdiction is excluded, except in the case of economic sanctions adopted under Article III-224,[31] and monitoring compliance with Article III-209 (policing the borderline between the CFSP and other Union policies).

The position of the Commission is more ambivalent: the 'special provision' on the CFSP, Article I-39, only mentions the Commission once, as supporting proposals for action from the Minister for Foreign Affairs. In Article I-25, the Commission's role (inter alia) is to 'ensure the Union's external representation', but this is with the exception of the CFSP. Primary responsibility for policy making and ensuring that the Union's objectives and principles are complied with is given to the European Council, the Council of Ministers and the Minister for Foreign Affairs.[32] Delegations in third countries which are currently, somewhat oddly, 'Commission delegations' are to become Union delegations. And yet this virtual invisibility of the Commission is offset by the key role to be played within the CFSP by the Minister for Foreign Affairs, and this Minister will be a Vice-President of the Commission as well as a member of the European Council and Chair of the Foreign Affairs Council.[33] The Minister is intended to bridge the gap not only between the Council and the Commission, but also between the CFSP/CSDP and the other elements of Union external policy. This 'double-hatting' approach has been welcomed by the Commission, which referred to it as a 'major achievement'.[34] It does, however, give rise to a number of concerns, notably the fact that the Minister will be working under a mandate from the Council of Ministers[35] but will also be a full member of the Commission and thus subject to collegial responsibility. Given the creative tension between the two institutions, the potential for conflicts of interest is clear. The separation of powers between legislator and executive within the Union is blurred and the increased power and influence wielded by the new Minister is likely to alter the balance of power in ways which we cannot yet foresee.

4.3. LEGAL INSTRUMENTS

One of the noticeable characteristics of the current CFSP is the different set of legal instruments it employs.

[. . .]

One further comment may be made about the ostensible simplification of legal acts available for the conduct of the CFSP. An attempt to simplify what is inherently complex can lead to ambiguity and lack of transparency. Alongside the aim of simplification, the Convention was clearly attempting to 'carry over' into the new Treaty as much of the existing CFSP as possible. Thus, although common strategies, common positions and joint actions are no longer separate legal acts, the Union is still empowered to adopt European decisions which essentially reflect these existing acts.

[. . .]

Thus, although there is only one type of legal act available, in practice there are several different versions of that act, adopted by different institutions and with different legal consequences. On a superficial level, this may appear simpler, but a precise indication of the action taken will require the use of cumbersome portmanteau phrases instead of the relatively simple descriptive labels we currently use. More important, the distinctions between common positions and joint actions, although in the early days of the CFSP somewhat obscure, are now well understood, as are the characteristics of common strategies, even if not much used. Unless one is familiar with the previous history of the CFSP, it is not at all obvious what the difference is between 'strategic interests and objectives' which must be adopted by the European Council by way of European decision,[36] and 'general guidelines' and 'strategic lines' which are 'defined' (not by a European decision) by the same institution.[37] Yet they have different effects: the former, but not the latter, entitles the Council of Ministers to adopt implementing decisions by QMV.

4.4. VOTING

The draft Treaty does extend the use of qualified majority voting within the CFSP, but not very widely.[38] [. . .]

5. The Common Security and Defence Policy

The common security and defence policy (CSDP) has a separate five-Article section within the chapter on the CFSP in Title V of Part III,[39] as well as the 'special provision' in Part I.[40] This reflects the development of the CSDP since the Cologne European Council in June 1999 and the Nice European Council in December 2000.[41] There is no space here for an account of these developments or the full significance of the draft Treaty provisions, but a few points can be made. The first is the statement on 'common defence'. The current wording in Article 17 TEU does not contain a firm commitment: 'the progressive framing of a common defence policy, which might lead to a common defence, should the European Council so decide'. This phrasing is echoed in Article I-15 of the draft Treaty which also uses the word 'might'. However Article I-40(2) states that the progressive framing of a common Union defence policy 'will lead to a common defence, when the European Council, acting unanimously, so decides'. The 'will' implies certainty, but the following sentence undermines the effect by stating that the result of the European Council decision will merely be to 'recommend' to the Member States the adoption of such a decision in accordance with their respective constitutional requirements. One is forced to conclude that the 'will' is a statement of political intent rather than creative of any legal obligation.

Second, there are new references to operational capacity which will draw on both civil and military assets. Member States will be under an obligation to make these capabilities available to the Union,[42] and this capacity will be used for 'joint disarmament operations, humanitarian and rescue tasks, military advice and assistance tasks, conflict prevention and peace-keeping tasks, tasks of combat forces in crisis management, including peacemaking and post-conflict stabilization'.[43] The military capabilities of the Member States are to be improved with the help of a European Armaments, Research and Military Capabilities Agency which is to promote effective procurement, engage in multilateral projects and support defence technology research and joint research projects.[44] The objectives and scope of CSDP tasks and the conditions for their implementation will be set by European decisions adopted by the Council of Ministers acting unanimously, and the Minister for Foreign Affairs will have a coordinating role. These tasks may be entrusted to a group of Member States 'having the necessary capability and the desire to undertake the task'.[45] However, those Member States will then be committed to the task as defined in the relevant European decision; they will not have complete freedom of action, and if it should prove necessary to amend those parameters, a further European decision by the whole Council of Ministers will be necessary. These provisions give a Treaty basis to practice developed within the framework of the European Security and Defence Policy, such as the operations in the former Yugoslav Republic of Macedonia and the Democratic Republic of Congo during 2003.

Third, in addition to these ad hoc groups of Member States entrusted with particular CSDP tasks set by the Council of Ministers, the draft Treaty makes provision for a sub-group of Member States who fulfil higher military capability criteria and who wish to 'establish structured cooperation within the Union framework'.[46] This is a specialized form of enhanced cooperation, as envisaged under Articles I-43 and III-322 to III-329 and (subject to exceptions) is governed by those provisions. Those Member States which make an initial commitment to structured cooperation in security and defence will be identified, along with the details of the commitments undertaken, in a Protocol, but it will be open to other Member States to join the group in the future subject to a vote by the Council of Ministers.[47]

Yet another form of closer cooperation is envisaged by the draft Treaty, designed to operate in the indefinite period before a 'common defence' is established. This closer cooperation is for 'mutual defence' and the participating States will pledge to assist by all the means in their power, including military, other participating Member States should they be the victim of armed aggression on their territory.[48] The link with the collective defence obligations under Article 5 of the Brussels Treaty is clear, and from that perspective it is striking that there is no reference any longer to the WEU in the CSDP chapter of the draft Treaty. In contrast, the general no-prejudice clause in relation to NATO[49] is reinforced in the context of mutual defence, with references to cooperation between the Union and NATO and a confirmation that rights and obligations arising under the North Atlantic Treaty will not be affected. Participation in this form of closer cooperation is voluntary and open to all Member States.

A wider form of mutual assistance is envisaged by the Solidarity clause, under which all Member States undertake to assist another Member State should it be the victim of a natural or man-made disaster, or a terrorist attack.[50] Both Union instruments and military resources of Member States may be used, acting under coordination within the Council of Ministers.

The extended CSDP provisions in the draft Treaty, as well as providing a more extensive basis for the development of an increasingly important aspect of Union external policy, are also characterized by their emphasis on flexibility. Smaller – or larger – groups of Member States will take on more extensive commitments, on both a long-term and on a case-by-case basis. This is the way that the CSDP has developed and it makes pragmatic sense in terms of the very different traditions and capabilities of the Member States. The role of the European Council and Council of Ministers will however be crucial, in ensuring consistency and avoiding a multiplicity of Member State initiatives with insufficient coordination and linkage to other Union policies.

6. The CCP and other Union Policies

Article I-11, as we have seen, categorizes Union competence as exclusive, shared, and supporting, coordinating or supplementary, and specific competences are then allocated to these categories in the following provisions. As far as external policies are concerned, the common commercial policy and the customs union are exclusive competence under Article I-13. In addition, monetary policy (for those Member State participating in the euro), competition policy and conservation of marine biological resources under the common fisheries policy are also within exclusive competence, so the external policy dimensions of these fields of activity will be exclusive competence as well.[51] In addition, the draft Treaty reflects the case law of the Court of Justice in providing that in certain circumstances, exclusive competence for the conclusion of international agreements may arise, even where the Union's competence is not, per se, exclusive. This will be the case where the conclusion of an international agreement 'is provided for in a legislative act of the Union, is necessary to enable it to exercise its internal competence, or affects an internal Union act'.[52]

The clarity of this provision suffers from an attempt to express complex case law in a few words, itself a laudable objective. In particular, the phrase 'The Union shall have exclusive competence for the conclusion of an international agreement when its conclusion affects an internal Union act' is misleading. It is not the conclusion of the agreement by the Community which might or might not affect an internal act; it is the risk that the conclusion of a particular agreement by one or more Member States acting alone might, in the words of the Court of Justice, 'affect those rules or alter their scope'.[53] Further, the phrase 'an internal Union act' does not correspond directly to the Court's view that there must be, if not a common policy in existence in the field in question, then at least 'Community rules' designed to achieve a Treaty objective.

Exclusive competence will also arise, according to this provision, where the conclusion of an agreement is necessary to enable the Union to exercise its internal competence. This is clearly based on Opinion 1/76 as explained by the Court of Justice in Opinion 1/94. However in those cases, it was the need for an international agreement either before or at the same time as the adoption of an internal act, in order to achieve a Community objective, which was emphasized. In Opinion 1/94, which concerned the conclusion of the WTO agreements, it was the interpretation or scope of the 'Community objective' in relation to services and intellectual property rights that was critical to the issue of whether competence to conclude the GATS and the TRIPS was exclusive. The Court held that competence was not exclusive, as the Community's (internal market) objectives in these fields were not dependent on the conclusion of international agreements. While the difference between these two formulations may be resolved by interpretation, it is a pity to lose the explicit link between exclusivity and Union objectives.

The common commercial policy is in effect an example of this principle at work. Competence in the field of the internal market, including the free movement of goods, is shared, but in order to achieve the internal market objective of removal of internal border controls it is necessary to establish a common commercial policy, and this excludes the maintenance of an autonomous external trade policy by the Member States. In revising the existing provisions on the CCP, the Convention has made yet another attempt to extend the CCP beyond its traditional application to trade in goods while recognizing the concerns of the Member States over the extension of exclusive competence into ever wider fields. Chapter III of Title V reproduces Article 131 EC with one significant addition, and a revised version of Article 133 EC. Article 134 EC, under which the Commission may authorize protective measures in cases of deflection of trade, has finally disappeared. The most significant change appears in Article III-217(1): 'The common commercial policy shall be conducted in the context of the principles and objectives of the Union's external action.' As we have seen, these principles and objectives include not only the trade liberalization objectives already found in Article 131 EC (now Article III-216) but (among others) support for human rights and fundamental freedoms, sustainable development, 'the integration of all countries into the world economy', and environmental protection. Put together with the requirement added by the Treaty of Nice that international commercial policy agreements must be compatible with internal policies and rules,[54] this provision will encourage a greater coherence not only across the Union's external policy, but between external and internal policies. The objectives of the CCP are thus broadened beyond the uniformity inspired by its internal market rationale and WTO-inspired trade liberalization.[55]

The complex and cumbersome provisions of the current Article 133 EC have been simplified and rationalized. For the first time, the first paragraph of what is intended to be Article III-217 has been extended to include the conclusion of agreements relating to services and the commercial aspects of intellectual property, as well as foreign direct investment (the latter has also been added to Art. III-216).No special provision limiting the exclusivity of the CCP is made, so the extended CCP, including services and foreign direct investment, falls within exclusive competence. The drafters have, however, reflected the quite legitimate concern that exclusivity at the external level should not necessarily give rise to a loss of shared competence internally. Thus, '[t]he exercise of the competences conferred by this Article in the field of commercial policy shall not affect the delimitation of internal competences between the Union and the Member States'.[56] The provision for unanimous voting in cases where unanimity is required for the adoption of internal rules is also preserved, albeit in a simplified form.[57] Procedurally, the major change is the increased role given to the European Parliament. The CCP is to be implemented by means of European laws or framework laws, which are adopted according to the ordinary legislative procedure (co-decision).[58] Where an agreement is concluded, the European Parliament will for the first time be given the right to be consulted.[59] It may in fact be argued that the Parliament's consent is required, as the CCP is 'a field to which the legislative procedure applies'.[60] Overall, the revision and simplification of the CCP provisions is successful and to be welcomed.

External policies which fall within shared competence include development cooperation and humanitarian aid. However the principle of preemption, normally applied to shared competence,[61] will not apply here. The Union has competence to take action and to conduct a common policy but this will not prevent the Member States from exercising their own competence, subject to the overriding loyalty principle.[62] The specific legal base for humanitarian aid[63] is new, and takes its place alongside the Articles on development cooperation[64] and those on economic, technical and financial cooperation with third countries.[65] Humanitarian aid is designed to provide 'ad hoc assistance, relief and protection for people in third countries and victims of natural or man-made disasters', operating within the framework of the Union's overall external policy principles and objectives and in accordance with the international law principles of impartiality and non-discrimination. The latter in particular will reinforce the Union's current policy of continuing to provide humanitarian aid to the peoples of countries whose governments are the subject of sanctions or negative conditionality.

One further new policy initiative should be mentioned here. The draft Treaty creates a new policy on the Union and its immediate environment, under which the Union is to establish a special relationship with neighbouring States, with the aim of establishing an 'area of prosperity and good neighbourliness' founded on the values of the Union. This policy may lead to the conclusion of agreements with neighbouring countries involving reciprocal rights and obligations and the possibility of undertaking activities jointly. This language is reminiscent of Article 310 EC, on association agreements, which is reproduced in Article III-226 of the draft Treaty, with joint activities substituted for common action and special procedures. The reasons for the introduction of this provision are suggested by its placing: instead of being placed in Part III, Title V, with other external policies, it is placed in Part I, immediately before the Title dealing with Union membership and accession procedures. On the one hand the new neighbourhood policy is designed to allay fears that the current enlargement will create new dividing lines within Europe and to provide a mechanism for creating a new set of relationships with the countries surrounding the enlarged Union. It could be argued that the Part I position implies a certain special status to the relationship. On the other hand, however, the suggestion is that the neighbourhood relationship is an alternative to membership of the Union itself. The complex dynamic of these relationships will prove a major challenge for the Union's foreign policy over the next decade.[66]

7. Conclusion

What then will have been gained by the adoption of the Constitution as far as external relations is concerned? There are clearly some improvements, and here I will highlight four. First is the explicit statement of objectives covering the whole of the Union's external action; a coherent set of objectives has long been lacking and as the external activities of the Union and Community have expanded the need has become acute. Whatever the difficulties of achieving real coherence, this development will be a positive one. Second, is the benefit of a more transparent, systematic and (with the notable exception of the CFSP) precise delimitation of competence in external relations and a rationalization of substantive and procedural provisions. Third is the increased clarity of the provisions on the common commercial policy, and fourth is the provision of a new legal base for the provision of humanitarian aid and the provision for the accession of the Union to the European Convention on Human Rights.[67]

However, this inevitably selective discussion has also identified some significant problems. First among these is the failure to identify clearly the nature of the Union's CFSP competence and, in particular, whether it is intended that the existing international law status of CFSP acts should be retained. Second is the potential for upsetting the delicate institutional balance between the Council of Ministers and the Commission by creating the doubly-accountable Minister for Foreign Affairs. Linked to this concern is that over the shift in the balance of power towards the European Council and Council of Ministers. Opinions over the correct balance will of course differ; here the point is rather that the Minister for Foreign Affairs, by being made a member of the Commission but also required to act on his own and to implement Council policy, serves to obscure the extent of the change. Lastly, it may be regretted that it was not possible to achieve greater simplification. It is accepted that, with some exceptions, the Convention was attempting to represent the existing legal position. However the result is that the true import of some of the provisions is only really clear to those who have a good understanding of the pre-existing Treaty rules and the case law of the Court of Justice. This is hardly conducive to transparency.

Our starting point was the aim of integration: integration of the Treaties, of the pillars, of external policies and of action. It is striking that the heading to Title V of Part III is 'The Union's External Action', rather than External Policy, or External Relations. Maybe 'action' conveys an optimistic sense of dynamism. Maybe it is intended to cover both policies and procedures, both autonomous measures and contractual relations, a neutral word that encompasses foreign policy and 'classic' Community external relations (it was also the name given to Working Group VII). My personal preference would be for the mutuality implied by 'external relations' rather than the autonomy of 'action', but these are just words. The real question must be the extent to which the draft Constitution enables not merely an integration of treaties into one text, or even of policies under a single set of objectives, but an integration of objectives, policies and legal instruments into an effective mechanism for international action.

Document 9.5: Article I-28, Treaty establishing a Constitution for Europe

Article I-28 The Union Minister for Foreign Affairs

1. The European Council, acting by a qualified majority, with the agreement of the President of the Commission, shall appoint the Union Minister for Foreign Affairs. The European Council may end his or her term of office by the same procedure.

2. The Union Minister for Foreign Affairs shall conduct the Union's common foreign and security policy. He or she shall contribute by his or her proposals to the development of that policy, which he or she shall carry out as mandated by the Council. The same shall apply to the common security and defence policy.

3. The Union Minister for Foreign Affairs shall preside over the Foreign Affairs Council.

4. The Union Minister for Foreign Affairs shall be one of the Vice-Presidents of the Commission. He or she shall ensure the consistency of the Union's external action. He or she shall be responsible within the Commission for responsibilities incumbent on it in external relations and for coordinating other aspects of the Union's external action. In exercising these responsibilities within the Commission, and only for these responsibilities, the Union Minister for Foreign Affairs shall be bound by Commission procedures to the extent that this is consistent with paragraphs 2 and 3.

Document 9.6: Reprinted with the permission of Centre for European Policy Studies from Jeannette Ladzik, 'A European Diplomatic Service?', European Policy Brief, The Federal Trust for education & research enlightening the debate on good governance, issue 20, January 2006

One of the most innovative aspects of the now deadlocked European Constitutional Treaty was the creation of a European diplomatic service, known as the European External Service. Bringing together officials from EU institutions and staff seconded from the diplomatic services of the member states the task of the External Service is, according to the Constitutional Treaty, to assist and support the holder of the new post of European Foreign Minister. In the often confused discussion following on the rejection of the Constitutional Treaty by the French and Dutch electors, some commentators and politicians have expressed the hope that it might be possible to introduce the European External Service without waiting for the perhaps impossible final ratification of the Treaty. This Brief considers the legal, institutional and political questions now surrounding the setting up of a European External Service. Our conclusion is that no substantial legal or administrative obstacles remain in the way of an early move towards setting up such an External Service. The current impasse over the ratification of the Constitutional Treaty, however, acts as a considerable barrier to the mobilisation of political will necessary to create the External Service outside the Treaty.

Historical Background

The Treaty on European Union (TEU) signed at Maastricht in 1991 set as a goal for the European Union a Common Foreign and Security Policy (CFSP), with the objectives, inter alia, of safeguarding 'the common values, fundamental interests and independence of the Union', of promoting 'international cooperation' and of developing and consolidating 'democracy and the rule of law, and respect of human rights and fundamental freedom'.[68] With the Amsterdam Treaty of 1997, a number of amendments to the CFSP provisions of the Maastricht Treaty were agreed. The most important was the creation of a High Representative for CFSP, a role held since the Amsterdam Treaty by Javier Solana, who is widely regarded as having given what was originally seen as an administrative post a significant measure of political authority. The High Representative's position has been further reinforced over the past decade by the creation of a number of other new institutions in the CFSP field, notably the Policy Planning and Early Warning Unit, the Political and Security Committee, the European Military Committee and the European Military Staff.

Despite what most member states of the EU see as positive developments in recent years, few observers would deny that the European Union's Common

Foreign and Security Policy suffers considerable institutional fragmentation, both internally and externally. There is poor coordination between the central institutions of the European Union, and equally uncertain collaboration between national policy makers and their colleagues in Brussels. It was in the light of such concerns that the European Council of Laeken in 2001 asked the Convention on the future of Europe to consider how to improve the instruments of EU foreign policies so that the EU can become 'a power [. . .] to change the course of the world'. The two major proposals of the Convention in response to this challenge (both later taken up by the Constitutional Treaty) were for the creation of a European Union Foreign Minister, combining the current responsibilities of the High Representative and the European Commissioner for External Relations; and for the setting up of an integrated European External Service to support this Foreign Minister. There is little doubt that the members of the Convention saw these two proposals as inextricably linked. The failure of the Constitutional Treaty to be ratified in the French and Dutch referendums has led some commentators, however, to wonder whether it might not be possible anyway to set up an External Service. The task of this Service would be to support and improve the Union's already functioning attempts to evolve a coherent Common Foreign and Security Policy under the Maastricht and Amsterdam Treaties.

The Debate on the External Service at the Convention and IGC

The first proposers of a European External Service during the Convention were the former Italian Prime Minister Guiliano Amato and two MEPs, Elmar Brok (Germany) and Andrew Duff (UK). The precise text of their proposal stipulated that 'to strengthen the coherence and efficiency of the Union's action in the world, the Convention agrees on the need to establish as an integral part of the Commission administration, one joint service (European External ActionService)'. The concept of a 'European External Service' rapidly gained ground within the Convention and was enshrined in the draft Constitutional Treaty finally proposed by the Convention to the Intergovernmental Conference. But the Convention's agreement on the general principle of an External Service was despite important differences within its ranks on the nature and working of the Service.

In their original initiative, Amato, Brok and Duff had proposed that the External Service form part of the European Commission's bureaucratic structure. This was acceptable, indeed attractive, to the current of opinion within the Convention which saw the European Commission as the appropriate eventual executant of the European Common Foreign and Security Policy. It was less attractive to those who see CFSP as being, in the medium or even the long term, as being primarily an intergovernmental arrangement. This disparity of views within the Convention was left unresolved in the final draft

Constitutional Treaty, which said that 'the organisation and functioning of the European External Service shall be established by a European decision of the Council' and that the Council will 'act on a proposal from the Union Minister for Foreign Affairs after consulting the European Parliament and after obtaining the consent of the Commission'. In the same way as the Convention eventually compromised on the institutional affiliation of the Minister for Foreign Affairs (although a member of the Commission, he or she would take instructions from the Council of Ministers) so the institutional status of the External Service and the precise scope of its activities were left open by the draft Constitutional Treaty.[69]

When the EU member states finally adopted the Constitutional Treaty at their Intergovernmental Conference held in June 2004 in Brussels, they did not change the content of the Conventions' proposals on the External Service. Significantly, however, the relevant article was placed in the CFSP Chapter in Part III of the Treaty (Art.III-296 para.3). Arguably, this positioning limits the External Service simply to CFSP matters, a limitation which contradicts a central objective of the External Service, namely to integrate and consolidate the EU's whole range of foreign policy instruments. (Trade, aid, environment and energy questions are all long-standing areas of EU competence, which have substantial foreign policy implications, but remain outside the narrowly defined intergovernmental CFSP.) It should be observed, however, that the article in question states that the External Service will 'assist' the Foreign Minister. The Service's scope of action should therefore logically reproduce that of the Foreign Minister.

After the signing of the Constitutional Treaty, the member states decided that preparations should begin immediately for the setting up of the External Service. This instruction was followed by the European Commission, working together with Javier Solana, who had been designated as the first European Union 'Foreign Minister'. At the Brussels European Council in December 2004, the EU member states urged the Commission and Mr Solana 'to continue this preparatory work, in particular by identifying key issues, including the scope and structure of the future service'. While doing so, however, Mr Barroso and Mr Solana needed 'to ensure the full involvement of Member States in this process'. They were further instructed to 'prepare a joint progress report' for the June 2005 European Council.[70]

The Discussion about the External Service

During the first half of 2005, the EU's member states and institutions refined their ideas on the European External Service. The debate took as its starting-point the text of the Constitutional Treaty. Controversy centred on two main questions, the institutional 'location' of the Service and its organisation. As so often in such debates, underlying differences of view about the appropriate nature of the CFSP found their predicable expression in the positions adopted by the participants.

The European Parliament, for instance, demanded, in its report of May 2005, that the Service should be 'incorporated, in organisational and budgetary terms, in the Commission's staff structure.' This was consistent with the original proposals put forward in the Convention by the MEPs Duff, Brok and Dini. During the debates leading up to the report of May 2005, however, it had become clear that differing opinions existed within the Parliament on this issue. Mr Dini himself, for instance, argued that the most natural interpretation of the Constitutional Treaty adopted by the Intergovernmental Conference was that the Service should be a 'sui generis' entity, based on none of the existing European institutional models. Mr Dini was supported by the former President of the European Parliament, Klaus Haensch, who suggested that if the Service had been envisaged by the signatories of the Treaty as falling into any existing European institutional category, then they would have said so in the Treaty.

Among the EU member states, there is indeed something very like a consensus that the Service should represent a new institutional departure within the Union. There is emphatically no enthusiasm for it to become part of the Commission, and no obvious support among the member states for locating the Service in the Secretariat General of the Council, a proposal which has been put by some high officials of the Secretariat. Particularly on the part of the bigger member states such as the United Kingdom, there is a clear desire to restrict the autonomy of the new Service. But the oft-repeated call for a 'sui generis' entity seems to mask (albeit imperfectly) uncertainty and disagreement as to how this restriction can best be brought about. The role of the European Commission in this confused situation is an interesting one. It seems to recognise that its preferred solution, the incorporation of the External Service into the Commission itself, is unattainable at present. It seems reluctant, however, to endorse or advocate any other model.

Intertwined with the controversy about the institutional affiliation of the Service are the questions of its composition and organisation. If the Service were to be incorporated into the Commission or the Secretariat of the Council, significant reorganisation of these two latter bodies would need to take place. On the other hand, if the External Service were to be established autonomously of the Commission or the Council, some duplication of staff already engaged in the Commission and Council would be the inevitable consequence. The background is further complicated by the disparity in present staffing levels between the institutions. The Commission has over 3000 staff members working in the three Directorates General most directly engaged in foreign affairs, while the Council has only 225 equivalent staff, admittedly supplemented by a further 140 working on the Military Staff.

This disparity is naturally reflected in all the three main approaches canvassed for the internal structure of the External Service. The organisationally least ambitious approach would incorporate only the foreign affairs Directorate from the Council Secretariat and the Directorate General dealing with external relations from the Commission. With such limited personnel, the Service would probably be too weak to ensure consistency and coherence in EU foreign policies. At the other end of the spectrum, proposals have been discussed for bringing together in the External Service all officials dealing with the external relations of the Union (broadly defined) from the Council and the Commission, and adding to their number the officials who represent the Union in third countries. This body would certainly not lack for resources, but it might be wondered whether even the European Union's envisaged Foreign Minister would be able adequately to supervise all its activities.

A further complication arises from the stipulation of the Constitutional Treaty that the External Service shall not only comprise 'officials from the relevant departments of the General Secretariat of the Council and of the Commission' but also 'staff seconded from national diplomatic service of the member states'. How many such staff should be detached to the Service, how long they should work for the Service, whether their terms of employment should be the same as those for Council and Commission officials are obviously crucial and controversial questions, with obvious implications for the identity and political culture of the Service.

The Constitutional Treaty explicitly says that 'the service shall work in cooperation with the diplomatic services of the Member States'. Certain member states, indeed, hope that in the medium term it may be possible for the External Service to take over some at least of the representative and analytical functions currently fulfilled by their own expensive and over-stretched diplomatic services. Larger member states such as the United Kingdom and France are less sanguine. They view the External Service on the contrary as a potential rival to their national diplomacies. Ironically, this suspicion co-exists, at least in the United Kingdom, with a more positive view of the External Service, as a possible counterbalance to the increasing external profile of the European Commission. The British Foreign Secretary recently remarked that 'you find all sorts of odd bods from the European Union running all sorts of odd offices around the world and that it would be a good thing if arrangements for the European External Service gave us more control than we have at the moment'.[71] The contrast between Mr Straw's long-term aspirations for the workings of the External Service and that of, say, Mr Brok, could not be more stark. The 'odd bods' running 'odd offices around the world' are a major element of the general debate concerning the future work of the External Service.

The Constitutional Treaty clearly placed the external delegations of the

European Union under the authority of the Union Foreign Minister without making clear whether their staff should be drawn from the External Service. There are today 123 such delegations, not only monitoring EU development aid and agreements with third countries, but also reporting directly to the Commission and the Council and providing local support to the EU's many special representatives. If, as is intended by the Constitutional Treaty, the Union Foreign Minister eventually takes over the permanent chairmanship of the Foreign Affairs Council, it would seem most logical that the external delegations controlled by the Foreign Minister should take on the work relating to CFSP in third countries. Until now, much of this work has been carried out by the national delegations of the country holding the rotating Presidency of the Union. Small countries have found this an unwelcome burden, which they will be happy to lose. This unsentimental view is not entirely reflected among the larger member states, who remain at least hesitant before the prospect of reinforcing the autonomous role of the European external delegations.

Joint Progress Report

The first draft of the joint progress report to be written by Solana and Barroso was presented in March 2005 as a basis for discussions with EU member states. This draft acknowledged that the authors of the Constitutional Treaty may have foreseen a *sui generis* status for the External Service, and asked the EU member states to make proposals as to what this status should be. In the view of Solana and Barroso, the External Service should incorporate those services currently working in CFSP areas within the Council and the Commission as well as the military staff (with the possible exception of SITCEN) from the Council. The Service needed to comprise 'geographical desks which cover all the countries/regions of the world' and 'single thematic desks [. . .], on issues such as human rights, counterterrorism, non-proliferation and relations with international organisations such as the UN' in order to support not only the Foreign Minister, but also the other Commissioners and the President of the European Council. Areas such as trade, development policy and humanitarian assistance and enlargement negotiations would, however, be excluded from the External Service's remit, a substantial pruning back of the most ambitious aspirations for the Service. The draft paper made no recommendations on the external representations of the EU, or on the budget to fund the External Service.

Between March and June 2005, Solana and Barroso made some progress on finding consensual solutions among the member states on outstanding issues. The great majority of member states envisaged a *sui generis* status for the Service, 'under the authority of the Foreign Minister, with close links to both the Council and the Commission'. Most of the member states agreed with the organisation of the Service proposed by Solana and Barroso, namely to include in it the services dealing with CFSP in the Commission (DG RELEX) and in the Council (Policy Unit, DG-E and Military Staff), and to set up within its internal structure both geographical and thematic desks. Differences, however, persisted as to whether the service should incorporate the military staff from the Council or SITCEN. The member states agreed that Union Delegations should be an integral part of the External Service, although most member states thought this did not imply that 'all staff working in the Delegations would need to be members of the (External Service)'. A majority (but not all) of the member states also supported the idea that at some time in the future the Union Delegations might perform additional tasks such as consular protection and visas. Concerning the staff of the External Service, most EU member states argued that their national diplomats should become 'temporary agents' of the Service in order to guarantee that 'all staff in the External Service had the same status and conditions of employment'.

Two important issues, however, remained unresolved. For the European Union, the financing of the Common Foreign and Security Policy has always been a controversial matter, particularly as to whether it should be financed from the general budget of the European Union or as a result of a separate intergovernmental agreement. Solana and Barroso were unable to resolve this matter in regard to the External Service. Their report laconically concludes that 'budgetary issues required further examination'. Another controversial issue for the Solana–Barroso report was that of the chairmanship of the Council working groups dealing with issues affecting the external relations of the Union. Where these matters squarely concerned the Common Foreign and Security Policy of the Union, the chair should be taken by a member of the External Service. Where the subject for discussion was a topic such as development, the environment or agriculture, the chairmanship should be taken by a representative of the country holding the presidency of the relevant specialist council, even though the particular developmental, environmental or agricultural matter under discussion had implications for the general external relations of the European Union. It remains to be seen whether this theoretically acceptable division of labour would be workable in practice.

The Future of the External Service after the Referendums

After the rejection of the Constitutional Treaty by the French and Dutch voters, the European Council of June 2005 decided not to consider the Solana–Barroso report on the External Service. A number of member states had expressed the fear that the continuation of work to set up the Service might be interpreted by voters as a rejection of the negative outcome of the consultations in France and the Netherlands. In the six months following the French and Dutch referendums, the British Presidency of the Union studiedly avoided any discussion of the Constitutional Treaty's future, and discussion of the

External Service languished correspondingly. The new Austrian Presidency, however, has said that it wishes to promote discussion of the Treaty's future. It is entirely possible that the question of the External Service will once again figure on the political agenda. Two obvious questions present themselves in this context, whether the problems which the External Service was intended to address can only be solved by setting up such an External Service; and whether, if it is thought desirable or necessary, the External Service can be set up before the now doubtful final ratification of the Constitutional Treaty.

It has been obvious from the preceding discussion that the EU's member states have differing expectations among themselves as to the likely advantages of the European External Service. Some see it as an essentially coordinating body between other powerful actors on the European stage, others see it as an embryonic European Foreign Ministry and others see it as a potential way of saving money and other resources for specific tasks traditionally carried out in third countries by national diplomatic missions. Although some progress was made by Solana and Barroso in bringing these differing views together before the European Council of June 2005, it is difficult to believe that, starting afresh, the member states could be brought to a new common analysis of where the underlying administrative problems in formulating a European foreign policy lie. The need to come to at least some agreement regarding the setting up of the European diplomatic service envisaged in the Constitutional Treaty concentrated remarkably the minds of national governments in the first half of 2005. It is doubtful whether any such degree of consensus could have been achieved other than under the spur of the supposedly nascent External Service.

Theoretically and intellectually the argument can certainly be made that better coordination between existing institutions (the desirability of which seems common ground between all participants in the debate) could be managed simply between those institutions, without the compelling need for a new organisation such as the External Service. But the question remains why such coordination has demonstrably not occurred before now. Whatever else it may have been in the mind of some, the External Service was a serious attempt to improve this coordination, the equivalent at the official and administrative level of the European Foreign Minister to whom it was seen as subordinated. If a coherent European foreign policy demands a single figure to articulate it, then that single figure must logically need for the formulation and refinement of European foreign policy a single organisation primarily responsible to him or her. The political case for a European External Service is as powerful as it was at the time of the signing of the European Constitutional Treaty.

Regarding legal requirements, it has been argued that it would be illegal to set up the External Service before the Constitutional Treaty has been ratified. This argument seems, however, juridically highly doubtful. Nobody disputes that if they wish to do so the European institutions can conclude among themselves interinstitutional agreements to facilitate, as the Nice Treaty puts it, 'the application of the provisions of the Treaty establishing the European Community'. Such agreements may not amend or supplement the provisions of the Treaty and may be concluded only with the agreement of the Council, the Commission and the European Parliament. The considerable measure of agreement reached by the member state governments before the European Council in the middle of last year [2005] suggests that, if the political will exists now to set up a European External Service, then it should be possible to conclude an interinstitutional arrangement on the subject. It seems highly unlikely that such an agreement would run the risk of legal challenge by 'amending or supplementing' the existing Treaty.

Conclusion

Replying to a question from the British Member of the European Parliament, Charles Tannock, the British Presidency of the Union said in September 2005 that the establishment of the European External Service 'is one of the provisions of the Constitutional Treaty; as such, it shall take effect only when the Treaty itself comes into force'. This negative reaction certainly reflected the desire of the British government to talk and think as little as possible about the Constitutional Treaty after being saved from a difficult referendum on the Treaty in Britain by the French and Dutch votes. But it must be said that until now little political momentum has been visible behind the oft-voiced view of academic and other commentators that the creation of a European External Service is an attractive and relatively easily achieved element of the Constitutional Treaty for 'cherry picking'.

It is certainly true that surprising progress was made by Solana and Barroso in their attempts to flesh out the organisational infrastructure of the Service in 2005. But it is probably too early to say whether their relative success in this area will eventually bear fruit. It may be that in due course the member states of the Union, perhaps with different political leadership in a number of countries, will wish to make a concerted effort to rescue what can be rescued from the wreckage of the Constitutional Treaty. At that stage, the European External Service would be an attractive candidate. In the year 2000 Javier Solana drew an interesting comparison between the 14 123 American diplomats scattered throughout the world in 300 missions and the 39 000 European diplomats in 1500 missions, and ironically wondered whether Europe was a more powerful diplomatic force than the USA in consequence. When all the EU's member states have drawn from those statistics the conclusion Javier Solana wished them to draw, the future of the European External Service will be much easier to predict than it is now, within or without the European Constitutional Treaty.

Notes

1. See nonetheless *Yusuf*, paras 260–62 and *Kadi*, paras 209–11 and the copious case law cited.
2. See *infra*, B [not reproduced in this volume, note of the eds].
3. *Yusuf*, para. 267; *Kadi*, para. 216.
4. 'Such decisions shall be carried out by the Members of the United Nations directly and through their action in the appropriate international agencies of which they are members.'
5. *Yusuf*, para. 272; *Kadi*, para. 221.
6. *Yusuf*, para. 275; *Kadi*, para. 224. See also C-11/70 *Internationale Handelsgesellschaft* [1970] ECR 1125, para. 3; C-234/85 *Keller* [1986] ECR 2897, para. 7; Joined Cases C-97/87, C-98/87 & C-99/87 *Dow Chemical Iberica* v. *Commission* [1989] ECR 3165, para. 38.
7. *Yusuf*, para. 276; *Kadi*, para. 225.
8. *Yusuf*, para. 277; *Kadi*, para. 226.
9. J. Giraudoux, *La Guerre de Troie n'aura pas lieu*, Livre de Poche, no. 945, p. 111.
10. *Yusuf*, para. 281; *Kadi*, para. 230.
11. *Yusuf*, para. 282; *Kadi*, para. 231. Advisory Opinion of the International Court of Justice, 8 July 1996, *The Legality of the Threat or Use of Nuclear Weapons* (1996) ICJ Reports, p. 226, para. 79.
12. This would of course be a novel development to the generally accepted understanding of *ius cogens*.
13. Unfortunately there is no indication as to the source and content of the alleged rule of *ius cogens* which thus satisfies the quite legitimate requirements of European and Community legislation, which again confirms the ideological rather than legal nature of this judgment.
14. See in particular C-135/92 *Fiskano* v. *Commission* [1994] ECR I-2885, especially paras 39–40; C-462/98, *Mediocurso* v. *Commission* [2000] ECR I-7183, especially para. 36.
15. With the exception of the special case of the jurisprudence of the special international criminal tribunals.
16. Council Regulation EC No 881/2002 of 27 May 2002 imposing certain specific restrictive measures directed against certain persons and entities associated with Usama bin Laden, the Al-Qaida network and the Taliban, and repealing Council Regulation (EC) No 467/2001 prohibiting the export of certain goods and services to Afghanistan, strengthening the flight ban and extending the freeze of funds and other financial resources in respect of the Taliban of Afghanistan [2002] OJ L 139/9.
17. Case T-306/01 *Yusuf* v. *Council and Commission* and Case T-315/01 *Kadi* v. *Council and Commission*, judgments of 21 September 2005 para. 276.
18. Idem, para. 231.
19. Idem, paras 234–40.
20. Joined Cases 21–24/72 *International Fruit Company* [1972] ECR 1219.
21. *Yusuf*, paras 266–7.
22. See, for example, the discussion on the right to a fair hearing.
23. The values of the Union are set out in Art. I-2: 'The Union is founded on the values of respect for human dignity, liberty, democracy, equality, the rule of law and respect for human rights. These values are common to the Member States in a society of pluralism, tolerance, justice, solidarity and non-discrimination.'
24. Art. I-6 states simply, 'The Union shall have legal personality.'
25. A. Dashwood and C. Hillion (eds), *The General Law of EC External Relations* (Sweet & Maxwell, 2000).
26. Denza, 'Lines in the Sand – between Common Foreign Policy and Single Foreign Policy', paper delivered to the WG Hart Workshop, London, June 2003.
27. Under Art. I-11(3) the Union will also have 'competence to promote and coordinate the economic and employment policies of the Member States'. This too thus has a special status, and it is unclear how it differs from the supporting, coordinating and supplementary competences described in para. (5).
28. Art. I-13(4): 'In the areas of development cooperation and humanitarian aid, the Union shall have competence to take action and conduct a common policy; however, the exercise of that competence may not result in Member States being prevented from exercising theirs.'

29. Art. I-39(6) and Art. III-205.
30. Art. III-227(7).
31. Art. III-282.
32. See Arts. III-195–9.
33. See further discussion of the MFA below.
34. Commission Communication on the draft Constitution, pursuant to Art. 48 TEU, COM(2003)548, 17 Sept. 2003, para. 18.
35. See, for example, Art. I-39(4).
36. Art. III-194.
37. Art. III-196; c.f. Art. 13(1) and (3) TEU.
38. Provision is made for a possible future extension of QMV, by unanimous decision of the European Council: Art. I-39(8).
39. Art. III-210–14.
40. Art. I-40.
41. European Council Conclusions, Cologne June 1999, Annex III: European Council Declaration on Strengthening the Common European Policy on Security and Defence; European Council Conclusions, Nice December 2000, Annex VI Presidency Report on the Common European Security and Defence Policy; European Council Conclusions, Copenhagen, December 2002, Part III European Security and Defence Policy, and Declaration at Annex II. See P.J. Teunissen, 'Strengthening the Defence Dimension of the EU: An Evaluation of Concepts, Recent Initiatives and Developments', (1999) *EFA Rev.*, 327; S. Duke, 'CESDP: Nice's Overtrumped Success' (2001), *EFA Rev.*, 155; A. Missiroli, 'European Security Policy: The Challenge of Coherence' (2001), *EFA Rev.*, 177; A. Missiroli, 'Ploughshares into Swords? Euros for European Defence' (2003), *EFA Rev.* 5.
42. Art. I-40(3).
43. Art I-40(1) and Art. III-210.
44. Art. III-212.
45. Art. III-211.
46. Art. I-40(6) and Art. III-213.
47. Art. III-213(2). Only those Member States already taking part will participate in the vote.
48. Art. I-40(7) and Art. III-214.
49. Art. I-40(2).
50. Art. I-42 and Art. III-231.
51. On fisheries conservation, see Case 804/79, *Commission* v. *UK*, [1981] ECR 1045.
52. Art. I-12(2). For relevant case law, see *AETR* case; Opinion 1/76/EEC, [1977] ECR 741; Opinion 2/91, [1993] ECR I-1061; Opinion 1/94, [1994] ECR I-5267.
53. Opinion 2/91 [1993] ECR I-1061, para. 9.
54. M. Cremona, 'A Policy of Bits and Pieces? The Common Commercial Policy After Nice' (2002), *Cambridge Yearbook of European Legal Studies*, 61, at 75–6.
55. M. Cremona, 'The External Dimension of the Single Market: Building (on) the Foundations', in Barnard and Scott (eds), *The Law of the Single European Market: Unpacking the Premises* (Hart Publishing, 2002).
56. Art. III-217(5).
57. Art. III-217(4). Unanimity is also required for the conclusion of agreements on trade in cultural and audiovisual services 'where these risk prejudicing the Union's cultural and linguistic diversity'. Although an improvement on the current provision (Art. 133(6) EC), there is clearly scope for unconstructive argument over the application of this proviso.
58. Arts. III-217(2) and III-302.
59. Art. III-227(7).
60. Art. III-227(7)(e).
61. Art. I-11(2).
62. Art. I-13(4).
63. Art. III-223.
64. Arts. III-218–20.
65. Art. III-221–2.

66. For further discussion, see M. Cremona, 'Enlargement: A Successful Instrument of Foreign Policy?', paper delivered at the WG Hart Workshop, London, June 2003.
67. Art. I-7(2).
68. Treaty on the European Union., Title V, Art.J.1 para. 2, Maastricht 07.02.1992, http://www.eurotreaties.com/maastrichteu.pdf [17.11.2005].
69. Constitutional Treaty, Part III Art.III-296 para. 3, http://europa.eu.int/constitution/en/ptoc66_en.htm [01.11.2005].
70. Brussels European Council – Presidency Conclusion, 16/17.12 2004, p. 23, http://ue.eu.int/ueDocs/cms_Data/docs/pressData/en/ec/83201.pdf [01.11.2005].
71. David Allen (2004), 'So who will speak for Europe? The Constitutional Treaty and coherence in EU external relations', *CFSP Forum*, vol.2, issue 5, p. 3, www.fornet.info [01.11.2005].

Index